*F*ABRIC

*R*EFERENCE

Mary Humphries, B.A., M.A.

Fellow, Institute of Textile Science

PRENTICE HALL
Upper Saddle River, New Jersey 07458

Library of Congress Cataloging-in-Publication Data

Humphries, Mary,
    Fabric reference / Mary Humphries. — 2nd ed.
      p.   cm.
    Includes bibliographical references and index.
    ISBN 0-13-010575-9
    1. Textile fabrics. I. Title.
    TS1445.H85 2000
    677—dc21   99-33047
                             CIP

Acquisitions Editor: Elizabeth Sugg
Managing Editor: Mary Carnis
Director of Production and Manufacturing: Bruce Johnson
Editorial Assistant: Delia Uherec
Editorial and Production Services: WordCrafters Editorial Services, Inc.
Prepress Manufacturing Buyer: Ed O'Dougherty
Marketing Manager: Shannon Simonsen
Cover Director: Jayne Conte
Cover Designer: Liz Nemeth
Printer/Binder: R. R. Donnelley & Sons, Crawfordsville, IN

Printed in the United States of America

10 9 8 7 6 5 4

ISBN 0-13-010575-9

Prentice-Hall International (UK) Limited, *London*
Prentice-Hall of Australia Pty., Limited, *Sydney*
Prentice-Hall Canada Inc., *Toronto*
Prentice-Hall Hispanoamericana, S.A., *Mexico*
Prentice-Hall of India Private Limited, *New Delhi*
Prentice-Hall of Japan, Inc., *Tokyo*
Pearson Education Asia, *Singapore*
Editora Prentice-Hall do Brasil, Ltda., *Rio de Janeiro*

CONTENTS

PREFACE

This is a textiles book for anyone who needs accessible information on how fabrics behave and why. It provides up-to-date background on the many facets of a very technical subject, in as nontechnical language as possible. It is aimed to serve the needs of the university or college student in a program in which textiles is a significant component but not the entire focus. It should also offer unique help to those who are not formally studying textiles but are looking for clarification of the latest developments in this rapidly changing field. I believe that most aspects of textiles learning can be made clear to anyone interested in acquiring it, even without formal background study of its basis (which is in such disciplines as organic chemistry and physics), yet without "watering it down" until the idea is lost or meaningless because of fuzzy or inaccurate presentation.

The *Reference* first traces the elements that go together to make a fabric—fibers, yarns, fabric construction, and finishes including dyeing and printing. This covers the ground of most introductory textiles texts, but with this difference: If you want information on a major fiber type, for instance, you will find it on a page or two of this *Reference*—as opposed to a whole chapter in other texts—along with data on that fiber in relation to others, in summaries or comparisons. The other elements of fabric performance are dealt with in similar condensed format: yarn types, fabric constructions, the effects of finishing, and the impact of coloration—a distillation of the main points covered by most texts.

In contrast, you will find much fuller treatment here of many areas of applied textile knowledge that are sparsely dealt with in other textbooks, plus some aspects that are virtually ignored; I believe these to be among the most useful to any of you in many fabric-related fields.

There is an expansive section on the care of fabrics, while other texts treat this more briefly. This second edition includes care instructions indicated by approved ASTM symbols used in the United States and compares the U.S. system with those of other countries. I also discuss the far-reaching changes in commercial cleaning, which include wet cleaning as well as dry cleaning solvent use. I have included insights gained from my work with textiles testing, quality control, and extensive experience in dyeing. Anyone buying fabric will do so with more confidence if the basic colorfastness to be expected has been clarified, as it is here.

Because students should understand the importance of standard tests, I have included a brief section on fabric assessment. Home sewers, dressmakers, retail buyers, designers, or fabric buyers for garment houses can apply the "nontechnical" assessments to get valuable information about a fabric's likely performance.

As befits a fabric reference, this text includes a full section on metric in textiles, recording almost every aspect imaginable—the result of my work as the "textiles person" on a metric committee of the Canadian Home Economics Association. When we deal with most of the world, we encounter metric units, and people in laboratory work use them all the time.

The extensive section on fabrics and ecology is unique among current texts. It addresses such issues as: how we can keep warm in cold weather with the least impact on the environment; how we can keep cool and relatively safe from ultraviolet radiation in hot, sunny conditions; what is happening to combat pollution or promote recycling; and finally, what are some of the most forward and exciting developments for the early years of the third millennium.

Throughout *Fabric Reference* I have emphasized key terms that are found in the consumer marketplace: those that reach the public media; those that are seen on hangtags or in advertisements; specific phrases, such as "cotton rich," or "medium micron"; and, most pervasive of all, trademark names and the companies that own them. This has been much more difficult and complex than usual for this revision, as some giants left fiber manufacturing, and a number of mergers around the world created new titans in this industry. At the turn of the 21st century, uncertainties slowed some of this action, but the direction continued strongly toward change, improvement, and advanced technology coupled with environmental awareness. Although many of the new names are not familiar in consumer goods, it is notable how the application of "high performance" fibers, fabric combinations ("systems"), or finishes accelerates each year in consumer activewear. Another pervasive partner of change is microprocessor control of virtually every aspect of fabric production.

There is very little looking back in this *Reference;** instead I have emphasized today's and tomorrow's fabrics the results of leading-edge technology, which produces more and more astounding results.

In the previous edition I paid tribute to microfibers much finer than the wispy filaments from the spinnerets of caterpillar (silk), about which we are already becoming blasé but which are wonders, nonetheless. Now we have *nanofibers* in our near future—fibers about a molecule in diameter, and fabrics incorporating microthermal materials that respond to ambient temperature are also being developed, to insulate the wearer. In addition, research in biotechnology is yielding information affecting natural fibers, treatment of pollution, even fiber synthesis.

Fabric Reference is the distillation of many years' experience in the textiles field, a desire to present this as succinctly and clearly as possible, and a culmination of wide-ranging research into its fast-moving technology to record the most forward developments in the most accessible format. I hope this text offers a lifeline to students of textiles trying to get a focus on the essentials of this demanding subject, and hoping to work in one of the areas where knowledge of fabrics is crucial, those already involved in a textiles or clothing field, but without formal training, and to educators dedicated to leading students through this complicated and rapidly developing subject.

The information applies to many fields:

- Design and manufacture of fibers, yarns, or fabrics, and various aspects of finishing including dyeing and printing;
- Design and production of garments or accessories, whether in business and industry or by an individual in couture, commercial dress-making, or home sewing;
- Design and furnishing of interiors;
- Quality control of fabrics, garments, or other consumer textiles products;
- Any phase of merchandising of fabrics, garments, accessories, or home furnishings, including wholesale, retail, and display, plus staff training;
- Fabric care—laundering, commercial cleaning dry or wet, repair, storage, or conservation;
- Design and production of costume, whether for "living museums" where authentic reproduction costume is desired or for theater in its many guises;
- Preservation and display of historic costume;
- The myriad forms of textile crafts, including spinning, weaving, dyeing, surface embellishment, and needlework;
- Communications in all media concerning any of these areas.

To guide you into and through the exciting, fascinating, colorful world of textiles, I offer the *Fabric Reference*—may it prove a good companion.

Acknowledgments

I would like to lead off with an acknowledgment omitted from the first edition: to the superlative attention and guidance of my editors, especially production editor Laura Cleveland. Although I have done a lot of writing and editing, it was a revelation to me to be in the hands of such experts. There are fewer to thank for the changes and additions made in this second edition, but I thoroughly enjoyed "meeting" those involved by letter or telephone. The shared enthusiasm

*The history of textiles has been my extracurricular passion for many years, taking me as an amateur member into spinning and weaving guilds and as a very active member into costume societies. However, it is modern fabrics I have dealt with all my working life—first in the textiles industry, running a small research, development, and testing laboratory, while at the same time presenting information to consumers through print, radio, and television; and later teaching college fashion students.

of so many diverse people makes a revision like this exciting and a joy. Those who helped me most are listed here, arranged alphabetically by company or organization:

Akzo Nobel Fibres: Graham Allen. American Textile Manufacturers Institute, Inc.: Caroline Bruckner, Communications. Amoco Fabrics & Fibers Co.: David B. Gray. BASF: Andy Buffam. The Bata Shoe Museum: Susana Petti. *Canadian Apparel Magazine*: Hedi Badakhsham. *Canadian Textile Journal*: Roger Leclerc. Celanese via Eileen Brown Associates: Eileen Brown, Consoltex Inc.: Tim Colburn. Corterra via BRSG, Inc.: Sarah Semple. B. A. Crosbie: Consultant. C-Shirt Canada: Jeanne Boldt. Dan-Ric Marketing: Paul Beacock. Doubletex: Cory W. Haynes. The DuPont Company: Adelina Tiberio, Martine Thériault, John Burn. *Fabricare Canada*: Marcia Todd. Federal Trade Commission: Steve Ecklund. *Fiber Organon*, Fiber Economics Bureau: Stan Snowman. FoxFibre (Natural Cotton Colours, Inc.): Sally Fox. W. L. Gore & Associates, Inc.: Cynthia Amon. Michael Graves, Architect: Michael Graves. Hempline Inc.: Geoffrey Kime. Hoechst NA Holdings, Inc.: Vicki Bousman. Industry Canada: Chris Chiba. Intera Corporation: Jim Klopman. Betty Issenman (re: *Sinews of Survival*). JABA Associates: J. A. B. Athey. The 3M Company: D. Christine Shumsky. Meadowbrook Inventions, Inc.: Roberta M. Ruschmann. Micro Thermal Systems, Ltd.: Philip Johnson. Milliken & Company: Timothy Monahan. Department of Entomology, Mississippi State University: Dr. Gerald T. Baker. National Cotton Council of America: T. Cotton Nelson. Outlast Technologies, Inc.: John Erb, Dana Rogers (MPH). Park B. Smith, Inc.: Valborg Linn. Picanol of America: John Vanhee. PTFE® llc: Robert Gunn, Amy Mansfield. Raven Marketing Services, Ltd.: Lisa Chummun. Seneca College of Applied Arts and Technology: Bev Newburg. Solutia Inc. (re: Monsanto): Joan Murcar. Sulzer-Rüti AG: René König. Sulzer-Rüti USA: Heidi M. Jameson. Tencel Fibres Europe: Caroline Crouch. *Textiles Magazine*: Jack Smirfitt. *Textile World*: John W. McCurry, Jim Morrissey. T.G.I. Fabrics: Paul Triska. United Media, United Feature Syndicate: Anna Soler. University of British Columbia Press: Marnie Rice. School of Textile Industries, University of Leeds: Jill Bullock. Uvex Toko Canada Ltd.: Andrew Murdison. Catherine Vernon, Textile Con-

servator. The Woolmark Company: Kate Sumptner, Heather Stuart, Kirsten Mogg.

The illustration on the opening for Section Two is a wonderful mystery entry: It shows part of the surface of the egg of a giant wild silk moth. It is a scanning electron microscope (SEM) image at 360X magnification, winner of the Polaroid International Instant Photomicrography Competition, 1994. I am glad to celebrate this amazing picture, which evokes for me the wonder of nature and science. It was taken by Dr. Gerald T. Baker, Professor of Entomology at Mississippi State University.

Mary Humphries

Acknowledgments—First Edition

As I worked on the manuscript for this book, I often looked forward to preparing some record of thanks to the many who helped me. I realize now that countless others will not be formally acknowledged, starting with my instructors and colleagues over the years. However, a key influence and guide was Jessie Roberts Current, who directed my graduate work and later managed to get me to take over from her the National Textiles Committee of the Consumers' Association of Canada, in its heyday of volunteer consumer advocacy. Perhaps most of all I owe a great debt to my students, who have led me first to try to digest and keep current the sprawling body of information to do with textiles, and then to compress and highlight it for those who do not have the time or opportunity to absorb all the detail behind the working guides and conclusions presented here. Their questions, comments, challenges, and responsiveness have helped shape this presentation of *Fabric Reference*.

Of individuals directly connected to production of this book, I wish to thank Paul Beacock, my computer graphics wizard (who had not been familiar with textiles before!), and the stalwart "home team" of my daughter Nina Scott-Stoddart, my sister Lucy Noble, and my good friend Rosemary Webber for endless hours of effort. Support came also from Bev Newburg of Seneca College, Cathy Bell of St. Lawrence College, and Alistair Stewart, expert and patient photographer. Claire Becker shared fur expertise over the years in Seneca textiles classes. My reference on silk production was obtained for me by Debbie Boedefeld Cowan, a former student now living in Japan, and the essential translations from the Japanese were by Hiroshi Yamamoto. Critical appraisal of the jacquard loom diagram was made by Marceline Szpakowski. I also wish to thank the reviewers of the original draft of the manuscript for their input: M. Kathleen Colussy, Art Institute of Fort Lauderdale, Florida; Kay S. Grise, Florida State University, Talahassee; David Harrington, Bauder Fashion College, Atlanta, Georgia; Joan Laughlin, University of Nebraska, Lincoln; Ruth MacEachern, Emery Collegiate Institute, Toronto, Ontario; Joanne F. Magoldi, Mount Ida College, Chamberlayne School of Design and Merchandising, Newton Center, Massachusetts; Katie Parham, Cabot College, St. John's, Newfoundland; and Diane L. Shelly, International Academy of Merchandising and Design, Tampa, Florida.

So many more gave of their time and expertise, and often lightened the job with enthusiasm and humor; I hope most of these are in the following listing, arranged alphabetically by company or organization:

Akzo Nobel Textile Technical Institute: Wolfgang Luft. American Sheep Industry Association: Ron Pope. American Textile Manufacturers Institute: Gail Raiman, Anne Schmitz. Amoco Fabrics & Fibers Company: M. Normand Joly. BASF Canada: Owen Bird. Bayer Corporation: Ben Bruner. Bayer Faser GmbH: Dr. Türck, Dr. Reinehr, R. Dohm. Canadian General Standards Board: Ginette Chalifoux. Christina Canada Inc.: Myriam Cook. Ciba-Geigy Limited: Peter Warne. Cluett International (Sanforized): Andrew Gryszkiewicz. Coats Patons: Karen Glover, John Laurie. *Cocoon World* photographers Shigeki Furukawa and Masahisa Furuta. Consoltex Inc.: Paul Pinsler. Consorzio Merletti di Burano: Dott. Annibale Tagliapietra. Cotton Incorporated: Bill Daddi. Courtaulds Fibers Inc.: Don Vidler. Courtaulds Fibres: S. A. Frankham. Cranston Print Works Company: George W. Shuster, Christine Navarette. Dahlbrook Farm: Lars Dahl. Denver Museum of Natural History: Dr. Richard S. Peigler. Dominion Textile Inc.: Sylvain Dufort. Dorothea Knitting Mills Ltd.: Beryl Borsook. Down North: Wendy Chambers. DuPont Canada: Wolfe Brehme, Elizabeth Lam. Eco Fibre Canada Inc.: Judy Heifetz. eco-tex consortium: Christel Beuth. E. I. DuPont de Nemours and Company: Karen Galbraith. Environment Canada, Climate Information Branch: Gary Teeter and M. S. Webb. *Fabricare Canada Mag-*

azine: Marcia Todd. Federal Trade Commission: Steve Ecklund, Bret Smart. Gateway Technologies, Inc.: Bernard T. Parry. GINETEX Secretariat: Nathalie Gamet. W. L. Gore & Associates, Inc.: Lisa Wyre. Hafner Inc.: M. Adrian Spoerry, Shirley Horner. Health Canada, Product Safety: Kathy Wick. Hoechst AG: H. Dilley and Robert Jarausch. Hoechst Celanese: Maxine Speakman, Ellen Sweeney. Hoechst Celanese Canada Inc.: Wilma Wiemer. Home Laundering Consultative Council: Richard Crooks. Industry Canada, Consumer Products: Chris Chiba, Kathy Dobbin, Francine Chabot-Plante. International Fabricare Institute: Jill Handman. International Wool Secretariat (IWS): Rachel McCluskey. IPL Ingenieurplanung Leichtbau GmbH: Dr. Harmut Ayrle. ISO Central Secretariat: Anke Varcin. Italian Cultural Institute (Istituto Italiano di Cultura di Toronto): Dr. Francesca Valente. Kanebo New York: H. Jindo. Kuraray Company Ltd.: Junko Mori. Lenzing AG: Dr. Dieter Eichinger. Linda Lundström Ltd.: Linda Lundström. 3M Canada Inc.: D. Christine Shumsky. Malden Mills Industries, Inc.: Kelly Raadmae, Ernst B. Weglein. Malimo, c/o Karl Mayer Textile Machinery Corp.: W. Poenite. Masters of Linen/USA: Pauline V. delli-Carpini. McCord Museum of Canadian History: Nicole Vallières. Merrow Publishing: Dr. J. G. Cook. Messe Frankfurt Techtextil-Team: Michael Jännecke. Metropolitan Toronto Zoo: Toby Styles. Mohair Council of America: Christie Ingrassia. Monsanto Canada Ltd.: Joan Murcar, Dragana Zivanovic. Morrison Textile Machinery Co.: James Hamilton. National Cotton Council of America: T. Cotton Nelson. Polywert Faserrecycling GmbH: Katrin Näser. J. C. Rennie & Co.: Dr. J. Lawrence. Rhône-Poulenc, Textile Performance Chemicals: Jack Bennett. Arthur Sanderson & Sons: Tony Tenkortenaar. SATRA Footwear Technology Centre: Peter Larcombe. Sears Canada: Shirley Baker. Sears Roebuck: Nancy Pauer. Seneca College Fashion Resource Centre: Claire Becker. Shima Seiki U.S.A. Inc.: Anthony McBryan. Speizman Industries (Jumberca): Bob Speizman. Statistics Canada: Margaret Parlor. Sulzer Canada Inc.: Gary Zimmermann. Sunsoakers, Inc.: Sheryl Barber. Teijin Limited: S. Tsuji. The Textile Institute: Paul Daniels. Tribune Media Services: Mary Beth Pacer. Universal Press Syndicate: Carla Stiff. Valley-Tex Inc.: David Huffman. Wool Bureau of Canada Ltd.: Heather Stuart.

Mary Humphries

SECTION ONE

INTRODUCTION

Fabrics—Everyday and Extraordinary

There are many familiar fabrics around us, and we are well aware of most of them, for they make up our clothing, plus interior furnishings at home as well as in transport and at work. We give little thought, as a rule, to the myriad other uses of textiles, some of them *really* "far out"—as far as the space program has taken them. Our focus, quite naturally, is on textiles used in consumer goods, and to a lesser extent on what are called *industrial* or *technical* textiles.

However, before using this *Reference* to get a clearer picture of how our everyday fabrics behave (and why), let us indulge in a kind of trivia game to uncover the not-so-obvious uses of fabric, yarn, or fiber. While some are used right in our homes, many others are used in articles and applications definitely not for the general public, yet tremendous developments in the industrial and technical fields are increasingly driving the forward edge of consumer fabrics.

Consider the canvas behind an oil painting, the tape in a cassette, the stadium's "grass" carpet as you watch a game on TV, the "enhancement" by synthetic fibers of the turf on a horseracing track, the teabag you used for your "cuppa," the filter in your air conditioner, the cover for your pickup truck, the cords in the tires, the belts and hoses under the hood? If a handsome balloon floats overhead, that's more fabric—also lines (ropes), not unlike the combination of canvas and lines still so important to sailing. You may have been in a structure with a fabric roof (and not just a pup tent, either)—perhaps a sports dome that retracts in good weather.

A fabric made for camouflage but about as highly visible as anything can be was developed to mask scaffolding around the 555-foot-high Washington Monument while it underwent its first major renovation since it was opened to the public in 1888.[1] The National Park Service undertook the job with private funding, and project architect Michael Graves wanted the monument to look good all during the work on its granite exterior. Some 15,000 sq. yds. of BO-LITE® mesh fabric (by Bo-Tex, Hogansville, Georgia) were used in panels designed to look like the actual blocks of the monument's structure (well anchored against strong winds). That all added up to some 1.3 acres of

fabric—hard to miss—to hang until July 4, 2000, the date for the unveiling of the monument in all its restored glory (see Figure 1.1).

At the other extreme, it takes the mind's eye to see the fiber optics core your telephone message flashes along, the miles of electrical cables hidden in any town or city, fibers in car brake linings and clutch facings, or air bags before they deploy. There is extensive use of fabrics embedded in the ground (*geotextiles*), such as those lining roadbeds on our highways to control ground erosion or slippage. These are often what are called *nonwoven* fabrics, but may be woven or knit.

Some of our most advanced textiles were developed for spacecraft and equipment, including astronauts' suits. Such extraordinary materials often eventually find consumer applications, but before that, they may be used in safety and protective clothing

Figure 1.1 Washington monument as it would appear during a $9.4 million restoration, to be completed by July 4, 2000 (computer rendering). The bluish-grey panels of strong mesh fabric were assembled by the Sinco Group, and firmly tied to the 32 miles of aluminum scaffolding beneath. (Photo by Marek Bulaj. Courtesy of Michael Graves, Architect)

[1]John W. McCurrey, "Monumental Fabric Goes to Washington," *Textile World*, June 1998: 24 and "GA Fabric Will Dress Monument," *Textile World*, November 1998: 24.

or equipment for people functioning under extreme conditions: firefighters, police officers, and operating room personnel (who may also be inserting very special textile artificial body parts such as arteries) (see Figure 1.2). Consumer applications of these "high-tech" fabrics include super-high-strength fiber gloves worn by butchers and flame-resistant aircraft upholstery. Still superior or special, but closer to run-of-the-mill consumer goods are those termed *contract fabrics*, for use in commercial applications such as offices or hospitals, with strict performance specifications.

Carry on this challenge, and if you get excited, wave a flag—another textile! It is time to wade in to find out what you want or need to know about fabrics.

Guide to Using This Reference

This *Reference* is designed to provide:

1. A "skeleton textbook" in as nontechnical language as possible, to clarify the main terminology and vocabulary of the subject of textiles used in clothing, home furnishings, interior decorating, and other consumer goods. "Skeleton" does not imply a weak dilution of this material—rather it is the condensed essentials when a lot of detail ("flesh") is pared away. This covers fibers, yarn types, fabric constructions, and finishing including dyeing and printing.

2. Accessible information, condensed in graphs, tables, and diagrams, especially to clarify relationships and provide summaries of the data underlying this field, which expands ever more rapidly each year.

3. Clear focus on up-to-date developments in fabrics as used in the consumer market, especially fashion fabrics, with trademark names included where possible—you see and hear more about GORE-TEX® fabric than "microporous film." This book features trademark names (mainly for fibers or finishes) that convey significant information on the expected behavior of a fabric.

4. Hard-to-find information significant in work with fabrics, e.g., on care, laundering, commercial cleaning (dry or wet), stain removal, storage, colorfastness, function related to fashion (including activewear).

5. Emphasis on the relationship of fabric and the environment, including discussions of pollution and recycling—major concerns today. Also covered: how to keep warm in cold weather or cool (and safe from UV rays) in sunny, hot conditions. We also look at 21st-century developments.

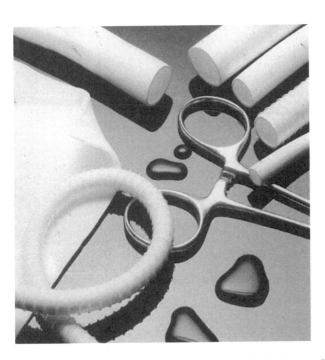

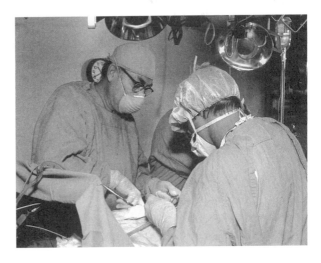

Figure 1.2 Tubes of expanded polytetrafluoroethylene replace human arteries in GORE-TEX® fabric vascular grafts. (Courtesy of W. L. Gore & Associates, Inc.)

6. Metric conversion data; even if the process in North America is stalled, the inch-pound system is an "island" in the world "metric sea."

7. A comprehensive index, to link all the data in this *Reference* with its companion *Fabric Glossary*. The best outcome of textiles study is a meaningful connection with specific fabrics. The *Fabric Glossary* gives detailed descriptions, with photos, of major "name fabrics" and comprehensive lists giving fabrics suitable for many end uses, in clothing as well as interiors. It is printed on heavier paper and provides templates to aid mounting of actual fabric samples for the best possible "illustrations." A Swatch Set designed for *Fabric Glossary* and related to Sections 2–5 of *Fabric Reference* is available; see *Teaching Aids and Resources*, and order form in back of this book.

Equipment Helpful in Fabric Study

The following equipment will be useful in studying and identifying fabric samples. Many items can be obtained from a laboratory supply house or special hobby or college store.

- **Scissors.** Sharp; *not* the pinking type.
- **Invisible or double-sided tape.** For mounting samples.
- **Magnifier.** A most useful item. Magnification of as little as four times (4×) will bring out features of fabrics and yarns in startling clarity. The best magnifiers incorporate a battery-operated light. Anyone involved with fabrics will find one handy. Available from laboratory supply companies, but also in optical stores and departments. (See Figure 1.3.)
- **Pick (dissecting) needle.** You also could use a hat pin or a darning needle with the eye in a cork. (See Figure 1.3.)
- **Pick or thread counter.** Also called a loop glass or linen tester. It gives some magnification and allows a count of the number of yarns or knit loops in a centimeter or inch. (See Figure 1.4.)
- **Microscope.** Need not be high quality; the type sold for children's hobby use is quite adequate. You will also need some slides and cover slips, and a dropper bottle for water is useful. (See Figure 1.5.)

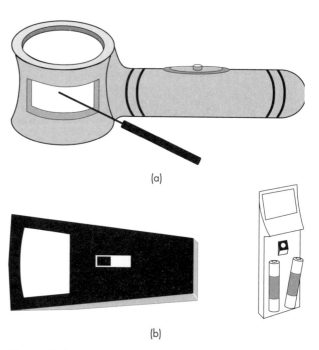

(a)

(b)

Figure 1.3 (a) Magnifier and dissecting needle; (b) optical department magnifier.

Figure 1.4 Pick counter.

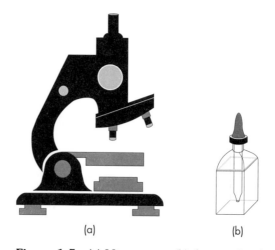

(a)   (b)

Figure 1.5 (a) Microscope; (b) dropper bottle.

Fabrics—An Overview

What Do We Want in Clothing?

We want clothing to make us look and feel good! As well as good appearance (what might be termed **psychological comfort**), today's consumer should get **physiological comfort** from clothing. In order to fulfill either of these requirements, apparel must fit the body and move well with it. Comfort also means keeping us warm in cold weather and relatively cool in hot weather. For most of us, part of comfort is the wearing of apparel that is fashion right as well. The shirts worn for playing tennis in Figure 1.6 are fashionable, fit and move well, *and* protect from the sun's ultraviolet rays. Today's consumer has extended that

Figure 1.6 These shirts, comfortable and fashionable, also provide protection from UV rays. They are C-SHIRT™ textile, which has a sun protection factor (SPF) of 100+ wet or dry. (Courtesy of C-Shirt Canada)

sense of rightness to include *environmentally friendly*—more on this in Section 7.

We have also come to expect that fabrics will be easy to look after—that it will not be hard to restore them to a neat, clean state, and that they will go on looking good even after considerable wear.

In almost every application, then, fabrics must serve *useful* as well as *decorative* functions. In order to select fabrics that are suitable to a particular end use, method of care, or price range, we must have an understanding of how they behave and why.

Groups of fabrics and fibers react differently from one another; these differences have affected the choice of textiles throughout history. With the introduction of manufactured fibers and complex finishing materials, the choice is much wider, but it is still governed by the behavior properties of:

Fibers

Yarns

Fabric constructions

Coloration and finishes

All of these will be examined in this *Reference,* but first we should define what a fabric is.

Fabric Definition

Fabric is known to us under several other names: textile, cloth, material, dry goods, and stuff. The derivations of these names are as follows:

fabric. (Latin *fabrica*) Workshop.

textile. (Latin *textilis*) Woven.

cloth. (Old English) Piece of woven, felted, or otherwise formed stuff.

(dry) goods. Manufactured soft wares (merchandise) as compared to hardware.

stuff. (archaic) Woven material of any kind.

So a regular dictionary definition of a fabric or textile usually includes woven, knitted, braided, twisted, or felted fabrics, but will not cover many materials we use as fabrics today, such as shower curtains of film or interfacings of nonwoven fabric.

A more cumbersome but inclusive definition of *fabric* would be:

a thin, flexible sheet of material with sufficient strength and tear resistance (especially when wet) for clothing; interior fabrics; and other protective, useful, and decorative functions.

While leather and fur may be considered to be natural fabrics, most **fabrics** are manufactured. Nearly all can be unraveled into **yarns,** and these further taken apart (untwisted) to give fine, hairlike **fibers.** (See Figure 1.7.)

Figure 1.8 gives a flowchart of fabric production and use.

Basic Terms Used with Fabrics and Fibers

Before using this *Reference*, you need to know some basic terms and special vocabulary used to describe fabrics and particularly to compare the character and performance of fibers.

Aesthetic Characteristics

hand. Feel or handle. It may be warm and dry or cool; smooth and slippery or fuzzy, rough, bumpy; soft or firm; "sleazy" or with good body; supple and drapable, even limp, or crisp, stiff, wiry.

flexibility. Suppleness, pliability; important to draping ability. Drapability as well as softness is related to fiber diameter (fineness); a fine staple fiber allows a fine, even, smooth, lustrous, strong yarn. Terms used for fineness are usually derived from yarn count (see Section 3), such as *denier* or *decitex* and wool quality numbers. The current

term *microfiber* represents a fiber with a diameter less than that of silk, which is approximately 1 denier or decitex.

luster. Subdued, pleasing shine or sheen; related to the fiber surface (smooth or rough) plus the shape of a cross section of the fiber. A round cross section will yield shine; a nonround or lobal cross section will yield luster. Manufactured fibers as made are bright; with the addition of a delustrant (white pigment) they are delustered or dull.

pilling. Fibers, worked out of a fabric, roll up into small balls on the surface. All staple fibers in spun yarns can form pills. Stubborn pilling, i.e., pills that cannot easily be brushed off, is a problem. This occurs with very strong fibers. (See Figure 1.9.)

oleophilic. "Oil-loving" or having a tendency to hold oily stains.

cover (opacity). Ability to create a dense-looking surface. (See Figure 1.10.)

sound. As in the rustle of silk.

Comfort Characteristics

absorbency. Ability to take up water. **Hydrophilic** or "water-loving" fabric takes up moisture; **hygroscopic** fabric takes up and holds moisture; **hydrophobic** or "water-hating" fabric absorbs little. Absorbency is of primary importance to comfort, for perspiration is a main body temperature control mechanism. We pass off about a liter (quart) a day of "insensible perspiration" as vapor; it is only when perspiration forms as water drops that we are aware of it as sweat.

Absorbency also affects collection of static electricity—electrostatic charges formed when two materials come into contact and are then separated. Moisture will conduct or "bleed" charges away, if present in a fabric; a fiber's electrical resistivity increases when dry. Olefin fiber (polypropylene) is an exception in that it absorbs almost nothing but does not tend to collect or build up static; it wicks moisture (*see wicking*). Further discussion of static buildup is presented under *Properties in Relation to Use (Synthetic Fibers)* in Section 2.

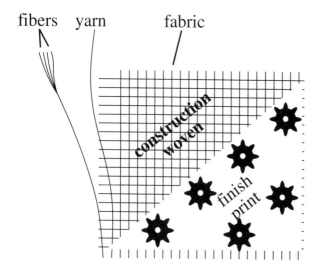

Figure 1.7 Most fabrics can be unraveled to yarns, which can be untwisted to fibers.

adsorbency. Moisture taken up on the surface, varies with the surface area available.

FABRIC PRODUCTION AND USE - FLOW CHART AND TIMING

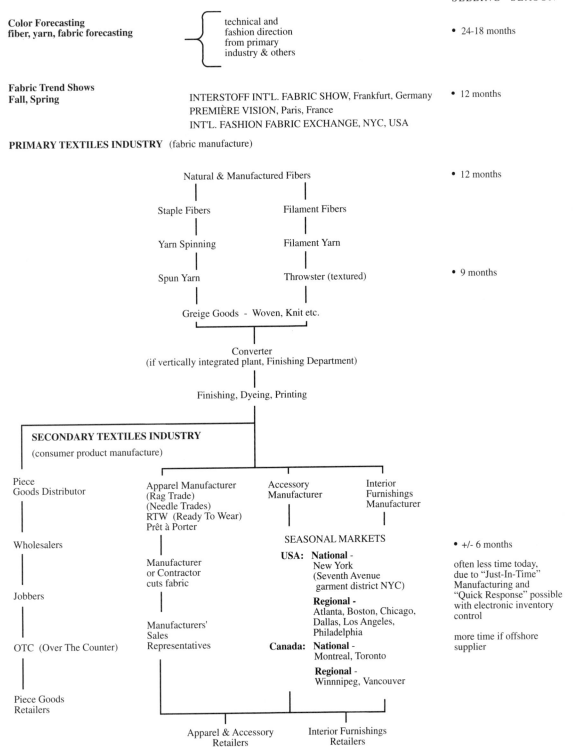

Color Forecasting
fiber, yarn, fabric forecasting

technical and
fashion direction
from primary
industry & others

• 24-18 months

Fabric Trend Shows
Fall, Spring

INTERSTOFF INT'L. FABRIC SHOW, Frankfurt, Germany
PREMIÈRE VISION, Paris, France
INT'L. FASHION FABRIC EXCHANGE, NYC, USA

• 12 months

PRIMARY TEXTILES INDUSTRY   (fabric manufacture)

Natural & Manufactured Fibers

• 12 months

Staple Fibers   Filament Fibers

Yarn Spinning   Filament Yarn

Spun Yarn   Throwster (textured)

• 9 months

Greige Goods - Woven, Knit etc.

Converter
(if vertically integrated plant, Finishing Department)

Finishing, Dyeing, Printing

SECONDARY TEXTILES INDUSTRY

(consumer product manufacture)

Piece
Goods Distributor

Apparel Manufacturer
(Rag Trade)
(Needle Trades)
RTW (Ready To Wear)
Prêt à Porter

Accessory
Manufacturer

Interior
Furnishings
Manufacturer

SEASONAL MARKETS

• +/- 6 months

Wholesalers

USA: **National -**
New York
(Seventh Avenue
garment district NYC)

often less time today,
due to "Just-In-Time"
Manufacturing and
"Quick Response" possible
with electronic inventory
control

Manufacturer
or Contractor
cuts fabric

Regional -
Atlanta, Boston, Chicago,
Dallas, Los Angeles,
Philadelphia

Jobbers

Canada: **National -**
Montreal, Toronto

more time if offshore
supplier

Manufacturers'
Sales
Representatives

OTC (Over The Counter)

Regional -
Winnnipeg, Vancouver

Piece Goods
Retailers

Apparel & Accessory
Retailers

Interior Furnishings
Retailers

Figure 1.8 Fabric production and use flowchart.

Figure 1.9 Pilling on a woven polyester fabric. (Courtesy of the Textile Institute [Shirley Institute photo])

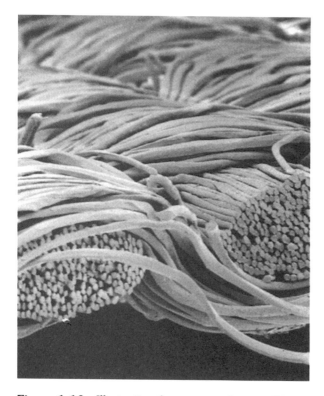

Figure 1.10 Illustrating the concept of cover: TREVI-RA FINESSE® microfibers provide good cover to this fabric surface; the fabric also keeps out wind and rain. (Courtesy of Trevira GmbH, formerly Hoechst AG)

wicking. Passing moisture along the length of the fiber, whether or not it absorbs. Because olefin fiber wicks well, it can be made into comfortable underwear or sportswear although it absorbs almost no moisture. Flax fiber both absorbs and wicks well; this is the reason linen has long been preferred for clothing in hot, humid climates.

resiliency. Ability to spring back when crushed. This most obviously affects crush or wrinkle resistance. (What is measured in testing is wrinkle recovery.) Resiliency of the fiber also affects the insulative property of a fabric. If a fabric with air spaces in it for insulation is made of resilient fibers, the air spaces will not be lost by the fibers "packing down." Such a fabric will prevent loss of body heat and be a good insulator, because one of the best insulators known is a layer of still air (the same principle used in double- or triple-glazed windows).

loft. The volume or amount of space taken up by a given weight of fiber. It is related to low specific gravity or, more simply, to low density, but is not equivalent to weight alone. A lofty fiber such as wool will give a thick material, for example, a heavy coat fabric, that is not nearly so heavy as one made of a denser fiber such as cotton.

crimp. Waviness along a fiber. The finest wool fibers have a great deal of crimp.

elongation. Ability of a fiber to stretch before it breaks; the amount it "gives." (See also *modulus*.)

elasticity. Elastic recovery is the relative ability to return to original length after stretching. A truly elastic fiber (an elastomer) can be stretched to several times its original length, with immediate and complete recovery, time after time.

skin irritation. Rough fibers, such as coarse wool, can cause itchiness and feel prickly.

Performance Characteristics

strength. Strength, which affects durability, is of several kinds:

- *tensile strength* (termed **tenacity** for fibers). Resistance to pulling or tearing forces.

- *resistance to abrasion.* Resistance to rubbing or scraping.

- *flex strength.* Resistance to bending.

- *modulus.* Resistance to stretching. High modulus is little stretch for a given pulling force.
- *wet modulus.* Ratio of wet strength to breaking elongation.

reaction to heat and flame. Fabrics vary in their reaction to heat and to flame.

- *thermoplastic.* Becoming soft and eventually melting when heated, allowing molding and heat setting. Fibers that do not melt will char with heat. All major manufactured fibers, except reconstituted cellulose fibers, are thermoplastic.
- *heat sensitive.* In this *Reference,* taken to indicate a fiber that would soften in home washing, a hot dryer, and at any but the lowest setting of an iron.
- *very heat sensitive.* Indicates a fiber that must be kept away from dryers, hot radiators, and even a low setting of an iron.
- *flameproof (nonflammable, noncombustible).* Will not burn.
- *flame resistant.* Can burn, but extinguishes when not in contact with flame (self-extinguishing).
- *flammable.* Can ignite and burn.

felting. Matting together of wool and hair fibers; the result in fabric is thickening and shrinkage.

dimensional stability. Ability to keep size, neither shrinking nor stretching.

wet press retention. Ability to hold a press if damp or wet.

Other Basic Terms

polymer. Having many parts: the submicroscopic structure of all fibers. Long molecular chains of small units (*monomers*) join together like a string of pop beads to make a *high polymer, macromolecule,* or "giant molecule." To give an idea of molecular size scale, G. R. Lomax of the Shirley Institute, Manchester, U.K., explained that "a 1 cm cube of polyethylene contains approximately one million, million, million molecular chains, each consisting of some twenty thousand monomer units."[2]

crystalline. Structure of a solid aligned into a repeating pattern. It is hard to realize that a fiber (think of one of your own hairs) is a crystal, just as a diamond is. This paradox can be explained,[3] but here it is simply recorded, since the more (perfectly) crystalline a fiber is (molecular chains closely packed), the stronger it is. Less well organized parts of a fiber are called *amorphous* and are usually more absorbent. The names come from Greek: *crystal* meaning "clear ice"; *amorphous* meaning "having no shape." A fiber may have some areas more crystalline, others more amorphous. Only one fiber type, novoloid, has no crystallinity.

orientation. Another term having to do with organization of a fiber's molecular chains; in this case, how nearly parallel they lie to each other. The more oriented a fiber, the stronger it is. If the long chains lie at all angles to each other, it is called a random arrangement. Again, a fiber may have more- and less-oriented parts. The chief method of orienting manufactured fibers is by drawing, and filaments not fully drawn are called POY—partially oriented yarn. (See *Synthetic Manufactured Fibers* in Section 2.)

[2]G. R. Lomax, "Polymerization Reaction," *Textiles,* 1987 vol. 16 #2:50.

[3]"Crystal Gazing," *Newscience,* The Ontario Science Centre, May 1991: 1.

SECTION TWO

Textile Fibers

Fibers Are Fundamental

Most basic of all in selecting fabrics is the behavior of the **fibers,** the smallest visible components of most fabrics.

The two main divisions in fibers are **natural** textile fibers (found in nature *as fibers* that can be used to make fabrics) and **manufactured** (MF) fibers (formerly called "man-made")—a fiber-forming raw material in the form of a thick, sticky liquid is "spun" or extruded through spinneret holes, forming streams that are solidified into fibers. The raw material for MF fibers may be natural, but it is converted into textile fibers by a manufacturing process. While there are MF fibers made of natural rubber (as well as of synthetic rubber), there is no such thing as a natural rubber fiber. Similarly, TENCEL® lyocell is not a natural fiber; it is an MF fiber made of a natural material, cellulose.

Textile fibers may be staple or filament. **Staple** fibers are relatively short, measured in millimeters or inches. **Filament** fibers are relatively long, measured in meters or yards. Most natural fibers are staple; the only natural filament fiber is reeled or cultivated silk. On the other hand, all MF fibers can be staple or filament; they begin as filament, and in this form can give silky or (reeled) silk-like fabrics. They can also be cut or broken into staple to give fabrics that look and feel more like wool, cotton, or linen.

Textile Fibers Are Special

Many fibrous materials are not suitable to make into fabrics, e.g., corn silk or wood slivers. Textile fibers must have certain properties: flexible, thin (but not too thin), long (enough), cohesive, and strong (enough).

Textile fibers must be flexible. Wood fibers do not bend easily—you cannot make fabrics from slivers! Textile fibers are also very thin—long in relation to diameter. To be mechanically spun into yarn—drawn out and twisted—staple fibers must have sufficient length, strength, and cohesiveness (fiber-to-fiber friction). Many seed fibers are too short, weak, and slippery to spin into yarn; kapok, for instance, can be used only for stuffing.

Of course, for a fiber to be used a great deal, there must be a reasonable supply and price.

What's in a Name? (Generic Names)

Fibers are classified into groups, each of which is given a **generic** name or "generic." For natural fibers, this generic is the name of the plant (cotton) or animal (camel) from which the fiber comes, or an accepted name, such as wool or mohair. For MF fibers, the generic name is given to a family of fibers of similar chemical makeup and is specified in textile labeling regulations in the United States, Canada, and many other countries (see *Fiber Content Labeling*).

A full listing of generics and their relationships is shown graphically as a textile fiber "family tree" in Figure 2.1 and as flowcharts in Figures 2.3 and 2.4. Only a few of these are used extensively by consumers; these *major generics* are shown in Figure 2.2 as a "pruned" textile fiber family tree. All are summarized and discussed in this section.

Note that some generic names legitimate in Europe or Canada are not recognized by the United States. Textile Fiber Products Identification Act, although all are known internationally (ISO 2076—1977). Some of these are: *cupro, chlorofibre, modal,* and *vinylal.* Conversely, ISO rejected *rayon* as a generic name in 1971, although it remains a legitimate generic name in the United States and Canada.

Some names are not official in the United States or Canada:

polynosic (a term for one type of HWM viscose rayon)

fibranne (a term for viscose rayon used in France)

PVC (an acronym for polyvinyl chloride, United States generic vinyon)

PVA (an acronym for polyvinyl alcohol—vinal)

polyacrylonitrile (PAN) or polyacryl (terms for acrylic)

Fiber Content Labeling

In the United States, the Textile Fiber Products Identification Act[1] (TFPIA), enforced by the Federal Trade Commission, specifies requirements for labels,

---

[1]"Rules and Regulations under the Textile Fiber Products Identification Act," from Bureau of Consumer Protection, Federal Trade Commission, Sixth and Pennsylvania Avenue NW, Washington, DC 20580.

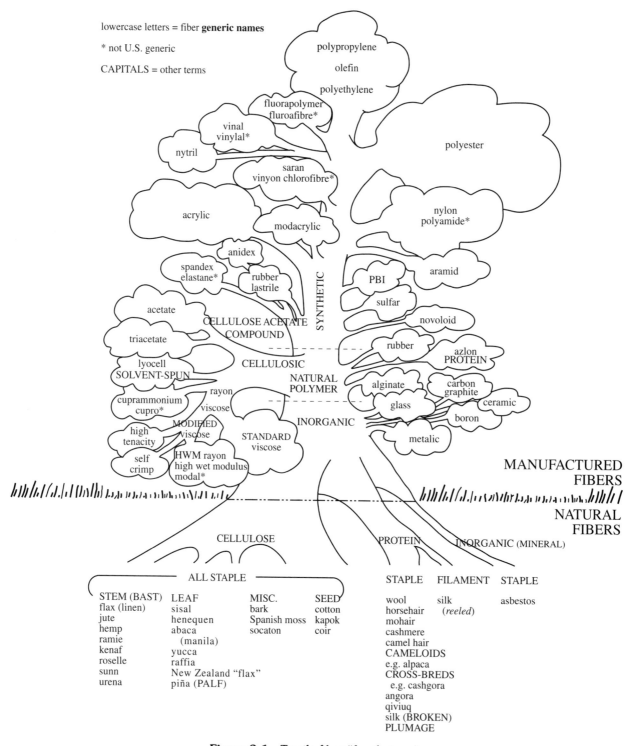

lowercase letters = fiber **generic names**

* not U.S. generic

CAPITALS = other terms

polypropylene
olefin
polyethylene

fluorapolymer
fluroafibre*

vinal
vinylal*

nytril

polyester

saran
vinyon chlorofibre*

acrylic

modacrylic

nylon
polyamide*

anidex

spandex
elastane*

rubber
lastrile

SYNTHETIC

PBI

sulfar

aramid

acetate

CELLULOSE ACETATE
COMPOUND

novoloid

triacetate

CELLULOSIC

rubber

azlon
PROTEIN

lyocell
SOLVENT-SPUN

NATURAL
POLYMER

alginate

carbon
graphite

cuprammonium
cupro*

rayon

viscose

glass

ceramic

high
tenacity

MODIFIED
viscose

INORGANIC

boron

self
crimp

HWM rayon
high wet modulus
modal*

STANDARD
viscose

metalic

MANUFACTURED
FIBERS

NATURAL
FIBERS

CELLULOSE

PROTEIN

INORGANIC (MINERAL)

ALL STAPLE				STAPLE	FILAMENT	STAPLE
STEM (BAST)	LEAF	MISC.	SEED	wool	silk	asbestos
flax (linen)	sisal	bark	cotton	horsehair	(*reeled*)	
jute	henequen	Spanish moss	kapok	mohair		
hemp	abaca	socaton	coir	cashmere		
ramie	(manila)			camel hair		
kenaf	yucca			CAMELOIDS		
roselle	raffia			e.g. alpaca		
sunn	New Zealand "flax"			CROSS-BREDS		
urena	piña (PALF)			e.g. cashgora		
				angora		
				qiviuq		
				silk (BROKEN)		
				PLUMAGE		

Figure 2.1 Textile fiber "family tree."

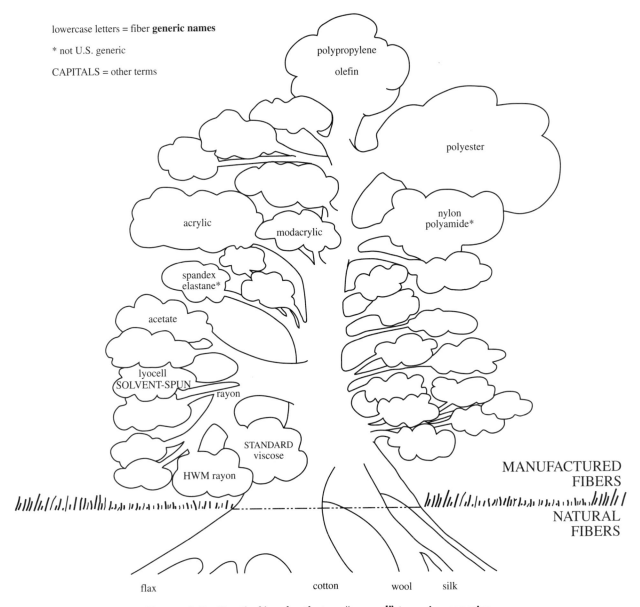

lowercase letters = fiber **generic names**

* not U.S. generic

CAPITALS = other terms

polypropylene

olefin

polyester

acrylic

modacrylic

nylon
polyamide*

spandex
elastane*

acetate

lyocell
SOLVENT-SPUN

rayon

STANDARD
viscose

HWM rayon

MANUFACTURED
FIBERS

NATURAL
FIBERS

flax   cotton   wool   silk

Figure 2.2 Textile fiber family tree "pruned" to major generics.

invoices, or advertising for most textile fiber consumer products (there are some exemptions); in Canada, the Textile Labelling and Advertising Regulations made under the Textile Labelling Act, administered by Industry Canada, give similar specifications.[2] Labels should state in English (Canada: English and French) the con-

tent by generic name (not capitalized) of each fiber present in an amount of 5 percent or more, listed in descending order of percentage. A fiber present as less than 5 percent, unless it clearly has functional significance, and excluding decoration, is labeled "other fiber." Generic names are defined in the regulations. A trademark name (see the next section) may be added in immediate conjunction with and in type of roughly equal size and prominence to the generic. When the fiber content cannot be determined, terms

[2]"Guide to the Textile Labelling and Advertising Regulations," Fair Business Practices Branch, Competition Bureau, Industry Canada, 50 Victoria Street, Hull, QC K1A 0C9.

NATURAL FIBERS

lower case letters = generics
CAPITALS = other terms

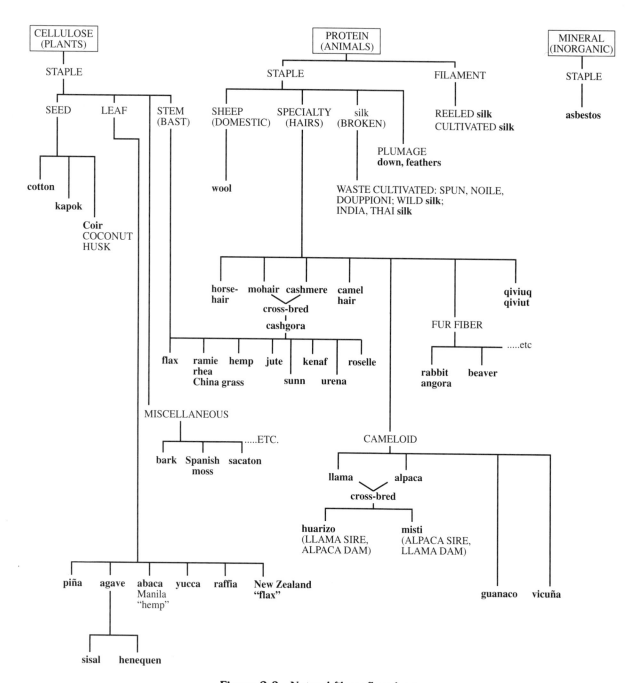

Figure 2.3 Natural fibers flowchart.

MANUFACTURED FIBERS

lower case letters = generics (+ PBI)
CAPITALS = other terms (except PBI)
* not USA generic

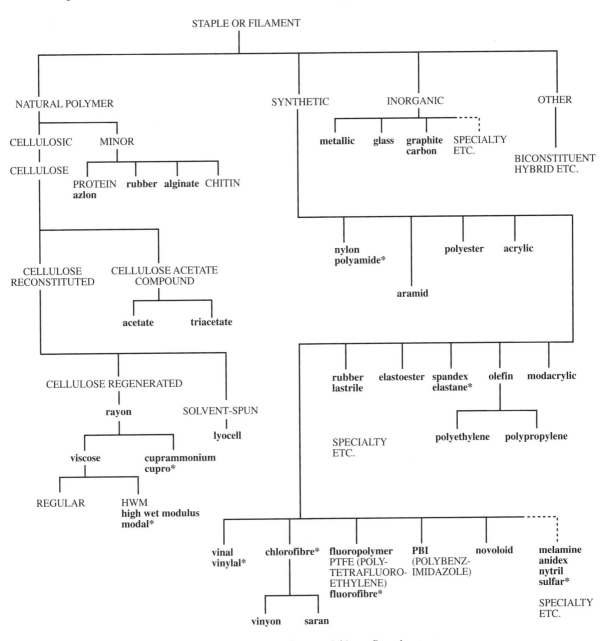

Figure 2.4 Manufactured fibers flowchart.

such as "unknown fibers" and their origin, such as "waste materials" are allowable. A company name or registered identification number must also appear on the label, and each act details declaration of the country where the textile product was processed or made.

What Is a Trademark Name?

With many fashion-forward, "high tech," or "Space Age" articles, consumers are much more familiar with the trademark names than with the fiber generic names; some examples are the trademark names ANTRON® in nylon, FORTREL® in polyester, and ACRILAN® in acrylic. Although this is especially true with names of fibers, it also occurs with trademark names in yarns (SUPPLEX®), fabrics (ULTRASUEDE®, GORE-TEX®), and finishes (SCOTCHGARD®).

Trademarks (brand, house, or trade names) are names or symbols given to a product by a company or association that has registered and owns the name. Many names we use indiscriminately for any

of similar products are actually trademarks of well-known products, such as COKE, KODAK, and KLEENEX.

These are powerful promotional tools, especially when they include or use a memorable *logo* (word in distinctive type) or symbol (such as the interlocking rings of the Olympic games). An example is shown in Figure 2.5: the SEAL OF COTTON symbol (a stylized cotton boll) plus the logo used by the trade association Cotton Incorporated for use with products made 100 percent of U.S. American Upland cotton.

Figure 2.5 The "SEAL OF COTTON" is a registered servicemark/trademark of Cotton Incorporated. **(Courtesy of Cotton Incorporated)**

Table 2.1 *Fiber Properties*

Fiber Group	Tenacity (Tensile Strength)	Abrasion Resistance	Absorbency	Static Resistance	Bulk and Loft
cotton	+++	++	+++	++++	+
flax	+++(+)	+/–	+++(+)	++++	—
wool	—	+++	++++	++	+++(+)
silk	+++(+)	*	+++	++	*
viscose rayon	+	+	++++	++++	+
HWM rayon	++	+(+)	++++	++++	+
lyocell	+++(+)	++	++++	++++	+
acetate	—	—	++	+	++
triacetate	—	—	+	+	++
nylon (polyamide)	++++	++++	+	+/–	++(+)
polyester	+++(+)	+++(+)	—	—	++(+)
acrylic	++	++	—	+/–	++++
modacrylic	++	++	—	+/–	+++(+)
olefin (polypropylene)	+++(+)	+++(+)	—	++++	++++
glass	++++	—	0	*	—

++++ excellent   +++ good   ++ fairly good   + fair   +/– fair to poor   — poor or deficient

A great deal of money can be invested in establishing a trademark with positive connotations; manufacturers naturally wish these to remain distinctive but part of their corporate image, rather than drifting into the dreaded area of a generic name, as *aspirin* has done. In this text, trademark names are given in capitals, and every effort has been made to add the appropriate symbol and give the name of the company that owns the trademark in brackets immediately after, at least for the first use on a page; in advertisements you will usually find a footnote used to denote ownership, such as "ABCD is the Registered Trademark of Wxyz Company." Such well-known trademarks carry a definite promise of quality to the consumer; see *Private Sector Labeling with Implications for Care* in Section 6.

Fibers or fabrics sold without a trademark name or end product certification are termed *commodity fibers* or *goods*.

Legal Framework of Trademarks

The symbol for a registered trademark is ® (™ if pending), and for a certification mark, ©. Such a trademark is owned as "intellectual property" and may legally be used exclusively by the company that applied for it.

The owner may license others to use the mark, within provisions of legislation in each country. In the United States, this falls within the jurisdiction of the Department of Commerce, through the Patent, Trademark and Copyright Information Office. A trademark, if for interstate commerce, may be registered with the federal Patent and Trademark Office. In Canada, the governing legislation is the Trade Marks Act, administered by Industry Canada.

Since trademarks or brands are such an important factor in advertising and hence in competition, governments handle registrations but leave policing of the system to those who own the trademarks. Infringement of trademark rights is pursued through the courts.

A few words and symbols cannot be used (e.g., *United Nations*; national, territorial, or civic flags; and the Red Cross symbol).

Fiber Properties

Section 1 listed the various properties by which a fabric or fiber may be evaluated; Table 2.1 gives the specifics of these properties for each fiber group.

Wrinkle and Crush Resistance	Wet Press Retention	Resistance to Heat	Resistance to Sunlight	Other Sensitivities
—	—	+++	++	Mildew, acid
—	—	+++	+++	Mildew, acid
++++[1]	+/−	+	*	Insect larvae, alkali, bleach[2]
+++	—	+	—	Perspiration, alkali, bleach[2]
—	—	+++	++	Mildew, acid
—	—	+++	++	Mildew, acid
—	—	+++	++	Mildew, acid
+	+/−	+	+/−	Acetone dissolves
++(+)	++++	++(+)	+/−	Acetone disintegrates
++(+)	++++	+	—[3]	Strong acid
++++	++++	+	+++	Strong alkali
+++	++	+	++++	Strong alkali, steam
+++	++	+	++++	Warm acetone
+++	*	—	—	Oxidizing agents, chlorinated solvents
++++	*	++++	++++	None

*Data either not relevant or not available.
[1]When dry.
[2]Hypoclorite or "chlorine."
[3]Without UV light stabilizers.

Properties of Major Fiber Groups— Important Relationships and Summaries

Table 2.2 gives the outstanding advantages and significant drawbacks of each of the major generic fiber groups. The following summarizes the properties of fiber groups and indicates relationships among the groups:

hand (feel):

cool: Cellulose fibers, especially flax (linen)

woolly (soft, warm, and dry): Wool; acrylic; modacrylic

silky (smooth, drapable, lustrous): Silk (cultivated or reeled); filament acetate; fine and/or lobal forms (e.g., nylon; polyester)

absorbency:

most (comfortable, nonstatic): Protein natural; cellulose natural; reconstituted cellulose MF

least (less comfortable, collects static [except olefin], dries quickly): Synthetics

wicking: Flax among natural fibers; olefin among MF fibers

resiliency (wrinkle and crush resistance, good insulation): Protein (wool especially); polyester; acrylic; modacrylic

loft (helps air-trapping or insulation with light weight, good cover): Olefin (lightest); polyester; acrylic; wool

strength (resists rubbing wear or abrasion and tearing, but stubborn pilling with staple fibers): Nylon; polyester; olefin

wet strength:

greater than dry: Cotton; flax (linen)

less than dry: Wool; silk; cellulosic MF fibers (includes viscose, lyocell, acetate)

no significant change: Synthetics

thermoplastic (softens, then melts on application of heat; moldable; can be heat set): All major MF fibers except reconstituted cellulose fibers

Permanent heat set in this *Reference* means that a yarn or fabric made 100 percent of that fiber can be set at a high enough temperature into crimps, pleats, smoothness, etc., that these will not alter in normal use and care (hot water, high dryer heat [not hot ironing!]) for the life of the article. (Care related to fiber content is discussed in Section 6.)

heat set permanent: Nylon; polyester; triacetate

heat set durable: Other major thermoplastics

heat sensitive (can be damaged or affected by heat, e.g., dryer set on high): Olefin; modacrylic; acetate; acrylic

heat resistant: Cellulose natural and reconstituted cellulosic MF fibers (there are other heat-resistant fibers, but these are special synthetic or minor generics)

flame resistant (self-extinguishes): Modacrylic (there are other special or minor generics that are flame resistant)

economical to produce: Cotton among natural fibers; cellulosic MF fibers among all MF fibers; olefin among synthetic fibers

expensive to produce, limited supply: Silk; specialty hairs; finest (Merino) wool; flax among natural fibers

expensive to produce: Spandex (elastane) among MF fibers

Properties in Relation to Use

General Advantages of Natural Fibers

From prehistory to almost 1900 A.D. fabrics were made of natural fibers, the major ones being cotton, wool, flax, and silk. These and minor naturals are shown in Figure 2.1 as the roots of a textile fiber family tree. In our marketplace today, they are used to make the fabric for most of the top-quality and top-price consumer textile goods. We still value them, then—why? They are all absorbent, comfortable to wear, and collect little static. All have a pleasing hand, texture, and appearance, although they differ a great deal one from another. Our standards of comfort and aesthetics are therefore still set by the natural fibers, which are also a renewable resource.

General Advantages of Manufactured Fibers

As the bar graph of world fiber production (Figure 2.6) shows, we use more and more MF fibers, especially synthetics, which have different characteristics from the CMF fibers. However, all MF fibers have the tremendous advantage of being free from most of the

Table 2.2 *Outstanding Advantages and Significant Drawbacks of Major Fiber Generics Used in Clothing and Household Textiles*[1]

Group	Advantages	Drawbacks
cotton	Absorbent; strong wet; ample supply; soft (fine); cool hand	Wrinkles; swells in water (fabric shrinks); mildews
flax (linen)	Absorbent; strong dry and wet; wicks; smooth; lustrous; cool hand	Wrinkles; limited supply; mildews
wool	Absorbent; soft, warm, dry hand; moldable; elastic recovery; lofty	Felts; weaker wet; eaten by insect larvae; limited supply; can irritate skin
silk	Absorbent; lustrous; smooth; soft, dry hand; drapes well; strong; good elastic recovery	Weakened by light and perspiration; limited supply
viscose rayon (cupro less NB)	Absorbent; economical to produce	Wrinkles; swells in water (fabric shrinks or stretches); mildews; fair strength; much weaker wet
HWM rayon (modal)	Absorbent; economical to produce; dry strength fairly good—better than that of standard viscose; loses less strength wet	Wrinkles; swells in water (fabric shrinks); mildews
lyocell	Absorbent; good strength	Wrinkles; swells in water (fabric shrinks); mildews; loses some strength wet
acetate (as filament)	Drapes well; soft, silky hand; smooth; economical to produce	Weak: low abrasion resistance; fairly heat sensitive; much weaker wet
triacetate	Economical to produce; permanent heat set	Weak; much weaker wet; low abrasion resistance
nylon (polyamide)	Greatest strength and resistance to abrasion; permanent heat set	Collects static; low UV light resistance; stubborn pilling (staple)
polyester	Good strength and resistance to abrasion; permanent heat set; resilient.	Collects static and oily stains; low perspiration absorbency; stubborn pilling (staple)
acrylic	Soft, warm hand; resilient; lofty	Collects static; low perspiration absorbency; somewhat heat sensitive
modacrylic	Soft, warm hand; resilient; flame resistant	Collects static; low perspiration absorbency; heat sensitive
olefin (polypropylene)	Strong; lofty; static resistant; wicks; most economical synthetic; almost no absorbency (stain resistant)	Very heat sensitive; low resistance to oxidizing agents; lowest UV light resistance
spandex (elastane)	Elastic; up to 10 times the strength of rubber; can be used uncovered; more resistant to oil and dry heat than rubber; takes dye	Yellows in chlorine bleach

[1]References are to standard forms of fibers (except HWM rayon); special forms of various generics are discussed under *Modifications of Manufactured Fibers* later in this section.

TEXTILE FIBERS - WORLD PRODUCTION

(excluding coarse fibers such as jute, hemp)

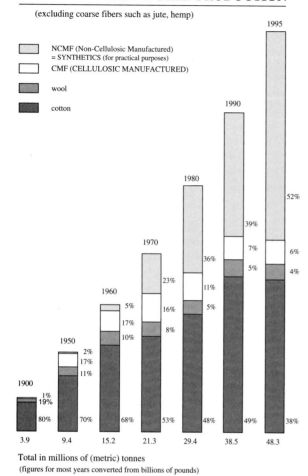

NCMF (Non-Cellulosic Manufactured) = SYNTHETICS (for practical purposes)

CMF (CELLULOSIC MANUFACTURED)

wool

cotton

Total in millions of (metric) tonnes
(figures for most years converted from billions of pounds)

Figure 2.6   Bar graph of world textile fiber production (excluding coarse fibers such as jute, hemp). (1995 figures courtesy of *Fiber Organon 69/6*, June 1998, Fiber Economics Bureau, Inc.)

hazards of agriculture, that affect production of natural fibers: seasonal variations of weather (sun, wind, rain, floods) and variations of nutrients, with the addition of disease and infestations (sheep tick, boll weevil).

MF fibers are produced all year around and indoors, and require less labor and relatively little space. (One of the reasons for the limited supply of wool is the amount of pasture needed for flocks of sheep, even when otherwise arid land is reclaimed.) Production, and so quality, is controlled with MF fibers, much more so than with natural fibers.

The other main advantage stems from this control—the versatility of MF fibers. MF fibers can be

any length (staple or filament); even, or thick and thin; any diameter (fish-line coarse or microfiber fine). The cross-sectional shape of the fiber can be altered; variations of chemical makeup can be made; and materials can be added to the fiber.

General Advantages of Cellulosic Manufactured (CMF) Fibers

The raw material for the first MF fibers was cellulose, which is obtained from wood, a renewable resource in large supply (though there is concern about de- and reforestation these days). Cellulose is a long-chain polymer, one of the main materials of plant structures. It comes to us, then, ready-made, a natural high polymer, and this is the most economical way to make a fiber. It is more expensive to synthesize such a polymer, by building small units and joining them together into very long chains, as we do to make a synthetic fiber.

CMF fibers have all the general advantages listed for MF fibers, but the two types within this grouping, reconstituted cellulose fibers and cellulose acetate compounds, cannot be described together beyond their economy of production from a renewable base. See the discussion of each or the summaries in this section for the specific advantages of each type.

General Advantages of Synthetic Fibers (and Some Drawbacks)

Synthetic fibers have the general advantages listed for MF fibers, but their special properties relate mainly to good performance. Because they are thermoplastic, synthetic fibers can be molded and heat set to give durable or permanent pleats or creases, garment shape, filament yarn texture, surface smoothness or texture, good wet press retention, and dimensional stability. Most have fairly good to excellent resistance to abrasion and tensile strength or tenacity (spandex is an exception), and their wet strength is much the same as dry. Because synthetics absorb little moisture, they do not swell and distort as easily as natural fibers or reconstituted cellulose fibers, and they dry quickly.

It is this superior performance that makes synthetic fibers so important in consumer goods today, especially polyester, now the most-used synthetic.

There is no such thing (so far) as a *miracle fiber*, however, and there are drawbacks to the synthetics, as with natural and CMF fibers. They require a finite resource, petrochemicals, for raw materials, although it is worth noting that only about 5 percent of the oil used worldwide goes to make chemicals, plastics, *and* fibers.

There are other sides to many of the properties valued for performance—durability and ease of care—that must be seen as disadvantages. The flip side of high strength is stubborn pilling, a problem met when staple fibers roll into balls on a fabric surface and are too strong to be brushed off easily. Low absorbency gives us quick drying, but makes for less comfortable fabrics that also tend to collect static electricity; a notable exception is the group of olefin fibers that absorb almost no moisture but exhibit wicking of moisture to a high degree, leading to transfer of perspiration away from the skin and a low tendency to collect static.

Static. Static is a pervasive problem with most synthetics, and in dry air it makes fabrics cling to the body, crackle with sparks, and attract bits of lint and other airborne particles such as soot.

A charge is built up when fabrics are brought together and separated, as a person moves, so that layers of clothing rub against each other and the body. The material in most clothing, footwear, and furnishings does not conduct electricity well, while the body is a good conductor but is often insulated so that charges do not escape gradually. Then, when a conductor is touched, the discharge can be great enough to give an electric shock or a spark. Static is also generated as fabrics are tumble dried. A *triboelectric series* can be made to show what type of charge is induced on various materials when they are rubbed together; one such series is shown in Figure 2.7.

Static is usually simply annoying, but in medical or industrial situations, it can be very dangerous (if flammable or explosive materials are around) or damaging (to delicate electronic equipment, either as it is assembled or in operation).[3] Buildup of static is especially common in winter conditions, when cold air holds little moisture, and humidifiers are not operational in many buildings.

[3]Sue Rolfe, "Problem Solving with Specialist Antistatic Fibres," *Textiles*, 1993/2: 9–11.

positive

wool
nylon
viscose rayon
cotton
silk
human skin
acetate
polyester
acrylic
polypropylene
vinyon
modacrylic
polyethylene
PTFE

negative

Figure 2.7 Triboelectric series. (From N. Wilson, Shirley Institute, "Fabric Cling: The Problem and Some Remedies," Textiles 7/2, 1978: 54; and "Static Electricity and Textiles, *Textiles* 16/1, 1987: 18)

Fibers—Relative Position in World Production

World textile fiber production is shown in the bar graph in Figure 2.6; note that this excludes coarse fibers such as jute. In 1900, 80 percent of this was *one* fiber, cotton! Although more and more cotton was grown, with total fiber use expanding, cotton's portion fell to 50 percent in 1975. In the 1990s, it fell gradually to about 25 percent, and the total amount used also fell slightly in some years. However, cotton is even now the most-used single fiber (when coarse fibers such as jute are excluded from the summary). It earns its name of "King Cotton," although it is no longer absolute monarch.

It may be hard for us to realize that in 1800, at least in European countries, cotton accounted for only 4 percent of fiber use, with wool at 78 percent, flax at 18 percent. (Silk, then as now was a luxury fiber only, at less than 1 percent.) Cotton did not become "king" until after the Industrial Revolution got well underway in the 19th century, after beginning in the 18th century with machine spinning of cotton yarn. This explains why a fabric such as lawn, originally made of flax and so historically of the flax or linen family, is today definitely considered a "cotton," since it has long been made predominantly of cotton.

The total amount of textile fibers used worldwide since 1900 increased tenfold by 1990, and (at over 50 million tonnes by 1997) is expected to reach fifteenfold by the end of this century. The turn of the 20th century marked the earliest stages of use of MF fibers, those from cellulose: reconstituted, as in rayon, or cellulose compounds, as in acetate. In 1938, the first synthetic fiber—nylon—was introduced, and synthetics established themselves after World War II, in the 1950s. Textile fiber consumption increases almost directly with development of countries and the rise in standard of living. So, while some fierce competition between fibers for certain end uses exists, seldom does one major fiber drive another from the marketplace.

Of the MF fibers, it is the noncellulosic (NCMF) fibers that have shown the most notable growth in amount used; compare 1950 to 1995 in Figure 2.6. This group, for all practical purposes, is comprised of synthetics, since only a few very minor MF fibers are made from a natural polymer base other than cellulose. Among the synthetics, nylon led in growth and amount used until 1972, when polyester took the lead; by the end of the 1990s, polyester was not only the dominant synthetic, but accounted for over 50 percent of all fibers used. Greatly increased fiber output capacity in the Far East, notably China, Taiwan, South Korea, and India, led to overproduction in the late 1990s, at a time when polyester producers in Western Europe and the United States were realigning. Polypropylene (olefin) which has long been a dark horse in this fiber steeplechase, has moved rapidly into prominence, especially for activewear, industrial floor coverings, and disposable nonwovens; it is now the second most used MF fiber.[4] Acrylic has steadily lost ground, along with other members of the related vinyl families. Spandex, although present in small amounts in most applications, gains steadily in importance, and a specialized fiber, aramid, has also found many uses for its flame and heat resistance.

Cellulosic MF (CMF) fiber production has been out-distanced by the synthetics, especially polyester, and use of CMF fibers decreased from 1980 to 1995, with the HWM rayons never reaching their full

stride. However, by 2000, the closely related CMF fibers of the lyocell type, led by TENCEL® (staple, originally from Courtaulds) and NEWCELL® (filament by Acordis), deliver excellent properties and performance, and are environmentally acceptable in raw material and process used.

The increase in production of synthetics from 1980 to 1995 (and continuing) is truly startling. It should be kept in mind by any student of textiles, as a verifier of the importance of the advantages of the synthetics discussed in this section. A major advantage is the specialized forms and modifications that multiplied in the 1990s, many of them suitable for the myriad industrial and technical applications or consumer gear that use "high tech" materials. The growth also reflects hugely increased MF production in areas other than the United States, Western Europe, and Japan, what are called "emerging markets,"—especially Taiwan, China, South Korea, and India. Economic uncertainties at the end of the 1990s slowed production, but the pattern remains clear.

Natural Fibers

Cellulosic Natural Fibers

Cellulose is a main building material of plants, likened to the (protein) flesh of animals. The woody plant material *lignin,* found in the stiffer plant parts, especially in trees, acts like bone, while binders such as plant pectins act like animal ligaments.

Cellulose is a carbohydrate, composed of carbon (C), hydrogen (H), and oxygen (O), making simple sugar units (β–Δ–glucose). These *polymerize;* that is, they join together, with water (H_2O) given off, to form very long molecular chains of 2,000 units or more; this makes cellulose a *polysaccharide.*

A representation of this unit commonly used for many years is shown in Figure 2.60 under Cellulose Acetate Compounds; the more modern "puckered ring" diagram for the structure of these units is shown in Figure 2.8. It is interesting to note that the unit of starch, another very large carbohydrate molecule, is also a glucose but in a slightly different form; it produces long chains, but is less suitable for a textile fiber.[5]

[4]"Decades Later, Polyester Forges New Image," *Textile World,* January 1999: 56–60.

[5]G. R. Lomax, "The Polymerization Reaction, Part 2: Natural Textile Polymers," *Textiles,* 16/3, 1987: 77.

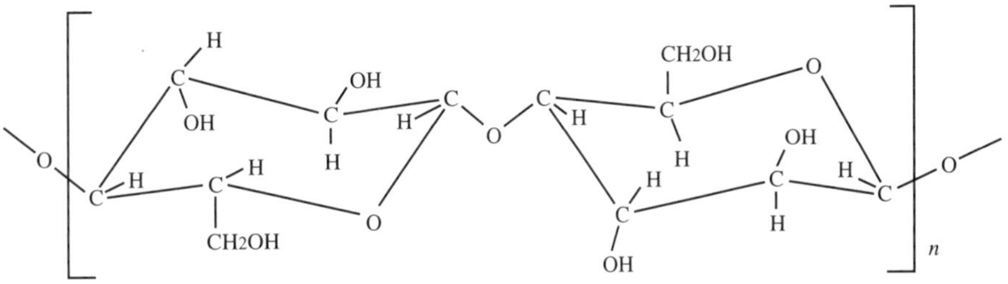

Figure 2.8 Unit of cellulose: two β–Δ–glucose residues in "puckered ring" structure.

Cellulose is sensitive to mineral (strong) acids, but not to alkali or chlorine bleach; it can be attacked by mildew growth (fungi), rot (bacteria), and silverfish. It has a cool hand (conducts heat well) and good heat resistance (cellulose fiber fabrics scorch only under a hot iron). Cellulose is fairly rigid or stiff (not resilient). Cellulose fibers swell in water, and, although they return to their original size when dry, fabrics made of them shrink when the fibers are wet and swollen. Cellulose is flammable, burning quickly with the familiar odor of burning plant material, such as wood or leaves, and glows for some time after a flame is extinguished.

Cotton—A Seed Fiber

Cotton still accounts for a quarter of all fiber use (when coarse fibers such as jute are excluded). It certainly has desirable properties, but the success of "King Cotton" lies in production: the fiber is readily available from the plant.

Cotton Production.

Cotton production requires a semitropical climate (nearly 200 days frostfree), with sun and water needed to produce the best fiber. Principal cotton-producing countries with percentage of world production in 1997 were: China (23 percent); the United States (21 percent); India (13 percent); Pakistan (8 percent); Uzbekistan (6 percent); Turkey and Australia (4 percent each); and Brazil, Syria, Greece, and Egypt (2 percent each).[6]

Cotton is in the mallow family (Malvaceae), genus *Gossypium*, and there are many species. The best types for textiles develop fibers called mature cotton or *lint*, which can be spun into yarn; other types pro-

duce only immature cotton or *linters,* also called fuzz, that cannot be spun into yarn.

By far the predominant type of textile cotton grown in the Americas is *G. hirsutum*. This species produces both mature cotton and fuzz. The longest types (*long staple*), such as Sea Island, Pima, and Egyptian, are varieties of *G. barbadense* and *G. peruvianum* produce no fuzz but account for only a small percentage of production. The Old World species are the *short-staple* types grown in Asia and Africa: *G. arboreum* and *G. herbaceum*.[7] All wild cottons produce only fuzz.[8] The best long-staple cotton grown in the United States is labeled *SUPIMA*, grown in the "Pima Belt": Arizona, New Mexico, Texas, and the San Joaquin Valley of California.

Cotton seed is planted, weeded, and cultivated during an 8- to 12-week period until the plant, grown to a height of 1–2 m (3–6 ft.), forms flowers. These are cream colored at first, then, over 3 days, turn to deep red and the petals fall, leaving the seed pod or boll, which is about the size of an egg. A boll contains about 30 seeds, and fibers (each a single cell) grow out on the surface of each seed. (See Figure 2.9.)

During the first 24 days after pollination, a fiber develops only in length, folding back on itself inside the closed boll and reaching a length up to 1,000 times its diameter (see Figure 2.10). During this time, the fiber has only a thin *primary wall,* lying under the very thin, outer, waxy cuticle. Fibers that start to grow in the first 2–3 days after flowering will go on to develop the *secondary wall* of mature (lint) fibers; those that start to grow later never develop more than the primary wall and are called immature cotton, linters, or fuzz. They cannot be spun into yarn

---

[6]Figures for 1997 courtesy of the National Cotton Council of America.

[7]Lewis Miles and Peter Greenwood, "Cotton," *Textiles,* 1992/3: 6, 7.

[8]W. Bally, "Cotton," *Ciba Review,* 95 (December 1952): 3400–3403.

Figure 2.9   (a) Cotton boll; (b) open boll with fibers (Courtesy of National Cotton Council of America); (c) cotton seeds.

Days after Pollination	4	12	24	36	48 →
Boll					
Fiber (Lint) Length	—				
Fiber Wall Thickness					

Figure 2.10   Growth of the cotton fiber. (Courtesy of *Ciba Review*)

for textiles, but are used for cotton batting or as a cellulose base for manufacture of rayon.

After 24 days, then, a fiber does not grow longer but begins to thicken, maintaining a central canal (*lumen*) carrying the plant juices that nourish it. Each day, a layer of cellulose is laid down in the fiber in a spiral arrangement that reverses each day; this thickening of the secondary wall continues for about 24 days more, when the boll opens. The fibers, which have been almost cylindrical in shape, dry, flatten, and twist to form the reversing convolutions so typical of cotton seen under the microscope (see *Fiber Identification*, later in this section). These folds and twists are very important in spinning fine yarns, and are one of the main reasons why such a (relatively) short fiber can be spun into yarn—the only seed fiber that provides a textile fiber among so many thousands of types.

Cotton in the open boll is almost pure cellulose available for use. While some waxes and pectins, protein, coloring matter, and minerals are present, only 4–12 percent of the fiber is anything other than cellulose! It needs only to be picked (by machine mostly today) and separated from the seed, a process carried out in the cotton gin. *This* is the reason cotton is "king" (along with its excellent properties, of course).

The cotton gin pulls the fibers from the seed and carries them away (see Figure 2.11[a]). The heart of the operation is the gin stand, lower right—see also Figure 2.11(b). Here saws, operating between closely spaced ribs, pull the fibers from the seed. The lint is removed from the saw by a rotating brush or a blast of air. Bits of plant material (*trash*) and the seeds are collected separately. Cotton seeds are pressed to give an important polyunsaturated oil, while their hulls are used for animal feed or fertilizer. Some trash gets in with the usable lint fibers, and can be seen in a fabric such as unbleached muslin (see *Finishing the Natural Fibers* in Section 5 Osnaburg and under *Fabric Glossary:* SHEETING, APPAREL).

Cotton Properties. Cotton properties, when summarized, do not seem to account for its status as "king" of textile fibers. It is used, however, for bulky household textiles, such as towels and sheets, and for workwear and summer wear, when we want a fiber that

- is absorbent, comfortable, with a cool hand and good static resistance; and

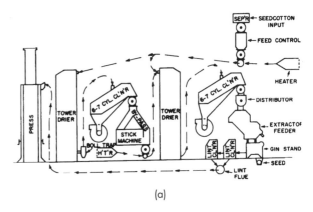

(a)

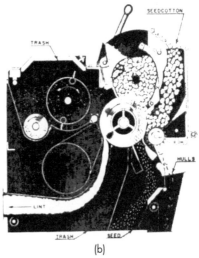

(b)

Figure 2.11 (a) Ginning of seed cotton, from input through the gin stand to pressing of lint fiber into bales. (b) The heart of the ginning operation is the gin stand, where lint fiber is separated from seed. (Courtesy of National Cotton Council of America)

- withstands vigorous machine washing and drying, using effective alkaline builders and even bleaches with detergents.

As well as resisting alkaline agents, cotton, which has good strength when dry, gets about 25 percent stronger when it is wet. However, cotton is certainly *not* easy care without special Durable Press treatment, since it wrinkles readily, swells in water so that fabrics made of it shrink, and can mildew, as anyone knows who has left a damp towel lying about. Cotton fabrics also lose a crisp press when damp (poor wet press retention).

Cotton Quality. Cotton quality is based largely on length. As mentioned, lint cotton is the only seed fiber long, strong, and cohesive enough to be spun into fine yarn.

- Short-staple, coarser cotton is 10–25 mm (½–1 in.) long. It is grown in China, India, South Africa, and southeastern Europe.

- Medium-staple cotton is 25–35 mm (1–1½ in.) long. These varieties are mostly American Upland.

- Long-staple cotton is the highest quality: 35 up to 60 mm (1½–2½ in.) long, and are the varieties with no fuzz: Sea Island, Pima, and Egyptian (see *Production of Cotton*). These are not only the longest, but the finest, softest, and strongest; plus, when mercerized, as much top-quality cotton is, these give the most luster. These long-staple cotton fibers will be spun as fine, combed yarn; made into top-quality fabric; given the most careful, artistic finish, coloring, and trims; ready to be turned into well-designed, best-made articles carrying the name of a designer or established firm: the top of the market.

A similar litany of factors contributing to the highest-quality, usually most expensive textile articles, both clothing and fabrics for interiors, can be repeated for every fiber, natural and MF. When the very best fiber is selected, it will almost always be used to make a superior product, with the concomitant expenditure on quality at the level of yarn preparation, fabric construction, finishing, coloring, trim, design, and manufacture of the final garment or home furnishing article, and culminating in the labels, tags, and promotional material.

Other Seed Fibers

Kapok. Kapok, from the seed pod of a tropical tree (*Ceiba pentandra*), is a soft fiber that is buoyant because it is hollow; it is used for stuffing in furnishings and life jackets, largely replaced now by foam or polyester fiberfill.

Coir. Coir, from the husk of the coconut (*Cocus nucifera*), is coarse, stiff, and strong even when wet; it is used for rough matting and cordage (twine, rope).

Flax (Linen)—A Bast (Stem) Fiber

In textiles study, the fiber is termed *flax*, while the fabric made of it is called *linen*; however, both are legitimate fiber generic names. The fiber bundles lie between the outer bark and the core of the stem of *Linum usitatissimum* (the meaning of the Latin is "the most useful linum"; many of the *Linum* genus grow wild). As mentioned, *linen* is a legal name for the fiber; it is *flachs* in German, giving the English name *flax*. (See Figure 2.12.)

Flax has been in limited supply and expensive because processing the fiber from the plant to get top-quality fiber is long and labor intensive, and fine yarns could not be spun with any but top-quality fiber until relatively recently.

Flax Production. Flax grows in temperate climates, the best quality coming from the moist area of northwestern Europe: France, Belgium, the Netherlands, and Ireland; coarser flax from eastern Europe, New Zealand, and Australia. Another variety of flax is grown for oil from its seeds; linseed oil has long been used as a quick-drying oil base for paints.

It takes 100 days for the plant to grow from seed to its height of 80–120 cm (2–4 ft.); while the stem is still pliable, the plant is pulled and dried (see Figure 2.13[a]). *Rippling* removes the seeds.

Next comes the central process, *retting*, which is really rotting—a natural breakdown of the stem materials and pectins that bind the fiber bundles to the stem. Dew, pool, or river retting takes 4–6 weeks. Lukewarm water retting in tanks takes 3–5 days, after which the bundles are dried for 1–2 weeks. Chemical retting speeds up the process, but when the stem

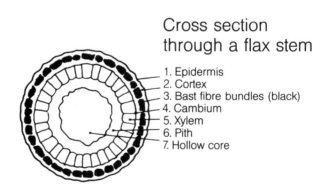

Cross section through a flax stem

1. Epidermis
2. Cortex
3. Bast fibre bundles (black)
4. Cambium
5. Xylem
6. Pith
7. Hollow core

Figure 2.12   Cross section of flax stem. (Courtesy of MASTERS OF LINEN/USA)

(a)

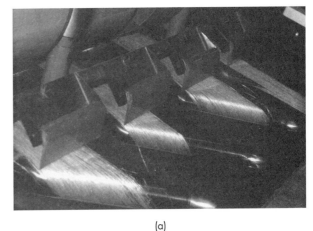

(a)

(b)

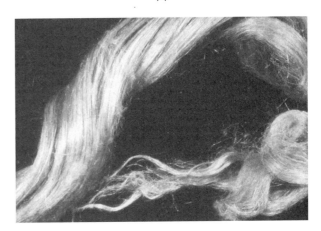

(b)

Figure 2.13 (a) Flax harvested with pulling machine. (b) Worker at flax scutching machine, where stems are broken up. (Courtesy of MASTERS OF LINEN/USA)

Figure 2.14 (a) Hackled (combed) flax ready for spinning. (Courtesy of MASTERS OF LINEN/USA) (b) Line flax.

materials are so attacked, the fibers are also weakened and harshened. Top-quality fibers today are often still *dew retted,* where the cut flax is left in the fields to let the action of moisture from dew and the action of microorganisms break down the outer stem.

After retting and drying, the stems are broken up by *scutching* with wooden breaker rollers (see Figure 2.13[b]), then the straw is beaten out as waste or *shivs* for use in chipboard. The fibers, separated into "hands," are then *hackled* or combed to take out short waste fibers called *tow* and to lay parallel the long fibers called *line;* these may reach 500 mm (20 in.) long. (See Figure 2.14.)

Wet spinning of flax (immersed in hot water) is done for the finest yarns, to soften the natural gums

holding fibers together; dry spinning is used for other qualities.

Flax Properties. Flax properties are outstanding—it is a fiber that is still valued after some 10,000 years. It has better dry strength than cotton, and like cotton it gets 25 percent stronger when wet. It absorbs more moisture (for comfort and static resistance), *and* it wicks; it is longer, smoother, and more lustrous than cotton.

A number of symbols are used to identify the top quality of this prestigious fiber and its fabrics; some are shown in Figure 2.15.

Linen has been enjoying an upsurge in popularity as technological developments have reduced spinning

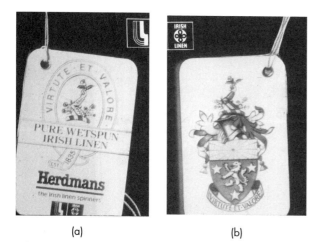

(a)   (b)

(c)

Figure 2.15 Tags and logos identifying high-quality linen: (a) wet spun tag, (b) Irish Linen Guild logos, (c) MASTERS OF LINEN labels identifying products using West European quality 100 percent linen and blends with minimum 50 percent linen (flax). (Courtesy of MASTERS OF LINEN/USA)

costs by achieving fine yarns with middle-quality flax, and also by allowing blends of flax with other fibers, on spinning machines that can handle long- and short-staple fibers together.[9] Although linen is a legitimate name for flax fiber, and bedding or table fabrics made of any fiber may be called "linens," there is a definite profile of the apparel fabric *linen:* traditionally bottom weight, with slubs in both warp and weft

[9]"Textiles and Clothing in the New Europe," *Textiles,* 1993/4: 9.

yarns, in a balanced plain weave. (See *Fabric Glossary:* LINEN.)

Flax Quality. Flax quality is well established with consumers. The best long, smooth, lustrous line fibers give us strong and beautiful fabrics with a cool hand that absorb and wick moisture well, so that clothing is comfortable in hot, humid weather, while dish towels or handkerchiefs, after absorbing well, dry quickly without linting.

An old-fashioned test to distinguish linen from cotton was to drop water on the fabric; if it spread quickly along the yarns, it was (probably) linen. Linen fabric is noted for slubs, since the fibers are bundles of cells and vary in thickness. These bundles of cells can be affected more easily than cotton by chlorine bleach; bleaching of linen should be carried out less vigorously than with cotton.

Fine table linen (see *Fabric Glossary:* DAMASK) seems to get softer and more lustrous as it is used, laundered, and ironed. And *ironed* it must be! Linen fabrics do wrinkle badly, and are the opposite of "easy care." In apparel a small amount of spandex blended with flax helps avoid some wrinkling—more under *Blending of Fibers.* Care of linen including bleaching, ironing, and storage is discussed in Section 6.

Other Bast Fibers

A number of fibers from plant stems are used in considerable amounts, and to get at the fiber, all are retted in much the same way as flax (see Figure 2.16). These fibers are not included in the figures on the world fiber production chart in Figure 2.6, as they are considered to be "coarse fibers," used mostly for sacking, carpet and linoleum backing, and cordage (twine, cord, and rope). The only one not considered coarse is ramie, and since it has been expensive to produce, it has been used in small amounts.

Jute. Jute is one of the most easily spun and cheapest fibers but is also one of the weakest, most brittle, and least durable. It comes from plants of the *Corchorus* genus (*C. capsularis, C. olitorius*), grown mainly in India and Bangladesh, but also in China, Nepal, and Thailand. Fibers range in length from shorter than 25 mm (1 in.) to about 300 mm (12 in.). Retting takes 2–3 weeks, and fiber yield is less than 10 percent of the total stem weight. We have used a great deal of jute for coarse twine and cordage and as burlap in sacking and carpet and linoleum backing

Figure 2.16 Retting hemp—"rafts" submerged with rocks. (Courtesy of *Ciba Review*)

(see *Fabric Glossary:* BURLAP). Jute cannot be used in water (e.g., for fish nets) as it deteriorates quickly when wet.

The International Jute Organization is promoting jute bags for the food industry, produced using a vegetable jute batching oil instead of a petroleum-based oil. Further, as the use of jute in sacking, cordage, and especially carpet backing has been replaced extensively by polypropylene, other uses for it have been actively sought, especially in geotextiles, such as fabrics used to prevent erosion on hillsides.

Hemp. Hemp is an old bast fiber of the Mulberry family Moraceae, and like flax, the fibers are removed from the plant stems by retting (see Figure 2.16). Hemp has many of the good properties of flax, and is one of the strongest natural fibers, even when wet. It has been used mostly for coarser products, such as strong twine and other cordage, fish nets, canvas (see *Fabric Glossary:* CANVAS), and a better quality of burlap. It can give a fabric hard to tell from linen, and historically, fine fabrics as well as good paper have long been made from hemp in China. Hemp seed oil compares in yield to rape or sunflower oils, and the woody core of the stem can be made into building materials as well as paper, so there are nontextile uses as well. Plants grow quickly in temperate climates to heights of some 4 m (10–14 feet) in 3 months, resist weeds, and need little application of pesticides or agrochemicals. The large root system aerates the soil it grows in.

However, one of the major impediments to its growth is apparent from its plant genus and species:

Cannabis sativa—the same as marijuana and hashish, and so its growth has been prohibited in North America since 1938, and in a number of European countries, under narcotics control legislation. (It remained legal in China, France, Spain, and many former Eastern Bloc countries such as Yugoslavia, Romania, Hungary, Poland, Ukraine, and Russia.) By the mid-1990s, with the introduction of specially-bred low-narcotic varieties of hemp (and vigorous lobbying), farmers were growing hemp as a legal commercial crop in the United Kingdom, Germany, the Netherlands, and Australia; Canadian farmers were able to be so licensed in 1998 (see Figure 2.17). These varieties of hemp are low in the psychoactive or hallucinatory substance tetrahydrocannabinol (THC) present as 3–5 percent of marijuana plants; this is some 10 times the amount that is in hemp. Like all bast fibers, the long outer fibers of the stem are expensive to obtain from the plant stem; hemp has more lignin than flax, and the fiber bundles are harder to separate to give fine yarns. Research and development efforts therefore concentrate on improving retting methods,

Figure 2.17 Hemp for fiber may now be legally grown in Ontario, Canada. (Courtesy of Hempline Inc.)

machinery to harvest the fiber, processing to soften it, and spinning methods.[10]

Ramie. Ramie (China grass, rhea) is a minor fiber but can rival linen in strength, beauty, and absorbency. It is a nonstinging nettle of the Uticaceae family, genus *Boehmeria (B. nivea* and *B. tenacissima),* is stiffer than flax, and is even more difficult than flax to loosen from the plant stems without chemical treatment, which harshens the fiber. The ramie called China grass is grown in China, while the type called rhea comes from Malaysia, Africa, and Mexico. A good deal of ramie appeared on the North American market in the 1980s, blended, usually with cotton, in both knit and woven fabrics. This influx was a result of its exemption, as a minor fiber, from the duties and quotas put on cotton in the Multifibre Arrangements; blends of ramie (often just over 50 percent) with cotton could be imported at an advantage from low-cost sources: India, China, and Southeast Asian countries.

Kenaf, Roselle, Sunn, Urena. Kenaf, roselle, sunn, and urena are minor bast fibers used for the same purposes as jute. Kenaf (*Hibiscus cannabinus*) is grown in India, Bangladesh, China, Thailand, and other parts of Southeast Asia. Other minor bast fibers are roselle (*Hibiscus sabdariffa*), sunn (*Crotalaria juncea*), and urena (*Urena lobata*). As the uses of jute rise or fall, so will those of these fibers.

Leaf Fibers (also called Hard Fibers)

Textile fibers are obtained from the long, fleshy leaves of tropical plants and trees. These are usually removed not by retting, as bast fibers are, but by *decorticating*—ripping out the cortex cells that lie in the center of the leaf (see Figure 2.18).

Sisal. Sisal, family Amarylklidaceae or Agavaceae, is one of the best known of the *Agave* genus of plants (*A. sisalana*) (see Figure 2.19). The bundles of fibers, which are coarse and woody, may be up to 1 m (3 ft.) in length, held together by resin. Sisal is used for totebags, summer handbags, matting, cordage, and bristles. The plant is a native of Mexico, but is now grown in East African countries, as well as Mexico, Haiti, Cuba, and Brazil. These fibers cannot be used for fish nets, as saltwater degrades them.

[10]Gordon Mackie, "Hemp: The Acceptable Face of Cannabis . . . , *Textile Month*, 1998: 49–51.

Figure 2.18 Decorticating leaves for fiber. (Courtesy of Ciba Review)

Figure 2.19 Sisal growing. (Courtesy of *Ciba Review*)

Henequen. This is another of the Agavaceae *family,* used mostly for twine.

Abaca. Abaca, Manila "hemp," "sisal hemp," "sunn hemp," or manila is a fiber from the leaves of a member of the banana family (*Musa textilis*), used for cordage, matting, and some clothing.

New Zealand "Flax," New Zealand "Hemp."

New Zealand "flax" (*Phormium tenax*) is a leaf fiber of the Liliaceae family, and is similar to abaca.

Yucca. Yucca is in the Agavaceae family, genus *Yucca*. The most common in northern Mexico and the southwestern United States is *Yucca cassava*. Fibers from the rigid, sword-shaped leaves have been used for a long time. The Anasazi people who lived

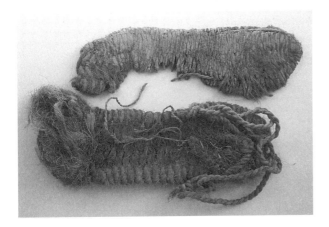

Figure 2.20 Anasazi sandals, pre-Columbian, circa 1300, yucca fiber soles. (Courtesy of the Bata Shoe Museum)

from approximately A.D. 1 to 1300 in the region known as the Four Corners—Utah, Colorado, Arizona, New Mexico—produced footwear by weaving, plaiting, and twining yucca plant fibers into sandal soles and binding them to their feet with cordage ties. (See Figure 2.20.)

Raffia. Raffia (rafia) is a type of palm of the genus *Raphia*, a soft fiber from the leaves of *R. ruffia* and *R. taedigera*. Often used for craft work, raffia can be dyed to many colors. It is typical of many minor fibers and other plant materials like reeds and even paper, made into yarn and used to make chair seats, rugs, and wall or window coverings.

Piña. This is the fiber (known as PALF for pineapple leaf fiber) from the leaf of the pineapple plant, a member of the Bromeliaceae family. There are many species of the genus *Ananas*, such as *A. sativa*. This is the only fine leaf fiber, giving exquisite fabrics, crisp and sheer, or soft and flexible. It is usually hand stripped from the leaves, but is also retted. This fiber has not been produced in commercial amounts but rather as a boutique or craft material, for example as a base for craft embroideries. A charming article in *Dress* (Journal of the Costume Society of America) argues that historically the fabric was brought to New England from the Philippines in souvenirs, not as an article of commerce in itself.[11] Designer Romeo Gigli

[11]Linda Welters, "Dress as Souvenir: Piña Cloth in the Nineteenth Century," *Dress*, 24, 1997:16–26.

used gauzy woven material of piña in couture designs for summer 1991, and a cottage industry in the Philippines has produced *jusi cloth,* made with piña and silk. India in the 1990s has concentrated on its possible commercial use in textiles.

Other Miscellaneous Cellulosic Natural Fibers

Bark Fiber Cloth (Tapa). Bark fiber cloth (tapa) is made using fibers from the inner bark of the paper mulberry tree (*Brousonnetia papyrifera*), pounded into bark cloth (tapa) in the Pacific islands, to give a kind of "natural nonwoven" fabric (see Figure 2.21).

Spanish Moss. Spanish moss, a relative of the pineapple, has been used in the southern United States as an alternative to horsehair for stuffing.

Sacaton. Sacaton, a root fiber from Mexico, has been used as a stiff bristle in brushes.

Inorganic (Mineral) Natural Fibers

Asbestos

Asbestos, or "rock wool," is a fiber formed in rocks, which can be spun and made into fabrics. It has been known from ancient times because it is flameproof; the name comes from the ancient Greek, meaning "will not burn." Asbestos *can* melt, but only at 1450–1500°C (2580–2670°F), the temperature of lava in a volcano. There are various types of asbestos, hydrated silicates of magnesium and calcium, with

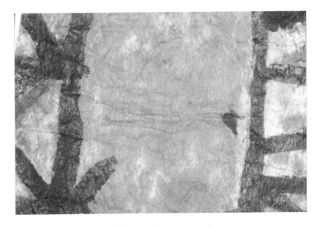

Figure 2.21 Bark fiber cloth (tapa).

other minerals; the best fibers for textiles come from chrysotile asbestos, much of it mined in the Eastern Townships of Quebec. The fibers subdivide to fibrils and, since they never rot, are very harmful if breathed into the lungs; mining and use of asbestos today are therefore carried out much more carefully than in the past, and we no longer use asbestos where it is exposed to air, as for oven mitt palms.

Protein Natural Fibers

Protein is a major building material of animals; flesh, skin, hair, antlers, plumage, and spider webs are all proteins, differing from one another according to their function and the creature that made them.

Proteins are *polypeptides,* and have the most complex makeup of any fiber polymer. The units are *amino acids,* joined together with *amide or peptide linkages* (see the discussion under *Nylon,* later in this section). Long chains are formed, some folded, others lying in spirals or helixes. The protein of silk (*fibroin*) is folded; that of wool (*keratin*) is a single spiral or helix, with some cross-links (see Figure 2.22); while the *collagen* of leather is a triple helix (see Figure 4.87).

Each type of protein has its own assortment of amino acids made up of carbon (C), hydrogen (H), oxygen (O), and nitrogen (N), plus, in some units of hair fibers, sulfur (S); these last two (N and S) account for the different burning smell of wool from cellulose fibers, which are made up only of C, H, and O.

Protein fibers have a dry, warm hand, are weaker wet, and are sensitive to alkali and chlorine bleach, but not to acid.

Wool—The Major Hair Fiber

Wool is taken in this *Reference* to be the hair of the domestic sheep; what we will call *specialty hair fibers,* such as camel hair, are not usually termed *wool* in textiles or fashion. Domestic sheep raised for wool have been bred with less and less *guardhair,* the coarse outer coat that protects wild animals and is found on all fur-bearers, even domestic cats. This layer is distinct from the fine, insulating *undercoat* called "down." Wool from most breeds of sheep contains a portion of guardhair as coarse white fibers called *kemp* that do not take dye; they may be used as *effect fibers* in fabric such as tweed (see *Fabric Glossary: TWEED*).

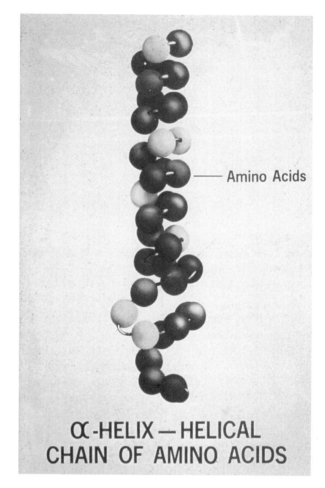

— Amino Acids

α-HELIX — HELICAL CHAIN OF AMINO ACIDS

Figure 2.22 The α-helix form of wool keratin. (Courtesy of the Woolmark Company, formerly IWS)

Wool Production. Production of wool involves many breeds of sheep all over the world and requires a great deal of grazing land, although in many key sheep-raising areas, formerly unproductive land has been reclaimed for grazing pasture. Australia, with 130 million sheep, 75 percent of them Merino, produces one third of the world's wool, and over 50 percent of all Merino wool (the finest). Next is New Zealand with 60 million sheep, supplying 50 percent of the world's carpet wool (coarser). South Africa raises over 35 million sheep, 70 percent of them Merino. South America produces significant amounts, especially Uruguay with over 25 million sheep.[12]

[12]*A Guide to Wool,* The Woolmark Company, 1997. (See Resources under the Woolmark Company.)

Figure 2.23 Shearing the fleece from a sheep. (Courtesy of the Woolmark Company, formerly IWS)

Figure 2.24 Coat of a Merino sheep parted showing close, crimped fibers. (Courtesy of the Woolmark Company, formerly IWS)

Sheep are sheared once a year in most countries, and the wool just shorn from a sheep is called a *fleece* (see Figure 2.23). With such a valuable crop, research is intensive and unending for improvements, some of which involve treating sheep to repel pests such as blowflies, to produce mothproof wool,[13] or injecting a chemical that causes wool growth to be stopped for about one day, after which the effect disappears almost at once. When this interrupted point in the wool fiber reaches the skin surface, the wool can be *peeled* off; sheep can be handled this way two and a half times as fast as with shearing.[14]

Wool is only a portion of each fleece, with up to half the weight made up of wool grease (lanolin in purified form), suint (perspiration), and all kinds of dirt and plant matter (twigs, burrs), especially with the Merino (see Figures 2.24 and 3.8). Wool is generally washed (*scoured*) and treated to remove plant matter (*carbonized*); for details, see *Finishing the Natural Fibers* in Section 5.

The Merino sheep is the ultimate wool producer (see Figure 2.25), with no kempy wool in its fleece and an annual yield of greasy wool up to 4.4 kg (9.7 lb.), compared to 1 kg (2.2 lb.) from some types of sheep in China or India. Merino wool has all the qualities we rank as best in wool for finer fabrics—a fine fiber with scales tightly packed, which gives a soft hand, plus lots of crimp. The finer the wool, the finer the yarn that can be spun from it. The Merino as we have it now was developed in Australia from a type of sheep that was prized from Roman times, developed

Figure 2.25 Group of Merino sheep. (Courtesy of the Woolmark Company, formerly IWS)

Figure 2.26 Romney sheep. (Courtesy of the Woolmark Company, formerly IWS)

[13]*Textiles*, 1992/1: 15.
[14]*Textiles*, 1993/1: 6.

in Spain, and taken by a circuitous route to Holland, South Africa, and eventually the emerging British colony in Australia. Over half of the world's fine clothing wool comes from there now. The Rambouillet, developed in France and raised prominently in the United States, also produces very fine wool.

Coarser wools have their place, too, and are better for very hard wear, as in carpets or for a sturdy, sporty fabric such as tweed. Romney sheep, the main breed raised in New Zealand (see Figure 2.26), give coarser wool that is much valued (see *Wool Quality* and Figures 2.33, 2.34), as is that from Lincoln sheep. Hair from mountain sheep is shaggy and coarse as well, to protect them from inclement weather (see Figure 2.27). Medium-fine wools come from many crossbred sheep, for example the Corriedale, a cross of Merino rams and British Longwool ewes. Some special wools come from sheep living in unique conditions, such as Iceland or the Shetland Islands, an island group northeast of Scotland. The number of fibers in the coat of one sheep varies from 10 million for coarse wool to 100 million for fine wool.[15]

Wool Structure. Wool protein is *keratin,* of which our fingernails as well as our hair are also made. The molecular chains of joined amino acid residues lie in *alpha-helix* coils (see Figure 2.22); some sulfur-containing amino acids can form *cystine* cross-linkages between chains, and side chains on others can give *salt bridge* links. The result is a springlike coil, giving wool and hair fibers resilience and elastic recovery (springiness).

The outside layer (*cuticle*) has overlapping scales in three layers (Figure 2.28), the outermost being thin and porous. The edges of the scales project, so that the fiber is rougher from tip to root than from root to tip. When fibers are moved about, there is a kind of ratchet effect, so they move in the direction of their root ends; the fibers tangle together, a process called *felting,* discussed further under *Wool Properties.*

Under the cuticle is the *cortex,* made up of spindle-shaped cortical cells, which can take up and hold moisture (Figure 2.29). Wool is the most absorbent fiber of all, and is also *hygroscopic*—takes up moisture without feeling wet. The cells are of two types, *ortho-cortex* and *para-cortex,* twisted together along the length of the fiber, making it *bicomponent* (Figure 2.30); the two sides behave differently as a

[15]*A Guide to Wool*, The Woolmark Company, 1997.

Figure 2.27 Sheep with coarser wool than Merino. Left to right: Scottish Blackface, Welsh Mountain, Lincoln Longwool. (Courtesy of the Textile Institute)

Figure 2.28 Wool fibers with outer scale covering. (Courtesy of the Woolmark Company, formerly IWS)

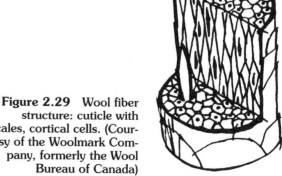

Figure 2.29 Wool fiber structure: cuticle with scales, cortical cells. (Courtesy of the Woolmark Company, formerly the Wool Bureau of Canada)

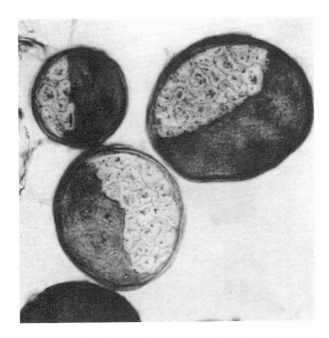

Figure 2.30 Cortex of wool stained to show the bicomponent nature of the cells. (Courtesy of the Woolmark Company, formerly IWS)

wet fiber dries, one shrinking more than the other, resulting in a spiral crimp (Figure 2.31). The cortical cells are made up of *microfibrils,* which are finally composed of the coiled molecular chains. In the center of some coarser wools is a *medulla* with air spaces (Figure 2.32).

Wool Properties. The properties of wool result from its structure, adding up to a fiber that makes up into fabrics well suited to keep us warm in cold

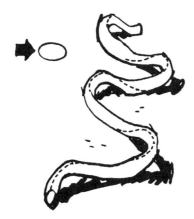

Figure 2.31 Three-dimensional wool crimp. (Courtesy of the Woolmark Company, formerly the Wool Bureau of Canada)

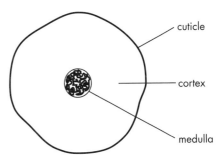

Figure 2.32 Cross section of wool.

weather and comfortable under many other conditions.

First, wool has a dry and warm hand because it is protein material, and it is light (low specific gravity). Next, it is very resilient, so wool fabrics insulate well; this, along with great loft, allows warmth with little weight. The resilience plus good elastic recovery mean wrinkle recovery. Wool can have a luster, but the finer the scales, the duller the fiber. However, when fine fibers are spun into worsted (combed) yarns, with fibers laid nearly parallel, we see the quiet luster evident in fine suitings.

Wool has low tenacity (tensile strength); pilling is not a great problem in wool fabrics. Pills can be removed with a stiff bristle brush, and so are not classed as "stubborn." However, wool does make very durable fabrics, with good abrasion resistance, which can be restored to good looks over a long wear life. There is a tribute to the restorability of wool in the report that 12,000 square yards of tufted all-wool carpet in the World Trade Center in New York City survived the 1993 bomb blast, but was left uncovered while a cleanup of other surfaces took place, since it was assumed that the carpet would have to be replaced. Although all kinds of soot and grease were ground into it, the carpet was found to have no physical damage, and cleaning removed *all* the soil and stains.[16]

All hair fibers (and leather), since they are protein, can be molded or shaped with steam. This is used in tailoring to give a temporary set, and is an important adjunct to shaping apparel in hard tailoring, where interlinings such as tailor's or hair canvas hold the structured shape of a jacket or coat. It is, of course, lost if a cheaper tailor's canvas of tapelike

[16]*Textile Chemist & Colorist,* 25/6, June 1993: 8.

rayon fiber (cellulose) is used instead of a wiry hair fiber and wool. (See *Fabric Glossary:* CANVAS, HAIR or TAILOR'S.)

The coarser the wool, the more prickly it will be; this can cause itching and redness that is often taken for an allergic reaction. Since wool is the same protein as our own hair, a truly allergic reaction is rare, and most people can wear fabrics made of fine wool in finer, smoother yarns without discomfort.

Hair fibers (sulfur-containing protein) are eaten by some insect larvae, notably those of the clothes moth and various carpet beetles. Materials can be treated to be mothproof; this is especially important with articles such as carpets and valuable or seasonal clothing (see Section 5). Details and directions for home storage protection are given in Section 6.

In caring for any protein fiber, treat it like your own hair: wool is harmed by alkali and chlorine bleach, is harshened by heat, and is also weaker when wet. Care procedures are discussed in Section 6.

Felting of wool described under *Wool Structure* is looked on as a disadvantage insofar as it is produced by machine washing and drying of wool articles with resulting matting and shrinkage, unless they have been given an antifelt treatment (see Section 5). However, it is often done on purpose, e.g., to make *felt* (see Section 4 and *Fabric Glossary:* FELT). In finishing, gradual felting is called *fulling*, giving closer, warmer fabrics—a definite advantage in uses such as winter coats (see Section 5 and *Fabric Glossary:* MELTON).

Wool Quality. Wool quality is related to wool grade, and this is linked to fineness. There is not only a considerable range of quality (fineness) among various breeds of sheep, but there is a difference from one part to another of the fleece from one animal. Fineness also varies with year of growth and health of the animal (food, weather, etc.). Although the finest, softest wool is taken to be the highest quality, we must realize that this is not the strongest type; what we want for slacks or a dress is not best for a long-wearing overcoat or for carpet.

Fineness of wool is expressed in science as the diameter of the fibers in millionths of a meter, termed a *micron* (symbol μ) or in international metric usage a *micrometre* (μm or 0.001 mm—see Section 9, *Metric in Textiles Use*). Figure 2.33 records various wool qualities by grade, related to diameter (fineness), uses, and various sheep breeds.

Wool fineness in commerce is more commonly related to the old British worsted yarn count numbers, such as 50s, 70s, and so on; the higher the number, the finer the wool. Figure 2.34 shows the length and crimp of various wool qualities by number. Fine wools have shorter fibers, 40–110 mm (1½–4½ in.), with the most crimp; coarser wools have longer fibers, 110–150 mm+ (4½–6 in.+), with less crimp.

Most terms for high-quality wool relate to fineness: low micron figure (diameter), high number (fine yarn = fine fiber), botany, lamb's wool, or Merino.

Pure Merino Wool and *Merino ExtraFine.* These two brands (see Figure 2.35) are backed by the Woolmark Company and quickly became established in fashion fabric vocabulary. They were brought out in 1997 to celebrate the 200th Anniversary of the arrival of a few Merino sheep in the struggling British colony at Sydney, Australia. **Pure Merino Wool** is self-explanatory, while **Merino ExtraFine** is in the range of 19.5 μm (μ) diameter or less, and so conforms to the category termed Superfine, as well as guaranteeing the wool is Merino.

botany. 60s or better-quality wool, in a worsted yarn; all Merino wool is 60s or finer.

Wool Grade	Diameter (µm; µ)	Length (mm; inches)	Uses	Sheep Breeds
Superfine	15–18	–40; –1½	apparel	Merino, some Rambouillet
Fine	18–24	40–110; 1½–4½	apparel	Merino, Rambouillet, most lamb's wool
Medium	24–31	110–150; 4½–6	apparel (coats, tweeds)	Crossbred, e.g., Corriedale
Coarse	31–40 (most), can go to 70	150 up; 6 up	carpet	Romney, Lincoln

Figure 2.33 Wool quality by grade, related to fineness.

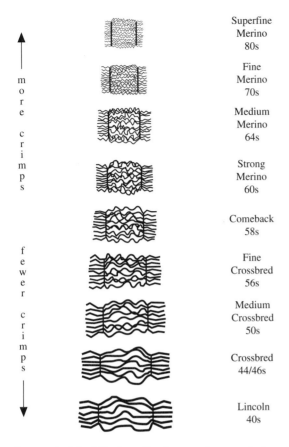

Superfine Merino 80s	
Fine Merino 70s	
Medium Merino 64s	
Strong Merino 60s	
Comeback 58s	
Fine Crossbred 56s	
Medium Crossbred 50s	
Crossbred 44/46s	
Lincoln 40s	

more crimps → fewer crimps

Figure 2.34 Wool quality by number—note length, degree of crimp.

pure merino wool

merino extrafine

Figure 2.35 Logos for PURE MERINO WOOL and MERINO EXTRAFINE. (Courtesy of the Woolmark Company)

Superfine. 80s or better-quality wool (some may give a higher number, such as **Super 100s**); this term may be woven into the selvage in some worsteds (see Figure 2.36). There is a very limited supply of these very finest fibers, and they amount to a kind of modern "golden fleece" (see *Golden Bale*, Section 3). The finest and rarest, **Super 170s,** is "1PP" wool, highest of the Australian Wool Trading Authority's 975 grades, and would represent only 0.0002 percent of the annual Australian wool production. The limited supply of these finest wool fibers is being extended by judicious blending (see *Blending of Fibers*) and by new spinning techniques (more on these and ultrafine wool as part of the cost of combed yarns in Section 3).

"Medium micron" is a somewhat confusing term for Merino wools that fall at the coarse end of the Merino scale but are still *very* high quality! Since there is a larger supply of these than of the Superfine, spinning technology has concentrated on producing fine yarns with them to give lightweight worsteds that are more affordable.

lamb's wool. The first clip of a young sheep (6–8 months old), with each fiber tapering to a tip—finer and softer than wool from adult sheep. It is accepted in the trade that an article labeled "lamb's wool" should contain about a third of this first-clip wool.

The WOOLMARK®, with its famous logo (see Figure 2.37), is an overall assurance of the quality of the article, which must be of 100 percent new (virgin) wool. The mark is licensed by the Woolmark Company (formerly the International Wool Secretariat—the Wool Bureau in the United States and Canada), with

Figure 2.36 Worsted suiting made of Superfine wool may have the word woven into the selvage.

PURE NEW WOOL

WOOLMARK

WOOLBLENDMARK

Figure 2.37 WOOLMARK® and WOOLBLEND-MARK®—trademarks of the Woolmark Company. (Courtesy of the Woolmark Company)

strict quality standards laid down. The WOOLBLEND-MARK® mark (see Figure 2.37) is licensed for certain products made in a "wool-rich" blend, with at least 60 percent new wool in a blend (55 percent in blends with cotton) and quality assurance as with the WOOLMARK®. Two other trademarks are used for WOOLMARK fabrics: LIGHT WOOL and COOL WOOL (see Section 7 and *Fabric Glossary:* TROPICAL WORSTED).

The New Zealand Wool Board promotes high-quality but sturdier (coarser) wool through its WOOLS OF NEW ZEALAND brand, launched in 1994 for carpets. These growers separated from the Woolmark Company, which does not allow country of origin to be indicated in use of its WOOLMARK.

Wool Products Labeling Act. The United States passed the Wool Products Labeling Act in 1939 to clarify descriptions of the stage of use of this fiber:

virgin wool, new wool. Wool that has never been previously manufactured or used, never reclaimed from any woven or felted wool product.

recycled wool. Wool reclaimed from new fabric or fabric used by the ultimate consumer. Until the July 1980 Amendment to the act these were called *reprocessed* and *reused* wool, respectively.

These terms, while informative, do not relate to quality, which can vary widely within either category. Fiber is reclaimed by garnetting, a process in which textile material is torn apart to fiber. Garnetted fiber has usually sustained some damage, but could still be higher-quality fiber than some virgin wool.

Specialty Hair Fibers

We use hair from many animals besides domestic sheep; most cost more than wool and all have special advantages or properties for them to be used instead of wool—this is what we will concentrate on. See the summary of information in Table 2.3, a comparison of specialty hair fibers.

Horsehair. Horsehair (from the mane and tail) is very wiry, and has been used to stuff sofas or for millinery and hem braid; it is now used mainly in tailor's canvas to help in garment shape retention (see *Fabric Glossary:* BRAID; CANVAS, HAIR or TAILOR'S).

Mohair. Mohair comes from the Angora goat, thought to originate in Asia; the name for the goat comes from Ankara, Turkey, also (confusingly) the origin of the name of the rabbit (with hair called angora). Mohair grows very long, up to 200–300 mm (8–12 in.), if the animal is sheared once a year, but shearing is usually done twice annually (see Figure 2.38[a]). The United States is the leading mohair producer in the world; two million Angora goats are raised on 23 million acres, 85 percent in southwestern Texas. Almost all of this production is exported. South Africa is also a major producer. The logo of an international association and the Mohair Council of America (Figure 2.38[b]) reflects the length of the fibers in mohair fleece. Mohair has relatively large, platelike scales that give a smooth, lustrous, dirt-shedding surface; it is still used for paint roller covers because it releases the paint. It is stronger than wool and gives very durable fabrics; however, when used in crisp worsteds, creases should not be pressed hard over and over in the same place, or the fabric can split. This fiber is often used in bouclé loop yarn to give a light, airy, but warm fabric (see *Fabric Glossary:* LOOP YARN). For its wiry property, like horsehair it is used in braids and tailor's canvas (see *Fabric Glossary:* BRAID; CANVAS, HAIR or TAILOR'S).

Table 2.3 *Comparison of Specialty Hair Fibers*

Fiber/Animal	Geographical Source	Special Property or Advantage vs. Wool
horsehair/horse (mane & tail)	Worldwide	Wiry, smooth, coarse
mohair/Angora goat	United States, South Africa, Turkey	Wiry, smooth (large scales)—lustrous, dirt-shedding, long, strong
cashmere/cashmere goat	Kashmir, Himalayan Mountains, white from Mongolia (China), brown or gray from Iran or Tibet (China)	Undercoat very fine, buttery soft, rather dull
camel/two-humped Bactrian camel	Mongolia (China), mountains and desert	Distinctive tan color, thermostatic, makes very warm fabric
Cameloids: llama/llama	Peru, Chile, Andes Mountains	Various natural shades from cream to dark brown
alpaca/alpaca	Peru, Chile, Andes Mountains	Same shades as llama, long, lustrous, soft
vicuña/vicuña	Peru, Chile, Andes Mountains	Cinnamon-color undercoat finest, softest, rarest hair
angora/Angora rabbit	China, France, Chile	Limply soft, lustrous, smooth, slippery, lofty
qiviuq or qiviut/musk ox	Northwest Territories, Alaska, Yukon, Greenland, Russia	Undercoat very lofty, fine, soft, shades of taupe (gray/brown), makes very warm fabric

Figure 2.38 (a) Angora goats, source of mohair. (Courtesy of the Mohair Council of America)

Cashmere. Cashmere, as used in sweaters, is the very fine, soft underhair of the cashmere (Kashmir) goat, combed out as the animal molts; coarser hairs are used in overcoats (see Figure 2.39). Most white cashmere, needed for light-colored articles, is from Mongolia (China); natural colors, such as brown or gray, come from Iran or Tibet (China).

Articles of widely different prices can be 100 percent cashmere, but the more expensive will be made of the (hand-sorted) longest underhair, spun into worsted yarn, which pills less. These will probably be of 2-ply yarns for better wear, and the fibers will be the finest and softest as well. Finally, when this much care is taken in selection of the raw materials and spinning of the yarn, the same high quality will be

Figure 2.38 (b) Mohair logo. (Courtesy of the Mohair Council of America)

Figure 2.39 Cashmere goats. (Courtesy of the Textile Institute)

built in with the knitting, color selection, finishing, trim, findings—all aspects of the finished article.

Cashmere was the fiber originally used (sometimes with silk) to make the elaborately patterned Kashmir shawls that were prized in Europe from the mid-18th century. The basic design motif, which we call *paisley,* has been widely developed and used from the 19th century on (see *Fabric Glossary:* PAISLEY).

Cashgora. This is the long yet soft hybrid fiber produced by a cross between an Angora goat sire (the source of mohair) and a cashmere goat dam.

Camel Hair. Camel hair is obtained from the two-humped Bactrian camel of Asia, of which only about 1,000 have been estimated to be living wild today in a remote part of northwestern China.[17] However, this animal has long been domesticated and used as a beast of burden on ancient caravan routes over mountains and across deserts (see Figure 2.40). Its coat therefore protects it from both heat and cold—a *thermostatic* property, keeping temperature constant. It makes fabrics that keep us very warm. It is a distinctive tan color.

The fiber is gathered in the molting period, the coarse guardhairs separated by hand from the fine, soft undercoat. As with cashmere, the coarser hair will be used for overcoats; the finer, usually in a worsted yarn, for knitwear and lighter wovens.

Hair of Cameloids. Cameloids, living in the Andes Mountains of South America, are believed to be the

[17]John Hare, *The Lost Camels of Tartary* (New York: Little, Brown, 1998)

originals of the camel family, which crossed to Asia when there was a land bridge between Alaska and Russia; the Bactrian camel and the one-humped dromedary of the Middle East developed from these. They became extinct in North America some 10,000 years ago, with llamas reintroduced in the late 1800s.

Llama and **alpaca** are domesticated cameloids used to carry burdens in the mountains, the alpaca being more important commercially for fiber (see Figures 2.41 and 2.42). The hair on the alpaca is very long, with properties as listed in Table 2.3.

Vicuña and **guanaco** are wild cameloids, living very high in the Andes. The vicuña is much prized for its undercoat, often listed as the finest, softest, rarest hair fiber (however, this was before qiviuq entered the fringes of the commercial fiber supply). Vicuña were almost extinct, having been hunted and killed to get the small amount of hair from each. They have been strictly protected for some years, and there has been some success in "ranching" them in order to take hair without harm to the animal. Guanaco hair is not much used in textiles. Vicuña and alpaca have been cross-bred to obtain soft hybrid fiber of greater length; see the natural fibers flowchart (Figure 2.3) earlier in this section.

Angora. Angora fiber comes from either the French or the English Angora rabbit, the latter having tufts on the ears. The hair is combed at molting time, and although there are many natural colors, white-haired types are needed for fabrics that will be dyed pastel shades. Angora is really a fur fiber, with air cell spaces in the center of the fiber, visible under the micro-

Figure 2.40 Bactrian camel of Asia. (Courtesy of the Metropolitan Toronto Zoo)

Figure 2.41 Llama and young (cria). (Courtesy of Lars Dahlberg, Dahlbrook Farm, for the Ontario Llama and Alpaca Club)

scope. The rabbits are raised today in China, France, and Chile. (See Figure 2.43.)

Qiviuq. Qiviuq (or qiviut) comes from the musk ox, species *Ovibos moschatus* ("musky sheep-cow"), living far above the tree line in the Arctic tundra (see Figure 2.44). The undercoat is very fine and lofty, much warmer than wool, and in a subtle, pleasing range of taupe colors. This fiber is just beginning to be used beyond craft products, as the basis of an Inuit industry. The largest population of musk oxen is in Canada's Northwest Territories (NWT) and Nunavut, primarily on the Arctic islands, and these herds are growing rapidly. Beginning in 1975, musk oxen from the NWT and Alaska were reintroduced to Russia, where the animal had been extinct for some 2,000 years. The herd, in the Taimyr Peninsula, is well established, if not large.

Figure 2.43 Angora rabbit.

(a)   (b)

Figure 2.44 Musk ox, source of qiviuq fiber.
(a) Logo, courtesy of Folknits formerly Down North;
(b) Canadian stamp issued 1991.

Figure 2.42 Alpaca. (Courtesy of the Metropolitan Toronto Zoo)

Other Specialty Hair Fibers. **Yak hair** is used in Tibet (China) where this animal is used to carry burdens. **Reindeer hair** is used for effect fibers; it is similar to caribou. **Caribou hair** (not available commercially) has a cellular core that traps air and provides excellent insulation. Caribou skins are used by the Inuit (see Section 7), but it has been suggested to blend the hair with wool for increased insulation. **Cow hair** and many other hairs have occasional uses. **Fur fibers** (except angora) are used mostly to make the best, most lustrous felt for hats; **beaver fur** undercoat makes exceptionally fine felt.

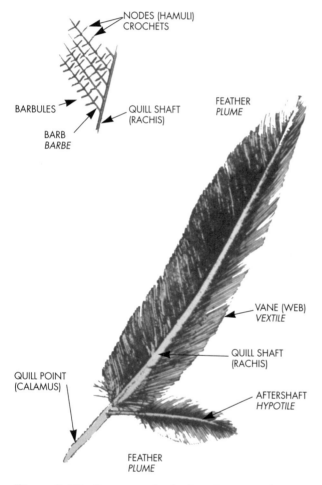

Figure 2.45 Structure of a feather. Reprinted from National Standard of Canada CAN/CGSB-139.1-M86, "Feathers and Down—Terminology and Characteristics." (Courtesy of Canadian General Standards Board. Structure of down is reprinted from the same source under *Typical Features* under *Microscopic Fiber Examination.*

Plumage—Feathers, Down

Plumage—the outer body covering of birds—has been used in a variety of ways for fabric, including as a skin, complete with feathers (a superlight and super warm parka made of such duckskin is on display in the Glenbow Museum, Calgary, Alberta).

More often, plucked feathers are used for stuffing, being very lofty and resilient. Feathers have a quill shaft and vanes (see Figure 2.45) and are used mainly for pillows and upholstery (in most cases today, they are replaced by rubber or polyurethane foam or by polyester fiber). Feathers are also used, as is fur, to make the long, snakelike boa scarf.

Down, the undercoat of waterfowl, is a marvellous structure with fine, barbed filaments growing from a quill point (see Figure 2.46). It is very light and fluffy, highly insulating with little weight, and softer because it lacks the quill shaft or vanes of feathers.

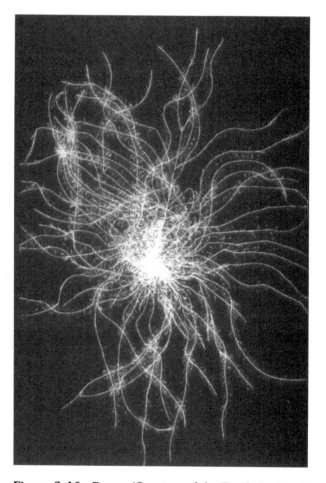

Figure 2.46 Down. (Courtesy of the Textile Institute)

The best (most lofty) is goose down, followed by eider duck down, with white being more expensive than gray. Down is being challenged today by hollow and microfine manufactured fibers.

Silk Filament

Cultivated or **reeled silk** is the only filament natural fiber, discovered and developed in China and often called the "queen" of fibers. The character given only by using a *filament* (very long fiber) is shown in fabrics typical of the silk family; refer to the *Fabric Glossary:* CHINA SILK; CREPE DE CHINE; GEORGETTE; ORGANZA; TAFFETA; and more than any other, SATIN.

We use other silk fibers, including silk in staple form, but when we talk about "silky," we imply continuous filament and a fine, lustrous, white fiber. To get such a long fiber, nearly the entire length of the very fine filament making up the cocoon of the silkworm has to be reeled off *unbroken,* and when a sticky gum is removed, what we recognize as silky silk emerges. Only one combination of factors in all of nature and history has given this product.

Silk Production. *Sericulture* is the raising of silkworms for production of reeled silk; Figure 2.48 shows the life cycle, while Figure 2.47 outlines the set of conditions that give us reeled silk. These begin

Moth (*Bombyx mori*) lays 400–600 eggs, eggs can be kept dormant in cold. Incubation takes 10–12 days.

↓

Egg hatches into a tiny caterpillar ("silkworm")(see Figure 2.48[b]) which begins to eat after 1–2 hours. To produce silk, caterpillar must be fed leaves of white mulberry (*Morus alba*) especially in the final part of the 28–34 days as it matures. The caterpillar molts 4 times as it grows.

↓

The caterpillar grows in length from 3 mm to 90 mm, through 5 *instars*—periods between moltings. It increases in weight 10,000 times, with a spurt of eating and growth after the last molt. Quarters must be airy, and kept clean (labor intensive!).

↓

Caterpillar spins cocoon from its head (see Figure 2.48[d]); head moves in a "figure 8" pattern. Spins about 20 m/hr (yd./hr.) for 2–5 days, a total of 400–1500 m (440–1640 yd.). Figure 2.48(e) shows mature silkworms at various stages of producing a cocoon. Occasionally one will wander into another's compartment. Two caterpillars spinning together, produce doupion (slubby) silk.

↓

Caterpillar changes to chrysalis (pupa). Cocoon is about the size of a peanut shell; weighs approx. 2 g (0.07 oz.).

If silk is to be reeled:

Chrysalis is killed (stifled with steam or dry heat).
Cocoons are gathered, inspected, graded, and sorted.
Cocoons are put into boiling water to soften gum, and silk filament is reeled (see Figure 2.49). It takes 45,000 cocoons to give 1-kg of raw silk.*
Silk filament is thrown (twisted, or combined with twist to form yarn—done by a *throwster*).

If moth is to breed:

Chrysalis is allowed to develop into moth (takes 1–2 weeks), which dissolves cocoon with alkaline saliva, and emerges leaving a hole in end of cocoon (see Figure 2.48[f]), to mate (see Figure 2.48[g]), after which female lays eggs (see Figure 2.48[a]) to complete the cycle.

*"Silk Facts," for exhibition "*Bombyx mori,* The Wonders of Silk: 4,000 Years of History," sponsored by UNESCO at the Montreal Botanical Garden and Insectarium, May–October, 1995.

Figure 2.47 The Silk Production Cycle.

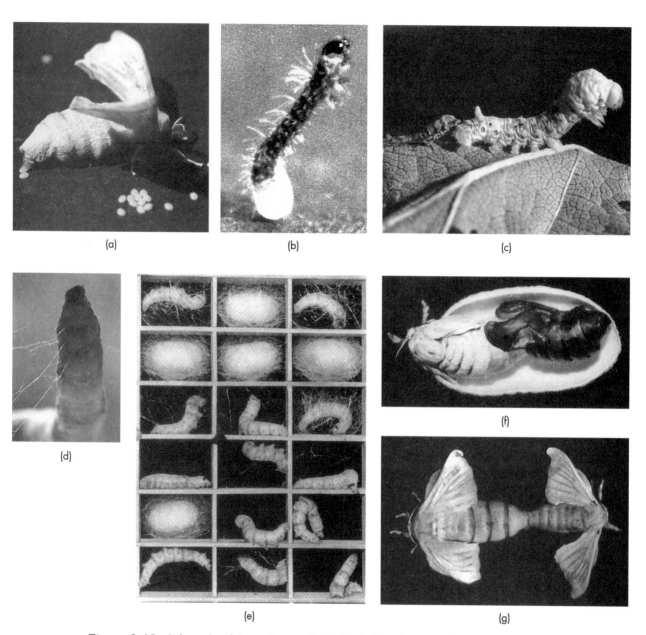

(a)

(b)

(c)

(d)

(e)

(f)

(g)

Figure 2.48 Life cycle of the "silkworm": (a) Moth *Bombyx mori* lays eggs. (b) Tiny caterpillar covered in black hair hatches from the egg. (c) Caterpillar eats and grows, molting four times as it matures over about 4 weeks. (d) After the last molt, the caterpillar has a final spurt of eating and growing, then is ready to spin. The silk filament is extruded from the spinneret below the mouth. (e) Each caterpillar usually gets on with spinning in its separate compartment or mount. (f) Inside the finished cocoon the caterpillar becomes a hard chrysalis (pupa). When silk is to be reeled, the cocoon is treated with heat to halt the cycle, but when metamorphosis is allowed to proceed, the moth develops, dissolves the end of the cocoon, and emerges. (g) Female (left) and male (right) moths mate, after which the female will lay her eggs to complete the cycle. (Courtesy of Shigeki Furukawa and Masahisa Furuta, *Cocoon's World*, Yousei Printing Co., October 1994)

with the "silkworm"—the caterpillar of one species of moth, *Bombyx mori* (family Bombycidae), although there are many varieties. This moth is uncamouflaged (white) and unable to fly or look after itself after centuries of domestication. The larva or caterpillar that hatches from an egg must be fed the leaves of the white mulberry (*Morus alba*) and in a form that it can manage when it is tiny. Much research has been done to develop alternative foods, but especially in the final growth period, nothing else will do. Given the right diet, the caterpillar of this specific moth spins its cocoon of a filament that can be reeled off in an unbroken strand, giving us "silky" silk. The final condition, then, is that the chrysalis or pupa inside is not allowed to emerge as a moth, which breaks the filaments; it is killed or *stifled* with steam or heat (hot air or sun).

Since a very few "wild" silk-producing types of silkworms are "cultivated," and a few others spin cocoons that can be reeled, the term "mulberry silk," rather than "cultivated" or "reeled silk," would probably be more accurate, but centuries of commerce and about 99 percent of silk production for textiles enforce the use of the terms "cultivated silk" and "reeled silk."

When the silkworm is ready to spin, it has stored a liquid protein, *fibroin,* in two glands running back into the body. These lead, in the head of the caterpillar, to a tube, opening at the *spinneret.* The silk fila-ment is extruded (spun) from the spinneret as a twin stream (*brins*) of sticky liquid, to which has been added a coating of the protein gum *sericin* from another pair of glands. (See Figure 2.48[d], [e].) This liquid hardens to form the twin filament (*bave*), which has no internal structure, but in which the dividing line of the original two brins can sometimes be seen under the microscope. Fibroin contains no sulfur, which makes this protein somewhat different from the *keratin* of wool and hair fibers, detectable in a burn test.

This is raw silk—*in the gum*—one of the most misused terms in fashion fabrics. It is *not* the same as wild silk; gum makes raw silk dull and stiff and of an ecru color. It does not become *silky* until the gum is removed.

Before reeling (Figure 2.49), the gum is softened in hot water and the cocoon brushed to find the outside end of the filament, which is then reeled in combination with about eight others. These are next combined again, with a small amount of twist, to make a multifilament yarn; this process is called *throwing*—a term that has persisted into MF filament yarn, with production done by "throwster" firms. Raw silk filament yarns or fabrics made of them are termed **net silk** or **nett silk** as compared to spun silk (see Figures 2.49, 2.50).

Degumming of silk is done by a wash that takes off the gum, and is necessary before silk will become

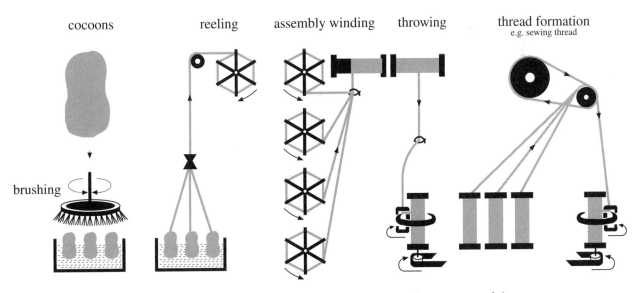

Figure 2.49 Reeling and throwing of filament (net, nett) silk. (Courtesy of the Textile Institute)

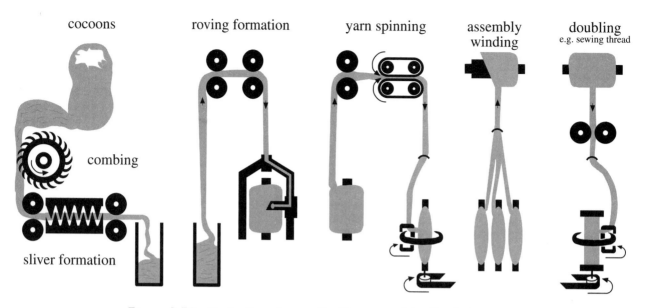

cocoons   roving formation   yarn spinning   assembly winding   doubling e.g. sewing thread

combing

sliver formation

Figure 2.50 Production of spun silk. (Courtesy of the Textile Institute)

silky. This leaves the filaments 25 percent or more lighter, showing them characteristically smooth, lustrous, soft, and drapable—in a word, silky (see Section 5). The time and method of degumming has been found to be important to the resulting fabric. A more lively and supple woven fabric results if degumming is done after weaving and without tension, in a batch method, to allow warp yarns to relax (develop crimp) and to take advantage of the thinning of the fabric as the gum is washed away. While the gum is left on, yarns need have little twist, since the gum holds them together and acts as some protection during processing.

Reeling was long a skilled, hand process, but has been automated. A single bave is so fine (about 1 dtex or denier—there is no point in exact conversion in this sort of comparison), it is virtually never used alone as a monofilament. (See definitions of denier and dtex under Yarn *Classified by Linear Density* in Section 3.) MF microfibers were first defined as being fibers of less than 1 dtex or denier—rivaling the spinneret of the caterpillar. Since they are now being made much finer than that, the emphasis is on describing them as finer than any of the natural fibers.

Silk production has been intensively studied over thousands of years, and in Japan, especially, efforts have been made to make a food that will allow hatching and feeding of caterpillars all through the year (with the natural cycle, the eggs are kept dormant by cold and hatch in the spring, just as the new leaves of the white mulberry are available). There is now even computer control of hatching! Needless to say, the breeding is carefully controlled to produce and select eggs (seed) of the most disease-resistant, best silk-producing moths; *grainage* is the term applied to this specialized procedure of seed production. A percentage of the food can be other than mulberry leaves until the final stages of growth, but then, for best quality and yield, nothing but mulberry leaves will do.

It takes silk from over 100 cocoons to make a necktie, nearly 650 for a blouse. China, where silk originated, has increased its production of silk a great deal in recent years, after a long period when Japan was the leading producer. By 1995, China was producing 75 percent of the world's silk, but cut back sharply on its production toward the end of the 1990s. India and Japan are prominent in raw silk production, with Russia, North and South Korea, Brazil, and Thailand increasing output. As labor costs have risen in Japan and silk production has fallen, it has imported raw silk to meet fabric manufacturing and printing needs. Although Japan has produced much less raw silk (in 1981 about 15 percent of 1930), improvements in the care of eggs and feeding of caterpillars have more than doubled efficiency (yield per box of eggs, field of mulberry bushes, or silk reeled per cocoon). *Renditta*, a specific measure of productivity, is the mass in kg required to produce

1 kg of raw silk; the lower the renditta, the less waste there has been.

Silk Quality

Momme (mommie) is a Japanese unit of weight (see Section 9 for the exact weight equivalent) used for silk fabrics and sometimes cited in advertisements for silk blouses, etc. Fabric of a higher momme will be heavier, from use of heavier yarns and/or a closer weave.

Weighted silk (British: *loaded*) has had (cheap) chemicals added to make up for the body lost in degumming; it makes the silk stiff and lowers durability. While there was a good deal of this rather fraudulent practice when only silk could give filament fabric characteristics, it is not a problem today. However, one term linking it with lower quality still persists: *pure dye silk;* since weighting was done in the dye bath, pure dye silk was defined by the U.S. Federal Trade Commission in 1932 to mean no more than 15 percent weighting for black, 10 percent for other colors. See also Section 5.

Silk has a crunchy, dry hand sometimes called *scroop,* but this term usually means the rustle typical of taffeta, produced by an acid treatment of silk.

Washed (sanded, chafed) silk and *washable or washer silk* are all modern treatments to give silk fabrics an informal, sometimes preworn look that demands less care than traditional silk fabrics require. Presumably, washable silks have colors that are fast to washing, but silk must never be washed under the same conditions as cotton. See Section 5 for a discussion of sand-washed silk and Section 6 for silk care.

Silk Properties. Silk properties are unique, even though silk is a protein fiber like wool. The silk protein, *fibroin,* is simpler than wool keratin, without the coiling and cross-links, so silk is not as resilient as wool. It has low wet resiliency and wrinkles easily when wet—watch for this when caring for washable silk.[18] Silk has a degree of elastic recovery or give.

It has a warm, dry hand and can be a good insulator, although we seldom use it as a fabric to keep us warm. Silk absorbs well, and is strong when dry, although it does lose strength when wet.

Silk can be weakened by long exposure to sunlight. More seriously—for most of us who do not have

---

[18]*Textile Chemist & Colorist*, May 1994: 25.

---

silk furnishings to worry about—perspiration can attack silk clothing. Proteins are not sensitive to acid but are to alkali; fresh perspiration is mildly acidic, but is acted on by bacteria on the skin, breaking down ammonium compounds to form alkali. However, it is only after time that this can concentrate and do damage to the fibers and to dyestuffs, so silks should be cleaned soon after wearing; home care is discussed in Section 6.

We value silk most for its beauty, the result of it being a smooth and fine filament: lustrous, soft, drapable. The supply is limited and price high because of its expensive (labor-intensive) production.

Staple Silk (Spun)

We use and treasure silk in many ways other than as reeled filament.

Cultivated Silk Waste. Waste fibers occur at the start of reeling (*floss* or *frison,* the short fibers on the outside of the cocoon) or at the end, and from damaged cocoons, e.g., those from which moths have been allowed to emerge for breeding purposes. Silk waste is used as staple fiber to give spun silk. Production of spun silk is shown in Figure 2.50. (See *Fabric Glossary:* SPUN.)

The shortest waste silk is called *noils* and gives little bumps on the surface of the fabric called *noile.* Double cocoons cannot be reeled and give the slubby *douppioni (dupion) silk* that may also be used for "silk linen," discussed in the *Fabric Glossary* under SHANTUNG.

Wild Silk. Wild silk comes from various types of moths, many of the family Saturniidae (called "giant silk moths"), genus *Antheraea*—varieties that give *tussah, eri, and muga* silk. Seed may be spread on trees such as oak, castor, or polyanthus, but most of the caterpillars forage for themselves, and the moths emerge, leaving cocoons with a hole in the end (see Figure 2.51) and broken filaments. The *S. eri* silk moth has been domesticated and cannot live on its own, but the silk has the character of wild silk: coarser than cultivated (mulberry) silk and gum that is darker and cannot be removed entirely. Silk from some of the wild varieties of India, such as **tasar** (from which tussah comes), cannot be reeled, whereas **muga** (mooga, moonga) silk can be reeled but the silk is coarse and golden brown (see Figure 2.51). Besides the fabric names **tussah** and **muggah** (see

Figure 2.51 Muga moth (India), opened cocoon, fabric made from this wild silk. (Photo by Rick Wicker, Courtesy of the Denver Museum of Natural History)

Fabric Glossary: TUSSAH), those connected with North China are **shantung, honan,** and **pongee** (see *Fabric Glossary:* SHANTUNG).

Thai Silk and Indian Silk. These silks traditionally have had slubs, especially in the weft. In most cases, these uneven yarns result from the moth being allowed to mature and leave the cocoon, rather than being killed with dry heat in the chrysalis stage (it is against Hindu teaching to kill any creature knowingly).

Spider Silk

For many years, the strong and complex silk spun by spiders from a spinneret in the abdomen has been used for the cross-hairs in gunsights or microscopes. There is an interest in exploiting this remarkable filament for specialized yarn and textile uses, and silk is actually taken from spiders for research into these applications. A spider spins a number of specialized types of filament from several spinnerets in the abdomen. These protein lines have a unique combination of tremendous strength coupled with ability to absorb impact forces without breaking, as when a bug flies into a web (for forward research on ballistic fibers see Section 7, Third Millennium Problem Solving and Innovations). They also show what is called *supercontraction;* when wet, spider silk shrinks to almost half its length. All sorts of possibilities exist with this unique and complex type of fiber.

Manufactured Fibers

The silkworm was the direct inspiration for manufactured (MF) fibers, since the process could be seen and is simple: a sticky liquid is ejected in a thin stream, which turns into a solid as a filament. Furthermore, silk has been long prized as one of the most desirable textile fibers. The first MF fibers were made using a naturally formed polymer, cellulose, as the raw material. This was imitating the silkworm which eats leaves (cellulose); but the silkworm produces a protein, very different from cellulose (just as a cow eats grass but produces milk). Eventually, in the development of MF fibers, the polymer raw material was synthesized as well, to give synthetic fibers.

Most methods begin with a solid raw material that is converted to a sticky liquid, forced through holes in a spinneret in streams (*extrusion* or chemical spinning), and turned into a solid filament. It is a matter of awe to hear what heights engineering has reached in this area of chemical spinning—not only in construction of spinnerets with tiny, sometimes specially shaped holes, but in extruding these filaments at speeds such as 400 km/h (250 mph), while keeping the precise physical properties of each fiber constant.[19]

The flowchart of MF fibers (Figure 2.4) shows three main divisions: ready-made natural polymers, minor-use specialized fibers made from inorganic materials, and synthetic fibers.

Spinning Manufactured Fibers

Spinning Methods

Several spinning methods are used:

- **Wet spinning.** The fiber-forming liquid is extruded into a bath of liquid, in which the filament is solidified; an example is viscose. (See Figures 2.52, 2.57.)

- **Dry spinning.** A solid raw material is dissolved in a solvent that evaporates, leaving the solid filament; an example is acetate. (See Figure 2.53.)

[19]Dr. Albin F. Turbak, Professor, School of Textiles, Georgia Tech. and U. of Georgia, talk given to the Institute of Textile Science, Toronto, Ontario, April 12, 1989.

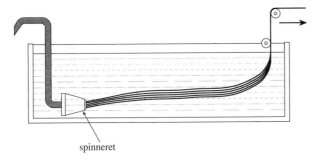

Figure 2.52 Wet spinning of manufactured fiber.

- **Solvent spinning.** The fiber-forming material is dissolved in a solvent, then extruded and coagulated in a liquid bath with no chemical combination intermediate; an example is lyocell.

- **Melt spinning.** A solid raw material is melted and spun, and forms the solid filament as it cools; an example is nylon. (See Figure 2.54.)

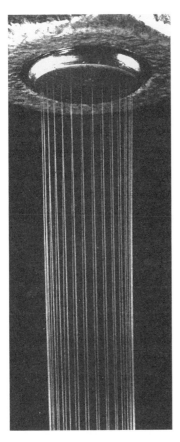

Figure 2.53 Closeup of spinneret; dry spinning of acetate filament. (Courtesy of the Textile Institute)

- **Gel spinning.** The fiber-forming material, as a very thick (viscous) liquid, is extruded and the filament is set as a gel; an example is the very high molecular weight high-tenacity fiber SPECTRA.

Spinneret Types

Spinneret types differ for filament or staple fiber. When filament yarn is intended, the number, size, and in some cases the shape of the spinneret holes are engineered so that the product of that spinneret can be wound up as the yarn—hence the term *chemical spinning*. When it is planned that filaments should be broken or cut into staple fiber for eventual mechanical spinning into spun yarn, much larger spinnerets with many more holes are used, and the product of several of these is gathered together to give *tow*—a thick rope of MF filaments intended for conversion into staple. (See Figure 2.55.) (Note that the same term, *tow,* is used for short flax waste, for who knows what reason.)

Drawing Manufactured Fiber Filaments

When MF fibers are spun, the long chains of polymer often lie at all angles to one another—what is called a *random* or *disoriented* arrangement. Such disarray produces a fiber with less tensile strength than if the molecular chains are aligned nearly parallel to each other in an *oriented* arrangement and packed closer together in a more crystalline structure. *Drawing* or pulling out of the fiber after spinning can accomplish this and is an integral part of production of our strongest fibers, such as nylon and polyester. After the filament is drawn it is thinner, and tests demonstrate the changes this brings: tenacity testing reveals the increased strength, while x-ray diffraction testing indicates a more crystalline structure. The aligning of molecular chains is shown in Figures 2.56 and 2.63.

Cellulosic and Minor Natural Polymer Manufactured Fibers

Of those MF fibers using natural polymers for raw material, some are minor, such as fibers from proteins, seaweed, or chitin; most of our discussion of this type will be of the cellulosic MF (CMF) fibers, which use cellulose as the raw material. Of these, those that reconstitute cellulose in the MF fiber by regeneration

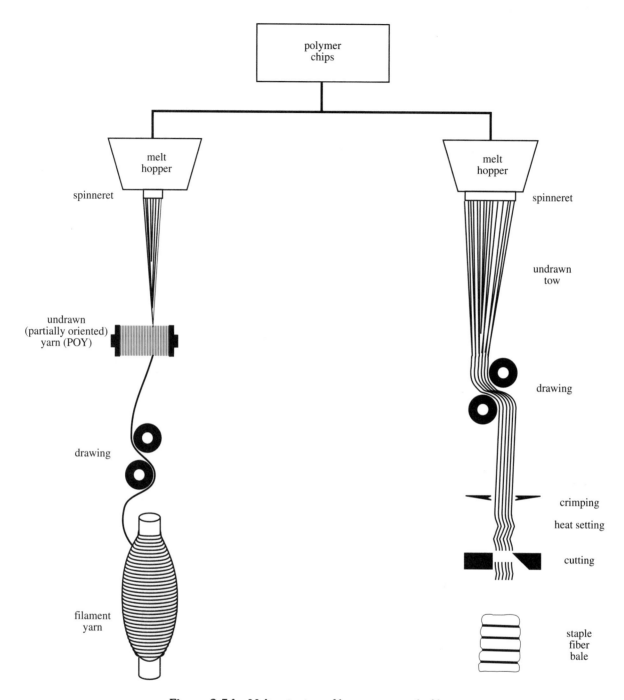

Figure 2.54   Melt spinning—filament or staple fiber.

or precipitation are much more important commercially than the cellulose acetate compounds. It can be noted that until 1953 in the United States all CMF fibers were classified as rayon. After that (much later in Canada), rayon was reserved for fibers regenerated by the viscose or cuprammonium process, while cel-

lulose acetate compounds were given a separate generic grouping.

General advantages of MF fibers and of CMF fibers have been noted earlier in this section. In the 1990s, a new type of reconstituted cellulose fiber, lyocell, was introduced commercially. It is produced

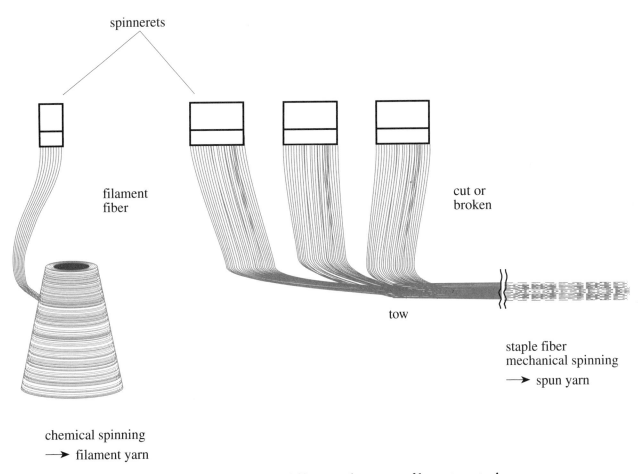

spinnerets

filament fiber

cut or broken

tow

chemical spinning
→ filament yarn

staple fiber
mechanical spinning
→ spun yarn

Figure 2.55 Manufactured fiber may be spun as filament or staple.

(a) Undrawn polymer; no orientation or crystallinity (amorphous).

(b) 3:1 draw ratio; alignment of some chains and crystallinity introduced.

(c) 6:1 draw ratio; high degree of chain orientation and crystallinity.

Figure 2.56 Effect of drawing on molecular orientation. (Courtesy of the Textile Institute)

by reconstituting cellulose from a solvent, using chemicals and processing methods that give superior CMF fibers and have little impact on the environment. This has a profound effect on the position of the more traditional fibers that regenerate cellulose from an intermediate form, as with viscose, or a complex, as with cuprammonium. However, we should still examine the older methods, especially the long-time commercially successful viscose process.

Reconstituted Cellulose Fibers

Rayon, the oldest MF textile fiber, has accounted for the greatest part of world CMF fiber production, and almost all of this has been viscose, with cuprammonium minor in production. (It should be noted that Europe and the ISO withdrew support for the generic group *rayon* in 1971,[20] while in Canada, lyocell, as well as viscose or cuprammonium, can come under the generic of rayon.)

Viscose Rayon Production. Viscose is made by the odd, complicated viscose process; this is a rather inelegant way of converting cellulose (solid) to a liquid form, then spinning it, to regenerate it as an MF fiber filament (solid), but it has worked well since its development in England in 1892–1905. Further, it is multistage and allows many modifications to produce special versions, the most important being HWM rayon (modal). The wrapping film cellophane is viscose rayon in another form.

The standard viscose process results in a fiber with a skin/core structure, depending on the speed of regeneration of the fiber in the spinning bath. Because of the wrinkled outside of the fiber, the lengthwise appearance under the microscope shows many striations, while the cross section shows an almost serrated edge. Some modifications have made use of the skin/core structure to make self-crimping viscose. The viscose process is shown in Figure 2.57.

Trademark names for standard viscose rayon are not often seen; the better-known trademark names are those given to HWM forms of viscose. Some years ago, Akzo Nobel set up a certification system to license the name GOLDLABEL© to products of

[20]International Organization for Standardization (ISO) Recommendation R2076, July 1971; British Standard (BS) 4815: 1972.

logs → wood pulp → purified pulp →cellulose (in sheets like thick blotting paper)

[steeped in sodium hydroxide (NaOH), very strong alkali, also called caustic soda or lye.]

→ alkali cellulose (alkcell) [shredded or ground] → crumbs [aged, + carbon disulfide (*xanthation* process)] → sodium cellulose xanthate (intermediate)

[+ weak NaOH] → thick, syrupy, (viscous) orange liquid [ripened, filtered, gas bubbles removed] [wet spun (see Figure 2.52) into dilute sulfuric acid bath, with some other chemicals]

→ solid filament of regenerated cellulose

[stretched around Godet wheels] → filament yarn or tow [washed]

Figure 2.57   The viscose process.

ENKA® CIRCLE OF QUALITY indicating viscose made to high-quality standards.

Cuprammonium Rayon (Cupro) Production. Cuprammonium rayon (generic name is *cupro* in a number of countries) is made by a process that is much simpler than that for viscose. Cuprammonium, a deep blue solution of copper in ammonia, converts the cellulose to a liquid form believed to be a complex formed with cellulose by the cuprammonium solution. Cellulose from purified wood pulp is combined with the cuprammonium solution, and when the resulting sticky liquid is spun and washed with water, cellulose is regenerated as filaments. Since spinning takes place downward through a funnel, the fibers are stretched somewhat, making them finer and slightly stronger than those from the standard viscose process. Cuprammonium rayon is most often used in high-quality lining fabrics, since it is made in a finer filament than most viscose. Cuprammonium does not regenerate slowly as viscose does, and so does not show a wrinkled surface; it has a round cross section.

This form of CMF is still made in Europe by Bemberg Italy, marketed under the trademark name BEMBERG®, used since the fiber was developed by the Bemberg Company (Germany) in 1890.

Viscose and Cuprammonium Rayon Properties. Properties will be similar for any standard viscose or cuprammonium rayon. Since it is composed of cellulose, like cotton, it is absorbent—in fact, it absorbs more than cotton, so it is comfortable to wear, with good static resistance and cool hand. Rayon has good heat resistance, but like cotton it wrinkles, has poor wet press retention, and allows mildew growth. Since it swells as it absorbs moisture, rayon in fabrics tends to shrink even more than cotton.

The main area of difference from cotton is in strength, especially wet strength. Cotton has good strength when dry and gains significantly when wet, but these rayon fibers have only fair strength when dry and lose about half of that when wet. In converting the cellulose to fiber, the molecular chains end up shorter and less oriented than those in cotton—making a weaker fiber. This low wet strength makes these fibers less able to stand up to machine washing and drying in consumer use, and unsuited to the wet finishing in fabric manufacture that can give resistance to wrinkling and shrinking (Durable Press)—to deliver the ease of care consumers want: fabric articles that are machine washable and dryable and require little or no ironing.

Most viscose and cuprammonium is used as staple fiber (spun rayon), but filament rayon is found in linings, apparel velvet, trims, and furnishing fabrics such as damask drapery material.

High Wet Modulus (HWM) Rayon (Modal).
The viscose process can be modified to leave the cellulose chains longer, with more orientation, giving an HWM rayon (the generic name is *modal* in a number of countries) that comes closer to cotton in strength. Its strength when dry is fairly good, better than standard rayon, and it loses less strength when wet.

The higher wet modulus means that the fiber is less prone to stretch when damp or wet; heavy drapes of standard rayon, for instance, lengthen in high humidity and shorten in dryer air—what is called an "elevator effect." Otherwise, HWM rayons behave like any rayon. The main trademark name for HWM rayons is ZANTREL® (by BASF), with LENZING MODAL using the (non-United States) generic name modal. There is also an *unofficial* term, *polynosic*, for one type of HWM rayon. Vincel (by Courtaulds) is no longer produced.

Lyocell is a solvent-spun cellulosic fiber—an innovation of the 1990s in this oldest group of manufactured fibers. Research went on at Courtaulds Fibres Plc., U.K. from the late 1970s, with the pilot plant stage reached in 1988; during this time the fiber was referred to by the name "Genesis." The first of this type marketed in North America was TENCEL®, a staple fiber made by Courtaulds, with the first commercial production plant in Mobile, Alabama, in late 1992. By the late 1990s, Courtaulds had turned over this fiber to the Dutch firm, Akzo Nobel, which had held the original patent on the solvent spinning process, and Tencel Fibres Europe was formed to forward applications of TENCEL staple there. TENCEL is used alone and blended with cotton, flax, polyester, and wool, plus some blends with spandex. Akzo Nobel, expert in high-speed spinning of filament yarns, and building on work done by American Enka, formed a separate fibers company and introduced the first filament lyocell under the trademark name NEWCELL® (by Acordis), with resulting wider applications of this fiber type in "silky" fabrics.

Lyocell as a generic name was established promptly in Europe, where the generic *rayon* has not been used since the 1970s, and was later accepted as a generic in the United States. In Canada it can be used as a generic or classified as another rayon.

Lyocell Production. Lyocell is made by dissolving purified cellulose from wood pulp in an amine oxide, n-methylmorpholine oxide (NMMO), an organic solvent that is much less harmful or irritating than others used in fiber production. After the clear, viscous (thick, sticky) liquid is filtered, it is extruded (spun) in a bath of dilute NMMO, where the fiber coagulates as reconstituted cellulose. It is then washed and dried. The process is shown in Figure 2.58. Like cuprammonium, lyocell has a smooth surface and a round cross section. Since virtually all the solvent can be recovered and used again, the process is largely pollution-free. A similar process was developed by Lenzing in

---

logs → wood pulp → purified pulp →cellulose

mixed with organic solvent amine oxide (n-methylmophaline oxide—NMMO)

→ heated, cellulose dissolves→ clear, viscous liquid

→ filtered → extruded (spun) in bath of diluted amine oxide

→ coagulates to solid filament of cellulose

→ washed → dried

diluted solvent from washing → purified

→ recovered by evaporation of water → totally recycled

Figure 2.58 Solvent spinning of lyocell.

Austria (LENZING LYOCELL), and other countries have followed suit.

Lyocell Properties. Lyocell has dry strength comparable to cotton and some polyester, very high wet modulus, and although it does lose some strength when wet, it will stand up to home laundering, and to wet mill finishing to give Durable Press, for instance, so wrinkling and poor wet press retention can be counteracted. Of course, being made up of cellulose, it has the advantages of good moisture absorption, good static resistance, cool hand, and good heat resistance.

Lyocell fibers can have a tendency to *fibrillation*—to splitting off if abraded when wet, forming surface fibrils (see Figure 2.59). These give a very soft "peach skin" hand, which can also be promoted in finishing by physical abrasion, by enzyme treatment, or by chemical (alkali) treatment. In making some industrial fabrics, a "fast fibrillating" type is useful to generate microfibrils, as for filters. However, the tendency to fibrillation can also result in a difference in light reflection from the surface that may be interpreted as graying. As well, without fibrillation, different hands can be achieved that are desirable for certain products; therefore a non-fibrillating variation is available, TENCEL® A100 (by Tencel).

Cellulose Acetate Compounds

Cellulose will combine with acetic acid to produce new compounds with very different properties from the original cellulose, and therefore different from cellulosic natural and reconstituted cellulose MF fibers. Attempts to make fibers of cellulose acetate compounds were made from the late 1890s, at a time when there was intense experimenting to put cellulose into a liquid form to extrude into textile fibers.

Cellulose acetate compounds of two types are made into fibers. **Triacetate** is the one discovered first but not commercially made until, as Arnel, it was marketed in 1954 by American Celanese. Production of triacetate was phased out in North America in 1987 because the solvent used was considered environmentally unacceptable; it was still produced under the trademark names Arnel in Belgium and Tricel in Italy (by Novaceta), and also made in Japan, but has faded with the 1990s. The generic called simply **acetate,** introduced about 1905, is a *secondary cel-*

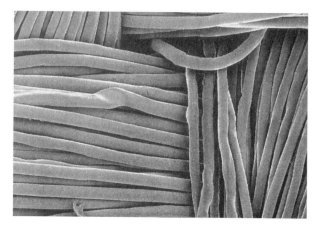

Figure 2.59 Fabric of TENCEL® lyocell, before and after fibrillation, plus TENCEL logo. (Courtesy of Tencel Fibres Europe)

lulose acetate compound, sometimes called a "diacetate"; in Europe, trademark names for acetate are DICEL® and SILENE® (by Novaceta).

Cellulose Acetate and Triacetate Production.

The relationship of these fibers comes from the structure of the cellulose chain unit, which is a residue of the sugar glucose, shown in Figure 2.8 in the discussion of Cellulosic Natural Fibers. The reaction to produce a cellulose acetate compound is shown in a different style in Figure 2.60. On each unit, there are three active hydroxyl groups (OH) where chemical reactions can take place. If cellulose (purified from wood pulp) is steeped in very strong (*glacial*) acetic acid, eventually an acetyl group (CH_3COO) will attach itself to each of the hydroxyl groups, with water (H_2O) lost. Since there are three OH groups, the result is cellulose triacetate.

Cellulose acetate production follows the same procedure, but acetic anhydride is added when the reaction to form cellulose triacetate is complete, and then the solution is aged. The compound is reduced slightly until there are approximately two acetyls per unit, giving a secondary cellulose acetate with the generic name acetate.

The compound is solidified and broken up into white flakes, which are dissolved in acetone for dry spinning; the solvent evaporates, leaving the solid filaments, just as liquid nail polish quickly becomes solid. The first cellulose acetate was used in large amounts, not to make fibers, but as "dope" to paint the fabric of early airplanes. Although the solvent in nail polish is not acetone, it is related closely enough that it will affect acetate or triacetate fabrics.

Triacetate is disintegrated by acetone, but does not form a smooth solution for spinning, as acetate does. In fact, it was the search for a suitable solvent that delayed introduction of triacetate half a century, (no one wished to use the known one, chloroform). The one used eventually, a mixture of alcohol and methylene chloride, was also a difficult chemical to work with; methylene chloride is known as a strong paint stripper.

Cellulose Acetate and Triacetate Properties. These two types of fibers show both similarities and differences, since they are closely related, yet individual—like family members.

Cellulose acetate and triacetate are thermoplastic—they soften and melt on application of heat. Both are weak fibers with low abrasion resistance and tenacity, and both lose much of this low strength when wet. In burning, both fibers have an odor of vinegar, which relates to their composition; vinegar is weak acetic acid. On the other side of the scale is the important economic advantage of cost; CMF fibers are more economical to produce than synthetics.

Triacetate softens at a higher temperature than acetate and can be given a heat set in garment manufacture, using carefully controlled presses, that is permanent for the life of the article in normal use and care; pleats, for instance, will stay sharp through washing and drying. It also withstands a fairly high iron heat, although care must be taken with any thermoplastic. It is a stiffer fiber than acetate, although with a softer hand than, for instance, nylon.

Acetate is produced almost entirely as filament, and in this form has good luster; a soft, smooth hand; and pleasing drapability. In other words, it can give very silklike fabrics. This allows very pleasing, silky, yet inexpensive fabrics, often used in linings. Acetate is fairly heat sensitive; this means pressing heat must

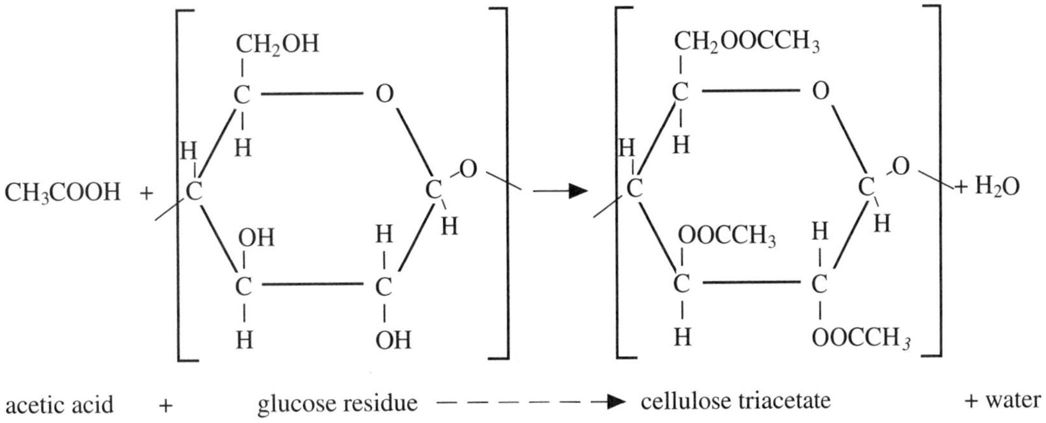

Figure 2.60 Formation of cellulose triacetate.

be low to avoid "sticking" (melting). Acetate cannot be given a permanent heat set and with its low strength, especially wet, is anything but an easy care or high performance fiber. Within its limitations, however, it gives satisfactory fabrics, mostly classified as dry-cleanable; only more informal fabric styles such as crushed satin are presented as washable and "no iron."

Trademark names for acetate: ESTRON® (by Eastman); and DICEL®, NOVALENE®, SILENE®, and SILNOVA® (by Novaceta). Celanese no longer uses its trademark Celebrate!, but simply labels its product acetate.

Minor Natural Polymer Manufactured Fibers

Azlon (Protein). A number of fibers have been made from proteins, in attempts to make a wool-like MF fiber, from before World War I until just after World War II. However, many of these used proteins for raw material from sources that are complete or first-class proteins in a nutritional sense—having all the amino acid building blocks humans and animals need to make protein in their bodies. It is not surprising that these fibers are of minor use today, when there is so much malnutrition, especially a lack of complete proteins. Furthermore, synthetic fibers, particularly acrylic, give wool-like properties with much better performance than protein-based MF fibers.

The generic name *azlon* was given to MF protein fibers, and they can have a soft, warm hand; have good absorbency; and take dye well, as wool does. Such fibers are weak, and weaker wet, and some, like Vicara from corn protein, *zein*, were golden or tan in color. Others used in the 1940s and 1950s were Aralac, Fibrolane, Lanital, and Merinova, all made using milk protein, *casein*; and Ardil, from peanut protein, which was in production for many years. There is some milk protein used in a fiber made in Japan, CHINON, discussed under Bicomponent Fibers.

Alginate Fiber. Alginate is fiber made from alginic acid, derived from seaweed, and converted into calcium alginate to form a filament. This fiber is used because it will dissolve in an alkaline solution, such as of washing soda (sodium carbonate) and can be used for sewing or looping articles together temporarily or as a ground material that is to be removed eventually.

It has also found use in medicine, since alginate will help stop bleeding and does not irritate.

Chitin Fiber. Chitin is a polymer based on a sugar-like unit that resembles cellulose (see Figure 2.61 compared with Figure 2.60). It is the main part of the hard outer covering of insects, arachnids, and crustaceans, as well as forming reinforcement in the cell walls of fungi, molds, and yeast. As such it is the most abundant organic compound after cellulose. It can be made into a fiber; in medicine it is absorbable as sutures and has been found to speed healing greatly when used as wound dressings. Its derivative *chitosan* may also be used to remove offensive color from dyebath effluent, in combating water pollution (see Section 7 *Textiles and the Environment, Wastewater*).

Synthetic Manufactured Fibers

The general advantages of MF fibers in general and of synthetic fibers in particular were noted earlier in this section.

Manufactured fibers were inspired by study of the production of much-prized silk filaments by a caterpillar, turning a thick, sticky liquid into solid filaments.

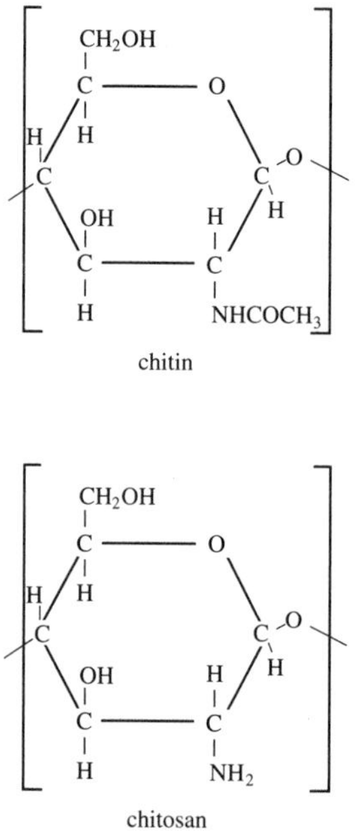

Figure 2.61 **Structure of chitin and its derivative, chitosan.**

However, it was a giant step to go from using a complex natural polymer, cellulose, as the raw material, to synthesizing such a fiber-forming material out of simple chemicals to create the very long molecular chains necessary to make a useful textile fiber.

This was the area of research chosen in the 1930s by a team of organic chemists at E. I. DuPont de Nemours and Company, Inc., headed by Dr. Wallace Hume Carothers. They knew that all the natural fiber-forming materials (cellulose, protein, rubber) were such long-chain or "giant" molecules, also called "high polymers." The research team was looking for small units that would have a reactive group at either end so that they might be made to join together into very long chains, rather like making up a necklace of pop beads.

The work of this team is widely regarded as one of the most significant (and probably the last) examples of "pure research"—the luxury to explore any area of knowledge, without necessarily coming up with any practical or valuable results. In this case, the team "hit the jackpot" in producing not only the first synthetic textile fiber, nylon, but one which is still, so many years later, in the forefront of desirable and useful fibers. Nylon is also employed in many forms other than textile fibers, from bristles for paint-, hair-, and toothbrushes to buttons to cog wheels to liquid coatings.

On the way to developing the type of polymer that was eventually called nylon or polyamide, the team tried hundreds of units that did not work out, and along the way, touched on a number of families that would eventually be explored more fully (and successfully). Among the compounds tried by the DuPont team was one that could be stretched like "pull toffee" to some four times its length, at which point further stretching would break it. It would not return to its original length so was not a truly elastic fiber. This was the type that led to nylon.

This story has been well told by the man who in 1941 delivered the second synthetic, polyester, also a success and now by far the most-used synthetic fiber. Dr. J. R. Whinfield narrated an ICI film called *Point of New Departure*, tracing efforts to create first manufactured fibers and then synthetic.

Synthetics are made using fossil fuels (oil, gas, coal) plus air, water, and other chemicals as the raw materials. From these, chemicals are obtained to make the simple materials that will be the units of the fiber polymer. These units must have reactive groups at both ends; in *polymerization,* these groups join to form very long chain molecules with fiber-forming properties.

Nylon (Polyamide)—The First Synthetic Fiber

Nylon was first marketed in 1938 as bristles and fishline, and in the early 1940s as nylon hosiery or "nylons."

Nylon contains carbon, hydrogen, oxygen, and nitrogen. There are now several types, but the generic name is defined by the amide linkage between units (see Figure 2.62); an alternative generic in many countries is *polyamide,* the name most commonly used in Europe. The original type has a unit made from the reaction between the *comonomers* hexamethylene diamine and adipic acid; there are six carbons in each, giving this the name *nylon 6,6.* "Deep dye nylon," called *nylon 6,* has six carbons in the caprolactam unit or *monomer;* Trademark names for this type are: CAPROLAN® (by Allied), and in Europe, ATLAS, BAYCO, DORIX, PERLON (by Bayer). There are also other types: *nylon 4, 11,* etc. A very silklike variation of nylon, developed by DuPont under the trademark name Qiana, is no longer manufactured, more for marketing reasons than for any performance lack in this fiber.

Polyamides containing 85 percent or more aromatic units were given a separate generic, *aramid,* discussed under *Flame- and Heat-Resistant Organic Fibers.*

Nylon Production. Nylon production starts with the basic chemicals for any one type of nylon, combined to form the unit compound; then polymerization takes place under heat and pressure. The polymer, a thick, sticky liquid, is solidified and broken into white flakes or chips. The chips are melted and spun (shown in Figure 2.54 under *Spinning Manufactured Fibers*) and the resulting fiber drawn to orient the molecular chains (see also Figure 2.63). Partially oriented yarn or POY is often produced if filament texturing is to follow, when the drawing will be completed.

Figure 2.62 Amide linkage in nylon (polyamide).

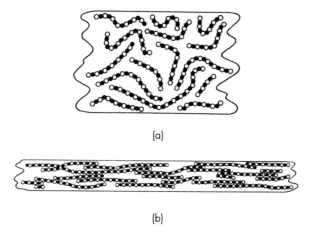

(a)

(b)

Figure 2.63 Polymer molecules in fibers: (a) undrawn and (b) drawn and oriented. (Courtesy of the Textile Institute)

Nylon Properties. Nylon's properties are outstanding; although no longer the most-used synthetic, nylon is still the strongest major fiber in its standard form. It was first used as filament in place of silk to give strong, light materials such as parachutes and women's sheer hosiery.

Although nylon is not a true elastomer, it has low modulus, so it "gives" when stretched. This contributes to its outstanding abrasion resistance and tenacity; nylon can withstand abrasion even when under strain, as in hosiery, and even small amounts of nylon blended with wool, for instance, extend the life of carpets or socks. However, this also means that in a blend with a more rigid fiber such as cotton, nylon elongates and leaves the cotton to take wear. A special **low elongation** type, Nylon 420 (by DuPont) is used for cotton blends. Nylon is not ideal for sewing thread, either, because stitching can stretch and then contract, leaving a puckered seam.

The great strength of nylon can also be a disadvantage; it results in stubborn pilling. Balls of short fibers rolled up during wear cannot be brushed off, as they can with wool, but must be cut off with a sharp blade such as a razor. Electric pill removers are sold for the purpose; the pumice-stone used on rough skin has also been recommended to rub off pills. Stubborn pilling can be a problem with any very strong fiber used in staple form.

Nylon softens at a temperature high enough that yarn or fabric made 100 percent of it can be given a permanent heat set as defined in this *Reference.*

Nylon absorbs less moisture than natural fibers, which means less comfort in clothing, but its absorbency is not as low as acrylic, polyester, or olefin (in decreasing order).

Lower absorbency also signals collection of static electricity in dry air. When nylon clothing is worn next to polyester, as often occurs with nylon underclothes and polyester outerwear, there can be a particular problem; see the triboelectric series in Figure 2.7. Because of its fairly low absorbency, however, nylon is quick drying.

Nylon in standard form is weakened by sunlight; much nylon produced today has antioxidants or other stabilizers incorporated in the fiber to make it more resistant to the ultraviolet (UV) rays of sunlight.

Nylon is used for its strength, abrasion resistance, and heat settability in home furnishings, lingerie, loungewear, eveningwear, sportswear, activewear, footwear, and luggage. In some uses, thickness of yarn may be listed, usually as denier (in the order of 1,000 denier for luggage). CORDURA® (by DuPont) is a trademark for very tough nylon. ULTRATURF (by Toray) is a trademark for a nylon pile covering for playing fields. Figure 2.64 portrays the general acceptance of nylon as the strongest standard fiber ("super-strength" fibers are discussed later in this section).

Some trademark names for standard nylon exist besides those listed for "deep dye nylon"— ANSO® and CAPROLAN® (by Allied), EXCEL (by DuPont in Europe), LILION (by SNIA), MERYL® (by Nylstar, a joint company, Rhône-Poulenc/SNIA), ULTREL (by Kraus), and ZEFTRON® (by BASF)—however, most nylon trademark names are for special versions, such as ANTRON® or ULTRON®, discussed under *Modifications of Manufactured Fibers.*

Polyester—The Most-Used Synthetic Fiber

Polyester was the second synthetic fiber type to be developed (1941) and is now by far the most widely used, due to a balance of properties that gives it great versatility plus a less expensive manufacturing process compared to nylon.

There are several types of polyester, since the generic is defined as the ester of a dihydric (two hydroxyl groups) alcohol and an aromatic dicarboxylic acid. The original type is called PET for polyethylene terephthalate, the result of linking and then polymerizing ethylene glycol (antifreeze) and terephthalic acid.

Figure 2.64 The superior strength of nylon is well known! (Reprinted by permission: Tribune Media Services)

The acid component gives part of many trademark names for polyester, beginning with the first, Terylene (by ICI). Polyester is made up only of carbon, hydrogen, and oxygen (no nitrogen, as there is in nylon); the carbons in the acid are in rings, making this, in organic chemistry terms, an *aromatic* acid.

Polyester Production. Production of polyester follows steps similar to those outlined for nylon; it is also melt-spun and drawn after the fiber is made, and filament intended for texturing may be made as POY (see Figure 2.54).

Polyester Properties. Properties of polyester can appear very similar to those of nylon, so it is important to clarify how they differ. One thing is certain: If an MF fiber does not have *specific, significant* advantages over others, it will not be, or continue to be, produced.

Polyester has strength and abrasion resistance next to nylon and also takes a permanent heat set—all "first-class" fiber properties, from the point of view of performance. The further characteristics that finally put polyester ahead of nylon in amount used are good resilience (the nearest to wool of any MF fiber) and high modulus; these mean that it is springy and can recover well from strain, yet resists stretching better than nylon.

This combination of properties has led to many uses: polyester can be used instead of or with wool (e.g., in suiting fabrics) and it is ideal to blend with cotton, rayon, lyocell, or flax, since it has wrinkle resistance and yet is fairly rigid, so no special form has to be made of it for blending with cellulose fibers, as was the case with nylon. It *is* "fiberfill" for pillows, insulation, batting, etc. Its better stability gives it an advantage over nylon as well as for sewing thread textured filament yarn in fabrics for more tailored articles. Further, it has good sunlight resistance (excellent behind glass when the UV component is removed), so it is used for sheer curtains (see *Fabric Glossary:* VOILE [filament]). Finally, filament polyester has been successfully altered to look and feel very much like silk. Current developments, especially in microfibers, are turning this "workhorse" fiber into more appealing "thoroughbred" types.

Polyester does have particular drawbacks, too, one being that it holds oily stains tenaciously. It absorbs very little moisture, so it is less comfortable to wear in its standard form. It is also a static collector.

(Of course, less absorbency means quick drying.) Like nylon, polyester fabrics show stubborn pilling because of the great strength of the fiber.

Some of the *many* trademark names for polyesters are DACRON® (by DuPont), DIOLEN® (by Acordis, formerly Akzo Nobel), ENCRON® (by BASF), FORTREL® (by Fiber Industries), KODEL® (by Eastman), SETILA, TERGAL (by CEP), TERITAL (by Montefibre), TETORON (by Teijin, Toray), TREVIRA® (by Trevira), and WISTEL (by SNIA). Trademark names for special versions are found under *Modifications of Manufactured Fibers.*

Aromatic Polyester (PTT). CORTERRA® (by Corterra) is an aromatic polyester, polytrimethylene terephthalate, patented by Whinfield and Dr. J. Dickson at the same time the first polyethylene terephthalate (PET) was developed, to be joined by another—polybutylene terephthalate (PBT). For technical and cost reasons, PTT was not worked on until the 1990s, with introduction by Shell Chemical of CORTERRA in 1995.[21] In long-term walker tests on carpet, it performed as well as nylon and definitely better than PET polyester (see Figure 2.65). It is inherently resistant to water-borne stains, although not to oily stains, and generates low static charges. (See Figure 6.3 under *Home Treatment of Spots and Stains.*)

Acrylic Fibers

Acrylic fibers are made up of 85 percent of the unit acrylonitrile (vinyl cyanide; see Figure 2.66); they contain carbon, hydrogen, and nitrogen. Since 15 percent of the fiber can be a copolymer (containing other chemicals), acrylics produced by different companies can have a variety of characteristics, or one company can market differently dyeing acrylics, for example.

Acrylic Production. Production may be by wet or solvent spinning (see *Spinning Manufactured Fibers*). One solvent for acrylonitrile is dimethylformamide.

Acrylic Properties. The properties of acrylic fiber include the most wool-like hand of any MF fiber: warm, dry, and soft. Acrylics are also lofty (of low density) with good resilience—a combination to make

[21]"Corterra: A new polyester fibre," *Textiles Magazine,* 1, 1998: 12–14.

into wool-like fabrics that are warm with little weight. All acrylic in consumer use is staple fiber, and much is used in place of, or with, wool, since acrylic is much less expensive than wool, does not felt in machine washing, has fairly good strength, and does not lose strength when wet. Acrylic has taken over much of the market of wool in blankets and moderate- to lower-price clothing, especially for infants and children. Acrylic has been successfully used in upholstery, especially as velvet, giving a pleasant hand, crush and stain resistance, cleanability, and resistance to light. It also resists chemicals and even weather.

Acrylic has quite low absorbency, giving stain resistance and cleanability, as noted, but exhibiting static collection and lowering comfort in clothing.

Acrylic is more sensitive to heat than nylon or polyester—it is well to remember this when tumble drying articles of acrylic; see Section 6.

Acrylic cannot be permanently heat set, although it will take a durable heat set. It is "meta-stable" in very hot, wet conditions, and will shrink if steamed. If stretched or put under tension, it will relax when heated; by combining fibers that have been relaxed with those that are still under tension, yarns (Hi Bulk) can be produced in which the shrinking fibers "elbow out" the relaxed or stable fibers to create a bulkier yarn. Using this same latent shrinkage in acrylic (and modacrylic) fibers, sliver-knit pile fabrics can be created with a very furlike guardhair/underfur look and feel. The sliver is made by blending heavier fibers that have been stabilized with finer fibers that will shrink when steamed; after knitting, the fabric is steamed, and when the fine fibers shrink, they lie under the coarser ones (see *Direct Spinning*, Figure 3.11 and *Fabric Glossary:* FUR-LIKE).

Major trademark names for acrylics are ACRILAN®, DURASPUN (for socks), and FI-LANA (craft yarn) (by Solutia), COURTELLE (by Acordis), CRESLAN® (by Cytec), DRALON (by Bayer), LEACRIL® (by Montefibre), TORAYLON (by Toray), VELICREN (by SNIA), and ZEFRAN® (by Mann). DuPont ceased production of the first acrylic, Orlon. Asahi ceased European production of Cashmilon at the end of 1997. The name Dolan is no longer used since Hoechst went out of fiber production.

Fibers Related to Acrylic

Vinyon, saran, and modacrylic are all related to acrylic in varying degrees; all feel soft, warm, and dry like wool, and all are more heat sensitive than acrylic.

Figure 2.65 CORTERRA® PTT polyester is suited to various carpet types from plush cut pile to a tight loop to a soft berber. (Courtesy of Corterra Polymers)

Vinyon and Saran (Chlorofibre). Vinyon and saran are both given the generic *chlorofibre* in many countries including Canada, but not in the United States; vinyon contains at least 85 percent vinyl chloride, saran at least 80 percent vinylidene chloride. The chlorine component makes them flame resistant (see *Performance Characteristics* in Section 1 for the definition of flame resistant), but all melt and are sensitive to tumble dryer heat. Trademark names are RHOVYL® and ISOVYL® (by CEP).

Modacrylic. Modacrylic is a "modification of acrylic" in that it is a copolymer with units of both acrylonitrile and either vinyl chloride or vinylidene chloride.

Modacrylic is used where flammability could be dangerous, as fabric traps air, such as with wigs or deep-pile "fake furs." in coats and rugs. The only trademark name left in modacrylics is KANECARON (KANEKARON) (by Kanebo, for fake furs and airline blankets); the oldest, Dynel, was discontinued in 1975, and gone are Verel, Elura, and SEF. The latter was developed by Monsanto as a modacrylic that would give flame resistance for children's sleepwear

Figure 2.66 Acrylonitrile unit.

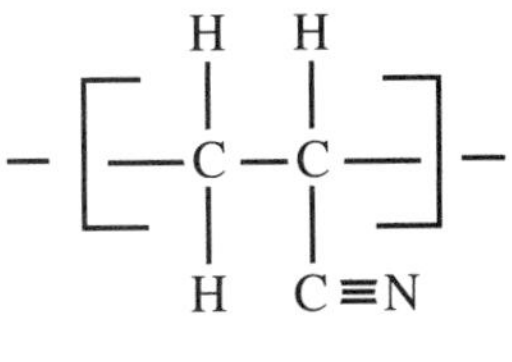

and withstand tumble drying. Teklan disappeared when Courtaulds went out of fiber production.

Vinal (vinylal). Vinal is made up of vinyl alcohol with various acetal units. As first made, this produces a fiber soluble in water, useful as a ground for lace or in blends to give sheer fabric when it is dissolved away, or as a connecting thread in knitting (see also the discussion of alginate, the other soluble fiber, under *Minor Natural Polymer Manufactured Fibers*). Further treatment develops a strong fiber with good elongation that melts but is self-extinguishing, with good chemical and rot resistance. It has been made for some time in Japan as KURALON® (by Kuraray) and MEWLON® (by Nichibo).

Nytril. Nytril is another minor and related generic, made up mainly of vinylidene dinitrile. This fiber was made in the United States as Darvan, used for furlike fabrics, but was discontinued.

Olefin Fibers: Polypropylene, Polyethylene

Olefin has been the least familiar of the major generics, but has many outstanding and interesting properties and is rapidly coming of age in widening its uses from furnishings to consumer apparel.

Olefins are paraffin-like (waxy), with rather simple units, which makes them the most economical synthetics to make. The most usual member of this family in textile consumer goods is polypropylene.

The other family member, polyethylene, is more often put to nontextile use in squeezable toys and kitchenware (TUPPERWARE); it is sometimes used in textiles, for example as tent floors, as well as nonwovens, e.g., TYVEK® (by DuPont) (see *Nonwoven, Spunbonded*).

Polypropylene is produced not only by melt spinning but by the economical split-film method of fibrillating (see *Continuous Filament Yarn* in Section 3 and *Fabric Glossary*: SPLIT-FILM YARN). It has the lowest density of any fiber (specific gravity less than 1.0, lighter than water—like wax) and so is very lofty, giving good cover for low price. It has good tensile strength, abrasion resistance, wrinkle recovery, and chemical resistance. Its modulus is between that of nylon and polyester, and in spite of almost no moisture absorbency, it has good static resistance. All of the foregoing have ensured its use in carpets and home furnishing fabrics. However, again in spite of almost no moisture absorbency, olefin wicks, and so moved into use in garments, first as staple (spun yarn) in underwear, but later as filament in a wide variety of activewear. INNOVA® (by Amoco) has performed well in specialized sportswear such as for warm weather diving, paddlesports wetsuits, surfing, bike tights, and aerobicwear (see Figure 2.67). Low absorbency gives olefin stain resistance in furnishing fabrics and quick drying in garments. With almost no absorbency, olefin is difficult to dye; solution dyeing is the most effective way to color the fiber; INNOVA is solution-dyed, so colors cannot fade in light or during washing, and are not affected by chlorine.

Because polypropylene is less complex to make than other synthetics, an increasing number of carpet makers manufacture their own bulked continuous filament (BCF) polypropylene yarn in the heavier filaments used (most at 2,600 denier, some at 1,300–1,500 denier).

Olefin is very heat sensitive, having the lowest melting point of any major fiber; do not use tumble dryers for garments, watch out for any hot embers on upholstery or carpet, and do not drape any over hot radiators. Olefin is very low in resistance to UV rays. In coarser fibers, olefin has an unpleasant, waxy hand.

In microfiber form, olefin gives enormous surface area for air-trapping insulation in a thin layer of fibers (e.g., THINSULATE™); see *Microfibers and Very Fine Fibers*.

Besides the trademark names listed, MERAKLON® (by Montefibre) is a long-standing one for staple

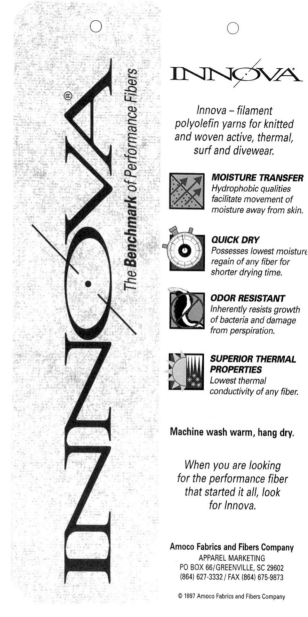

Figure 2.67 Hangtag for INNOVA® olefin filament yarns used in activewear and multisport garments. (Courtesy of Amoco Fabrics and Fibers Company)

polypropylene, and there have been some underwear brands such as Lifa and Wickers. Much is sold simply under the generic name olefin or polypropylene.

Elastomers—Rubber, Spandex (Elastane), Elastoester

Elastomers are different from any fibers discussed so far; they can be stretched to several times their length and they will recover immediately. For many years the only elastomer was rubber, both natural latex (the sap of the rubber tree) and synthetic rubber.

The major synthetic elastomer, spandex (elastane), should be compared only to rubber in properties. It does not conform to the general behavior of synthetic fibers, since its strength is relatively low. Lastrile is an elastomer now classified by the United States as a type of rubber, composed of a diene and acrylonitrile; another elastomer, anidex, was marketed as ANIM–8 (by Rohm & Haas) but has been discontinued for some time.

Elastomers are needed to provide power stretch in garments that compress, control, or support the body during wear; see *Fabric Glossary:* STRETCH, POWER. Smaller amounts can provide stretch for comfort, fit, or fashion; see *Fabric Glossary:* STRETCH, COMFORT or FIT.

We are clothed in a "stretch fabric"—our skin! (See Figure 2.68.) The amount the skin stretches when the body moves is shown in Table 2.4.

Rubber. Rubber occurs as a natural compound, latex, the sap of a tree, but is also synthesized (e.g., neoprene). It is a good elastomer but is always used as a core, wrapped or covered. It does not take dye so it

Table 2.4 *Skin Stretch*

	Percent Skin Stretch	
Body Movement	*Horizontal*	*Vertical*
Back—in tieing shoe	47	—
Elbow—full bend	15–20	50–51
Seat—hip to hip, when sit down	15–20	27
Knee—deep bend	28–29	49–52

Source: "A Practical Guide To Stretch," DuPont International, SA.

"grins through" if the covered yarn is stretched so the core shows. A trademark name is LASTEX.

Rubber has low strength; it is deteriorated by oil and dry heat, both encountered in wear and care, especially with garments worn next to the body that are washed and tumble dried often, such as power stretch articles or underwear with waistband elastic.

Spandex (Elastane). Spandex is segmented polyurethane—some blocks or segments of the molecular chains (polyurethane) are "hard" while other segments (polyether or polyester) are "soft" or elastic. As Figure 2.69 shows, when the fiber is relaxed, the soft chains are tangled together; they straighten out under tension, but always pull back to the shortened tangle. Spandex can stretch up to seven times

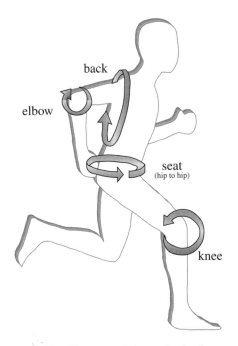

Figure 2.68 **Skin stretches as the body moves.** (Adapted courtesy of the DuPont Company)

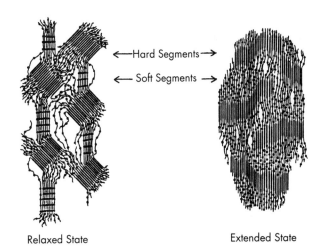

Figure 2.69 The action of the elastomer spandex (segmented polyurethane) in DORLASTAN®. (Courtesy of Bayer Corporation)

its original length and recover instantly when tension is released.

Spandex is the most complex and expensive of all synthetic fibers to make, originally developed by DuPont; production under their trademark name LYCRA® still dominates the market worldwide and is one of the most-recognized consumer brands (see Figure 2.70).

The early use of spandex seldom went beyond applications in which rubber had been used, such as elastic waistbands and what is termed "intimate apparel." Even in these basic applications, technology is being developed to give better performance. LYCRA® SOFT (by DuPont) is aimed to deliver comfort (a softer fit) along with good control in waistbands or body-shaping apparel.

Spandex is now being used in an ever-widening array of articles, for wovens as well as knits, in amounts from about 3 percent to upwards of 50 percent in combination with other fibers. A Technical Bulletin of February 1995 from Bayer Corporation[22] indicated use of their DORLASTAN® spandex in a range of 2–10 percent in outerwear; 2–25 percent in underwear (and a similar range in swimwear); 2–40 percent in pantyhose; 10–45 percent in foundation garments; and 35–50 percent in medical hosiery.

Beyond these, there has been a considerable increase in the use of spandex in all kinds of active-wear. This parallels consumer preference trends to clothing especially designed for vigorous sports (athletic compression garments) as well as for "second skin" clothing fashions. There are demographic changes as well, with older consumers representing more of the market and wanting comfort stretch in, for instance, jeans. A strong turn to cotton knits brought introduction of blends with spandex, since recovery in cotton knits, especially at cuffs, is better with a small amount of spandex in the yarns. There has also been a positive response by consumers to wearing traditional tailored clothing made of fabric that provides more ease of movement and holds its shape better; this has been seen with clothing of wool and of linen.

None of this would promote this relatively costly synthetic, however, if it did not have great advantages over rubber. It is much stronger and can be used uncovered; this means that power stretch can be

Figure 2.70 Hangtag for LYCRA® spandex, a brand name with high recognition by consumers. (Courtesy of the DuPont Company)

obtained with a much finer yarn than with rubber, allowing much lighter "contour fashions": foundation garments, swimwear, and all kinds of actionwear, to say nothing of medical support stockings. It is also used in a number of other yarn "configurations" as a core wrapped with staple or filament of other fibers, as shown in Figures 2.71 and 2.72.

Spandex also has good resistance to dry heat and oil and can be dyed as rubber cannot, so it does not "grin through" in a stretched-out fabric, as a rubber core would. The fine, uncovered yarns have had a tendency to break and protrude through swimwear after wear, and one of the few basic drawbacks of spandex has been yellowing in chlorine bleach. Use of more colored articles and changes in care procedures make yellowing less troublesome, and changes have been made in the fiber as well. A special type of LYCRA is offered by DuPont for swimwear, with chlorine resistance and more durability.

Use of a small amount of spandex with regular filament nylon in pantyhose results in a smooth feel with good fit, an improvement over the use of textured stretch nylon yarn, which is duller and more easily snagged. Here, again, DuPont offers a special form for knitters of hosiery, in blends with any fiber to ensure a consistent body-hugging fit; it may be given the trademark LYCRA® 3D when DuPont's construction standards have been met.

The muscle vibration encountered by many sports participants can be reduced by wearing compression garments. However, it took intensive research to develop fabrics and garments that would do this and still allow unrestricted movement. Results of a five-year study done at Penn State Center for Sports Medicine were released in 1998 by DuPont. Garments incorporating the then-newly developed LYCRA® POWER and made to specification were reported to give a 10–20 percent average improvement in force and power production in subjects who were "fatiguing" after standard repetitive jumping tests. So, all that sleek athletic wear can offer definite physiological advantages—making you feel right as well as look right.

[22]"Dorlastan® Bayer Spandex Technical Brochure," Bayer Corporation, February 1995.

Figure 2.71 Corespun/core-plied yarns have staple fibers spun around a core of stretched LYCRA® spandex. The resulting yarn has the hand and texture of the covering fiber with stretch. (Courtesy of the DuPont Company)

The few trademark names for spandex other than LYCRA® and DORLASTAN® are GLOSPAN® and CLEERSPAN® (by Globe), LINEL® and LINEL® COMFORT (by Fillattice), and OPELON™ (by DuPont/Toray).

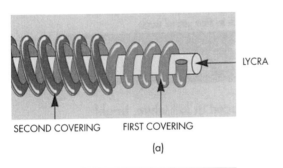

SECOND COVERING   FIRST COVERING

(a)

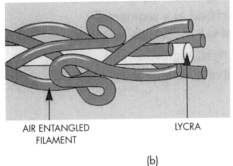

AIR ENTANGLED FILAMENT   LYCRA

(b)

Figure 2.72 (a) Stretch LYCRA® spandex can be wrapped with one or two strands of a nonelastic filament to give a smooth stretch yarn. (b) Stretched LYCRA® spandex fed through an air jet with a multifilament nonelastic yarn so that the textured filament partially covers the LYCRA core. (Courtesy of the DuPont Company)

Elastoester. A generic name was given to a Japanese development of a polyurethane-ester fiber that can be melt-spun, which is preferable to dissolving with most organic solvents. The elastoester can be processed more readily with polyester than spandex, which is usually used more with nylon than with polyester.[23] The first trademark name was SPANTEL® (by Kuraray).

Flame- and Heat-Resistant Organic Fibers and Other High Performance Fibers
(See also *Inorganic Manufactured Fibers, and High-Tenacity Fibers* under *Physical or Chemical Properties Modified, Flame Retardant* under *Additions to MF Fibers Before Spinning*, and CORDELAN under *Bicomponent Fibers*.)

It may be helpful to distinguish between *flame resistance* or retardancy and heat or *temperature resistance*.[24] Flame retardancy is measured by the amount of oxygen needed to support combustion (Limiting Oxygen Index or LOI); fibers with an LOI greater than 25 are said to be flame resistant or retardant, that is, there must be at least 25 percent oxygen present for them to burn. Glass, for instance, will not burn even in an atmosphere of 100 percent oxygen. Glass is also very resistant to heat, but other fibers may be flame resistant yet heat sensitive, such as the modacrylics.

[23]*Canadian Textile Journal*, March/April 1998: 42.
[24]William C. Smith, "High-Performance Fibers Protect, Improve Lives," *Textile World*, October 1998: 53–64.

Aramid. Aramid is a separate generic assigned to aromatic polyamides because of their special properties, and is divided into the subgenerics *meta-aramids* and *para-aramids* according to the position of joining of the aromatic rings relative to one another (see Figure 2.73).

Meta-aramids are both flame resistant and heat resistant. This is not from any chemical element, such as a halogen (e.g., chlorine) or phosphorus, but from the fiber structure: When exposed to heat, it tends to char, not melt, and is self-extinguishing, giving off little smoke. It has been used for filters, aircraft furnishing fabrics, lampshades, and protective clothing for firefighters or racecar drivers. Filament yarn rather than spun has been tried for strength with light weight. Complex tests with instrumented mannequins can be carried out to determine the effectiveness of these fibers in protective clothing (see Figure 2.74).

Trademark names include the first and best known, NOMEX® (by DuPont), TEIJINCONEX® (by Teijin), plus KERMEL® (by CEP), a polyamide imide that can be classified here.

Para-aramids are fibers of very high orientation, which results in *very* high strength at low density (five times stronger than steel for the same weight). Fibers also have good flexibility, good resistance to stretching (high modulus), and tremendous resistance to heat or flame.

KEVLAR® (by DuPont) is the best-known trademark name. It is used in safety and protective clothing such as gloves to offer cut protection (see Figure 2.75), plus body armor and firefighters' coats. It is used also for cables, coverings (e.g., protection of optical fibers), and reinforcing. This fiber type is strong but lighter than glass fiber and so is good in tires. It has been used to provide very special reinforcement for sport sock heels and toes, and in patches at shoulders or elbows of skiwear. Its use in sophisticated

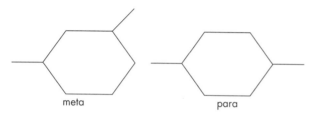

Figure 2.73 Relationship for aramids: meta-, para-.

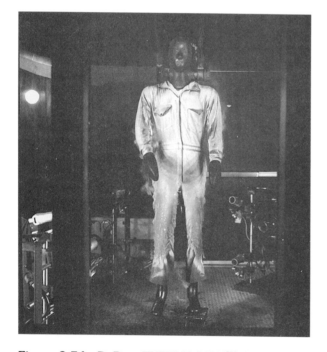

Figure 2.74 DuPont THERMO-MAN^{SM} thermal Instrumented Mannequin System evaluates the relative predicted body burn a wearer would receive in a simulated flash fire, to measure the efficiency of clothing made of heat-resistant fibers. (Courtesy of E. I. DuPont de Nemours and Company)

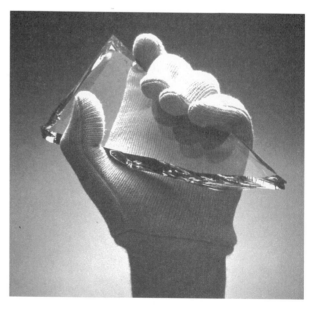

Figure 2.75 100 percent DuPont KEVLAR® para-aramid is used in hand and arm protection to offer outstanding cut and heat resistance. (Courtesy of E. I. DuPont de Nemours and Company)

sports equipment prompted a writer for the newsletter of the Ontario Science Centre to comment some years ago that "Until recently, sports equipment was made from steel and natural materials including wood, bamboo, leather and gut. . . . Sports equipment catalogues now read like works of science fiction, complete with futuristic designs and exotic materials."[25]

DuPont is developing new forms of KEVLAR fibers, among them one for body armor inspired by the unique ballistic properties of spider silk, noted in this section. For more on this, see Section 7, *Third Millennium Problem Solving and Innovations.*

Trademark name fibers are KEVLAR® (by DuPont), TECHNORA® (by Teijin), and TWARON® (by Acordis).

Aramid fibers are increasingly used in contract furniture coverings, e.g., for hospitals and hotels, to meet strict fire safety standards.

Novoloid. Novoloid is a fiber unique in having *no* orientation (no crystallinity); in the most intense heat or flame, it turns to carbon, keeping its form without melting, burning, or giving off smoke. Novoloid is a *novolac,* a cross-linked phenolformaldehyde polymer, better known by the trademark name KYNOL® (by Kynol). The fiber is not strong and is golden in color, so is of limited, very specialized use.

PBI (Polybenzimidazole). PBI, a trademark name of Celanese, is a fiber type that does not burn or melt and stays intact even if charred. It is strong and absorbs well, although it is difficult to dye. PBI is used in protective clothing and in furnishings.

Other Minor Organic Synthetic Fibers

Fluoropolymer (fluorofibre). This is well known by the trademark name TEFLON® (by DuPont) but is not often seen as a fiber in consumer goods. TEFLON is composed of polytetrafluoroethylene (PTFE). The properties that make it useful as a coating on cooking pans or as a textile finish that repels both water and oil (see Section 5) are useful in specialized fabrics made of the same substance in fiber form. It has no absorbency at all; has a very slippery surface; does not conduct electricity; and is inert to chemicals,

light, and insects. As we might guess from its use on cookware, it is very heat resistant—it will eventually melt but cannot burn. PTFE has been used as covers for hot head presses. Since human tissues do not react to PTFE, it has been used to make such body replacement parts as artificial blood vessels and heart valves (shown in Figure 1.2).

With TEFLON filament yarn knitted in at the toe, heel, and pad of BLISTER GUARD™ socks (by PTFE®), this specialized fiber found another application in "low friction clothing" (see Figure 2.76). Reduction of friction between the foot and shoe in hiking or active sports reduces the chance of developing blisters; field tests with football and field hockey teams and with soldiers on maneuvers, where previous experience of blisters was high, confirmed the effectiveness of the socks. Many other applications are possible for this unusual fiber; for information call 1-888-5222-7625.

Sulfar. Sulfar is polyphenylene sulfide (PPS), an aromatic polysulfide. This fiber is gold in color and strong with good elasticity. It is resistant to most chemicals. It can melt but is very flame resistant. Low absorbency limits its use in apparel. Trademark names are PROCON® (by Toyobo), RYTON® (by Amoco), and TORAY PPS (by Toray).

Melamine. Melamine fiber (BASOFIL® by BASF) is heat resistant, does not melt, and has been used for thermal insulation in filters.

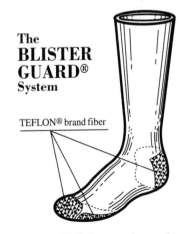

The BLISTER GUARD® System

TEFLON® brand fiber

Figure 2.76 TEFLON® fluoropolymer filament at heel, toe and pad of BLISTER GUARD® socks. (Courtesy of PTFE® llc)

[25]"Dressed for Success," *Newscience,* Ontario Science Centre, 13/3, Summer 1988: 1.

Carbon. Carbon fibers conduct electricity and are incorporated into other filaments or fabrics to confer permanent antistatic properties. See Section 7, *Third Millennium Problem Solving and Innovations* for use of such fibers (GORIX®) as heating elements. A carbon fiber, PANOX® (by RK Carbon), when preburnt to remove all combustible elements, can be made into a fire-resistant material suitable for racing drivers' outfits, or if coated with aluminum, for firefighters. Other trademark names are FORTAFIL (by Acordis), PANOTEX (by Lantor Universal Carbon), TENAX (by Tenax-JV Akzo/Toho), THORNEL (by Amoco), and TORAYCA (by Toray).

Polyetheretherketone. PEEK (by Shakespeare, H-C) is another heat-resistant fiber used in industrial applications including aviation. Although expensive, PEEK can be recycled easily since it does not degrade on remelting.

PBO (Polyphenylenebenzobisoxazole). PBO is very strong and exceptionally flame retardant. Its trademark name is ZYLON (by Toyobo).

Polyimide. Polyimide fibers (P-84 by Inspec) have good flame and chemical resistance and a unique lobal cross section.

Polyarylate. Polyarylate fibers are melt-spun from a liquid crystal polymer. They have very high strength and have been used for cables, sports goods, and stab- or puncture-resistant materials. The trademark name is VECTRAN (by Celanese).

Many other specialized fibers are discussed later in this section under *Modifications of Manufactured Fibers.*

Inorganic Manufactured Fibers

(The inorganic natural fiber, **asbestos,** was discussed under *Natural Fibers.*)

Glass. Glass as a fiber gives fabrics that are flameproof, as well as being very strong; nonabsorbing; and inert to light, weather, age, and most chemicals (think of a windowpane). Silica sand and limestone, plus other ingredients such as soda ash (sodium carbonate), are melted at about 1370°C (2500°F) to make the special glass that is formed into marbles about 15 mm (⅝ in.) in diameter. In the usual spinning method, each perfect marble is melted in a small

furnace and extruded through tiny holes in a platinum bushing to form filament or staple fiber.

Glass fiber is used for drapery fabrics, window screening, tires, thermal and electrical insulation, reinforcing in plastic to form composites for trays and many other products, filters, and of course, the core for fiber optics in communications systems.

Owens-Corning produces glass fiber under the best-known trademark, FIBERGLAS®, and developed the CORONIZING process to give a heat set to fabrics and add finishing resins, printed designs, etc. Fiberglas Beta, a virtual microfiber introduced in the 1960s, was flexible enough to be promising in more home uses, but the low abrasion resistance of glass and the skin irritation that results from cut or broken fiber ends reversed this development.

Glass fabrics should be washed (not dry cleaned) separately and gently to prevent abrasion.

Metallic Fibers. Metallic fibers, notably stainless steel, have been made as a high-strength fiber for tire cords and used in blends to conduct static electricity, especially in carpets. BRUNSMET® is a trademark name (by Brunswick).

Most metallic, however, is more a yarn than a fiber, and is discussed under *Novelty (Fancy or Complex-Ply) Yarns* in Section 3; see also *Fabric Glossary:* LAMÉ.

Miscellaneous. Other inorganic MF fibers are made, such as boron and ceramic, but these are still experimental and/or for extremely specialized uses.

Modifications of Manufactured Fibers

One of the great advantages of an MF fiber is the possibility of producing it in many shapes and forms. One major area of modification gives us special versions of the major synthetics that are more pleasing and/or more comfortable—in other words, closer to natural fibers in aesthetics, but maintaining excellent performance. Japan has given us a name for such new synthetic fibers—*shingosen.*

Specialized Physical Modifications

Solid Fibers with Nonround Cross Section. These are produced to alter the characteristics of fibers that have a standard form with a round cross section; this applies to the two main synthetics, nylon and polyester. Nonround or irregular cross section can give a shape with lobes, like a clover leaf (trilobal, pentalobal, octalobal, or often just lobal). (See Figure 2.77.)

The main thrust of this development has been in filament fibers, to give a different light deflection off the fiber. Silk has a nonround cross section, roughly triangular in shape, and its beautiful luster sets a standard. When light falls on a rodlike, round cross section fiber and is deflected in broad beams, it gives off a hard shine; with fine filaments of a nonround fiber, light is broken up to give that silklike subdued luster. In coarse filaments, a nonround cross section results in a glitter or sparkle; this has been used to make "sparkling nylon" pantyhose or glittering organza for holiday season wear.

Lobal filaments also have a drier, less slippery hand, again more silklike, plus somewhat improved moisture absorbency and/or wicking action, giving more comfort, less static collection, and better soil release.

A major trademark name is ANTRON® nylon (by DuPont), which is made in many specialized forms, such as ANTRON® III, permanently antistatic with inclusion of carbon in some filaments (see Figure 2.78). (ANTRON® III HF and ANTRON® PLUS are discussed under *Air Spaces Incorporated into Manufactured Fibers*.)

Other lobal trademark names are:

- *In nylon:* CAPROLAN TOUCH and ANSO V (by Allied), ULTRON® (by Solutia), GOLDEN TOUCH® and SILKY TOUCH® (by BASF)

- *In polyester:* SOIRESSE fabric (by Lagran) of ULTRAFIL yarn, TERGAL VP (by CEP), TREVIRA® STAR, and TREVIRA® 353 (by Trevira)

Figure 2.78 Hangtag for ANTRON® III antistatic trilobal nylon. (Courtesy of the DuPont Company)

- *In viscose:* ENKA PROFILE® (by Acordis)—star-shaped cross section gives a matte (low luster) silk effect

COOLMAX© (by DuPont) is a polyester with a definitely irregular cross section; it has four channels or grooves that increase surface area (by 20 percent), moisture absorption, and wicking ability. This gives a polyester that has been found comfortable for activewear. This unusual cross section is informally dubbed "Mickey Mouse ears" (see Figure 2.79). Fibers with such an irregular cross section pack together less in a yarn than those with round cross section and so give better airflow through fabrics.

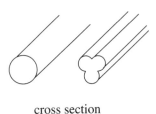

cross section

round   trilobal

Figure 2.77 Round vs. lobal cross section.

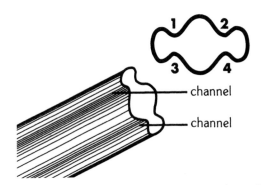

Figure 2.79 COOLMAX© cross section shows four channels running the length of the fiber to promote moisture wicking. (COOLMAX is a DuPont certification mark.) (Courtesy of The DuPont Company)

Morpho-structured fiber is an interesting modification from Kuraray of Japan (see Figure 2.80). The fiber combines different kinds of flat profile and multispiral formations, taken from the shape of the wing scales of the Morpho butterfly; the result in fabric is to give changeable color, like the iridescence of a butterfly's wings. See also the discussion of "chameleon" porous fibers, under *Air Spaces Incorporated into Manufactured Fibers.*

Flat Filament or Tapelike Fiber. This form produces a glittery look; a traditional fabric has been called "crystal acetate." Rayon with a wide, flat cross section can give a linenlike look and hand to a fabric. Very wide, flat rayon fiber is used for strawlike hats in millinery. Flat rayon filaments are also used extensively to replace the wiry hair fibers, mohair and horsehair, in much tailor's "hair" canvas interfacing; these are cheaper, but cannot be molded with steam in tailoring as the hair fibers can. (See *Fabric Glossary:* CANVAS, HAIR or TAILOR'S).

Air Spaces Incorporated into Manufactured Fibers

Voided Fibers. Voided fibers, with hollow channels or air spaces inside, have been used for carpets and other furnishings, since they have soil-hiding ability (see Figure 2.81). They may also be made antistatic and/or soil resistant; two trademark names are ANTRON® III HF (for hollow fiber) and ANTRON® PLUS (both by DuPont).

Hollow Fibers for Insulation. These are widely used for their air-trapping ability and lightness, as fiberfill for pillows, comforters, mattress pads, and quilted outerwear. The fiber may have a hollow center, rather like macaroni, or may have four or more channels running through it (see Figure 2.82). The extra channels add insulation for cold weather clothing. They also give better loft and resistance to crushing, and so are suitable especially for pillows and comforters. Trademark names have multiplied, coming many times from the fiber maker, but there are also store private labels: HOLLOFIL®, QUALLOFIL® (by DuPont); DUVELLE; KODOFILL, KODOSOFF (by Eastman); FILLWELL, WELLENE, WELLON (all by Wellman); POLARGUARD® HV (by KoSa); QUATTRO (by Hudson's Bay Company); SEAROFIL (by Sears); TREVIRA® LOFT (by Trevira); ULTRAFIL—

Morpho Butterfly

Morpho-Structured Fabrics

Color-producing scales of Morpho Butterfly

Figure 2.80 The morpho-structured fiber is flat with a multispiral form to imitate the wing scales of the Morpho butterfly of South America for the same visual effect. (Courtesy of Kuraray Company Ltd.)

Soil Resistance

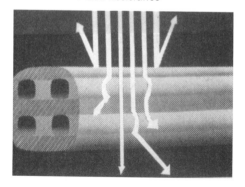

Figure 2.81 Voided fiber hides soil; ANTRON® III HF. (Courtesy of the DuPont Company)

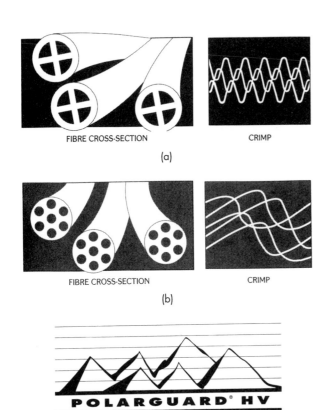

FIBRE CROSS-SECTION CRIMP

(a)

FIBRE CROSS-SECTION CRIMP

(b)

POLARGUARD® HV

HIGH VOID CONTINUOUS FILAMENT

(c)

Figure 2.82 (a) HOLLOFIL® is made of four-hole crimped fibers for resiliency that promotes warmth and loft. (b) QUALLOFIL© is made of seven-hole crimped fibers. (Courtesy of the DuPont Company) (c) Trademark and logo for another "high-void" insulating fiber, POLARGUARD® HV. (Courtesy of Celanese Corporation, trademark now of KoSa)

many with II, III, etc., following to indicate degrees of firmness or other changes. HOLLOFIL®, for example, is made of 100 percent DACRON® polyester (by DuPont), in staple, crimped fibers in single or multi-hole versions; these may be treated with a silicone finish to fluff up more easily in a filled product, so there is less chance of them clumping together. The name COMFOREL® (by DuPont) covers sleep products fibers that may be hollow, or "cluster fibers" that look like the quill point of down (see Figure 2.45).

Some hollow fibers are used for clothing insulation, such as THERMASTAT® (by DuPont) (see Figure 2.83). These hollow-core DACRON® polyester fibers, used for close-fitting clothing such as socks, long underwear, or turtlenecks, trap air and with their

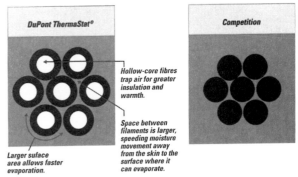

Figure 2.83 THERMASTAT® polyester with its hollow core traps insulating air and allows faster evaporation of perspiration. (Courtesy of the DuPont Company)

large surface area, allow for faster evaporation of perspiration.

Hollow Viscose. Hollow viscose gives loft; bulk; and a firmer, less limp hand. It also absorbs even more than regular viscose and contributes to insulation. This form had the trademark name of Viloft (by Acordis).

Hollow Fibers for Dialysis. Hollow fibers are used in artificial kidneys; blood is pumped through a fabric made of some 7,000 special hollow cuprammonium fibers of the right pore size to let waste products go through but retain blood. Hollow nylon fibers and a reverse osmosis process allow purification of seawater; the salty water is pumped through the hollow fibers, and drinking water comes through the walls of the fibers, while concentrated salty fluid emerges out of the end. This trick is also turned around, to allow concentration (getting rid of water) of liquids like some juices that do not take kindly to heating to drive off the water.

Crater Fibers. These have a pitted surface, which increases absorbency. A solid crater polyester has been given the trademark name SN 2000 (by Kuraray) (see Figure 2.84[a]). Another even more specialized fiber is both cratered and hollow: WELLKEY® is a TETORON® polyester (by Teijin), that provides even more absorbency; see Figure 2.84(b).

Porous Fibers. Porous fibers are a significant development, with channels running through them side to side, as well as end to end, to give a microporous

Ultra-micro Crater Fiber "SN 2000"

Regular Polyester

(a)

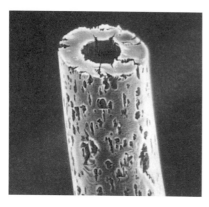

(b)

Figure 2.84 (a) SN 2000® crater fiber. (Courtesy of Kuraray Company Ltd.) (b) WELLKEY®, a hollow fiber of TETORON® polyester with a cratered surface for greater absorption. (Courtesy of Teijin Limited)

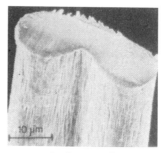
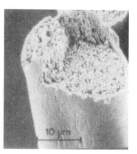

Dralon X100®   Dunova®

Figure 2.85 Structure of DRALON® standard acrylic compared to the core/sheath structure of the now discontinued absorbent acrylic fiber Dunova. (Courtesy of Bayer AG)

structure. Such channeled fibers go beyond the cratered surface of a solid fiber already discussed, although most are aimed at the same purpose—increased absorbency. Acrylics of this type have been made, such as Lumiza (by Kanebo) and Leaglor (by Montefibre). Dunova acrylic (by Bayer) was another, with a special porous structure: an outer sheath and a spongey core, rather like wool (see Figure 2.85). This allowed it to absorb a great deal of moisture without feeling wet—the *hygroscopic* property valued in wool but not possessed by cotton (when cotton gets wet, it feels wet!). The fiber did not swell when wet, either, so water vapor could still pass through. This core-sheath acrylic was also light and quick drying.

Production of Dunova, however, was discontinued at the end of 1993. Part of the reason might be

that some years before this, application in suitable uses in competition with cotton, such as towels, was hindered by the habit of European consumers of washing cotton at high temperatures, a procedure definitely harmful to an acrylic.

Porous fibers also feature in some of the "chameleon" or *polychromatic* fabrics that can change color with variations in light or temperature. This is done by means of dyes held in the channels of the fiber that react to changes in light or temperature. (They may also be applied in a coating, as with SWAY—discussed in the *Fabric Glossary:* COLOR VARIABLE.)

Microfibers and Very Fine Fibers

A *microfiber* is taken to be one finer than silk, approximately 1 dtex or 0.9 denier (these are terms that measure linear density of yarns, but are used as measures of fineness in fibers; they are defined under *Yarn Classified by Linear Density* in Section 3). Since the figures for denier and dtex are so similar, only dtex will be quoted in the rest of this discussion. Conventional fiber spinning through finer spinneret holes, plus drawing, can produce filaments down to about 0.3 dtex; *ultra-microfibers* down to 0.1 dtex (3 μm or μ diameter) and lower are made by other means, discussed under *Bicomponent Fibers*. Heralding ultra-ultra-microfibers are *nanofibers*, possible by technology that could produce fibers down to 3 nm (0.0000001 dtex)—see Section 7, *Third Millennium Problem Solving and Innovations*.

Filament Microfibers. Filament microfibers will be discussed first, for the early concentration was mainly on making fabrics more silklike in attempts to equal the finest natural fiber and the only natural filament. Filament microfibers can give finer, softer, lighter fabrics, even when yarns of equal size are used. Yarns made of microfibers have a higher number of filaments compared to yarns made with standard fibers. This gives a more silklike hand, drape, and even color brilliance. When made of polyester, as many are, they deliver high performance and ease of care as well.

Microfilament yarns are as strong as standard yarns, but individual filaments are more easily broken by emerizing (see Section 5), giving the popular peach-skin surface; see *Fabric Glossary:* SUEDED.

However, other dimensions of microfilaments are being discovered. One is that, aside from aesthetics, the packed microfilaments in yarns of a woven fabric give materials that deliver the high performance combination of being permeable to moisture vapor (perspiration) to let the body "breathe" while blocking rain and wind—and this without adding a film (see *Compound Fabrics* in Section 4) or putting on a coating (see *Coatings* in Section 5). Figure 2.86 shows water beading on the outside of such a fabric, made of TREVIRA® FINESSE® (by Trevira) microfilaments.

Figure 2.86 TREVIRA® FINESSE® **gives breathable yet highly water resistant fabric, plus protection from wind, through the high number of densely packed microfilaments. (Courtesy of Trevira GmbH, formerly Hoeschst AG)**

Some trademark names in the microfilament arena are:

- *Polyester filament:* DIOLEN® MICRO (by Acordis, formerly Akzo Nobel), made in 0.5–0.7 dtex filament, regular or textured; FORTREL® MICROSPUN (by Fiber Industries); MICRO-MATTIQUE™ (by DuPont), nearly twice as fine as silk; SETILA® MICRO (by CEP); SILKY TOUCH® (by BASF); (in fabric) TECHNO (by Toray); TERI-TAL ZERO.4 (by Montefibre, 0.4 dtex); TREVI-RA® FINESSE® and MICRONESSE® (by Trevira). MICROTHERM (by KoSa) is a flat microfiber.

- *Nylon filament:* SUPPLEX® microfiber (by DuPont), can give close, light, yet strong fabrics, much more wind resistant than regular nylon and more water repellent; MERYL® MICRO (by Nylstar); TACTEL® MICRO (by DuPont de Nemours Int. SA) for softer nylon microfilaments. (For a description of standard SUPPLEX® or TACTEL® nylon, see *Loop Texturing,* Section 3).

- *Rayon filament:* ULTRAFINE 2001 (by Acordis, formerly Courtaulds).

The list grows, as microfilaments show up in fabrics for all kinds of apparel end uses and in price ranges from those of exclusive designer lines to mass produced. It would be well to have some firm standard for the term, as it has been given to many fibers that are quite fine but not microfine. CAPTIVA® nylon (by Allied) and GOLDEN TOUCH® ENCRON® polyester (by BASF) seem to be fine but not microfine. At the other extreme, terms such as "Ultrafine" or "ultra-microfiber" are already being coined, with no standard definition.

Notation of filament yarns can be confusing, yet to be able to "read" information given about these new developments, we need to understand one term used: **denier per filament (dpf).**

High denier per filament really means the opposite of what it suggests: it means a great many, very fine filaments in a yarn; Figure 2.87 shows a diagram contrasting a high-dpf yarn of SUPPLEX® nylon (by DuPont) with a yarn of comparable size made up of fewer, standard-diameter filaments. High-dpf yarns give better hand and drapability and a softer luster than the same weight of yarn made of fewer, coarser filaments. A detailed notation, in dtex as well as

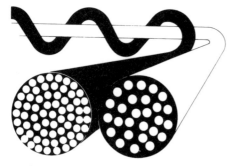

SUPPLEX   Standard Nylon

Figure 2.87 SUPPLEX® high-dpf (denier per filament) yarn compared to a yarn of comparable size made up of fewer, standard-diameter filaments. High dpf gives yarn that is soft and supple. (Courtesy of the DuPont Company)

denier, is given in Section 3, along with factors for conversion between the two systems.

Staple Microfibers. Like filament microfibers, staple microfibers are being explored in a trend to augment or substitute for the most desirable features of wool, cotton, and even flax; Figure 2.88 compares fineness of an MF microfiber, TREVIRA® MICRONESSE® (by Trevira), to these three important natural staple fibers as well as to silk.

Developments in staple microfibers are as follows:

- *Polyester staple:* Japanese firms Microfibric polyester blended with wool has been promoted to extend the supply of the very finest wool for suitings. This is a very different use of blending from just "diluting" wool with a cheaper fiber. Trademark names are MICROMATTIQUE™ (by DuPont); MICROSPUN™ (by Fiber Industries); and TERITAL® MICROSPUN® (by Montefibre), 0.85 dtex.

- *Acrylic staple:* LEACRIL 130 ULTRAFINE (by Montefibre); DRALON® MICROFIBRE (by Bayer), 0.6 dtex.

- *HWM rayon staple:* LENZING MODAL MICRO (by Lenzing), 1.0 dtex.

A caution: as the fibers become finer, the tendency in fabrics to pill increases.

Suedelike fabrics, to come very close to the velvety hand of real suede, must have ultra-microfibers on the surface, on the order of those on the surface

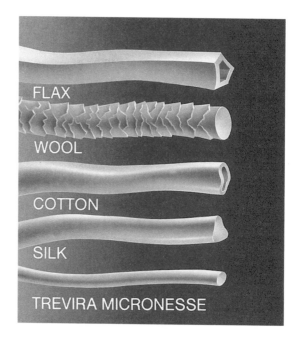

FLAX

WOOL

COTTON

SILK

TREVIRA MICRONESSE

Figure 2.88 Relative diameter of flax, wool, cotton, and silk compared to TREVIRA® MICRONESSE® microfiber. (Courtesy of Trevira GmbH, formerly Hoechst AG)

of a mushroom. One such advanced technology fiber is BELIMA X® (by Kanebo), the secret of BELLE-SEIME fabric, licensed as SUEDE 21. The individual filaments split from a petal-shaped bicomponent are as fine as 0.15 dtex (see Figure 2.89; see also *Bicomponent Fibers*). These very "real" suedelike fabrics often incorporate polyurethane foam to give the sponginess as well as the softness of suede skin. The construction of most of these is nonwoven, discussed in Section 4.

Some other major trademark names are CLARINO AMARETTA® or AMARA® (by Kuraray); ECSAINE® (by Toray, licensed as ALCANTARA® in Italy, ULTRASUEDE® in the United States—Skinner Division of Spring Mills); FACILE®, a very thin, fine, soft, suedelike fabric (by Toray, licensed as FACILMO in the United States, MOSSO® in Europe); LAMOUS (by Asahi); and SUEDEMARK I, II, and III. AQUA-SUEDE® (by Teijin) is one of the few based on a woven fabric.

Insulation in a thin layer is possible using microfibers because they provide a tremendous amount of surface area in a small amount of fiber. When that microfiber is olefin (polypropylene), there is the added advantage of the least dense fiber we

Figure 2.89 Formation of ultra-microfiber BELIMA X®. A single petal-shaped bicomponent filament is split into 9 to 13 parts, which may be as fine as 0.15 dtex. (Courtesy of Kanebo Ltd.)

have, giving a very thin, light layer of highly insulating material.

THINSULATE™ (by 3M) is a widely known name, the original thermal insulation version being made of microfibric (0.2 dtex) olefin, in some lines with standard size polyester (see Figure 2.90). It is said to give insulation equivalent to down in a layer about half the thickness. Furthermore, olefin will not rot or get wet. Caution with heat is necessary, especially steam heat in dry cleaning.

THERMOLITE© MICRO (by DuPont) is a very fine microfiber intended to give excellent insulation with a thin layer of soft fiber, which is resistant to migration.

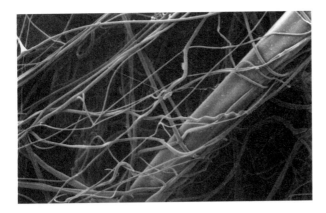

Figure 2.90 THINSULATE™ thermal insulation made up of microfibric olefin and standard polyester fibers. (Courtesy of 3M)

Physical or Chemical Properties Modified

Some of these modifications have already been discussed, such as HWM rayon, low elongation nylon, and less heat sensitive modacrylic.

Better Absorbency for Nylon. This is provided in HYDROFIL® (by Allied) by a copolymerization with ethylene glycol to give increased absorbency and wicking. The fiber was early made into a taffeta lining fabric.

High-Tenacity (High-Strength) Fibers. High-tenacity fibers have been made in many generics, including rayon, nylon, and polyester. Dolanit was a high-tenacity acrylic made by Hoechst for industrial use; KURALON® T 7901 (by Kuraray) is a high-tenacity vinal, introduced in 1994, of interest since it gives an economical high-strength fiber.

HDPE (High-Density Polyethylene). The strongest fiber yet made is a form of high-molecular-weight polyethylene (extra-long molecular chains) with "super strength." Trademark names are SPECTRA® (by AlliedSignal in North America) or DYNEEMA (by Toyobo/Dyneema, DMS in Europe and Asia). SPECTRA is used as a replacement for tough body connectors such as tendons and for protective clothing, especially to protect from shearing forces, such as in gloves for meat cutting. To give an idea of relative strength, if viscose is about 3 grams per denier (gpd), nylon about 6 gpd, and KEVLAR® (by DuPont) aramid about 20 gpd, SPECTRA 900 is *40 gpd*. These special forms are obviously not your average consumer product fibers!

Low-Pilling (Pill-Resistant) Fibers or Fibers to Be Sueded. These are achieved by providing a fiber that can be broken so that pills can be brushed off in the manner of wool, or allowing easier finishing in giving a suedelike or softened surface.

PIL-TROL® is a low-pill acrylic (by Solutia); Figure 2.91 shows the logo used for articles made of this, when tested and approved by Solutia.

Trevira GmbH makes the TREVIRA® 350 family of low-pill polyester fibers. The fibers behave like any others in spinning and weaving but have a complex molecular structure that will split up to some degree after final heat treatment so that pills developing in wear break off, even on very soft or stretch (textured yarn) fabrics. Figure 2.92 contrasts a pill formed on

LOW PILL CAREER APPAREL
TESTED AND APPROVED BY SOLUTIA

✓ Resists Pilling
✓ Stays Good Looking Longer
✓ Easy Care

Sweaters with the Pil-Trol® trademark are made with S-63®, a low pill acrylic fibre, and have been tested and have met Solutia's rigid standards. Pil-Trol fibre was developed to specifically answer your need for a high performance low pill sweater.

Pil-Trol and S-63 are registered trademarks of Solutia, formerly Monsanto.

Figure 2.91 Hangtag for PIL-TROL® apparel made with low-pill acrylic fiber. (Courtesy of Solutia, Inc., formerly Monsanto Fibers)

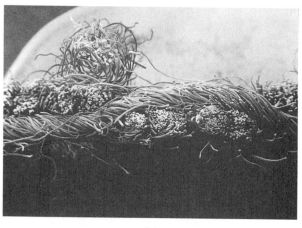

(a)

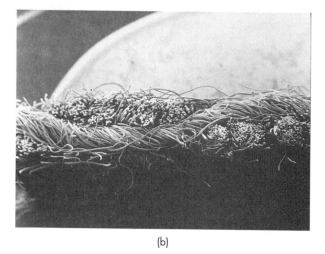

(b)

Figure 2.92 Electron microscope picture of a pill formed on a standard polyester fabric during wear compared with the clean surface on fabric of TREVIRA® 350 low-pill polyester. (Courtesy of Trevira GmbH, formerly Hoechst AG)

fabric of regular polyester with the pill-free surface of a similar fabric made with TREVIRA® 350 polyester.

More Dyeable Fibers. More dyeable fibers are made in a number of generics, but particularly in polyester. Acid-dyeable rayon is made so that it can take up the same type of dye as wool in blends.

Antistatic Fibers. Antistatic fibers often contain a very small amount of a material such as carbon that will conduct electricity; this is termed an *epitropic* fiber—one with an altered surface property.[26]

Additions to Manufactured Fibers before Spinning

Dulling or Delustering Agent. This is a white pigment, usually titanium dioxide, added to the liquid before the fiber is spun or extruded; an MF fiber with no dulling agent is often shiny and is termed *bright* fiber. The bright form is sometimes considered to have a hard shine that looks artificial and "cheap" com-

[26]*Dictionary of Fiber & Textile Technology*, Hoechst Celanese, 1990.

pared to the soft luster of silk or the light-absorbing *matt (matte)* look achieved by delustering. Heavily delustered fibers give a chalky appearance to the fabric. Delustering increases the tendering action of sunlight, since a dull fiber absorbs more light.

Bright fiber is desirable in some applications, such as when making a staple acrylic to look and feel like mohair, which has a definite luster, or when using filament nylon in lingerie fabric, where a gleam is desired.

Colored Pigment. Colored pigment added before spinning yields an MF fiber called solution-dyed (producer-, polymer-, spun- or dope-dyed). Such color is completely fast to any treatment or condition of use that will not damage the fiber itself; details and discussion are in Section 5. Trademark names are CHROMSPUN® acetate (by Eastman), DECORA polyester (by CEP), DU-REL (for upholstery) and SO-LARA (craft yarn) (by Solutia), KOLORBON™ rayon and ZEFKROME® acrylic (by BASF), LEACRIL OUTDOOR HT acrylic (by Montefibre), SILCOLOR acetate (by Novaceta), and STRUDON olefin (by Strudex).

Flame Retardant.

A flame-retardant agent incorporated into fibers helps to prevent propagation of flame; such fibers are in many cases identified with FR after the fiber trademark name, such as AURORA FR polyester staple and filament (by KoSa), LENZING VISCOSE FR (by Lenzing), TRACE FR olefin (by Amoco), and TREVIRA® FR polyester (by Trevira). TREVIRA CS has a flame retardant polymerised into the fiber as a co-monomer.

VISIL (by Kemira) has been called a *hybrid fiber*, but is a viscose fiber that achieves flame resistance when silica (as polysilicic acid) is added in the wet spinning process. This results in an organic-inorganic cellulosic MF fiber with polysilicic acid in it, very much like regular viscose in properties, with flame resistance. When it does burn, there is no problem with toxic gases or smoke as there is when other chemicals are added for flame resistance, such as phosphorus, or halogen-containing compounds.

Bacteriostatic or Biocidal Agent.

Incorporation of a bacteriostatic agent will inhibit the growth of bacteria, while a biocidal antimicrobial agent will kill bacteria or fungi. Such agents may also be applied in a finish (this is discussed, with trademark names, in Section 5). Whether the property is in the fiber or the finish, it acts to prevent the breakdown of perspiration by bacteria on the skin; it is only after this breakdown that perspiration develops an unpleasant odor.

BIOKRYL® (by Mann) is an acrylic fiber with a biocidal agent incorporated, while DIOLEN® BACTEKILLER (by Acordis, formerly Akzo Nobel) is a polyester. MICROSAFE AM (by Celanese with Microban Products Co.) is a trademark for antimicrobial acetate, staple and filament. RHOVYL'AS (by CEP) is used in tennis and hiking socks. An antimicrobial olefin, developed by Filament Fibers Technology Inc. and Microban Products Co., is used in AM MICROSTOP, circular knits from Coville Inc.; another is GYMLENE (by Drake Fibres Ltd.), used in hospitals and carpets. PERMAFRESH (by Plasticisers Fibres) is olefin fiber that can kill not only bacteria and fungi but dust mites—a first.

There is a complication to the development of more hygienic fabric: We usually wear several layers of clothing, and if each textile is not bacteriostatic, perspiration odor can develop there, just as it will on unwashed skin, and be transferred to other fabrics.

Antioxidant or UV Absorber.

Light-resistant nylon is achieved by incorporating antioxidants or UV absorbers into the fibers to prevent tendering by the UV rays of sunlight.

Cut-Resistant Particles.

Ceramic particles may be added before spinning to confer cut resistance to material made of the fibers. One application would be seat upholstery in trains or subways.

Bicomponent Fibers (includes Biconstituent [Bigeneric] Fibers)

Bicomponent fibers as originally defined covered only fibers made of two variants of the same generic type of polymer, but the term now is also used to describe what used to be called *biconstituent* or *bigeneric fibers*: fibers made up of two different generics.

Bicomponent Fibers (a).

In a fiber made up of two variants of the same generic of polymer, one variant shrinks more than the other, resulting in a self-crimping fiber. This development was the result of study of the crimp of wool, which was found to derive from its bicomponent structure, with two types of cortical cells lying next to each other in a spiral line the length of the fiber (illustrated under *Wool Structure*, Figure 2.30). When this structure is built into an MF fiber, the result is a crimp or curl forming as the fiber dries. With staple bicomponent fiber, this gives a more wool-like effect—better bulk and resilience—and has been applied in acrylic craft yarns with two well-known names, SAYELLE® and WINTUK® (by Caron). Articles made of such fibers after washing should be tumble dried or dried without tension (not hung) to let fibers develop crimp, so that the fabric recovers its original shape and size. The logo for BOUNCE-BACK®, a bicomponent acrylic fiber (by Solutia) used in craft yarns is shown in Figure 2.93(a).

Bounce-Back™

(a)

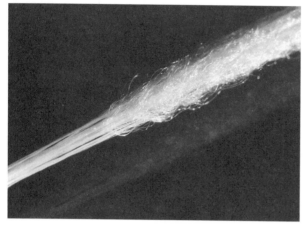

(b)

Figure 2.93 (a) Logo for BOUNCE-BACK®—a bicomponent acrylic fiber used in craft yarns. Articles made of BOUNCE-BACK® recover shape and size after washing and drying. (Courtesy of Solutia, Inc., formerly Monsanto Fibers) (b) DIOLEN® SEDURA®, a flat yarn of bicomponent polyester microfiber, develops bulk and a natural hand in finishing. (Courtesy of Akzo Nobel, now Acordis)

MIRAFLEX™ (by Owens Corning) is a bicomponent glass fiber that is soft, flexible, randomly twisted, and virtually itch-free. The trademark name of PINKPLUS® is given to home attic insulation made of the fiber.

Bicomponent filament has been used to produce hosiery that will return to a close fit after washing and drying. TACTEL® DUO (by DuPont) is a bicomponent nylon that gives sheer pantyhose with better stretch and cling. Development of bulk and crimp in an interesting flat yarn of bicomponent DIOLEN® SEDURA® polyester (by Acordis, formerly Akzo Nobel) is shown in Figure 2.93(b).

What has been termed a *heterofil* is a different application of a bicomponent fiber. In nylon, it has been used to fuse together a nonwoven fabric, since the "skin" of the fiber has a lower softening point than the core; see the discussion of "spunbonded" under *Nonwoven* in Section 4. WELLBOND polyester (by Wellman) is used in a similar way in thermal bonding.

Bicomponent Fibers (b). These are biconstituent or bigeneric fibers made up of two different polymers extruded in the same fiber. This may be in various arrangements:

- *Conjugate, side-by-side, or lateral:* from a spinneret with a double orifice.
- *Core/sheath:* from one spinneret inside another.
- *Matrix/fibril or islands-in-the-sea:* drops of one polymer in another, giving fibrils in a matrix—what is called islands-in-the-sea.
- *Petal-shaped or segmented-pie fiber of one polymer set in another:* multisplitting of such a petal-shaped fiber gives ultra-microfibers such as BELIMA X® (see Figure 2.89 under *Microfibers and Very Fine Fibers*).
- *Different polymers in layers:* splitting of such multilayer fibers can give flat ultra-microfibers down to 0.1 dtex.

When the generics can be separated later, as in the case of BELIMA X®, the bicomponent is called a *graft polymer*. When a matrix/fibril bicomponent is a graft polymer, if the matrix is dissolved away by a solvent that does not affect the fibrils, ultramicrofibers well below 0.1 dtex can also be produced. Conversely, if the fibrils are dissolved away, a channeled fiber results.

Some trademark names of bicomponent fibers are the following:

- CORDELAN® (by Kohjin), which is 50/50 vinyon/vinal, is called a *polychlal* fiber and is used for its flame resistance. It is heat sensitive, so use a low setting if tumble drying sleepwear.
- FILLWELL (by Wellman), which contains recycled polyester, is a conjugate filling fiber used in pillows and quilts. Its spiral crimp gives extra loft.
- TREVIRA® CS & NSK (by Trevira), which combines flame retardancy (CS) with low melting (NSK). The latter allows surface effects or reinforcing without coating.
- ANGELINA™ (by Meadowbrook Inventions), which is a flat staple fiber, made up of many layers of polyester or polyester acrylic, each with a different refractive index. These fibers can give ultimate glitter, or unique subtle glimmer, or iridescence.

Bicomponents that have come and gone, affected by market forces of competition from more effective fiber developments, include the following:

- Source (by Allied), which was 70/30 nylon/polyester, was a matrix type, made into carpets for the quality of color taken up by the two fiber types. It was developed originally to prevent "flat-spotting" with all-nylon tires. When heated during use these would soften enough that the weight the car when parked would flatten the tire and the nylon would set as it cooled until the tire warmed up again.

Monvelle (by Monsanto), side-by-side 50/50 nylon/spandex, was used in hosiery to give good fit and cling with smooth yarns, just as a combination of nylon and spandex is being used today.

Blending of Fibers

Fibers can be teamed together in fabrics in two ways:

1. **Combinations** (called *union* or *mixture cloths* in the United Kingdom) have yarns made up of differing fibers, as in the crash drapery fabric called *union linen* that has warp made of cotton with weft of flax (linen). Even one ply of a yarn might have a different fiber content from another. (I have examined a fine sari fabric to find that it was all silk, except for one very fine ply of the warp, which was rayon!) In a knit, one yarn feed might differ in fiber content from another, as in the case of the BLISTER GUARD® socks with TEFLON® in heel and toe (Figure 2.76).
2. **Blends** (also called *intimate blends*) are the result of mixing fibers together, before or as a yarn is spun. This is usually done only with staple fibers, although intimate blends of filaments can be produced. Such a filament blend comes only from an MF fiber producer, as it can be accomplished only at the time the fibers are extruded; for this reason they may be called *feeder blends*. It is impossible to have a blend of reeled silk (filament) with an MF filament; any silk blend must use silk as staple fiber. Trademark names are SITUSSA for yarns that combine SILENE or DICEL acetate with nylon, and DICELESTA for yarns that combine DICEL acetate and polyester (both by Novaceta).

Reasons for Blending Fibers

Economy. Blends are sometimes used because a more economical fabric can be produced by "diluting" a highly desirable but expensive fiber with a cheaper one, to retain some of the good properties of the more costly type. Specialty hairs such as camel, cashmere, or angora, blended with wool, are examples. With wool prices high, we see blends with polyester in suitings, or with acrylic in softer materials. To qualify for the WOOLBLENDMARK®, such a blend must have at least 60 percent new wool and meet the strict quality standards of the Woolmark Company; see wool quality terms under *Wool*, plus *Quality and Fashion* below.

Blending wool with cotton or rayon is usually mainly a matter of economy, since these fibers are much less expensive than wool and of very different behavior as well; see the discussion of improved performance from blends for a notable exception, VIYELLA.

Quality and Fashion. Blends using silk or flax with MF fibers are encouraged when fashion turns to "natural" appearances and textures. However, when such blends incorporate the *minimum* of prestige fibers allowed to be stated on a fiber content label, consumers are being offered something close to a gimmick, playing on the appeal of silk, linen, cashmere, etc., with little of the character of that fiber contributed.

Blends we are seeing now that combine the best and rarest natural fibers (e.g., Superfine Merino wool) with the best and most pleasing of MF fibers—microfibers—are a much more legitimate approach (see the discussion of staple microfibers under *Microfibers and Very Fine Fibers*). For example, a very lightweight blend of wool can be made with a microfiber nylon or polyester to give a high-quality fabric that still carries the ease of care associated with more practical but usually less pleasing and comfortable fabrics.

Comfort. We have seen a strong trend to using more comfortable (absorbent) fibers in clothing. This has led to using a higher percentage of cotton in blends with polyester. Instead of a blend of 65 percent polyester with 35 percent cotton we now often see blends of over 50 percent cotton—what is termed "cotton rich" or a "majority blend." NATURAL BLEND® means 60 percent or more of cotton.

Fashion and Comfort. The increasing use of spandex with many other fibers is driven by both fashion and comfort, as discussed under *Spandex.* Blends of wool and spandex appear in quite tailored clothing. Staid linen has spandex added for crease resistance. By the end of the 1990s, men's dress shirts were among the few garments that resisted the addition of spandex. Polypropylene, moving into apparel use, was usually blended with spandex, as INNOVA® (by Amoco) with LYCRA® (by DuPont) for activewear.

Dyeing Effects. Multicolor effects in dyeing are achieved by blending fibers that take up dyes differently. Most of the major MF fiber generics can be produced in a number of differently dyeing modifications. This means that a fabric could be 100 percent of one fiber generic and still allow this "magic" of what is called *cross dyeing* or *fiber mix dyeing,* or *differential dyeing; see* Section 5. Cross dyeing is used most often for carpets, to allow piece dyeing; this delays decisions on color which, if carpet were made up in fiber- or yarn-dyed colors, could leave warehouses stocked with giant rolls of less popular shades.

Flame Resistance. This is one special reason for a blend of modacrylic with acrylic, in deep-pile, furlike fabrics, including mats and rugs. These structures incorporate a lot of air, and so can be dangerous if made of a flammable fiber.

Improved Performance in Wear and Care. This is one of the notable reasons for blending fibers—part of what may be called *fabric engineering.* We can make up for a disadvantage or weakness in one fiber by picking the right partner. Blending of 10 percent nylon with wool in socks or 20 percent in carpets greatly increases the wear life of the wool.

For years, cotton has been mixed with wool to give a material that will not felt, mat, or shrink in machine washing and drying, yet will carry some of the warm, comfortable feel and loft of wool. The oldest member of the family of fabrics now given the trademark name VIYELLA® (by Coats Viyella) is a high-quality example of such a blend; this is a top-weight, twill weave flannel, 55 percent wool and 45 percent cotton, carrying the label shown in Figure 2.94.

Introducing nylon to strengthen cotton led to the development of a special form of low-elongation

Figure 2.94 Hangtag for the original VIYELLA® fabric, made of a 55 percent wool, 45 percent cotton blend.

nylon, Nylon 420 (by DuPont); see the discussion of nylon properties under *Nylon.*

There is an odd but long-made blend used for long underwear by Damart of the United Kingdom, knit of 85 percent vinyon blended with 15 percent acrylic. Its trademark name is THERMOLACTYL—just keep it away from heat, as it is *very* heat sensitive.

THINSULATE™ (by 3M) is often a blend of microfibric olefin and standard polyester (see Figure 2.90) to give high insulating value (much fiber surface area) in a very thin, light layer of material. A variation, THINSULATE™ LITE LOFT, gives maximum warmth in sleeping bags with the least weight. The air-laid nonwoven material is a blend of fine (not micro) fibers, with thermal bonding of the fibers to maintain the structure; see Figure 2.95. See *Care of*

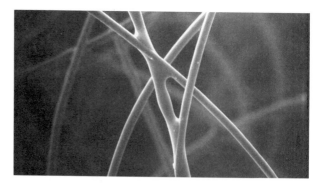

Figure 2.95 THINSULATE™ LITE LOFT insulation blends fine fibers in a nonwoven fabric with thermal bonding to maintain the structure for insulation. (Courtesy of 3M)

Special Items and a warranty offered under *Private Sector Labeling*, both in Section 6. THINSULATE™ FLEX INSULATION, developed for use with stretch fabrics, combines special elastomeric olefin fibers with regular size staple fibers to allow 40 percent stretch in all directions.

Each of THERMOLITE® ACTIVE, THERMO-LITE® PLUS, and THERMOLITE® EXTREME (by DuPont) is a special blend of fibers for insulation. Figure 2.96 shows the action of the last of these, combining very fine fibers for drapability and compactability; hollow-core, springy fibers to trap air and keep the filling lofty; and thermal bonding fibers to keep it in place.

Many tests and trials have produced the best blends we have now. This is where the term *engineered blend* is deserved. The manufacturer of such a blend uses a mixture of more than one fiber, not as a sales gimmick but to produce a fabric superior in

Three Ways Better: The Tri-Blend Fiber System

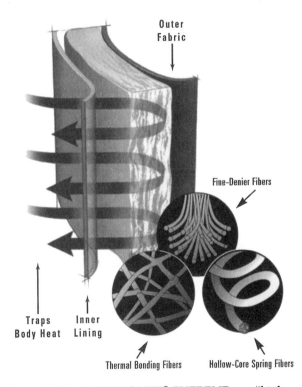

Outer Fabric

Fine-Denier Fibers

Traps Body Heat

Inner Lining

Thermal Bonding Fibers

Hollow-Core Spring Fibers

Figure 2.96 THERMOLITE® EXTREME is a "high-tech" insulation using a blend of fibers for optimum warmth with light weight. (Courtesy of the DuPont Company)

performance and/or more comfortable and more pleasing.

Fiber Identification

The first and most basic information about a fabric is fiber content. Although the way a fabric or garment is made and finished will affect its suitability for different purposes, nothing will counteract the mistake of using a fiber in riding pants, for instance, that cannot withstand abrasion.

Although most fabrics are labeled as to fiber content, there are many occasions when you might wish to determine or confirm this: You may have fabric that was a remnant, a gift, or acquired long ago, with content uncertain. In business, you may simply be unsure of the fiber content you are quoted; however, you cannot depend on your own determination in any legal sense.

For anyone studying the basics of textiles, few demonstrations are more convincing of the real differences between fibers or fabrics that may look and feel similar than a burning test or microscopic examination; these can also show that a relationship does exist between fibers that may look and feel very different!

Fiber identification is a useful skill and can develop into a kind of detective process. With very little equipment, you can at least determine a fiber's general type. Conclusive tests probably have to be made in a laboratory, sometimes with expensive equipment, certainly needing skilled staff.

Fiber Identification Methods

The following is general information on the methods of fiber identification; we will then examine several of them more closely:

1. **Burning test.** A burning test is often the simplest to carry out, as long as precautions are taken with open flame and there is a receptacle for burning or melting material. The test is useful if only a single type of fiber is present in a yarn; if any yarn contains a blend of fibers, the test will reveal only the presence of fibers with very characteristic odors, such as protein and cellulose, or of fibers that melt—but that is good general

information. If someone has told you that a fabric is "all silk" and you do *not* smell burning protein, you know there is no silk at all; however, if you do smell the characteristic odor of burning silk, you do *not* know whether it is 100 percent silk.

Discussion in detail of this procedure follows, with results of typical burning tests on various fibers.

2. **Microscopic examination.** A lengthwise (longitudinal) view of fibers is easy to get and *very* helpful. A cross section of fibers may sometimes be needed for positive identification, but is much more demanding to prepare. You do not need an expensive microscope; a child's or hobby type will do well, as fibers reveal most of their significant appearance at a magnification of 100 times (100×) or even less, and mounts made in water give a good, undistorted view, although they do dry up quickly. Detailed discussion of this procedure follows.

3. **Staining test.** A stain test provides a useful cross-check in identifying fibers, as long as they are not already too dark a color, either naturally or from having been dyed. The identification (ID) stain will have a mixture of dyestuffs in it that gives different colors on different fiber types—a variation of cross-dyeing. When microscopic examination is made of a sample that has already been stained, both appearance and color contribute information. For example, a number of major fiber groups are round in cross section and so appear structureless in lengthwise view—like a rod. Use of an ID stain, especially if a piece of *multifiber cloth* is included, often helps greatly to distinguish among these groups. Testing laboratories regularly use such multifiber cloth, woven with 5 cm or 10 cm repeats of a variety of fibers in strips. The makeup of a 13-fiber cloth and a result with one ID stain mixture are shown in Figure 2.97; for sources of multifiber cloth, *see* Section 8.

4. **Solubility or chemical test.** This kind of test is needed when an unknown is very dark in color, when two or more fibers are present in a blend (which makes a burning test inconclusive), when fibers have very little visible structure, and in general, as a conclusive cross-check to burning or stain tests or microscopic examination.

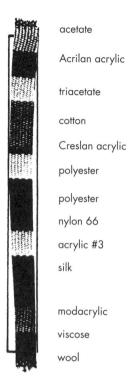

acetate

Acrilan acrylic

triacetate

cotton

Creslan acrylic

polyester

polyester

nylon 66

acrylic #3

silk

modacrylic

viscose

wool

Figure 2.97 A 13-fiber multifiber cloth stained with an identification stain, made up to give different colors on different fiber types.

One of the few specific chemicals readily available is nail polish remover, which, although it is not acetone, will affect only acetate or triacetate at room temperature. Most other chemicals needed in fiber identification are hazardous and used only in laboratories. However, a chart follows showing some key fiber solubilities.

5. **Fiber density, infrared spectrophotometry, gas chromatography.** These are all positive identifying tests, but are very specialized.

Burning Behavior

This topic touches far more than just fiber identification, so before proceeding with specific information on burning tests, we should consider fire safety as it relates to textiles. Fabrics are all around us—in clothing and household furnishings; in whatever transport we use; in schools, offices, theaters. Concern that dangerously flammable textile products should not be allowed on the market has led to increasing legislation in this area in a number of countries. In the United States, the original Flammable Fabrics Act (1953) was amended in 1967 to outlaw highly flammable fabrics for interiors as well as apparel. Since 1973, under the Consumer Products Safety Act, an independent agency, the Consumer Product Safety Commission, creates and enforces the rules for textiles (as well as other products). Standards in effect can be found in parts of Title 16 of the Code of Federal Regulations. In Canada similar regulations exist under the Hazardous Products Act (1969) administered by the Product Safety Program, Health Protection Branch, Health Canada. The standards in both countries establish a base level of safety for consumer apparel, with special standards for items such as children's sleepwear, carpets, and mattresses.

Fiber Type and Fire Safety. Just as fiber behavior is basic to wear, ease of care, or comfort of our textile articles, so it is to their relative flammability. The following lists describe behavior in flame and removed from it, by fiber category:

Most Flammable

- Cellulosic fibers (such as cotton, flax, viscose, lyocell). Once alight, these burn readily and so can "propagate" flame to other fabrics; can leave glowing embers.

Intermediate

- Acetate, triacetate. These melt as they burn; burn more readily than the groups listed next.
- Nylon, polyester, olefin (polypropylene), acrylic, spandex. These do not catch fire (ignite) readily; once ignited, burn and melt; tend to drip (especially nylon); the drops tend to carry the flame away, so the fabric self-extinguishes in some situations.

Less Flammable

- Protein (wool, silk). These do not ignite easily; burn slowly; tend to self-extinguish, except in very dry air or with very open fabric.

Flame Resistant

Will not continue to burn when the source of ignition is removed (self-extinguishing).

- Modacrylic, saran, vinyon. These melt.
- Aramid. These do not melt but char; tend to self-extinguish; give little smoke.

- Certain modifications. Some MF fibers are given flame resistance by agents put in before the fiber is spun.

Flameproof (Nonflammable)

- Novoloid, polybenzimidazole (PBI). These will not burn; do not melt; char, but stay intact.
- Inorganic fibers (asbestos, glass, metal, etc.). These will not burn; can melt, but at temperatures so high they do not figure in textile fire safety!

Fabric Construction and Fire Safety. The way the fabric is constructed is another very important factor in fire safety:

- Lighter-weight fabrics, especially light, sheer, or open fabrics, burn faster than heavier fabrics (of equivalent fiber types).
- Fabrics with a raised surface burn faster than smooth fabrics.
- Open, porous fabrics or those with a more sparse pile burn faster than those with yarns packed closely together.

Garment Design and Construction and Fire Safety. The style and construction of a garment affects flammability:

- Loose-fitting garments, with flaring skirts or sleeves, with gathers, ruffles, trim like lace, anything with a lot of air incorporated with it, will ignite more readily and burn faster than closely fitting, virtually untrimmed articles. This means that flowing, at-home garments should be worn with care around the kitchen stove or barbecue.
- Thread may be more flammable than garment fabric, so an article can burn preferentially at the seams.

In almost a summary of the preceding "lineup" of hazards from fiber type, fabric construction, and garment design, product safety authorities in the United States and Canada in August 1994 were warning about full skirts imported from India made up of rayon chiffon over gauze, some of which had been found to be dangerously flammable.

Other Fire Hazards. Other fire hazards involving textiles include the following:

- Bedding and upholstery made of fabric covering over foam present a fire hazard; the resistance to burning or even melting of the covering fabric is evidently crucial in preventing fire from reaching the foam, which burns readily because of the air trapped in its structure.

- One of the hottest fire sources is an unextinguished cigarette or cigar; a combination of one of these with a mattress or a wastebasket of paper is often deadly.

- Other areas of concern (and legislation) are tents, dining shelters, and the like.

- Clothes dryer fire hazards from lint and foam are noted in Section 6.

Fiber Identification Burning Test

You will be working with an open flame—from a Bunsen burner, a candle, or even a match—so **take care**, especially to keep long hair well clear of the flame. Samples for burning tests should be quite small, although if you use the recommended loose fibers or bundles of yarn, you will probably keep the sample small in any case. Fiber material burns very quickly when it is not held in a fabric, so twist fibers together and bundle yarn pieces, so they will not burn too quickly. Always hold the sample (or a flame source such as a match) in tweezers or tongs and work over something like a sheet of foil or metal tray, in case you drop burning material. Make sure the surface under the foil or tray is protected from heat.

The sampling procedure itself is very important if you wish to get the maximum information from your test. You should take yarns from warp separately from weft in a woven fabric, and if any contain more than one ply, test the plies separately. Twist short lengths of the yarns into a bundle; bring the sample *slowly* up to the flame source *from the side* (not pushed into the top of the flame); note what happens as the sample approaches the flame—does it "shrink away" as a thermoplastic fiber will?

Put the sample in the flame and note whether and how it burns. Remove it and see whether it goes out on its own (self-extinguishing), whether it smolders, or whether it goes on burning. Samples that burn and melt will often drip; take care with this molten material—it is very hot. If a sample burns

"fiercely," you may have to blow it out so it will not all be burned up.

As the flame goes out, note the type of smoke and its odor.

Finally, let the residue cool (use caution again with this) and examine its character: soft ash, crushable or hard bead, smooth or irregular.

Note that the dyes and finishes used on a fabric can affect its behavior in burning and the color of the residue.

Results for major fibers are presented in Table 2.5; the order is not connected with relative flammability as given in the opening of this segment; instead, it is one you might follow if you are doing a systematic series of burning tests, to prevent your sense of smell from getting fatigued early by the really acrid or pungent odors of the fibers listed furthest down the table.

Microscopic Fiber Examination

Every microscope is a carefully engineered optical instrument and should be handled with knowledge and care. The main parts are shown in Figure 2.98; the two lenses that do the magnifying are the eyepiece (*ocular*) and the *objective*. Many microscopes have a revolving turret nosepiece, allowing you to interchange objectives. An eyepiece of 15 times magnification (15×) used with an objective of 10× will give you a magnification of 15 × 10 or 150×. As mentioned in the introduction to this segment, that is more than enough for examination of fibers; in fact, for an inexperienced person, too high a magnification (in the order of 600×) can make locating the sample difficult, or give a very confusing picture.

Handle any microscope with care. A soft lens paper should be used to keep the lens system as clean as possible. Water from the slide or chemical reagents must never be allowed to come in contact with the lens. Care should also be taken that water does not seep between the slide and the stage.

Microscopic examination can be a good first step in fiber identification, and the microscope need not be an expensive one. You need as well some microscope slides, cover slips, two long needles, and a dropper bottle of a liquid medium such as glycerine or just water. Glycerine does have advantages over water for mounting all fibers except acetate: water evaporates quicker, swells many fibers, and does not allow as good definition. On the other hand, water is readily available, and there is little distortion as light passes through the glass, water, and fiber. For student

Table 2.5 *Burning Behavior of Major Types of Fibers*

Fiber Type	Behavior Up to Flame	Behavior in Flame	Behavior Removed from Flame	Odor of Smoke	Type of Residue
asbestos, glass	No effect	Glows	No change	None	NA
cellulosic such as cotton, linen, viscose, lyocell	No effect	Burns fiercely	Burns, can glow, smolders	Like burning wood, paper, leaves	Soft, gray ash
acetate, triacetate	Curls.	Burns, melts	Burns, melts	Like vinegar	Bead—can crush
nylon	Shrinks away	Melts, drips	Tends to go out	Like celery seed(?)	Hard bead
polyester	Shrinks away	Burns, melts	Tends to go out	Aromatic(?)	Hard bead
olefin (polypropylene)	Shrinks away	Burns, melts, black smoke	Burns, melts	Like wax	Hard bead
acrylic	Shrinks away	Burns, melts	Burns, melts	Fishy	Bead—can break
modacrylic	Shrinks away	Burns, melts	GOES OUT	Like animal waste!	Bead—can break
silk	No effect	Burns slowly	Tends to go out	Like burning feathers	Ash—can crush
wool	No effect	Burns slowly	Tends to go out	Like burning hair, meat	Ash—can crush

NA Not applicable.

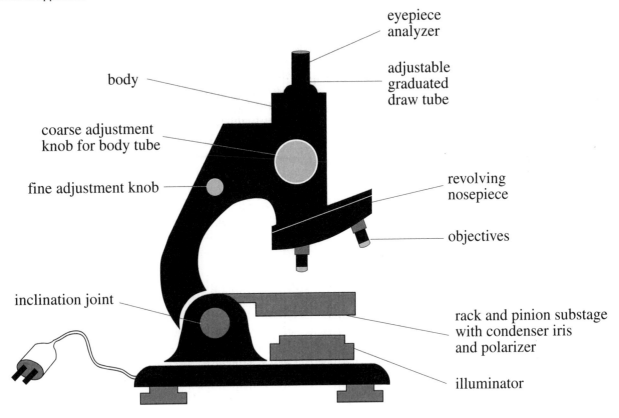

Figure 2.98 **Main parts of a microscope.**

use in introductory courses, or for amateur interest, water does very well. For the long needles, use dissecting needles, hat pins, or darning needles with cork on the eye ends.

The procedure outlined here will give you a lengthwise (longitudinal) view of fibers; to see the cross section, you must take a slice across the fibers, which requires some special equipment plus manual skill and practice.

Fiber "knowns" are an invaluable help in microscopic examination of fibers for identification. You can consult printed guides such as you find in this *Reference* and others, but if you can look at an actual sample of what you know to be that fiber, it is much more revealing and conclusive. A collection of known samples can be made, of which only a fiber or two is needed, to be mounted alongside an "unknown," to give you a great deal more assurance in making your identification.

Alternatively, you could assemble a set of permanent slides to give you a known to compare with an unknown. A permanent slide can be prepared by mounting in a medium such as *collodion*,[27] which hardens on drying. If using such a medium, take care to move the fibers in it as little as possible, or many bubbles will form; these are most distracting and misleading when you are examining what is on the slide. A set of such slides can be prepared more cheaply than buying a commercially available set, can cover many more interesting examples (e.g., wool fibers bitten by larvae), and, in my experience, can be prepared to a higher standard (fewer bubbles)!

See the sampling procedure described for the burning test. Ravel yarn off the cloth and untwist; if there is more than one ply, examine each separately, and look at warp separately from weft. In a fabric with yarns of different colors, you should really look at each color separately.

When the yarn is nearly untwisted, *do not pull it apart*—hold it over a drop of water or glycerine on a microscope slide and clip off a length of about 10 mm (½ in.), letting it drop onto the slide. Using two needles, tease the fibers to separate them; ideally, you should not have fibers crossing each other at various levels. It is a common mistake to have far too many fibers on a slide.

Drop a cover slip on top, and examine for air bubbles; if present, press gently on the cover slip with

[27]Collodion is available from a laboratory supply house.

the tip of a needle, *not your finger*. If bubbles are still present, hold a needle against one edge of the cover slip, and raise the slip with the other needle from the opposite edge, using the first needle like a hinge; introduce a *little* liquid, and lower the slip *slowly*. You may wish to use this technique in any case, rather than "dropping" the cover slip on. Blot excess liquid away; absorbent papers are available from laboratory supply houses, with the rather W. C. Fields-ish name of *bibulous paper*.

Place the slide on the microscope stage so that the fibers on the slide are in the center of the hole. Use an objective and eyepiece to give a magnification of 100–150× if possible, but even 60× will do. The microscope can be tilted by the inclination joint. Clips on the stage hold the slide in place, and there is usually an iris diaphragm below the stage to allow more or less light through. If a mirror is used, the concave side concentrates light more than the flat or plane side. An illuminator lamp, useful to throw a good light below the stage, may be clipped in place where a mirror would be, if a light source is not fitted to the microscope.

Focusing is done first with the coarse adjustment knob, then the fine. First, guiding yourself by looking from the *side* of the microscope, lower the objective until it nearly touches the slide. Then, with your eye to the eyepiece, turn *up* slowly, until the material comes into focus. (If you do not follow this procedure, you run the risk of grinding a lens into the slide.)

When the fibers have been brought into view, focus carefully using the fine adjustment knob. Sometimes details can be seen more clearly if the light coming into the microscope is reduced by use of the iris diaphragm. In other cases, such as with lobal MF fibers, you get a better impression of the shape of the fiber if you focus up and down through it. Try to keep both eyes open when using a microscope; this will result in less eye fatigue.

Typical Features. Following are descriptions of fibers seen through the microscope at magnification of 60–150×. Cross-sectional shape is described and shown as well as longitudinal features. With reeled silk and (particularly) MF fibers, it is important to know the shape of the cross section in order to understand the lengthwise view you see. You will not be able to see the cross section, however, unless a slice has been taken of the fiber; as noted before, this requires special equipment and a good deal of practice. What you will ordinarily be looking at is the lengthwise (longitudinal) view.

- **Natural fibers** have very definite characteristics in each type; e.g., hair fibers will have features in common, as will bast fibers; it is very difficult (if not impossible) to tell a cashmere fiber from very fine wool, or flax from hemp or ramie, but the *type* is unmistakable.

- **Cotton** (mature or lint fiber) looks like a twisted ribbon, with a central canal, the *lumen*, clearly visible at this magnification. Views seen in many textbooks and Figure 5.4(a), given by a scanning electron microscope, show the surface but not the lumen. Immature cotton is twisted, but has no inner substance.

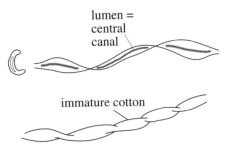

- **Mercerized cotton** shows few twists, since it has been swollen in caustic soda; the smoother surface after mercerizing gives luster (see Figure 5.4[a]). Immature cotton will not react in mercerizing, as there is no secondary wall to swell; it remains looking like (insubstantial) twisted ribbon.

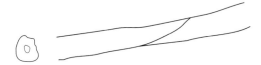

- **Flax and other bast fibers** show nodes—swellings along the length, like the "elbows" in bamboo—plus cross cracks.

- **Wool** shows overlapping scales, like shingles on a roof or fish scales; the edges protrude slightly toward the tip of the fiber. Coarse wools may show a *medulla*—a dark space in the center.

- The finer the hair fiber, the smaller the scales, so **cashmere** undercoat has very small scales that seldom overlap on one side of the fiber.

- **Mohair** has large, platelike scales that project hardly at all from the fiber; these account for the dirt-shedding character and luster of mohair.

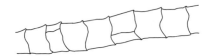

- **Angora** has an appearance typical of **fur fibers:** air spaces in the center of the fibers look like "box cars," scales project hardly at all.

- **Down** shows a truly wonderful construction: a quill point with fine branching arms, carrying tiny barbs. Since this is all made of a light material (protein), it gives air trapping with little weight. *Note:* Since down was intended to *resist* wetting, it is almost impossible to mount in water without a lot of air bubbles. Find a bit without too much intrusion from bubbles, and enjoy!

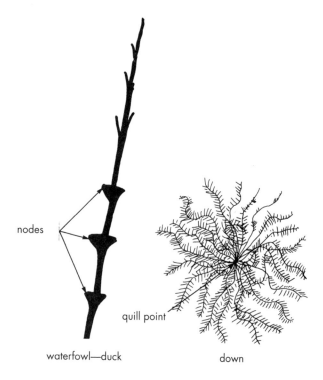

nodes

quill point

waterfowl—duck

down

- **Cultivated (reeled) silk** is the only natural fiber that is *structureless,* since it was formed by a liquid solidifying. Sometimes a faint lengthwise line can be seen to mark the joining as the fiber

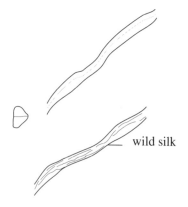

wild silk

was spun of the original two brins into one filament. Silk is always very fine and is irregular in diameter; the cross section is roughly triangular. **Wild silk** has a rather striated appearance and is much coarser than cultivated silk.

- Any **MF fiber** may appear clear, or with specks through the fiber, no matter which group it falls into according to the fiber shape and type. Clear fibers are called *bright* and will look shiny; the specks are granules of a white pigment dispersed in the fiber before it was spun, as a dulling agent or delustrant. Some fibers have very little delustrant, while others are heavily delustered; since light cannot pass through the (white) pigment granules, they look like dark specks.

Major features identifying various groups of MF fibers follow:

- Structureless MF fibers have a **rodlike** shape, with a **round cross section.** Among the many structureless fibers are cuprammonium, lyocell, standard nylon and polyester, olefin, glass, saran, and CRESLAN® and ZEFRAN® acrylics.

- **One line or "crease"** is the result of a **dog-bone** or **bean-shaped cross section.** Fibers of this type are LYCRA® spandex, some modacrylics, and some acrylics (Verel and Orlon were like this).

- **A few lines** are given by **lobal cross sections** of two differently appearing types:

1. Two to four lines lengthwise, the result of lobes a little like clover leaves, are found with acetate and triacetate.
2. A few wider, shallower grooves with more solid lobes, the swelling of which can be seen by focusing up and down through a fiber, can be seen in a lobal fiber such as ANTRON® nylon or in the coarse filaments used for most of the "sparkling" fabrics. (A few such sparkling fabrics may still be made of flat, tapelike filaments, such as "crystal" acetate.)

- **Many lines** are seen only in viscose, the result of a wrinkled, almost corrugated surface that gives a **serrated cross section.** This is a result of the fiber precipitating gradually in the acid bath.

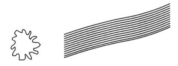

It is also interesting to look at a sample containing **microfibers,** to get an idea of just how fine these are. The tiny fibers in THINSULATE™ are on the order of the size of the fronds and barbs of down, and microfilaments can also be compared to silk.

Solubility or Chemical Tests

When other tests are inconclusive, solubility tests must be made using chemicals that are both hazardous to handle and not easily available. This portion, then, may largely be of limited interest, but is included for reference.

Sampling is done with very small clumps of fibers, short lengths of yarn, or (least desirable) small pieces of fabric. Comments on sampling for burning tests apply, in regards to trying to test each type of fiber present.

You should have at least 100 units of solution for every unit of sample. Leave the sample in the liquid for five minutes, stirring periodically. You may need a special light or background to see the effect on the sample.

The following are solvents specific for the fiber(s) mentioned, but often after other possibilities have been eliminated by burning, microscopic examination, or stain testing:

Solvent	Temperature (°C/°F)	Specific for
acetone	room	acetate (dissolves), triacetate (disintegrates), modacrylic, vinyon (softens)
cresol (meta-)	95/200 (hot)	polyester (if nylon and acetate have been eliminated)
dimethyl-formamide	95/200 (hot)	acrylic, modacrylic (if acetate has been eliminated and if saran, spandex or vinyon is unlikely)
hydrochloric acid (20% by weight, sp.gr. 1.096 at 25°C/75°F)	room	nylon
sodium hypochlorite (5% av. Cl)	room	wool, silk

SECTION THREE

Yarns—From Fiber To Fabric

Yarn Types and Constructions

Yarn is a continuous strand of textile fibers, filaments, or other material in a form suitable for knitting, weaving, or otherwise intertwining to form a textile fabric (ASTM definition). In other applications, it is called *thread*, e.g., for sewing or embroidery.

Filament yarn (also called continuous filament yarn) is formed by gathering a number of filaments together to give *multifilament* yarn, formed with or without twist; with MF fibers, a single continuous filament may form *monofilament* yarn. Most MF filament (and all reeled silk) yarn is multifilament. The main uses of monofilament yarn are in very sheer women's hosiery, as "color blending" sewing thread, and for wiry millinery and hem braids used in place of horsehair or mohair (see *Fabric Glossary*: BRAID).

Yarn may also be formed of one or more strips made by the lengthwise division of a sheet of material such as a polymer film, paper, metal foil, or other fabric, used with or without twist in a textile construction.

Spun yarn results from the mechanical spinning of staple fibers, twisted together and drawn out to form yarn (see *Conventional Processing* under *Spun Yarn*). Fabric names such as SPUN RAYON or SPUN SILK (see *Fabric Glossary*) indicate the characteristics given by spun yarn, in contrast to the "silky" character given by filament yarns.

Spun Yarns Compared to Filament Yarns

Look, Hand. Spun yarns, because of the protruding ends of fibers, have a duller, more fuzzy surface, more noticeable with carded than with combed yarns. Filament yarns (unless textured) are smoother and, more slippery, and will ravel or pull out of a fabric more easily, but will not shed lint or form pills as spun yarns do. Fabrics made of spun yarns have more loft, bulk, and cover but soil more easily than do those made of filament.

Comfort. The protruding fiber ends of spun yarns hold the yarn away from the skin. This creates still air space, which is a good insulator to prevent body heat from being lost in cold weather; it also makes spun yarn fabrics more comfortable on a hot, humid day. The comfort in hot weather of fabrics made of filament yarn, which lie close to the skin, depends on the absorbency of the fiber used and/or its wicking ability. Static buildup is closely associated with absorbency or wicking. Spun yarns, being more absorbent than filament *of the same fiber,* are more resistant to static buildup.

Textured filaments give yarns somewhat greater absorbency, warmth, bulk, and "spunlike" loft than standard (untextured) filaments; see *Textured Manufactured Filament Yarns.*

Durability, Strength, Cost. These can be compared only for yarns *of the same fiber type;* in this framework, filament yarns are more durable than spun, as they do not have fiber ends to wear away on the surface.

Moreover, in MF fibers, the filament form is purposely made somewhat stronger, as well as more even (uniform in diameter). Filament should be *stronger* because the strength of a filament yarn depends on the strength of each individual filament in that yarn; strength of a spun yarn depends more on the amount of twist and the length of the staple. Filament should be *more even* to prevent different shades in dyeing that can give streaks called *barré* or *barriness,* caused by any changes in fiber diameter. These show up much more in a fabric made of filament yarn, e.g., nylon hosiery or (especially) a warp knit such as tricot for lingerie. See *Dyes and Colorfastness* in Section 6 regarding nylon and practical results in colorfastness because of the dye type used to prevent barré.

All of this means that filament yarn costs more; offsetting this, the many steps needed to spin staple into yarn on conventional systems are also costly, especially those for very fine, even spun yarn. Newer, faster spinning systems, like open-end or direct, make some spun yarns cheaper.

Yarn Classification

The bulk of our discussion will be of **simple** yarns, those in which all parts are the same (as opposed to **novelty** or complex-ply yarns discussed later).

Yarn Classified by Ply

Figure 3.1 illustrates the types of yarn as classified by ply, as follows:

> **Single.** Made by any method, can be untwisted in one operation to separate into fibers.

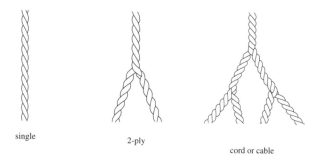

single   2-ply

cord or cable

Figure 3.1 Yarn: single, plied, cord or cable.

Plied or folded. Two or more singles twisted together for strength. For identification of plied yarns see *Yarn Notation*.

Cord, cable, or hawser. Two or more plied yarns twisted together for even more strength (e.g., cotton 6-cord sewing thread) or as a bulky cord for decorative ties or trim.

Yarn Classified by Twist Direction

Figure 3.2 illustrates the types of yarn as classified by twist direction, as follows:

S twist. Put in by a clockwise rotation; the spiral of the twist follows the direction of the slope of the letter *S*. In determining twist direction, it is often easier to note the direction in which the twist loosens: *S* twist loosens in a counterclockwise direction (to the left).

Z twist. Put in by a counterclockwise rotation; the spiral follows the direction of the slope of the

letter *Z*. This twist loosens in a clockwise direction (to the right).

Twist of plying is almost always the opposite of the twist of the singles, to prevent the resulting yarn from twisting and turning on itself (developing torque), which can make it unmanageable. A notable exception is the twist-on-twist used in the best voile; see *Yarn Classified by Amount of Twist* and *Fabric Glossary: VOILE* (cotton type).

Yarn Classified by Amount of Twist

Figure 3.3 illustrates the types of yarn as classified by amount of twist, as follows:

Zero twist. Possible only in *raw* reeled silk (filament) yarns, where the silk gum can hold the

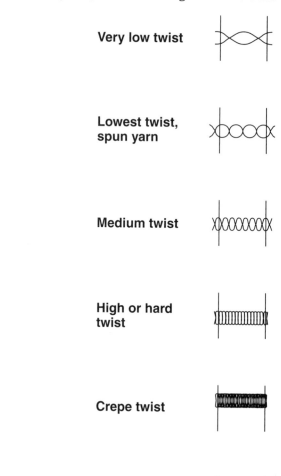

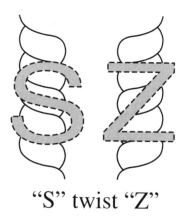

"S" twist "Z"

Figure 3.2 Direction of twist in "S" twist and "Z" twist yarn.

Figure 3.3 Degree of yarn twist from very low to very high (crepe).

filaments together. (See *Silk Production* in Section 2 for the significance of the stage and method of degumming silk to produce a "lively" fabric.)

Very low twist. 1–2 turns per cm or 3–5 per inch, possible with any filament yarn since the strength of the yarn does not depend on twist and fiber cohesiveness, as it does in spun yarns; all that is needed is enough twist to keep the filaments together during processing into fabric. The lowest twist in *spun* yarn, about 2–5 turns per cm or 5–15 per inch, is used in the weft (crosswise) yarns of a napped fabric, where the low or soft twist helps the tearing out of fibers, which are laid on the surface as nap. These are taken from weft yarns in wovens or from laid-in yarns in weft knits. Low-twist yarns are also used for the pile of candlewick fabric (see *Fabric Glossary*: TUFTED).

Medium twist. 8–10 turns per cm or 20–25 per inch, used for most spun yarns, e.g., sheeting. Strength increases with twist, up to a very high amount.

High or hard twist. 12–17 turns per cm or 30–40 per inch, used to give the firmness of voile. *Twist-on-twist* yarns are used for the highest-quality voile; these are hard-twist yarns formed by twisting the plies in the same direction as the singles to give a lasting firmness to the fabric (see *Fabric Glossary*: VOILE [*cotton type*]).

Crepe twist. 17–30 turns per cm or 40–75 per inch, the highest twist of all. When made of fibers that absorb moisture, the fibers swell in the wet-finishing creping treatment and form tiny bumps on the surface to give the pebbliness of crepe (see *Fabric Glossary*: CREPE and GEORGETTE). For plied crepe yarns, singles are first twist-set to make them less lively and "kinky," then plied with twist at 1–2 turns per cm.

The amount of yarn twist has a considerable effect on luster: Low-twist yarns of smooth filament have a high luster, while high-twist yarns such as crepe give a duller, matte effect and a lively, drapable fabric.

Yarn Classified by Linear Density (Count or Number)

Linear density, notated as count or number, refers to what the consumer would perceive as the thickness or weight (mass) of a yarn or thread. The size of a yarn and its notation (the way it is specified) are of particular importance to those working in the textiles industry or to designers of woven and especially of knitted fabrics. As well, certain quality terms used in merchandising are related to yarn number (see *Indirect Yarn Number* below).

Traditionally there have been two methods of recording yarn count: indirect and direct yarn number.

Indirect Yarn Number. This is calculated according to the length of yarn spun from a given mass; the larger the number, the finer the yarn. This system has been used for spun yarns of staple fibers, with a slightly different base for each of the major natural fibers.

A #1 yarn would be the following lengths weighing one pound (or spun from one pound of fiber): cotton (English system), 840 yards; linen (wet or dry spun), 300 yards, count called a *lea*; wool (worsted system), 560 yards; wool (woolen system), 256 yards. For woolen yarns there is also the *run* system, in which for a 1 run yarn a 1,600-yard hank weighs one pound. Woolen yarns are usually singles and range from 0.5 run (coarse) through those in tweed jackets (yarns of 2 to 3 run) to hosiery made of finest yarns, of 8 run.

Cotton sewing thread numbers are based on the English cotton yarn count, with #10 being a very heavy thread, #50 medium, #80 quite fine. A custom-made cotton shirt may be promoted as using "2-ply 160" yarn—stronger because it is 2-ply and fine, the equivalent of a single 80s (the *s* is added in textile circles but usually dropped in advertisements to the consumer).

Many of the indirect yarn counts have converted to *tex* (see *Direct Yarn Number*), but in the United Kingdom, the woolen and worsted counts persist. As noted in Section 2, wool fiber quality numbers are related to the count of worsted yarn, with 40s coarse, 60s finer (botany), and 80s or higher very fine (Superfine). Superior suitings are often described with these numbers, such as "Super 100s."

Direct Yarn Number.
This is calculated according to the mass of a given length; the larger the number, the heavier the yarn.

Denier has been the best-known direct system in traditional counts. It is based on the weight of a Roman coin, developed to describe silk (filament) yarns and used also for MF filament yarns. Denier is the number of 0.05 g units in 450 m of filament (or g/9,000 m). The range of yarn size in consumer articles is from 7 denier in some very sheer hosiery to over 1,000 denier in luggage and footwear.

The SI metric system (see Section 9 description) calculates the number of all yarns using a direct metric unit: *tex.* Tex is the mass in grams of 1,000 meters of the yarn (g/1,000 m). *Tex* will usually be used for spun yarns, with *kilotex* (*ktex*) (kg/1,000 m or g/m) for coarser units such as sliver or tow, and *decitex* (*dtex*) (g/10,000 m) for finer yarns, especially filament. It is easy to see that the decitex count of a filament yarn (g/10,000 m) will be close to denier (g/9,000 m), but the traditional spun yarn counts are very different from tex.

Yarn Notation

Notation is identification of yarn construction and count and differs according to the fiber the yarn is made from, as follows:

Cotton yarn. The notation 60s/2 means a 2-ply yarn made up of singles that are each of traditional cotton count 60s (9.8 tex); the resultant yarn is equivalent to a traditional cotton 30s (19.7 tex).

Worsted yarn. This notation is in the reverse order: a 2/60s also denotes two 60s singles plied, with the resultant yarn equivalent to a 30s. In marketing, this yarn number would probably be called 2/60 Nw, meaning two 60s singles plied, giving a "normal worsted" number (Nw). Yarns noted on the metric (tex) system would be identified as Nm or "normal metric."

Spun silk. A 2-ply yarn notated as 60s/2 means that the resultant yarn is a 60s count, made up of two plies of 120s count (4.9 tex).

If the count of a plied yarn is listed with "R" before it, this shows the resultant count and is giving the ply-to-single notation. After the "R" may be listed the direction and amount of plying twist, then a slash and the number of the singles in the plied yarn, followed if necessary by the direction and amount of twist. If the count (linear density) of the single is given, it is separated by a semicolon.

Yarns of fine filaments. These are notated as total yarn count in dtex or denier and the number of filaments in that yarn, in the formats shown below. To convert denier to dtex, multiply by 1.111; to convert dtex to denier, multiply by 0.9, as shown in the following comparison:

Total Yarn Count (dtex)	Number of Filaments	Total Yarn Count (denier)	Number of Filaments
166 f 32		150/32	
111 f 50		100/50	
78 f 136		70/136	

The different makeup of the third example—a fine yarn made up of a large number of very fine filaments—has commonly been referred to as *high denier per filament* or *high dpf* (see the discussion of filament microfibers under *Microfibers and Very Fine Fibers* in Section 2).

Spun Yarn

Conventional Processing

Hand methods of spinning, developed mainly for wool and flax, were the models for the machine spinning developed at the time of the Industrial Revolution; the machines, however, were applied first to spinning cotton. These machines developed from the first eight-spindle "spinning jenny"[1] in 1764 to pervasive power machine spinning by the early 19th century.

Today, electronic controls have been applied not only to spinning but to virtually all of the processes of textile manufacture; it is interesting to note that in the making of Harris tweed, which is still handwoven in the Outer Hebrides off northwestern Scotland, the rest of the operations are done by the most modern, automatic machinery. The wool fiber scouring, dyeing, and blending are all computer controlled, as well as the yarn carding and spinning and the fulling to finish the fabric.

---

[1]Jenny (pronounced "jinny") is a corruption of engine, in spite of the persistent tale that James Hargreaves named the machine for his daughter Jenny.

Main Conventional Processes

Today the main conventional systems for processing staple fiber into spun yarn are those developed for cotton and wool, as follows:

Carding. All staple fibers are carded when being processed into yarn on conventional machines; Figure 3.4 shows the stages. After opening of bales, loose fiber is blended and formed into a *picker lap,* which goes into the carding machine. Here, fine bent wires on revolving cylinders pull the fibers apart, remove waste, and begin to arrange the fibers enough that they can be spun into yarn; in cotton spinning, about 10 percent of the weight of fiber fed in is lost during carding. Fibers emerge from carding in a fine web, which is gathered together into a loose rope called a *sliver,* which is often coiled in cans. After carding (plus, for top-quality yarns, the additional processes of combing—see *Carded versus Combed Yarn),* fibers are taken through a number of stages to become yarn.

Drawing (drafting) and doubling. This is the process of running slivers between sets of rollers, each moving faster than the ones before, which draw out or draft a number of slivers to the thickness of one; this process is repeated until the fibers are well mixed.

Slubbing. Slubbing draws the sliver out to a strand about the size of a pencil, called *roving,* which is given a very slight amount of twist. This is the last stage before actual spinning into yarn.

Spinning. During spinning, the roving is drawn out to yarn size and given considerable twist to become yarn.

Types of Spinning Frames

Today, **mule spinning** is still done, with an *intermittent* action, adapted from the hand methods of

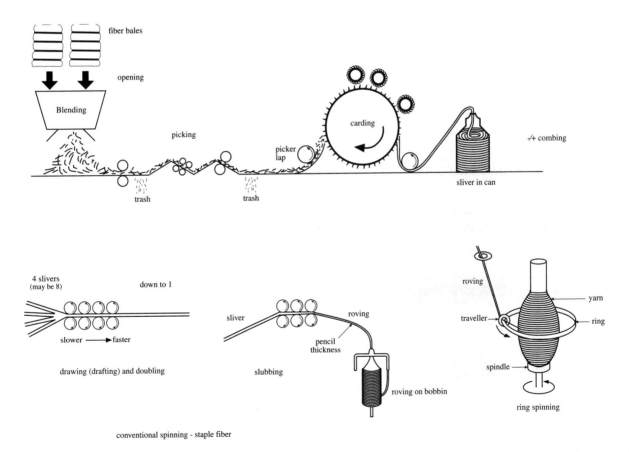

Figure 3.4 Conventional spinning of staple fibers into spun yarn.

the drop spindle or the large, single-belt wheel, where the drawing out and twisting was done as a first step, with the yarn wound up in a separate action. In mule spinning, a moving carriage on a frame draws out the rope of fibers, then the spindles insert twist; winding up is done as the carriage moves back.

The other types of spinning frames accomplish the twisting/drawing out and the winding up of the yarn as a *continuous,* rather than intermittent, process. Some spinning is still done on the earliest type of continuous spinning frame, the **flyer,** adapted from the hand spinning flyer wheel (Figure 3.5). This familiar spinning wheel, which was sketched by Leonardo da Vinci around 1516, allowed the spinner to sit down to this constant chore and was adapted to flax spinning as the Saxony wheel by Johann Jurgen in 1533. Some spinning of wool by **cap spinning,** another continuous type of spinning frame, is also still done today.

Most conventional spinning today (e.g., of cotton) is done on the **ring spinning** frame. In ring spinning (shown in Figure 3.4), twist is inserted as the fibers from the roving are carried by the *traveler* around the edge of the *ring,* inside of which is the faster-rotating *spindle.* The roving is drawn out to yarn size and is simultaneously wound up on this faster-moving spindle.

Figure 3.5 Hand spinning on a flyer wheel.

Carded versus Combed Yarn

Carded Yarn. Carded yarn has a fuzzy appearance and is loftier than yarn that is combed as well (see Figure 3.6). If spun on the cotton system, such yarn is called simply *carded;* on the wool system, it is called *woolen.* Fabrics made from yarn that is carded only have a more hairy surface and will pill more, and the weave or knit may be indistinct; this type of yarn in low twist is used for the weft in napped fabrics. Typical effects can be seen in most spun yarn fabrics.

Combed Yarn. Only the "elite" of spun yarns are combed as well as carded. Combing removes any shorter fibers and arranges the remaining longest fibers more or less parallel to each other (see Figures 3.7[a] and [b]). After combing, fibers are gathered into a loose rope called *top* in wool system spinning; in combing, about 15 percent further weight is lost.

When these fibers are spun into a tightly twisted yarn, it has a smooth surface. Spun on the cotton system, such yarn is called *combed;* spun on the wool system, it is called *worsted.* These special yarns are usually so identified in advertisements, whereas carded-only yarns are "no name." For typical combed yarn fabrics, see the *Fabric Glossary* Index under "combed yarns" and "worsted."

The main differences between fabrics made of combed yarns and those carded only are easier to see and feel with fabrics made of wool or blends. Worsteds (compared to woolens) will be relatively smooth, even, strong, and fine, and will have higher twist; most will have a firm hand (though worsted knitting yarns of fine wool will be soft). Woven fabrics made of worsted yarn will have a firm, smooth, often crisp feel, hold their shape better, take a sharp crease, show weave or knit distinctly (clear finish), and tend to develop less pilling.

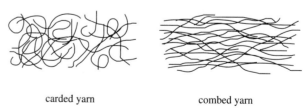

carded yarn   combed yarn

Figure 3.6 In carded yarn, fiber ends protrude; the surface of combed yarns is much smoother.

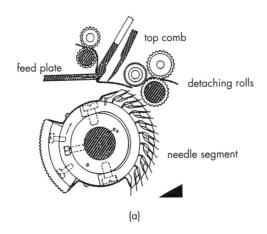

(a)

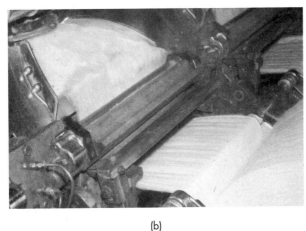

(b)

Figure 3.7 (a) The combing process removes shorter fibers and lays remaining fibers nearly parallel to each other. (b) Closeup of rectilinear combing machine. (Courtesy of Dominion Textile Inc.)

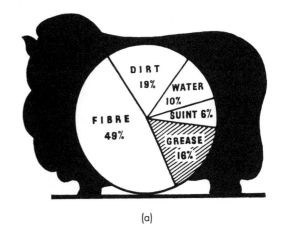

(a)

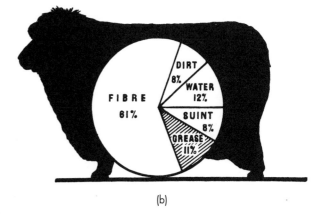

(b)

Figure 3.8 Amount of fiber compared to waste in Merino fleece (top) and Australian Crossbred (bottom). (Courtesy of the Woolmark Company, formerly IWS)

Combed yarns cost more because (in most cases):

- More raw material is used, especially with wool, with more waste (at least one-third waste). Part of this expense in wool is due to the greater amount of waste in relation to fiber (see Figure 3.8). A Merino fleece has much more grease (lanolin), suint (perspiration salts), water, and dirt than the coarser fleece from an Australian Crossbred sheep.

- The raw material is the best and hence the most expensive: a long-staple cotton variety for the finest, smoothest combed cotton yarn, or the finest, softest wool, such as Merino for worsted. "Golden Bale" yarns spun by Lumb's in England of very fine Merino wool net only about eight

pieces (150 suit lengths) in any year; the "Lansmere Super 170s" worsted suiting offered by the large tailoring fabric manufacturer, Cheil Industries of Taegu, Korea, is only enough for about 100 suit lengths in a year.

- It takes *many* passes through combing equipment to take out any shorter fibers and lay those that remain almost parallel to each other.

Some Twists on Conventional Processing

The Woolmark Company has developed the SIRO-SPUN technology to give 2-ply yarns by spinning two strands and twisting them together in one operation instead of having a separate plying (folding) process; this greatly cuts the cost of producing the yarn. Going even further, SOLOSPUN is the product of the Wool-mark Company's European Development Centre in Northern Italy; the technology allows lightweight yarns of wool to be woven as singles instead of having to use 2-ply. The technology that produces SIROFIL is called **bi-component spinning**; it allows a prespun yarn to be introduced into spinning of "medium micron" wool (see *Wool Quality*, Section 2). The prespun yarn may be regular spun or a synthetic filament, and the result can be a strong singles yarn and lower cost. Other yarns that can be all wool or wool with synthetic are **wrap spun**, as these can have a spun or synthetic filament core wrapped with wool.

Wool and cotton have been traditionally spun on different systems due to their different properties, but primarily for their different staple lengths. A process developed in Korea allows worsted yarn described as of fair quality to be processed on a slightly modified cotton system with ring spinning.[2]

Unconventional Processing

Open-End, Rotor, or Break Spinning. This type of spinning takes fibers from a sliver and in one machine, within a very small space, produces yarn (see Figure 3.9). This is in marked contrast to the succession of processes in conventional carding and spinning. The fibers from the sliver are laid into a groove inside a rotor by centrifugal force—like clothes flung against the drum of a washer in spinning extraction. The fibers are peeled off to join the end of already formed yarn. This method does away with many steps of conventional spinning and so is very economical; it is used mostly to spin coarser cotton yarns, e.g., for denim. To produce finer yarns, the rotor must turn faster, and this takes a lot of energy. MF fibers can clog the rotors. However, open-end spinning is now used widely throughout the world.

Air-Jet Spinning. This is the other major unconventional process to challenge ring spinning. Drafted sliver is led into first one, then a second nozzle, in which jets release air at high pressure, with the direction of airflow in the second nozzle being the opposite of that in the first. By this means, during passage through the nozzles, some fibers get wound around the main group, producing a yarn. This process is very fast, pro-

(a)

(b)

(c)

Figure 3.9 (a) Open-end spinning—sliver below to yarn above in a very small space. (b) Closeup of the rotor where fibers from the sliver are twisted into yarn. (c) Open-end spinning frame. (Courtesy of Dominion Textile Inc.)

[2]Peter Lennox-Kerr, "Worsted Yarn Spun on the Cotton System," *Textile Month*, June 1998: 21–23.

ducing yarn at higher speeds than open-end and many times faster than ring spinning.

A number of other nontraditional methods have been developed to spin fibers, already in staple form, into yarn, but none has yet made a significant impact in the marketplace: electrostatic, friction (DREF II, a variation on open-end spinning), "disc," twist, self-twist, false-twist (staple), and adhesive spinning.

Direct Spinning. Direct spinning takes MF fiber tow, breaks it into staple fiber, and then converts it into sliver or yarn on one machine (see Figure 3.10). Staple from this process will have tensions or strains in the fibers until it is relaxed, e.g., by steaming. When such fibers with "latent shrinkage" are blended

with others that have been shrunk or stabilized, a "Hi Bulk" yarn can be created; the fibers that shrink "elbow out" the others to give a more open, bulky yarn. BI-LOFT (by Solutia) is a high bulk acrylic yarn.

Furlike fabrics with guardhair/underfur effects (see Figure 3.11) can also be achieved, as mentioned under *Acrylic Fibers* in Section 2. Finer, high-shrink fibers are blended with coarser, stabilized fibers; after steaming, the finer fibers shrink to form the "under-coat" in a fake fur, while the coarser fibers remain on the outside, like the guardhairs of real fur (see *Fabric Glossary:* FUR-LIKE).

Continuous Filament Yarn

Cultivated or reeled silk is the only natural filament, with a maximum length of 1.5 km (nearly a mile) but one cocoon usually yields only 500–1,000 m or yards of usable fiber. MF fibers can be produced in virtually endless continuous filaments when extruded from the holes of a spinneret, and most are made this way.

Filaments can also be created by splitting film (usually polypropylene) into fine strips to make flat fibers (called split-film, fibrillated, stretched-tape, or slit-split filaments) (see Figure 3.12). This method is used to make twine and yarn for sacking, carpet primary backing, and for the backing for some sliver-knit pile fabrics; see *Fabric Glossary:* SPLIT-FILM. FIB-RILON (by Synthetic Industries Europe) is a solution-dyed, fibrillated polypropylene yarn.

Standard MF filament yarns are even in diameter and relatively smooth. Yarns are formed of such filaments by gathering them together as they are extruded from the spinneret (see *Spinning Methods* under *Spinning Manufactured Fibers* in Section 2).

(a)

(b)

Figure 3.10 Direct spinning takes fiber tow, breaks it into staple, and draws it out as sliver. (a) Shows breaking zone. (b) Shows tow coming in (vertical) and sliver drawn out, bottom right to left.

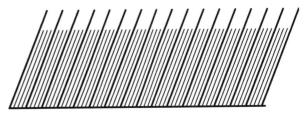

guardhair/underfur effect - through direct spinning

Figure 3.11 Guardhair/underfur effect—through direct spinning.

Yarns—From Fiber to Fabric **99**

Figure 3.12 Formation of split-film filaments by fibrillating polypropylene film. (Courtesy of the Textile Institute)

Textured MF filament yarns have had the filaments disarranged so that the yarn is no longer smooth and compact; these bulked continuous filament (BCF) yarns are often processed by throwsters using partially oriented yarn (POY), mentioned under *Nylon* and *Polyester* under *Synthetic Manufactured Fibers* in Section 2. In this case, the process is really draw-texturing, since the drawing of the fiber is completed along with the bulk texturing.

Textured Manufactured Filament Yarns

Textured versus standard filament yarn has more bulk and so has better insulating properties and creates better cover. It has less shine and snags more easily. There is better absorbency than with a standard filament yarn *of the same fiber.*

Specific texturing effects can be stretch, crimp, loop, or a texture more like spun yarns, but all of these are more economical and easier to produce than spun yarn from staple fiber.

Textured yarn of microfibers has even more bulk, since there are so many more filaments in a yarn of equal count; Figure 3.13 shows the increased bulk given by using DIOLEN® microfiber polyester (by Acordis, formerly Akzo Nobel) compared to a standard-size textured filament.

Stretch Texturing

Stretch-textured filament yarns have a springiness that has been heat set into the filaments by a number

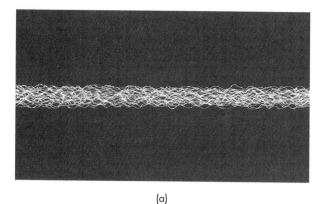

(a)

(b)

Figure 3.13 Textured yarn of DIOLEN® microfiber polyester has much greater volume and softness than one of the same count made of standard textured filament fiber: (a) 100 dtex f 36, (b) 100 dtex f 144 DIOLEN micro. (Courtesy of Akzo Nobel now Acordis)

of methods. Such stretch yarns are produced and used mainly in nylon and all kinds of body-fitting clothing, giving comfort stretch, fashion fit, or fewer sizes (see *Fabric Glossary:* STRETCH, COMFORT or FIT).

False-Twist. False-twist yarn is so-called because, if a filament yarn is held at two points and twist is inserted between these points, the twist in the left portion is equal and opposite to that in the right portion. If the twisting point is removed, the two twists cancel each other out and the filaments return to their untwisted state (see Figure 3.14[a]). However, in producing a stretch yarn by the false-twist method, thermoplastic filaments are not static; since they are moving through the machine, they are heat-set while they have a coil from twisting (Figure 3.14[b]), but the twist is *removed* as they come off the spindle to be wound, so they retain their crimped form (see Figure 3.14[c]).

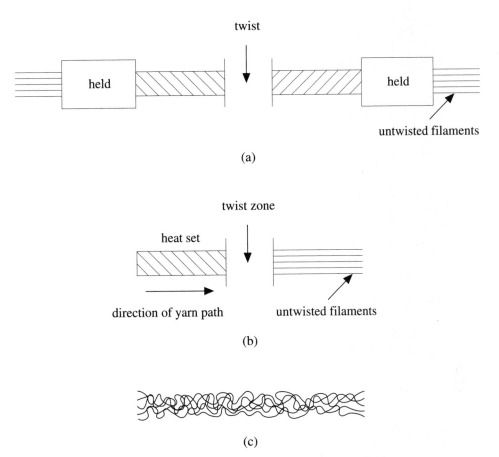

twist

held

untwisted filaments

(a)

twist zone

heat set

direction of yarn path

untwisted filaments

(b)

(c)

Figure 3.14 False-twist stretch texturing method.

This type of stretch yarn is the least expensive to make and can be single or ply, unlike HELANCA.® Some trademark names are FLUFLON and SUPERLOFT (by Leesona), and MERYL and MERYL MICRO (by Viscosuisse). A variation gives "auto-twist" yarn, as in DUO-TWIST (by Turbo).

Coil, Step-by-Step, Twist-Heat Set-Untwist. This is the oldest method, being the one by which HELANCA® (by Heberlein) stretch yarn is made. Twisting puts the yarn into a coil-spring shape, which is set by heat. The yarn now has stretch, but also tends to twist or torque; to counteract this tendency, each of these stretch yards is plied with another yarn twisted in the opposite direction. This method still gives the strongest stretch of any textured filament (see Figure 3.15) but cannot produce a monofilament (single ply) stretch yarn for sheer hosiery.

Knit-Deknit. This type is made by knitting up a tube of fabric, heat setting it, then unraveling and winding up the yarn, kinked in the shape of the knit stitch, on cones (see Figure 3.15).

Edge-Crimp. This gives a curl to yarn by drawing heated filaments over a knife edge and flattening them on one side, resulting in a randomly curly stretch yarn (the effect we get pulling giftwrap ribbon over a sharp edge) (see Figure 3.15). This method is used to make AGILON (by Milliken), and was important before the development of false-twist, since it gave a single-ply stretch yarn, needed where monofilament was to be used for sheer hosiery.

Textured Set. Textured set yarns are what we generally mean by *textured*. Yarn is first false-twist processed then steamed to remove the stretch and

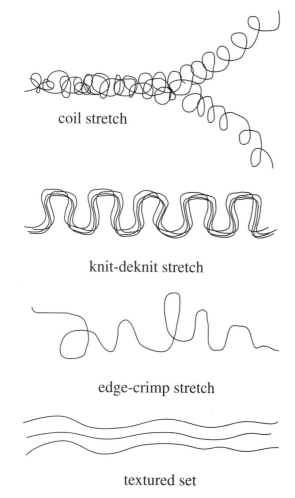

coil stretch

knit-deknit stretch

edge-crimp stretch

textured set

Figure 3.15 **Various filament stretch texturing methods (other than false-twist—see Figure 3.14).**

leave just a crimp (see Figure 3.15). A crepe yarn effect can also be given by these textured set yarns, although it usually has little of the drapability and liveliness of a true high-twist crepe yarn. Celara acetate (by Celanese) and Crimplene polyester (by ICI) were well-known trademark names in the doubleknit explosion of the 1970s. The general term *crimpknit* still refers to doubleknits made of textured set polyester yarns.

Crimp Texturing

Crimp yarns have some degree of stretch, plus some bulk. Filaments are given a wavy crimp by being fed into a heat setting *stuffer box* faster than they are led out so that they pile up in a wavy mass; Ban-Lon (by Bancroft) was a well-known trademark name of this type. Crimp is also put in by heated gear or tunnel methods.

Loop Texturing

Loop-textured or air-jet yarns are produced by feeding filaments over or past an air-jet faster than they are taken up by rollers. The blasts of air force some of the filaments into loops. Visible loops give a bouclé effect, texture, and bulk, but no stretch. This method can be used to give these characteristics to fibers such as rayon and glass (as well as to fibers such as nylon), since there is no heat setting involved. Trademark names are TASLAN® (by DuPont), CUPREL® (by Bemberg), and AEROCOR® (by Owens-Corning).

Spun-like Effect

Tiny loops, virtually invisible, give a spun-like effect to filament yarn; the process may also include random breaking of outer filaments. These yarns are now being made with microfibers to achieve a hand more like fine cotton or wool yarns. An earlier spun-like, Serell polyester (by DuPont) gave worsted-like fabric. Currently, SUPPLEX® nylon (by DuPont) has a cotton-like feel and is made of very fine fibers, in some cases microfibers (the trademark name TACTEL is used in Europe by DuPont de Nemours Int. SA). PONTELLA (by CEP) is an octalobal spun-like polyester. An older type of spun-like yarn was Lanese (by Celanese), a yarn used in curtains, in which a regular filament polyester core was wrapped with an air-bulked triacetate.

A different spinning and finishing process gives DIOLEN® SEDURA® (by Acordis, formerly Akzo Nobel), a flat yarn of bicomponent polyester microfiber that develops different shrinkage levels in finishing, giving bulk and a natural hand (see Figure 2.93[b]).

Novelty (Fancy or Complex-Ply)

Novelty (also called or fancy or complex-ply) yarns have a built-in irregularity; the plies differ in construction and/or are twisted together at different tensions or speeds.

The many types of novelty yarns are divided here into their main groups. Not all conform to the "classic" novelty yarn diagram and sample shown in Figure 3.16; these have three distinct components, but

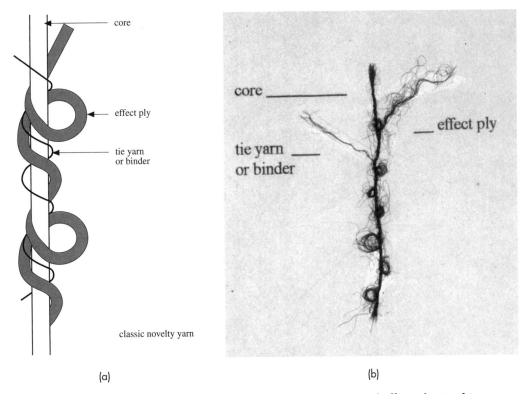

core

effect ply

tie yarn
or binder

classic novelty yarn

(a)

core _____

___ effect ply

tie yarn ___
or binder

(b)

Figure 3.16 (a) Classic novelty yarn, with core, tie yarn, and effect ply—in this case, forming a closed loop. (b) Sample of closed-loop novelty yarn, showing these classic three elements: core, tie yarn, and effect ply.

many will have one or two effect plies with a core or tie yarn, and some will be singles. In a classic novelty yarn, one ply forms a *core* or base. Another ply around it makes the *effect,* be it loop, nub, slub, or wrapping. Figure 3.16 shows a closed-loop type (bouclé). The effect ply is held to the core by a (usually fine) tie yarn or binder.

Main Types of Novelty Yarns

Loop Yarns. **Loop, curl, bouclé, bouclette,** and **gimp yarns** all have closed loops along the yarn, seen in Figure 3.16; gimp yarns give the small loops in ratiné fabric. **Spike** and **snarl yarns** have open loops. For more examples, see *Fabric Glossary:* LOOP YARN.

Nubby Yarns. **Nub, knop, knot, spot, nep,** and **bourette yarns** all have an effect ply twisted many times in the same place, or small tufts of fiber twisted into the core to give small lumps or thickenings in the yarn (see Figure 3.17). Tweed is a fabric in which

nubs, often of different colors, are characteristic (see *Fabric Glossary:* TWEED).

Slubby Yarns. **Slub yarns** are thick-thin, of irregular thickness, often with soft, untwisted places at intervals (see Figure 3.17). **Flake, flock,** and **seed yarns** are similar, with longish tufts of roving held by a tie yarn. Slubs are typical of linen fabric and of

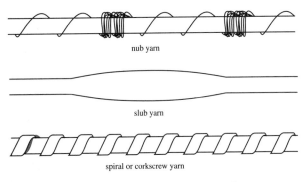

nub yarn

slub yarn

spiral or corkscrew yarn

Figure 3.17 Nub, slub, and spiral or corkscrew novelty yarns.

materials made of wild silk, such as shantung, pongee, honan, and tussah (see *Fabric Glossary*: LINEN; SATIN/SHANTUNG; SHANTUNG; TUSSAH).

Wrapped Yarns. **Spiral, corkscrew, covered,** and **wrapped yarns** have a core with wrapping around it (see Figure 3.17 and also Figure 2.72(a). In a decorative yarn, filament is usually wrapped around cotton (see *Fabric Glossary*: GIMP "BRAID"). For some purposes, as in display, the core may be a wire, so the yarn will hold the shape into which it is bent. Rubber yarns are always covered, usually with cotton yarns, and since the rubber core does not take dye, it can *grin through* when the yarn is stretched; spandex can be used unwrapped, but when it is the core in a wrapped yarn, it takes dye and does not grin (show) through.

Some novelty yarns do not conform at all to the classic construction discussed. Two of these follow.

Metallic Yarns. These are most often made of strips of foil, usually aluminum "sandwiched" between layers of film to prevent oxidation; coloring can be introduced in the film or the adhesive used for lamination. Yarns will differ in price, strength, and heat sensitivity according to whether the film is acetate or (better quality) polyester. Other metals used historically are either very expensive (gold) or tarnish badly (silver, copper). The fabric name connected with metallic yarn is *lamé* (see *Fabric Glossary*: LAMÉ).

Metallic yarn trademark names are LAMÉ (the same as the general fabric name referred to above), LUREX® (by BASF), and METLON. A letter *M* after the trademark name may indicate that the film covering is MYLAR® (by DuPont) polyester film.

A few metallic yarns are made with metallic particles incorporated in the filaments; this can give a fine, smooth yarn, more suitable for knitting.

Chenille Yarn. Chenille yarn is the "caterpillar" yarn, produced traditionally by a leno weaving process; see Figure 4.42 under *Types of Weaves* in Section 4. See also the photo and applications of chenille yarn in the *Fabric Glossary*: CHENILLE YARN.

There are also **mock chenille yarns,** made to give a fuzzy surface much more cheaply by various methods. A fairly soft, fluffy surface can be achieved by twisting together two spiral yarns in which the effect ply is soft and wound loosely around a finer core.

Thread

Thread, which holds fabric sections together in seams to create a garment or other textile article, is really a specialized yarn. It has to be strong so may be multiply or cord to give strength with pliability.

Thread strength will depend on how even the yarn is (few knots, slubs, or nubs) and its fiber content. Strength needed to sew will vary with the type of machine and speed; strength needed in use will vary with reaction to heat in sewing and pressing, perspiration, and chemicals met in cleaning. In general, it is better if thread tensile strength is less than that of the garment fabric, so that under strain, the seam will break before the fabric tears. As well as strength, colorfastness and shrinkage resistance of thread must be suitable for recommended fabric care methods. Flex resistance of thread is also very important to the life of a seam, with nylon and polyester having good flex abrasion resistance. Specialized garments need seams of like performance to the main fabric, e.g., water repellent or flame resistant.

Types of Thread

Cotton thread is the only natural-fiber thread in wide use; the other main types are synthetic, both spun and filament.

Cotton Thread

Cotton thread has the advantage of resisting high temperatures, either the heat generated in high-speed sewing or the heat of pressing garments. The best cotton thread is not only of cord construction but mercerized for added strength and luster. It is not really suitable for fabrics of high-strength synthetics, such as nylon and polyester, as the seam will then be of significantly lower strength and abrasion resistance than the fabric, and might shrink. Cotton thread is also more expensive than, for instance, spun polyester thread.

Cotton thread comes as *soft* (slightly fuzzy, with no finishes, and so less expensive) or in various finishes, of which *mercerized* has been mentioned. *Glacé* is polished (with a smooth wax, starch, or resin finish), and strong; it is used in making shoes and canvas goods. (The equivalent synthetic thread, filament or spun, is *bonded* to give a smooth, protective coating for heavy-duty sewing uses.)

Synthetic thread (nylon, polyester) is made in both **spun** and **filament.**

Spun Polyester

Spun polyester is now a standard for general sewing, giving good sewability, seam strength, stitch locking, and abrasion resistance. It adapts well to a wide variety of sewing machines, is least costly, and is not likely to cause seam puckering (as nylon is).

Filament Threads

Monofilament. Monofilament, also called *color-blending thread,* is usually made of nylon. This is a single filament, rather like a fine fishing line. Since it is translucent virtually no changing of thread is needed to match a complete range of fabric colors with just clear and dark monofilament thread. It is strong but stiff, unravels readily (from a chain-stitched hem, for instance), and may shrink in washing.

Multifilament. Regular multifilament gives a smooth yarn, stronger and with less bulk than spun, but with a tendency to slip. It is used in quilting and in lingerie sewing.

Bulked or Textured Filament. This has stretch and is used as serger thread, for hems, and in activewear. It is inexpensive and so is preferred for serging, which uses large amounts of thread.

Specialized Threads

Corespun is costly thread, but solves the problem of polyester fusing from excessive needle heating in high-power machine sewing by wrapping a polyester filament core with a (spun) cotton cover.

Elastic thread is usually a spiral-wrapped novelty yarn with a core of rubber or spandex.

Embroidery and buttonholes require specialized threads in home sewing, as in manufacturing.

Silk thread is rarely used by the home sewer but is still made, both filament and spun, for some high-grade custom work. It is strong, has a degree of give, takes good colors, and behaves well in sewing wool and silk fabrics.

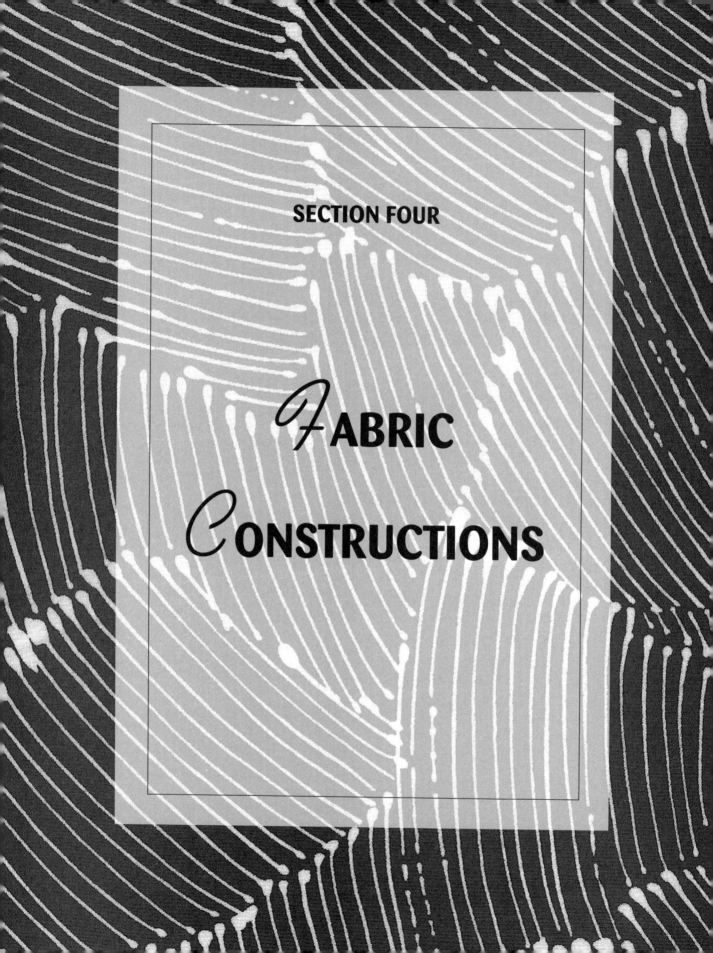

SECTION FOUR

𝓕ABRIC 𝒞ONSTRUCTIONS

Fabric was described in Section 1 as including products woven, knitted, braided, twisted, felted, and nonwoven, sheets of film or foam, even the "natural fabrics" leather and fur—all used today as textiles. This section will therefore discuss all these types of construction.

Fabric Right Side versus Wrong Side, Face versus Back

Many fabrics are *functionally reversible;* they have no built-in difference between face and back, though one side may be given a slight luster in finishing. These are often unprinted fabrics in plain weave and may have yarn-dyed checks or stripes; reversible compound weave fabrics are discussed in the *Fabric Glossary:* DOBBY—COMPOUND WOVEN, DOUBLE FACE.

Many fabrics do have a definite **face** (*usually* used as the **right** or upper side) as compared to the **back;** these concepts are discussed further in the *Fabric Glossary* under *Notes on Mounting Swatches.* There are some general rules for distinguishing the face of a fabric from the back; with fabrics, however, there may be an exception to any rule! Beyond these general guides, the face of many fabrics will be apparent when the particular characteristics of that fabric are known, as with the puffed surface of matelassé or the soft napped side of wool broadcloth.

General Guides to Fabric Right Side and Face

The right side will (usually):

- be more closely constructed (to take wear).
- be more lustrous (except antique satin [*Fabric Glossary:* SATIN/SHANTUNG]).
- show design (especially a print) brighter or more distinct.
- have more marked texture: twill line, ribs, cords, slubs, nubs, pattern with raised outline, puffed or blistered-looking surface, pile, nap (except fleece [*Fabric Glossary:* FLEECE KNIT]).
- have fewer imperfections; knots will be put to the back at the selvage (*Fabric Glossary:* SELVAGE).
- be folded to the inside as shipped from the manufacturer.

- have smaller tenter holes, rising in the shape of a volcano, usually on the face (*Fabric Glossary:* SELVAGE).

Particular Guides to Fabric Right Side and Face

Twill Line. Twill line with even twill weaves of the wool or silk family will be up to the right or *right hand* (*Fabric Glossary:* CHECK; MACKINAC; SERGE; SURAH; TARTAN); you must know the warp direction to apply this guide. Twill line with cotton family twills may be left or right (*Fabric Glossary:* CHINO; DENIM; DRILL). Warp face twills (such as gabardine [*Fabric Glossary:* GABARDINE]) have virtually no twill line showing on the back.

Stitch Side. In plain stitch (jersey) knit fabrics, the shank of the stitch is the technical face, though not always used as the right side (see *Fabric Glossary:* under Notes regarding Mounting Swatches). Similarly, the side of tricot knits that looks like jersey or plain (filling) knit is the technical face, though again not always used as the right side (see *Fabric Glossary:* TRICOT).

Weaving

Weaving has been used more widely than any other method of fabric construction and gives a tremendous range of fabric character; if you go through the *Fabric Glossary* and pick out just the simplest, plain weave fabrics, you will be amazed at the variety, to say nothing of all the more complex weaves.

Woven fabrics are formed by interlacing two or more sets of yarns at right angles to each other; these yarns lie parallel and perpendicular to the fabric edges. (This distinguishes a weave from a braid, in which the yarns are at right angles to each other but diagonal to the fabric edges.)

The yarns that lie parallel to the fabric edges—laid down first in the loom—are the *warp* yarns, also called *ends.* Yarns inserted in the crosswise direction are called *weft* or *filling,* also *picks* or (archaic, literary) *woof.*

The direction of the warp is called the *lengthwise grain;* the direction of the weft, the *crosswise grain* (see Figure 4.1). Most articles hang and wear better if cut so that the lengthwise grain is vertical; for this reason, it is also called *true grain.* Sometimes use is

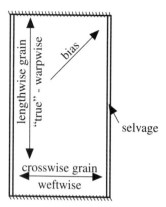

Figure 4.1 Grain (lengthwise, crosswise) and bias in woven fabric.

made of the "give" in the yarns when fabric is cut on the diagonal or *bias.* (See Figure 4.1.)

Types of Looms

Shuttle Looms

Shuttle looms (also called **fly shuttle**) are the standard, historical type; see the simplified diagram in Figure 4.2(a). With this type of loom, the weft yarn, wound on a *bobbin,* held in a metal-tipped *shuttle,* is hit across the loom by the action of a *picker stick,* through the *shed* or space created when a group of warp yarns (attached to one or more *harnesses*) is raised; thus the weft interlaces to form the weave. (The shed can also be clearly seen in Figures 4.3(c), 4.6, and 4.38—not all shuttle looms in these pictures.) The weft yarn (pick) is then *beaten up* (pressed into place) by the action of the *reed, batten, beater* or *sley (slay);* a different selection of harnesses is raised (*shedding*); and the shuttle travels back, carrying the weft yarn. The process is: shedding, picking, beating or battening, taking up (of finished fabric), along with the letting-off of more warp yarns. When yarn in the bobbin gives out, shuttle changing is automatic on modern power looms. The edge of the fabric just woven is termed the *fell.* The term *sley (reed)* is also used to mean the number of warp ends per inch; "high sley" then means many warp yarns per inch.

A **box loom** is a special shuttle loom that presents a shuttle of the correct color of yarn as required for a pattern with multicolor weft (vertical stripes are laid down in warping). A shuttle for each color needed in the weft is held at the side of the loom and is selected automatically as needed.

Dobby and *jacquard* are special loom attachments; see *Harness Control* and *Jacquard Control* for details.

Speed in weaving has been notated in picks per minute (ppm), i.e., insertions of weft per minute with the basic top speed of a shuttle loom at 200 ppm. With the varying widths of looms, a more uniform comparison of speed in weaving is meters per minute (m/min); basic top speed of a shuttle loom is 400 m/min. (There are no conversion figures given—weft insertion is quoted only in m/min and loom widths only in cm. When comparing widths with shuttleless looms, therefore, keep in mind that a loom 150 cm wide weaves the traditionally "wide" [60"] fabric; the widths capable on some models of the new looms are several times this.)

Shuttleless Looms

Shuttleless looms have increased the speed of weaving, are much quieter, and most take up less space on a weave-room floor. In all shuttleless looms, weft yarn is carried across from one side only (either premeasured and cut, or cut after insertion); this allows much larger yarn supplies than bobbins in a shuttle, and the shed can be shallower, putting less strain on warp yarns. See Figure 4.2(b) and (c), and Figure 4.4(a), as well as specialized shuttleless looms under *Jacquard Control of Complex Weaves* (Figure 4.27) and *Warp Pile Weaves, Slack Tension Warp Method* (Figure 4.39).

The following are the major types and speeds of shuttleless looms:[1]

> **Projectile,** in which a small gripper takes the cut yarn across the loom; these may work from one side or both (see Figure 4.3[a]). Speed is 430 ppm and up, and with wide looms (over 500 cm), weft insertion can be up to 1,400 m/min.
>
> **Rapier, rigid, or flexible** looms have two carriers mounted on flexible tapes with some guiding mechanism. The yarn is taken midway by one carrier and is picked up there by the other (see Figure 4.3[b]). Speed with a flexible rapier loom (see Figure 4.2[c]) is up to 700 ppm, with wide loom weft insertion of up to 1,500 m/min. Some models can be 500 cm wide.
>
> **Air-jet (pneumatic),** where a puff of compressed air carries yarn across (see Figure 4.3[c]).

[1]McAllister Isaacs III, "Loom Makers Get Ready For ITMA 99," includes Weaving Machines Chart, *Textile World,* May 1998: 86–109.

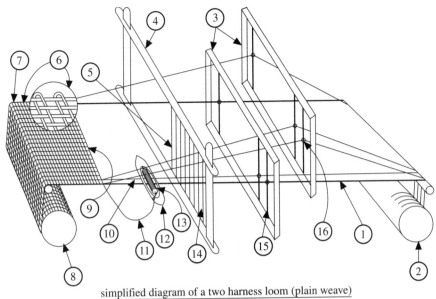

simplified diagram of a two harness loom (plain weave)

note: repeats of all parts not shown

1. warp yarn or end	7. woven cloth	12. shuttle
2. warp beam	8. cloth beam	13. bobbin, pirn or quill
3. harness	9. fell (edge of cloth as woven)	14. dent or split (space in reed)*
4. batten, beater or slay	10. shed (space for shuttle)	15. heddle, heald
5. reed	11. weft, filling yarn or pick	16. heddle eye
6. selvage, selvedge		

* If some warp yarns are left out, some dents will be empty, and a **latticed or ladder-like openwork strip** will result, called *skip-dent or à jour* (Fr. = "to the day{light}").

(a)

(b)

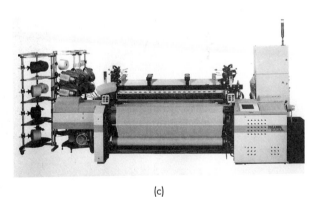

(c)

Figure 4.2 (a) Simplified diagram of important parts of a two-harness shuttle loom. (b) Modern automatic shuttleless looms in a weave room. (Courtesy of MASTERS OF LINEN/USA) (c) Flexible rapier weaving machine with eight-color capacity. As with all shuttleless looms, yarn is fed from one side only. (Courtesy of Picanol N.V.)

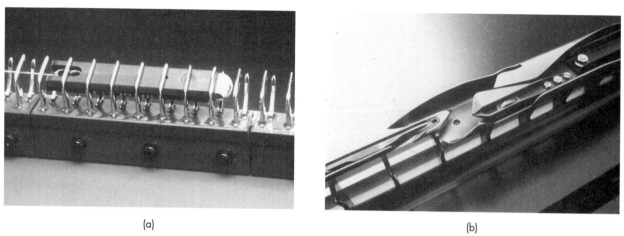

(a)   (b)

(c)

Figure 4.3 (a) Gripper carrying the weft yarn. (Courtesy of Sulzer Canada Inc.) (b) Two arms of rapier exchange weft yarn in the shed. (Courtesy of Sulzer Canada Inc.) (c) Weft yarn leaves the nozzle on an air-jet loom. (Courtesy of American Textile Manufacturers Institute, Inc.)

The width of such looms is limited, and stretch yarns are not laid in evenly. However, these looms are suited to spun yarns and can run at speeds up to 1,200 ppm, with a weft insertion of 2,200 m/min or more, and widths of up to 400 cm. An experimental upright, double-sided air-jet system has been demonstrated inserting 4,000 m/min and could reach 5,000 m/min.

Water-jet, in which a jet of water under pressure carries the weft across. This is obviously not suited to yarns of absorbent fibers, but reaches very high speeds when used with hydrophobic synthetics; speeds of 1,000 ppm or wide loom (up to

300 cm) weft insertion of 1,900 m/min are attained.

Multiphase, in which several picks are inserted in separate sheds at the same time, a departure worked on most of the last half of the 20th century.[2] Most work done from the late 1970s has been on the *wave-shed* principle of opening a number of sheds in the weft direction to insert multiple picks at once, beaten up as the weft went

[2]Alois Steiner and Dr. Ing Werner Weissenberger, "Multiphase Weaving—Historic Review and Outlook," OTEMAS, Osaka, Japan, October 1997.

(a)

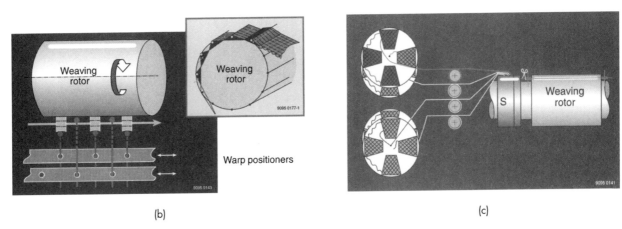

(b)   (c)

Figure 4.4 (a) Multiphase loom can insert nearly 3,000 ppm. (b) Warp positioners determine which yarns will be raised. (c) Weft yarn controller S, with its two disks, is located concentrically to the weaving rotor. It moves the yarns using compressed air to line them up with the insertion channels. (Courtesy of Sulzer Rüti AG.)

in. This type of machine has never succeeded much past testing stages, and mainly because a broken or badly tensioned pick (a *mispick*) is almost impossible to remove.

Another approach is the *multilinear or sequential-shed* action, with multiple wefts inserted through sheds formed in the warp direction. Many versions of this have been tried without showing an increase in speed over air-jet machines, until the Sulzer Rüti M8300 shown in Figure 4.4 (a), which has reached a speed of 2,850 ppm or 5,400 m/min, and

is expected to double that performance eventually. To achieve this, a different mechanism of weft insertion was developed, with four picks inserted at once.[3]

The warp is led over a continuously rotating drum—the weaving rotor (Figure 4.4[b]). Combs on the rotor form the sheds as well as guide channels for the weft. Four sheds are formed in the warp direction, one behind the other and in parallel, right across the loom, and into these the weft yarns are inserted

[3]Alois Steiner, "Breakthrough to the Next Magnitude?" *Sulzer Techical Review*, April 1995: 24–27.

simultaneously. Each time a comb goes into the warp plane, the warp yarn positioners determine which yarns are to be raised. Since these positioners are very light and move only a few millimeters, they can work at very high speeds. When the shed is formed all the way across, low-pressure compressed air carries the weft through the channel, and further weft yarns start to enter the combs that follow. As soon as the weft is right across, it is clamped and cut on the feed side.

The end of the weft yarn is led to the next free insertion position by the weft yarn controller "S" (see Figure 4.4[c]), made up of two disks each with a multichannel system arranged concentrically to the weaving rotor. Yarns in the controller are moved over a measuring drum by compressed air, so they line up exactly with the shed-forming combs and hence with insertion channels.

Selvage

The finished warpwise edges of a piece of woven fabric are called *selvages* or variations of this spelling, e.g., *selvedges* (literally, "self-edges"). In a shuttle loom, selvages are formed as the shuttle carries the weft yarn back and forth; in a shuttleless loom, various types of edges may be formed (see Figure 4.5):

Tucked-in—cut weft is tucked into the weave at the edges.

Fused by heat, when there are thermoplastic fibers in the fabric.

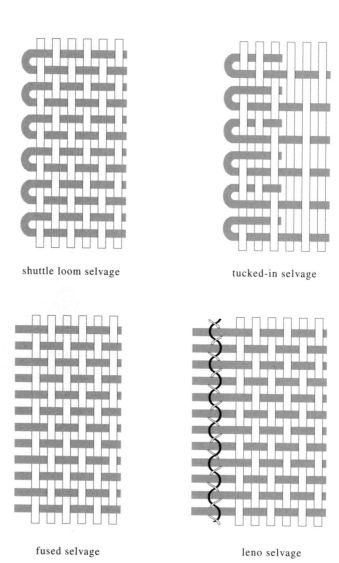

shuttle loom selvage   tucked-in selvage

Figure 4.5 Selvages formed on a shuttle loom and three types on shuttleless looms.

fused selvage   leno selvage

Leno weave at the selvage.
(*See Fabric Glossary:* SELVAGE.)

Warp versus Weft in a Weave

Before weaving can begin, there is a lengthy process of preparation of warp yarns and the "warping up" of the loom—the winding on of the hundreds or thousands of warp yarns, each held in precisely its correct place and under tension, with microprocessors greatly aiding in this operation. But then these yarns are selected and threaded through *heddle eyes* on a harness loom (Figure 4.6[a] shows two of four harnesses raised to create the shed). This threading is done by hand, and is termed *reaching in* or *drawing in* (see Figure 4.6[b]), after which yarns are passed through the dents in the reed. This means that, although electronic controls are used extensively in weaving (see Figure 4.7), as well as computer-assisted design (CAD) systems, there cannot be the "quick response" getting out a patterned woven fabric to meet a sudden or fleeting demand of fashion that there can be with some types of knits or prints.

Warp yarns are *sized* or stiffened with some sort of adhesive and a lubricant to prepare them for the weaving process. The adhesive has traditionally been a starch or gum, but today many other compounds are used, preferably those that can be removed before finishing with a simple wash. A sheet of warp yarns is led through the sizing bath, then dried. At this stage, the yarns are stuck together, and before they are wound on the warp beam, they are separated by splitting with what are called *slasher rods;* this is probably the origin of the odd name given the process: *slashing.*

Warp yarns are held under considerable tension in weaving (to prevent ripples and puckers). To withstand this strain, warps are selected to be stronger; if only one set of yarns is ply, or the weave is the *basket* variation of plain (more than one finer yarn taken as one), that will be the warp, for strength.

Balance in a weave means that the two sets of yarns (warp and weft) are much the same in type, size, and number. However, even in a fairly well-balanced plain weave or *square* construction, warp yarns are usually somewhat finer, higher twist, and set in more closely than weft, all for strength.

Since warp yarns are held taut, while weft yarns are not, the weft has more *weave crimp:* It looks wavier and there is a slight stretch or "give" in the weft direction.

(a)

(b)

Figure 4.6 (a) Close-up of two of four harnesses on a simple loom, as they form the shed through which the weft can be inserted. (Courtesy of the Woolmark Company, formerly IWS) (b) "Reaching in" to thread silk through heddle eyes.

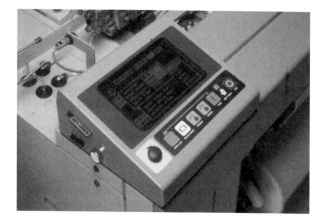

Figure 4.7 Controls on a modern automatic loom. (Courtesy of Sulzer Canada Inc.)

If one set of yarns is simple and one is novelty (fancy), the simple yarns will usually be the warp (but not invariably!).

Many finishing procedures give a *one-way lie* to yarns or fibers, and this will be in the warp direction.

The only absolutely sure guide to warp is the selvage, being parallel to the warp. However, many fabrics have a guide to warp direction in their "profile" of characteristics, such as the puckers of seersucker, the crossed warp yarns (leno) of marquisette, or the warp float of a filament-yarn satin weave. If the face of a twill weave fabric is known, the direction of the twill line in wool and silk family fabrics is right hand; this will indicate the warp.

Thread or Cloth Count

A *thread* or *pick counter* (also called a loop glass or linen tester) is a small magnifier with an opening of a square centimeter or square inch, marked in millimeters or fractions of an inch. With it, the fabric construction can be examined, but it is also used to count warp and weft yarns, to indicate *thread* or *cloth count* or closeness of weave (Figure 1.4).

The figure is recorded as the number of warp by (×) the number of weft, and the thread count is the *sum,* or the number of yarns altogether in the square.

At point of sale (POS) of consumer goods, thread count has most often been stated on a label for the fairly well-balanced plain weave of **sheeting**. Since this notation is not familiar to consumers in metric units, the following examples are given in the inch system:

	# warp × # weft = thread count
percale sheeting	92 × 88 (/in.) = 180
cotton broadcloth	122 × 58 (/in.) = 180

This example shows that thread count, of itself, does not give information on whether a weave is *balanced;* cotton broadcloth (see *Fabric Glossary:* BROADCLOTH [COTTON]) has at least twice as many warp yarns as weft yarns, giving the fine crosswise rib and firm hand of this dress shirt fabric (see additional note below), whereas sheeting, also a plain weave, is quite well balanced; as stated earlier, there will usually be a few more warp yarns than weft yarns.

For sheeting, then, thread count is a very useful comparison figure in relation to fineness of yarn and closeness of weave; the typical range has been:

Thread Count	Quality	Fabric Name
118	Quite open and "sleazy."	Called *muslin* (see *Fabric*
128	Medium weight, "Family" weight	*Glossary:* SHEETING,
140	close weave, sturdy	APPAREL)
180–350	Fine, smooth yarns, close weave, lighter weight	Called *percale* (see *Fabric Glossary:*
-600	Luxury sheets & very closely woven covers for down-filled duvets	SHEETING, HOUSE-HOLD)

Even though thread count in cotton broadcloth does not give as direct a reading of closeness of weave as that for sheeting, identification of the best quality in a dress shirt will often include thread count as part of the indication of quality (close weave and fine yarns); custom-made men's shirts could be described as made of long-staple cotton fibers (Pima or Egyptian), 100s 2-ply yarns, with thread count from 150 (good quality shirt) to 230 (superb).

Point Diagrams, Notation of Weaves

The way yarns interlace in a weave is often represented by a *point diagram* on graph paper, with each square representing the position of a yarn in the weave; three point diagrams are shown in Figure 4.8.

If a warp yarn has been raised when the weft yarn is passed through the shed, that yarn will lie on the surface of the fabric; its square is filled in (dark-

plain weave

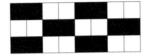

plain - 2x1 basket

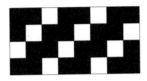

2/1 right-hand twill

Figure 4.8 Point diagrams of plain weave, plain 2 × 1 basket weave, and 2/1 right-hand twill.

ened) on the graph paper. When the weft yarn is on the surface, the square is not filled in.

A weave is described as "X up, Y down" (written X/Y), indicating how many warp yarns were raised at each passage of the weft and how many not, in groups across the loom—equivalent to how many harnesses were raised or not. The sum of this figure, then, is the number of harnesses, each one threaded differently, needed for that weave; this is also called the *shaft.*

A plain weave, the most commonly used, requires only two harnesses. They are raised alternately at each passage of the weft, so a plain weave is always a 1/1 weave. In two of the point diagrams shown under *Twill Weave* (Figures 4.12 and 4.13), the 3/1 twill weave is read "three up, one down" and the 2/2 is read "two up, two down," both requiring four harnesses. The 4/1 satin weave (in Figure 4.19 under *Satin Weave*) takes five harnesses and is described as a *5-shaft satin.*

Another convention of a point diagram is that it needs to be filled in only until there is a repeat of pattern so it will show the number of rows, each one dif-

ferent, needed to complete the pattern and one row of repeat; this is equal to the shaft plus one. For example, diagrams for two versions of plain weave are shown in Figure 4.8, both requiring only two harnesses to weave, so the "checkerboard" diagrams are only three rows deep. The 2/1 twill takes three harnesses to weave, and the diagram is four rows deep.

To understand why a twill direction is called *right* or *left hand,* begin (or "read") a point diagram from the *lowest* line, as if you were weaving a fabric; at each succeeding weft insertion, the interlacing moves over one in a simple twill. If this is to the right, the line will run "up to the right" and will be a *right-hand twill;* if to the left, the line will run "up to the left" and will be a *left-hand twill.*

Types of Weaves

Plain Weave

Plain weave, also called *taffeta* or *tabby weave,* is the simplest and most commonly used, representing over 70 percent of all woven fabrics worldwide.[4] The weft passes over and under alternating warp yarns across the cloth; in the next pick, the weft yarns go under and over alternating warp, then these two rows are repeated. This gives the maximum number of interlacings (crossings of warp and weft) you can have in a weave, so a plain weave can give great strength in a fabric such as tarpaulin. Note, however, that the twill and especially satin weaves allow more yarns to be packed into a given area since there are fewer interlacings with these. Plain weave tends to wrinkle, and shows soil more easily, although it is also more easily cleaned.

Plain weave requires only two harnesses, one with every even-numbered warp threaded through the heddle eyes, the other with every odd-numbered warp (see point diagrams in Figure 4.8). Although the interlacing in a plain weave is simple, the resulting fabric need by no means be plain! There are more distinctive "name" fabrics in plain weave than in any other construction. Any of these names that appear as a File page heading in the *Fabric Glossary* will be given in CAPITALS in the following discussion of plain weave variation; they can be found alphabetically in the *Fabric Glossary* File pages or through its Index.

[4]Adrian Wilson, "Italian Textile Machinery: Cautiously Confident and Ultimately Flexible," *Textile Month,* October 1998:18.

Balanced Plain Weaves. Balance was discussed under *Warp versus Weft*, and *Thread or Cloth Count*; there are many examples of balanced plain weaves besides those already mentioned: BATISTE; CANVAS; CHALLIS; GEORGETTE; GINGHAM; MADRAS; ORGANDY; ORGANZA; SEERSUCKER; TROPICAL WORSTED; VOILE; and more.

Unbalanced Plain Weaves. These occur when the number, size, or type of one set of yarns is different from the other.

Plain weave **rib** fabrics may show allover or occasional ribs. In those with allover ribs, the ribs run crosswise; this is a result of weaving with more (and usually finer) warp than weft. If such a ribbed fabric is closely woven (and most are), it will have firmness and good body. Besides the interesting texture of the rib, the closely packed warp yarns give good cover and often a pleasing sheen, while the fact that the weft is not packed so closely together makes for better hand and drape in the fabric, compared to a similar weight woven in a balanced plain weave.

The finest rib occurs when warp and weft are *similar in type and almost the same size;* the rib is formed when there are at least *twice as many warp as weft,* as in BROADCLOTH (COTTON); see discussion under *Thread and Cloth Count.* There is a similar fine rib in the silk family with TAFFETA.

Coarser, more visible, or prominent crosswise ribs develop when there are *more warp yarns than weft and the weft are definitely thicker* (see Figure 4.9), as with POPLIN in the cotton family. (Note that in the United Kingdom, the name *poplin* is used for fabrics as fine as cotton broadcloth [men's dress shirt fabric], as well as the sturdier type for

which the name *poplin* is usually reserved in North America.)

A large group of these crosswise rib fabrics is discussed in the *Fabric Glossary* under RIB WOVEN, ALLOVER, PROMINENT, in which the warp at least is **filament** yarn, completely covering over the weft, to give a "silky" face. They are faille, poult de soie (or just "poult"), bengaline, grosgrain, gros de Londres, (de Paris, etc.), and givrene. (Moiré is usually based on one of these fabrics, or on the finer rib taffeta; each of MOIRÉ and TAFFETA is discussed on a separate *Fabric Glossary* File page.) Any of these rib fabrics can show wear of the fine warp, or develop yarn or seam slippage (discussed under *Tender, Loving [Home] Care* in Section 6; see also the discussions of seam slippage under *Nontechnical Fabric Tests* in Section 8).

Two other fabrics with prominent crosswise ribs do not always have filament warp, but may be made of various fibers, including silk or MF filament, wool, cotton, flax, MF staple and therefore of filament or spun warp and weft. Ottoman (under RIB WOVEN, OCCASIONAL in the *Fabric Glossary*) has some heavy ribs (which may be bundles of yarns), while repp is in the RIB WOVEN, ALLOVER File.

Only a very few plain weave fabrics have a lengthwise rib, and then only **occasional** (under RIB WOVEN, OCCASIONAL). The best known is dimity, which always has an occasional lengthwise rib but may have the rib running both ways (crossbar dimity). A fabric with occasional ribs both ways, framing yarn-dyed checks, is called tissue gingham.

Note: Lengthwise *cords* are more complex weaves (see *Fabric Glossary*: DOBBY—COMPOUND WEAVE, SINGLE FACE).

Basket weave is an unbalanced variation of plain weave, having two or more yarns carried as one in the weft and/or warp direction. This gives more porosity (comfort) and wrinkle resistance to a plain weave fabric.

The weave is described according to the number of yarns carried together in the warp by the number in the weft, and is written "*X × Y.*" A 2 × 1 basket weave (two by one) such as OXFORD CLOTH shirting has double fine warp yarns while the weft is single, of softer twist and as thick as the two warp together. Other well-known basket weave fabrics are HOPSACKING and monk's cloth. Some CANVAS and CHINTZ (cretonne) may be basket weave, although these fabrics are often a balanced weave.

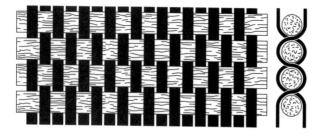

Figure 4.9 A prominent crosswise rib forms in a plain weave when weft yarns are much heavier than warp yarns.

Other Plain Weave Variations. Plain weave variations can be obtained by using yarns of different fibers, tensions (SEERSUCKER), degrees of twist (CREPE DE CHINE), or color (GINGHAM, MADRAS); or by using novelty yarns (LINEN; LOOP YARN bouclé; SHANTUNG). Shagbark fabric has occasional loops of warp yarn for surface texture—see Figure 4.10.

Many other variations may be achieved by means of finishing: applied design such as a print (CALICO), embroidery (EYELET), a glaze (CHINTZ), nap (FLANNELETTE, and FLANNEL [can also be twill]), or a finish such as PLISSÉ, which gives a three-dimensional effect.

Twill Weave

In a **twill weave,** a weft yarn may pass or *float* over two or more warp yarns, and interlacing progresses by one yarn to the right or left in succeeding rows, giving a diagonal line called a *wale;* this is a *progression* of one—also called *interval, step, shift, offset*—and is used with most twill weaves except broken twills, which are often found in fancy suitings (see Figure 4.11).

The simplest twill requires three harnesses on a loom (e.g., 2/1—see the point diagram in Figure 4.8). This is described as an **uneven twill,** as more of one set of yarns is on the face; a 2/1 is a **warp-face twill** (gabardine is usually made in this weave—see *Fabric*

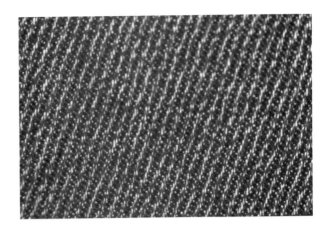

Figure 4.11 Broken twill fancy suiting.

Glossary: GABARDINE). Since warp yarns are stronger than weft, a warp-face twill will give better wear than an even twill (if fiber and yarn are equivalent). A 1/2 would be a **weft-face twill.**

A 3/1 left-hand twill (see Figure 4.12) has an even higher proportion of warp on the face than a 2/1, and so is even tougher; it occurs in the workwear fabric drill and in some denim (see *Fabric Glossary:* DRILL; DENIM).

An **even twill** has weft yarns passing over and under the same number of warp yarns each time, e.g., a 2/2 twill (see Figure 4.13); the diagonal wale is as noticeable on the back as on the face. This is the weave of many wool family fabrics, serge suiting, authentic glen checks, tartan, and mackinac (see *Fabric Glossary:* CHECK; MACKINAC; SERGE; TARTAN). When a *plaid* is woven in an *even* twill, such as a glen check or authentic tartan, lines match lengthwise and crosswise, producing a neat effect in garment construction; see Figure 4.14.

Figure 4.10 Shagbark has occasional loops of warp yarns, giving surface texture to a plain-weave fabric.

Figure 4.12 A 3/1 left-hand twill (uneven, warp-face).

Figure 4.13   A 2/2 right-hand twill (even).

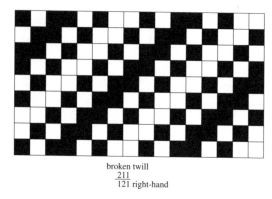

broken twill
$\frac{211}{121}$ right-hand

Figure 4.15   Broken or irregular twill weave.

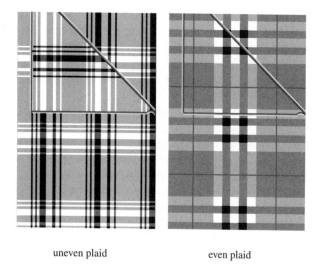

uneven plaid

even plaid

Figure 4.14   Matching is easier with an even plaid than with an uneven.

Figure 4.16   Herringbone—a reversing twill weave.

Broken or irregular twills have an irregular interlacing along each row (see Figure 4.15) and may also change direction to give such reversing patterns as herringbone (see Figure 4.16 and *Fabric Glossary:* HERRINGBONE).

Advantages of twill weave are a good balance between strength and wrinkle resistance (pliability) compared to plain weave, plus soil resistance, important for clothing that has to be worn day in and day out, such as suitings and workwear.

Twill weaves have fewer interlacings than plain, so more yarns can be packed in for strength and durability, especially in a steep twill. The closely packed yarns make fabric well suited to outerwear for cold or rainy weather (see *Fabric Glossary:* GABARDINE; the name for this typical trenchcoat fabric derives from "protection from the elements"). Twill weaves are, of course, more expensive to make than plain.

Twill Direction. This was discussed under *Point Diagrams, Notation of Weaves*; right-hand (RH) twill has the twill line up to the right from lower left to upper right), left-hand (LH) up to the left. Twills originally made of wool or silk are RH; today, of course, these may be of rayon, polyester, or any MF fiber, but the twill direction on the face is still RH. In addition to those already mentioned as examples of warp-face or even RH twills, there is foulard or SURAH, the only silk family twills (see *Fabric Glossary:* SURAH); in the wool family: barathea; CAVALRY TWILL; FLANNEL and TWEED (if twill weave, not plain); and WHIP-

CORD (see *Fabric Glossary* for Files of those names in capitals, or the index for others). If made in twill weave, wool fabrics for coats will be RH; see DUVETYN; FLEECE; and MELTON Files in the *Fabric Glossary*. Cotton family twills are traditionally LH, but this does vary. You will find much denim, for instance, with an RH twill line, although most North American denim is woven with an LH twill (see *Fabric Glossary*: CHINO; DENIM; DRILL).

Angle of Twill. This is classified as regular (45°), steep (63°), or (rare) reclining (23°); see Figure 4.17. If yarn type and twill interlacing are the same in two fabrics, when there are more warp yarns, the twill becomes steeper. Since warp is stronger than weft, a steeper twill will be more durable (see, for instance, in the *Fabric Glossary*: CAVALRY TWILL; WHIP-CORD). Figure 4.18 shows two gabardines, of which the one showing the steeper twill is of better quality and stronger. This is one case in which a very practical application can be made of a rather academic guide, without dissecting the fabric. A buyer finding two twill fabrics with a difference in angle of the twill line could choose the one with the steeper twill as the more durable, as long as the materials are quite similar in fiber content and weight.

Satin Weave

Satin weave is a highly unbalanced twill intended to produce a surface without apparent pattern, with interlacings as far apart as possible, and no two ever adjacent. One set of yarns passes in long floats (four or more) over the other set, then interlaces with a sin-

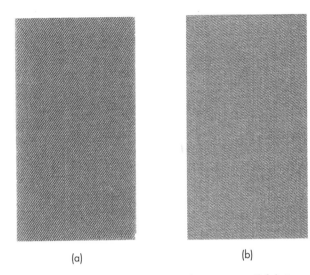

(a)   (b)

Figure 4.18 Two gabardines; the steep twill fabric on the left has more warp yarns and will wear better than the regular-angle twill sample on the right.

gle yarn; the number of harnesses used (the shaft) is always the number of the float plus one.

Only certain intervals or progressions will make a satin weave; these are numbers that add to the shaft number (reciprocals) but not including 1 (which would give a twill) nor any with a common divisor or that divide into the shaft number. Satin floats range from 4 to 12 or more, and so satin weaves are 5 shaft or more; the progression for a 5-shaft satin could be 2 or 3. Traditional peau de soie was 8 shaft (7/1, float of 7) but is now usually 5 shaft (4/1) (see *Fabric Glossary*: SATIN).

The original satin weave fabric, developed in China using cultivated silk (filament), had warp floats; any filament yarn satin weave, of silk or MF fiber, still has warp floats (smoother lengthwise) and so is a warp-face satin weave (see Figure 4.19 and *Fabric Glossary*: SATIN). This weave shows the maximum

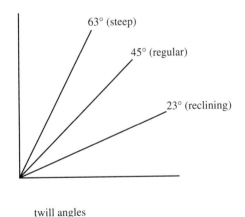

twill angles

Figure 4.17 Twill angles—steep, regular, or reclining—can reveal probable fabric durability.

4/1 satin weave (warp face)

Figure 4.19 A 4/1 satin weave (warp-face).

luster from smooth filament yarns, represented until about 1900 by silk. When cotton (spun yarn) is woven in a satin weave, it is usually a 1/4 weft-face version. This fabric will use fairly low-twist weft yarns floating across the fabric, and is called sateen (see Figure 4.20 and *Fabric Glossary:* SATEEN). When cotton is woven in a warp-face satin weave, yarn twist is usually higher to give a stronger fabric, which is called cotton satin or farmer's satin (see *Fabric Glossary:* SATIN). In a satin weave, most of one set of yarns is on the face of the fabric; if the other set of yarns is quite different in character, there will be a different look and feel to the other side (see *Fabric Glossary:* SATIN, BRUSHED-BACK; SATIN/CREPE; SATIN/SHANTUNG; another fabric is antique satin).

Satin weave has the fewest interlacings of the three "basic weaves," and so yarns can be tightly packed in to make a heavy fabric with good drapability, wrinkle resistance, and resistance to wind and rain. Even though satin can be woven to be rain resistant, it is not often used for raincoats because of the possibility of the long floats snagging and roughing up in hard (abrasive) wear. Satin is often used for linings because of its smoothness and drapability (see Figure 4.21[b]). On the other hand, satin that is not closely woven will feel cheap and sleazy (see Figure 4.21[a]). Satins will ravel easily and are more expensive to make than twill or plain weaves (other factors being equal).

See Table 4.1 for a comparison of plain, twill, and satin weaves.

Harness Control of Complex Weaves (Dobby)

Raising of harnesses for plain, twill, and satin weaves can be activated and the order controlled by means of *cams,* but a different direct control is needed for more

Figure 4.21(a) Close, heavy satin vs. sleazy, light-weight satin.

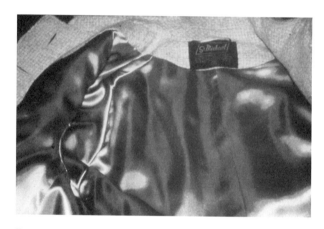

Figure 4.21(b) Satin is much used in linings for jackets and coats.

complex interlacing. The *dobby* (or *dobbie*) attachment on a loom can control the action of multiple harnesses (maximum 32, usually fewer) (see Figure 4.22[a]). A *pattern chain* (or *draft chain*) traditionally selected which harnesses were raised. This older chain worked with a continuous loop of strips with holes in them, into which projections on a cylinder fit, to raise a particular harness. Today a perforated paper strip or electronic tape can be used. Figure 4.22(b) shows a perforated strip controlling the action of a number of harnesses.

The dobby attachment allows a pattern with a repeat not greater than 32 rows of weft, and produces relatively small designs, usually geometric in shape (hard-edged, not curving) (see Figure 4.23[a] and [b]).

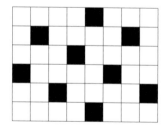

1/4 satin weave (weft face)

Figure 4.20 A 1/4 satin weave (weft-face).

Table 4.1 Weave Effects: Comparison of Plain vs. Twill vs. Satin*

Feature	Plain Weave	Twill Weave	Satin Weave
Right or wrong side (face or back)	None (unless printed)	Yes; twill direction changes from face to back	Yes; floats are on the face
Weave as base for finishing processes	Good background for applied designs, including prints	Seldom printed, except light, silky twills, since weave itself gives texture	Design usually achieved by changing float direction; sateen often printed
Strength, thread count possible	Highest strength; maximum number of interlacings of warp and weft, but cannot pack the most yarns in	Next highest; fewer interlacings allows higher thread count, yet float and interlacing well balanced	Lowest; minimum interlacings, so can have high thread count; if so constructed, get strength, body, wind and water resistance
Raveling, snagging	Ravels and snags least readily	Slightly more than plain	Most easily raveled, snags most from long floats
Wrinkle resistance, drapability	Least wrinkle resistant	Fewer interlacings give more wrinkle resistance, pliability	Most wrinkle resistance, drapability, pliability
Soiling, ease of cleaning	Most easily soiled and cleaned (most porous); soil shows on plain surface	Resists soiling, but harder to get dirt out; may become shiny with wear; soil shows less on uneven surfaces	Does not soil readily, but soil shows up against luster of threads
Comfort	Most porous; good for hot weather, especially basket version of plain	Closer-packed yarns better for cool weather	Can pack yarns very closely to give wind or water resistance
Basic appearance and variations	Often balanced; much same size and type of yarn for warp and weft, can be unbalanced (basket, rib). Interesting effects created by changing kind, color of yarns	Diagonal twill lines, varying in prominance, direction, or steepness; steeper twill = more warp yarns, therefore is stronger	Luster from long floats on face; satin = warp floats + filament yarn; sateen = weft floats + spun (cotton) yarn. Luster of satin looks best in soft (evening) light
Weight range made	Sheer to very heavy	Sheer fabrics seldom made	Light or medium as a rule; can be made with great body
Relative cost to manufacture	Least expensive (2 harnesses used)	More expensive (3 or more harnesses used)	Most expensive (5 or more harnesses used)

*Comparisons such as those in this table assume fabrics of roughly equal yarn type, fiber content, and weight (linear density).

Typical fabrics with a dobby design include armure, birdseye, honeycomb, huckaback, madras shirting, waffle cloth; these are discussed and most are illustrated in *Fabric Glossary*: DOBBY—DESIGN.

Dobby control of a fairly complex repeat of tiny floats in a weave is one way to produce the pebbly surface of crepe (see *Fabric Glossary*: CREPE WEAVE). It can also prevent yarn slippage in latticed effects that look like leno (at less expense, called *mock leno,* or a mesh-like cloth; see Figure 4.24); with yarns closer, it gives a basket-like weave (called *natté;* see Figure 4.25). See also the *Fabric Glossary*: DOBBY—OPENWORK EFFECTS.

The dobby loom is used to control most compound weaves, those using more than two sets of yarns and up to five in true double cloth (two sets each of warp and weft to weave the two sides, with a third set of warps weaving the two together) (see *Fabric Glossary*: DOBBY—COMPOUND WEAVE, DOUBLE FACE [reversible compound fabrics] and

(a)

(b)

Figure 4.22 (a) Dobby attachment on a loom allows weaves more complex than plain, twill, or satin. (b) A perforated paper strip controls multiple harnesses with this dobby attachment. (Courtesy of Dominion Textile Inc.)

DOBBY—COMPOUND WEAVE, SINGLE FACE [such as bedford cord and piqués of various types]). Of course, some compound fabrics with a more intricate design woven in have to be jacquard controlled, rather than dobby. *Stuffer yarns* may be incorporated in some of these corded fabrics; these do not interlace, but lie under the cords to raise them and add firmness. Diagrams of such weaves typically show a

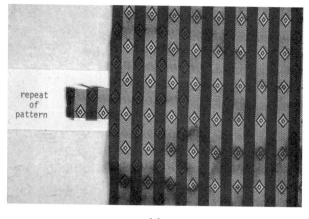

(a)

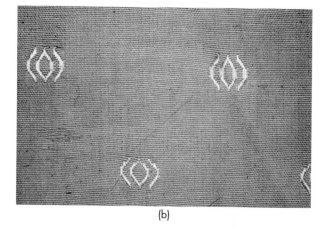

(b)

Figure 4.23 Typical dobby weave pattern repeat: small, geometric motif (a) in a lining fabric, (b) in sturdy pocket fabric.

cut edge, to render the depth of structure, as with a warp piqué (see Figure 4.26).

Jacquard Control of Complex Weaves

A *jacquard* attachment on a loom makes it possible to produce any design, however intricate, since *each warp yarn can be controlled separately for each pick* (insertion of weft). A very much simplified drawing of a common earlier version of the apparatus is shown in Figure 4.28, with views of the loom setup in Figures 4.27, 4.29, and 4.30.

The heddle (or *leish,* if it is a cord with an *eye*) governing each warp yarn is weighted with a *lingo.* The heddle is connected to another cord (see Figure 4.29[b]) that passes up through a *comber board* and is joined to the *neck cord.* This connects with a hook that can be moved if it is in the right position to be

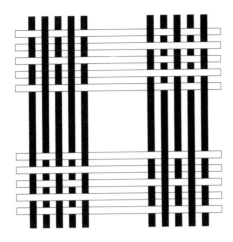

mock leno (dobby)

Figure 4.24 Dobby control can produce openwork effects where yarns do not slip or shift, and at less expense than with leno weave, hence the term *mock leno*.

Figure 4.25 A basket weave effect (natté) can be given with dobby weave, but is much more complicated than basket plain weave.

Figure 4.27 Jacquard loom. (Courtesy of Sulzer Canada Inc.)

caught by a *lifting knife* on the *griffe bar* as the bar goes up and down.

Each hook (and therefore the cord controlling a warp yarn) is linked at the top of the loom to a crosswise-placed, spring-loaded wire. Manipulation of warps is governed by cards that allow for a hole to be punched (or not) for each warp, with a row for each pick in the repeat of pattern. The cards—there can be thousands of them for a large design—are laced together and pass over the top of the loom during weaving (see Figure 4.30). They pass over a perforated cylinder, with a *needle board* in front, against which the spring-loaded wires push. If a wire encounters a hole in a card, it goes through and by this action puts the hook in a position to connect with the lifting knife on the griffe bar, and *the warp yarn is raised;* if there is no hole, the warp is not raised. As noted, this is a very much simplified presentation of the action, and many jacquard looms are considerably more complex,

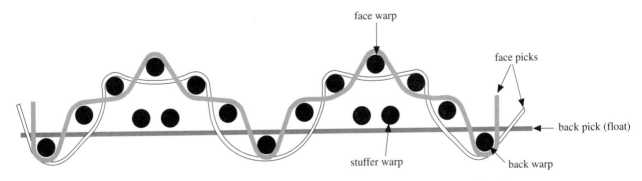

face warp

face picks

back pick (float)

stuffer warp

back warp

Figure 4.26 Structure of a warp piqué, viewed from a weftwise cut edge. The stuffer warp yarns do not interlace but pad the cord and add firmness.

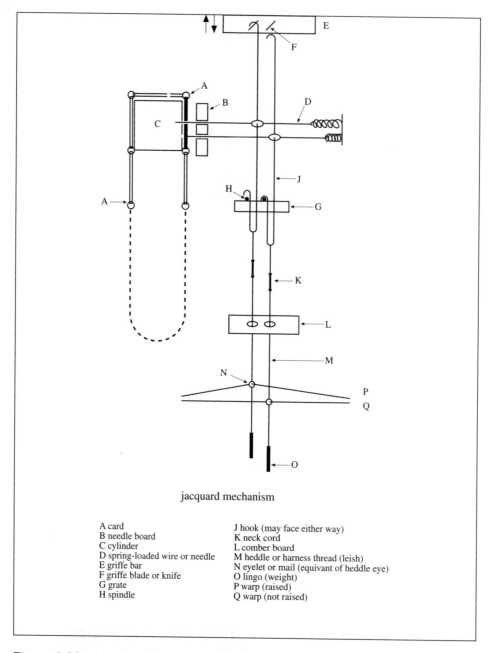

jacquard mechanism

A card
B needle board
C cylinder
D spring-loaded wire or needle
E griffe bar
F griffe blade or knife
G grate
H spindle

J hook (may face either way)
K neck cord
L comber board
M heddle or harness thread (leish)
N eyelet or mail (equivant of heddle eye)
O lingo (weight)
P warp (raised)
Q warp (not raised)

Figure 4.28 Selection of warp yarns by the jacquard mechanism, very much simplified to show one warp yarn raised, one not.

with double griffes, double cylinders, or even more than one jacquard attachment for very wide designs.

Continuous paper strips can replace the bulkier cards, and electronic controls are applied to key aspects of jacquard weaving. Computer-assisted design (CAD) today can greatly shorten the design and pattern-cutting preparation time, and electronic controls are now applied to simplify the actual weaving of these most complicated interlacings.[5] Designs

[5]Patricia M. King "Jacquards for Weaving," *Textiles*, October 1, 1981; pp. 10–17.

(a)

(b)

Figure 4.29 (a) Typical intricate, curving design in fabric being woven on a jacquard loom. (b) The heddles connect to cords that pass upward to the jacquard attachment that controls the raising of warp yarns.

Figure 4.30 Curtain of cards laced together, typical of jacquard attachments using punched cards to control raising of warp yarns.

can be transmitted directly to a fully electronic jacquard loom, such as one from Bonas Machine Co. Ltd.; the loom can have over 5,000 hooks on one machine, and there is electronic process monitoring.[6] This complex system can control 230-cm-wide air-jet looms running at speeds of 730 ppm, and any machine in a network can be connected to a central control computer.[7]

The jacquard mechanism was the first application of the principle of *binary selection,* by which telephone and computer controls work: each "deci-

sion" in a process is either path 1 or 2 (in the case of computer "bits," either 0 or 1, off or on). As an example of the astounding fineness achieved from the early days of this mechanism, the sample weaving "*l'hommage,*" sent by Jacquard to Napoleon as a demonstration piece, had a thread count of 1,000 per square inch and required 24,000 cards, each punched with 1,050 holes.[8]

Since there does not have to be a harness for each change of warp yarns raised as the weft is interlaced, a jacquard design can be intricate, curving, and/or large (see Figure 4.29 and *Fabric Glossary:* BROCADE; DAMASK; MATELASSÉ; TAPESTRY). When a yarn does not appear on the face, it may float on the back, as in many brocades (see Figure 4.31[a] and [b]).

A general term for smaller or less distinctive jacquard woven-in motifs is *figured,* often in connection with a name appropriate to the background weave if the figure is small and scattered. An example

[6]"Weaving Machinery," *Textile Horizons*, August 1994.
[7]"Weaving Technology: Portuguese Pioneer Sets Europe-Wide Standard," *Textile Month*, October 1998: 44.

[8]Charles Tomlinson, ed., *Cyclopedia of Useful Arts and Manufactures*, Geo. Virtue, London and New York, 1853.

(a)   (b)

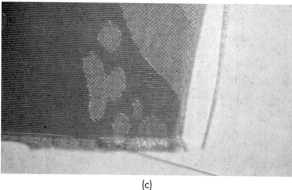

(c)

Figure 4.31 (a) Face of a brocade, woven with jacquard attachment; (b) the back of the fabric shows floats where a color is carried when it is not being interlaced. (c) Jacquard woven pattern on a plain ground weave, warp yarns low twist, weft yarns high (crepe) twist; might be called "figured crepe de Chine."

is shown in Figure 4.31(c), where the small but intricate designs are on a plain ground weave, with low twist filament warp and very high (crepe twist) weft; the name of this fabric would be "figured crepe de Chine." (See also *Fabric Glossary*: JACQUARD WOVEN.)

Leno Weave

Leno weave, also called *gauze weave*[9] or *doup weave,* requires a special *doup* attachment on the

[9]**Note:** The fabric called gauze (see *Fabric Glossary*: GAUZE) is plain weave. This is the much cheaper, open weave used in cheesecloth and gauze bandages, in which the yarns can and do slip easily.

loom that allows one of a pair of warp yarns to change position from side to side. By the time the fabric is wet finished, the warp yarns appear to have crossed in pairs, one yarn of each pair always in front of the other as it interlaces with weft (see Figure 4.32).

Weft yarns can be kept well separated yet held firmly so they do not slip, useful in sheer curtain fabric (see Figure 4.33), such as marquisette, or in mos-

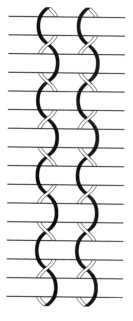

Figure 4.32 Leno weave is accomplished by crossing pairs of warp yarns from side to side so that weft yarns may be held apart without slipping.

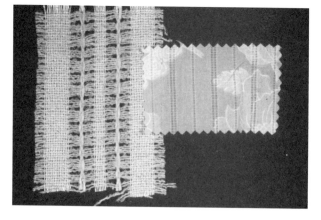

Figure 4.33 Semisheer leno curtaining, and latticed leno stripes in a dress fabric.

quito netting; grenadine is an allover leno weave apparel fabric (all are described in the *Fabric Glossary:* LENO). A *latticed* effect may be introduced into summer dress or shirt fabrics with strips of leno weave (see Figure 4.33), or a single warp may be moved from side to side to give a wavy pattern. Leno thermal cloth holds air for insulation, in blankets, for example.

Surface Figure Weaves

Patterns in weaves can be produced by figures woven into the base cloth using extra yarns. The three methods of accomplishing this are used to produce dotted Swiss (see Figure 4.34 and *Fabric Glossary:* DOTTED SWISS) as well as other surface figures..

Swivel. Extra weft yarns may be carried on small shuttles or swivels set along the width of the loom. The yarn from each swivel is woven with a group of warp yarns, and the yarn is clipped between the spots. This method (the original dotted Swiss from Switzerland), gives only two cut ends per spot, making this the most durable type of dotted Swiss but the rarest and most expensive.

Clip-Spot. Clip-spot (clip-dot, spot-dot) patterns are usually formed by shooting extra weft yarns across the width of the goods, interlacing only where the pattern is to be formed, i.e., floating between designs. After the cloth is woven, the floats are sheared or clipped; the design has two cut yarn ends for each row of weft (see Figure 4.35[a]). Clip-spot woven dotted Swiss (called American type) is good quality, though the dots are not held as firmly as by swivel weaving.

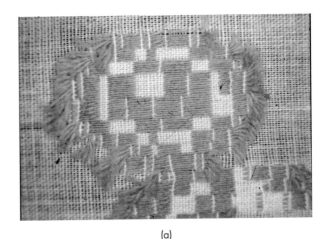

(a)

(b)

Figure 4.35 Clip-spot (a) and eyelash effect (b) surface figure weaves.

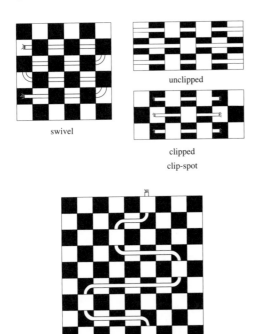

swivel

unclipped

clipped

clip-spot

lappet

Figure 4.34 Surface figure weaves.

Most clip-spot fabrics are plain weave ground; Madras muslin has clipped weft yarns, with figures held in leno weave (see *Fabric Glossary*: LENO WEAVE). In some clip-spot fabrics the spots are formed by extra warp yarns. With clipped ends in the vertical position, the resulting tiny fringe is called *eyelash* as with lappet.

Lappet. Lappet patterns are formed by extra yarns in the warp direction carried by needles set in a bar in front of the reed. These yarns can be moved to interlace with the weft yarns. The long floats that are formed between figures are usually left unclipped; if clipped, the result is called *eyelash effect* (see Figure 4.35[b]).

Pile Weaves

Pile weaves create a three-dimensional effect by weaving an extra set of warp or weft yarns into the basic structure of a fabric. These may be left uncut as loops or cut to give a plush effect.

Various methods are used to incorporate the extra yarns into the weave, but the ground is usually a plain or twill weave. **Twill back (Genoa back)** is likely to be more durable because the weave can be closer, so that the pile tufts can be held more securely. Plain weave back is also called **tabby back.**

The density of pile yarns is an important determinant of quality in any pile fabric. It is possible to pack in more pile tufts when weaving with extra warp than by the weft pile method. Woven pile is made of cotton with both warp pile (velour, cotton velvet) and weft pile (corduroy, velveteen). When an especially durable cotton pile fabric is desired, the warp pile weave is used; some cotton upholstery fabrics that look like corduroy are woven with warp pile for this reason. If you have a fabric sample, you can make a quick check by pulling a weft yarn; with warp pile weave, the weft will carry the warp pile tufts, like a caterpillar (see Figure 4.36[a]). In a weft pile fabric, the tufts hang on a warp yarn.

A woven pile fabric may have a V-loop construction or **"V" interlacing,** in which the pile loop is held by only one yarn of the opposite set, or it may have a **"W" interlacing** (sometimes advertised as "interlaced three ways"), much more durable, with each pile tuft firmly held in three places by yarns of the opposite set (see Figure 4.36[b].

Quality and durability in a woven pile fabric will depend on the fiber used, yarn quality, height of pile, ground weave (twill or plain), how the pile tufts are

(a)

"V" interlacing   "W" interlacing

(b)

Figure 4.36 (a) Velour (cotton) warp pile tufts hang on a weft yarn. (b) "V" interlacing; "W" interlacing.

held, and density of pile (see notes on carpet quality at the end of *Pile Weaves* for the term *grinning* when pile is sparse).

Warp Pile Weaves. These represent the original of pile weaves, by which velvet was made of silk. Three machine methods are used today for fabrics other than carpet, which can be woven by the third method described here plus a fourth unique to carpet:

1. **Double cloth method, face-to-face** (Figure 4.37; method described in the *Fabric Glossary*: DOBBY—COMPOUND WEAVE, DOUBLE FACE). Five sets of yarns are used, two pairs of

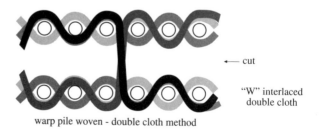

← cut

"W" interlaced double cloth

warp pile woven - double cloth method

Figure 4.37 Double cloth cut to form warp pile.

warp interlacing with weft, inserted by shuttles working one above the other, so that two fabrics are woven *face to face,* bound by a third set of warp yarns, which will form the pile [see Figure 4.38[a]). This *double cloth* is immediately cut apart (on the loom) to give two lengths of cut pile fabric (see Figure 4.38[b]). Most velvet and velour today is made by this method (see *Fabric Glossary:* VELVET; VELOUR WOVEN PILE); of course, a velvet with both cut and uncut pile must be woven by the over-wire method (see Method 3).

(a)

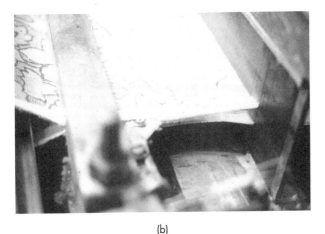

(b)

Figure 4.38 Double cloth weaving of velvet or velour with five sets of yarns. The two sheds, one above the other, are visible in (a) on the left, and there is a second shuttle working below the one that can be seen. In (b) the double cloth (jacquard pattern) is seen at the left, just before it is cut apart on the loom; two pieces of cut-pile fabric are wound up as the product of this weaving method—double cloth cut apart into two cut-pile fabrics.

2. **Slack tension warp method.** This is used for most terry cloth (see *Fabric Glossary:* TERRY). In a terry loom, a second warp beam supplies the yarn that will produce the pile loops, and this loom is engineered so that the tension on those yarns can be let off (see Figure 4.39). Suitable spacing of the weft yarn from the cloth fell must be allowed, with the number of weft yarns inserted per pile loop called the *shot*. In Figure 4.40, three picks have been inserted (a three-shot construction), and then tension is released on the pile warp yarns. When these warps are beaten up, this group of picks (weft) slide along the taut ground warp, and the slack pile warp yarn is pushed into loops, which can be formed on one side of the fabric or both sides. Loops can be made higher or lower according to the distance selected between the group of picks and the fell. Cut loops (terry/velour) are produced by shearing, as discussed in Section 5.

Figure 4.39 Terry loom with two warp beams. (Courtesy of Sulzer Canada Inc.)

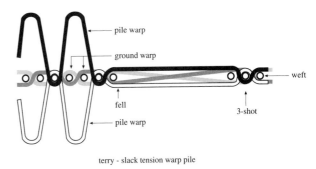

terry - slack tension warp pile

Figure 4.40 Weaving terry by the slack tension warp method.

3. **Over-wire method.** An extra set of warp yarns is held up in loops by a round wire or a metal strip inserted across the loom every few picks, instead of weft. Frisé (see *Fabric Glossary: VELVET*), with its uncut loops, is made by the over-wire method, as is a small amount of velvet and terry. This is the method used for a fabric with both cut and uncut pile, such as ciselé velvet (see *Fabric Glossary: VELVET*).

To produce a **cut pile,** as in plush, the "wire" has a sharp knife at the end, which cuts the loops as it is withdrawn. Some moquette has the loops cut.

Carpet, when machine woven, has long been made by the over-wire warp pile method. Over the last half of the 20th century, only a very small percentage of carpet was woven (however, note developments with Axminster looms under Method 4). The famous methods using the over-wire method that are outlined briefly here are of concern only to those in the interior design business at the top of the market.

One over-wire woven type still well known is **Wilton,** a cut-pile jacquard-controlled warp pile weave with not just two but three sets of warps working. **Brussels** is an uncut carpet made the same way. One group of *chain* warp (often cotton) interlaces with the weft to form the ground fabric, and a special group of warp does not interlace at all but is carried in the structure as *stuffer yarns* to give added body. (Because of these, one does not roll a carpet of this weave lengthwise!) The pile warp (usually wool) is carried on frames, one for each color required, a maximum of six frames. At each passage of weft, the appropriate colors are presented to be held up by wires in loops on the surface; with Wilton, the wires (metal strips) carry a knife end, and as they are removed, the pile loop is cut. Yarns in colors not forming pile at any point are carried in the body of the carpet—what has been called the *hidden value* of a Wilton (or Brussels) carpet. As a result, this carpet has a deep structure and is expensive to produce.

Velvet (cut loops) and **tapestry** (uncut loops) carpet is also warp pile woven, but without the complexity of structure of the Wilton.

4. **Precut warp pile.** One giant machine—the **Axminster** loom—follows original hand methods closely, in that it tucks into the weave a precut pile tuft. Here colored yarns, in order as they appear in a design, have been traditionally wound on spools or handled by grippers, a separate arrangement for each row of the design. When the appropriate yarns are presented to the loom, the pile tufts are cut, and they are woven into the ground. With this ingenious loom, a large number of colors for any size design has always been woven much more economically than by over-wire methods. As weaving enters the 21st century, a Fast Axminster Loom has been developed that rivals tufting in speed and has no backing of material that may be difficult to recycle.[10] Across a width of over 450 cm, the heavy weft can be inserted at 200 ppm (contrasted with 50 ppm achieved traditionally), and the pile insertion mechanisms, made strong and light, move short distances.

However, weaving by any method is a very small part of carpet making today—under 5 percent. Even rarer than machine-woven carpets, of course, are the warp pile *handwoven* carpets, such as **Oriental.** In these, warp pile tufts are tied in as the ground is woven; Figure 4.41 shows the traditional knots used: the Ghiordes or Turkish knot, and the asymmetrical Sehna or Persian knot, which can be packed in more closely to give the densest pile.

Quality in a carpet depends on the factors outlined for any pile fabric. A vivid trade term—*grinning* or *grin-through*—is used probably most often with poor-quality carpet, when sparse pile allows the ground to show when it should not! (The term is also applied to poorly covered woven ribs, double cloth not closely woven, or as noted in Section 3 under *Wrapped Yarns*, a rubber core showing when an elastic is stretched). In carpet, the number of warps per 10 cm in width is called the *pitch* of the carpet, the number of rows per 10 cm in length is called the *wires;* in the inch-pound system, pitch is warps per 27 in. and wires is the number of rows per inch.

The "touch-and-close" fastener VELCRO® is the trademark name of what is technically a two-part warp pile woven fabric of a most unusual sort, used in two layers that stick together. One layer is covered with loops (that feel like velvet), the other with tiny barbs (like crochet hooks) (thus the name, "vel-cro"),

[10]"New Axminster Loom 'World's Fastest,' " *Textile Month,* August 1998: 8.

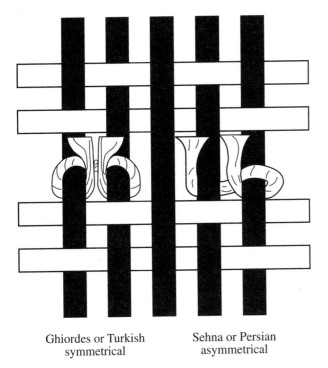

Ghiordes or Turkish
symmetrical   Sehna or Persian
                 asymmetrical

Figure 4.41 Two main types of knots used in hand-woven Oriental carpets with hand-tied knots.

all made of stiff nylon monofilament in standard VEL-CRO. The inspiration came from natural burrs, with their barbed prickles that stick tenaciously to any hairy surface.

The touch-and-close type of fastener represented by VELCRO has found myriad applications in clothing, household, and other consumer and industrial articles, and special high-performance versions have been made, including a fire- and chemical-resistant one made of a combination of NOMEX® aramid and PEEK fiber.[11] A really novel use suggested for a VELCRO-type fastener is to close wounds or rejoin blood vessels. Researchers at Carnegie Mellon University, Pittsburgh, invented a micro-sized fastener with tiny barbs that can attach to living tissue. It is predicted that a device like this could attach something like a heart pacemaker.

Weft Pile Weaves. In a weft pile, extra weft yarns float over the warp yarns.

Floats in lengthwise rows after cutting produce the vertical pile wales of corduroy, a cotton family fabric.

[11]"Velcro Finds New Applications," *Textiles Magazine*, 4, 1997: 11.

Types of corduroy, names, and wale sizes are defined in the *Fabric Glossary:* CORDUROY.

Velveteen is produced by cutting floats that are scattered over the base fabric, so there are no visible wales (see *Fabric Glossary:* VELVETEEN). The name denotes that this is a "lesser" fabric than velvet (warp pile originally of silk), being made of cotton and by the less-expensive weft pile method, with less dense pile possible.

Chenille yarn can make another type of weft pile woven fabric, although not a common one (see *Fabric Glossary:* CHENILLE YARN). A special yarn called *chenille fur* is first prepared on a loom, using leno weave, with fine warp yarns and heavier, softer-twist weft that will become the cut pile. The resulting fabric is cut into strips of fringed "yarn" (see Figure 4.42), which are then used in weaving as pile weft. This material is most often used for upholstery, but a few very high quality carpets are still made with chenille yarn pile. (It is also used in knitting and for decoration as with embroidery.)

Note: "Candlewick" chenille is produced by tufting; see *Tufting* this section, and *Fabric Glossary:* TUFTED.

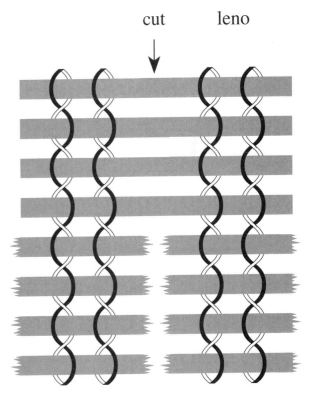

Figure 4.42 Making chenille yarn.

Knitting

Knitting is formed by a series of loops, intermeshing in rows, each hanging from the last. Each loop is called a *stitch;* a vertical row of stitches is a *wale* and a horizontal row of stitches is a *course.*

Knitting as a fabric construction method, according to surviving artifacts, is not as ancient as weaving. While knit fabric remnants exist from around the fourth century B.C., woven fabrics from ancient Egypt were sophisticated by the fourth millennium B.C.

Hand knitting became common only by the fifteenth century A.D.; a little later by 1589, the Rev. William Lee in England had developed a machine that could knit a coarse flat fabric in plain stitch.

Modern machine knitting is of two types, **weft** and **warp,** terms relating to the direction from which yarn is fed to the needles:

Weft knit. Yarn is fed to the needles from the side, and loops are formed across a course.

Warp knit. Yarn is fed to the needles from the end, a separate yarn feed for each needle, so loops are formed in the direction of the wales.

These two types are shown in Figure 4.43, along with a single loop and its parts. It is evident here also that knitting has an altogether different "geometry" from weaving. Because of the arrangement of yarns in loops, and the interdependence of adjacent loops (especially in weft knits), there are some significant differences between knitted and woven fabrics.

Knitted versus Woven

In Character
For a given quantity of yarn used, knits will:

- be lighter and more porous.

- be more easily distorted, leading to shrinking, or stretching and sagging. However, this also allows some degree of "give" in the structure (see next).

- have comfort stretch. Woven fabrics have "give" only on the diagonal or bias, not much on the grain lines *unless made with stretch yarns.* (See *Fabric Glossary:* STRETCH, COMFORT or FIT.)

The degree of comfort stretch varies with the type of yarn used, of course, but aside from that, it varies with the knit stitch, which in turn is governed by the kind of machine that produces it or the type of needle

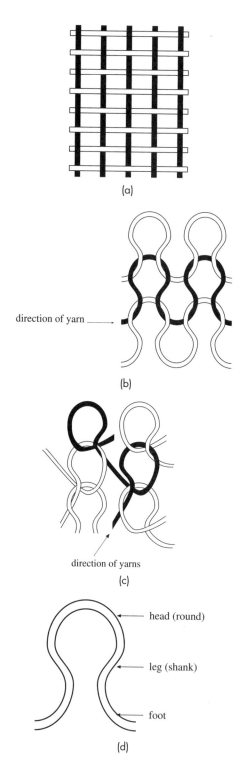

direction of yarn

(b)

direction of yarns

(c)

head (round)

leg (shank)

foot

(d)

Figure 4.43 Arrangement of yarns is contrasted: **(a)** weave (plain) **(b)** weft knit (plain stitch technical face), and a **(c)** warp knit (tricot); **(d)** parts of a knit loop.

used on that machine (see *Knitting Action, Types of Needles*).

So the character of knitted fabric depends on the type of machine used, much more than in weaving. Production of a fine, close-knit fabric is a good example, being dependent not only on using a fine yarn, but on having a machine with fine needles set close together. Fine yarn knit on a machine with coarser needles set farther apart just gives a lighter, more open fabric. Changing machines can be a very expensive step.

In Use

The effects of the differing geometry of knits compared to wovens are seen in comfort, wear, and care.

Comfort. Knits are more comfortable in cold, *still* air, since the porous structure insulates better; it holds more air (especially a rib knit) to prevent loss of body heat. However, in cold, *windy* weather, a closely woven fabric can give much more wind resistance.

In wet conditions, a knit will simply "strain the rain" without a water-resistant layer, usually woven, behind it or on top. (See Table 4.1 for a comparison of plain, twill, and satin weaves.)

In hot, humid weather, a crisp woven fabric, especially made of spun yarns and in a basket plain weave, will allow the best air circulation over the skin to help take perspiration away.

Wear. Knits, in general, are not as durable to hard wear as woven fabrics. Knits do have inherent wrinkle resistance, but can sag or bag in wear, especially single plain-stitch knits.

Care. Knits are more easily cleaned than wovens.

Resistance to relaxation shrinkage is best with wovens, or warp knits. Of the knits, warp knits and doubleknits generally show the best stability to care, such as machine washing and tumble drying.

Steaming a knit lightly will counteract bagging after wear. Let the fabric cool and dry in its pressed position.

Single knits should be stored folded or rolled, rather than hung; a shaped hanger is all right for most doubleknits or warp knits.

A heavy brooch should be pinned through fabric or tape put inside a knit garment to prevent sagging or damage.

Other aspects of care of knits are discussed in Section 6.

Handling in Garment Construction

Knits must be handled with special care and differently, in many cases, from wovens in garment construction.

Pattern. The pattern must be suitable to the amount of stretch in the knit fabric used. Doubleknits and tricot have more of the stability of woven goods; single knits, especially plain stitch, or knits with stretch yarns require specially adapted patterns with less ease allowed; see the knit stretch gauge in the *Fabric Case History* record in Section 8.

Layout. Put as little tension as possible on knit fabric; allow it to lie and "relax" before cutting.

Weft knits form "runs" one way. A silky interlock ("double jersey") may run easily; if so, lay it so the run direction is *up*. In construction, garment pieces can then be secured at the hem.

Watch for different stretch in wales versus courses direction; where there is a difference, lay all one way.

Marking and Cutting. Mark darts, etc., with tracing paper, chalk, or tailor's tacks, *not* with holes or nicks. Cut with sharp scissors, flat-blade preferable to pinking.

Lining. Lining and interlining should have "give" comparable to the knit.

Stitching. Polyester thread is often used for some "give." Seams must have some elasticity; use zigzag or other stitch to give some stretch. Wales-wise seams can be finished by double stitching and trimming close. A ballpoint needle in good condition is preferable, especially for knits from "silky" yarn, as it tends to part filaments rather than break them (see Figure 9.2). A straight needle must be fine and sharp (new). Pins should also be ballpoint, or fine and sharp.

Tape seams that take strain, as at shoulders. For a sharp crease, either stitch the crease or have it commercially pressed (heat set) if the knit is made of thermoplastic fiber.

Fasteners. The best continuous fastener for light knits is the coil type with tricot tape. With other fasteners, put some support behind the knit, or take care that the fastener is not so heavy that it will pull, as heavy buttons might on a light knit fabric.

Knitting Action, Types of Needles

Two main types of needles are used in knitting machines, and these have a considerable effect on the character of the fabric produced; they are **latch** and **beard** or **spring beard** (see Figure 4.44).

Knitting action—the formation of the stitches—is different with these two types of needles (see Figure 4.45). In any machine knitting, the needle hook must be *open* to receive yarn that will form a new loop, but it must *close* to allow the needle carrying the yarn to pass through the previous loop to form a chain. With a latch needle, the hinged latch closes as it touches the previous loop; a presser closes the flexible "beard" of the hook of the spring beard needle.

Latch needles can accept a wide range of yarn types, from finest to heavy and irregular; spring beard needles can knit only fine, regular yarns. **Hybrid** or **compound** needles are made to give some characteristics of each of the main types.

Terms relating to closeness of needles on knitting machines are somewhat confusing:

cut. A machine term, meaning the number of needles per inch around a circular weft machine; it is often applied to a fabric (fine cut, 18 cut), but is a general guide to stitch only, not a stitch count.

gauge. Varies in technical definition with different machines: It is needles per inch for circular weft knits and tricot; needles per 1½ inch for flat (full-fashioning) weft machines; needles per 2 inches for raschel machines.

The metric measure suggested for knits is stitches per 100 mm of fabric.

Some other knitting terms are:

plating (plaiting). Feeding two yarns to each needle, one covering the other; this can result in a different texture or color on either side.

gating (gaiting). The relation of one bed of knitting needles with another in a weft knitting machine. In *interlock gating*, the needles are exactly opposite each other, producing the structure shown in Figure 4.54. With *rib gating*, two sets of needles work at right angles, as in the machine shown in Figure 4.53. *Purl gating* occurs with flat or V-bed machines (Figure 4.50) with needles either two-ended or two sets but in the same plane.

weft insertion or laying-in also called **inlay** or **inlaid** (do not confuse with *intarsia*). A yarn is fed in (laid in) that does not loop, but is held in the loops.

flechage. Short row knitting, holding stitches of one area while knitting another, to fashion the knit material or even knit in effects such as pockets—see *3. Purl Stitch* under types of single knit machines.

Types of Knits

Weft (Filling) Knitting

Single Weft Knits. These can be made with one yarn forming loops; theoretically, a single yarn could form all the loops in a complete fabric. In practice, a number of yarn feeds or ends are usually used simultaneously in machine knitting.

Single knits may be **flat** or **circular:**

- **Flat knitting** machines are able to shape or fashion the sides of the knit fabric, creating *full-fashioned* articles. These are better fitting, and the pieces can be neatly joined by looping together, with no seam. This is also a good method of

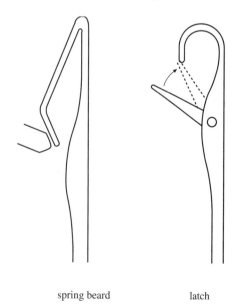

spring beard   latch

Figure 4.44   Two main types of knitting machine needles.

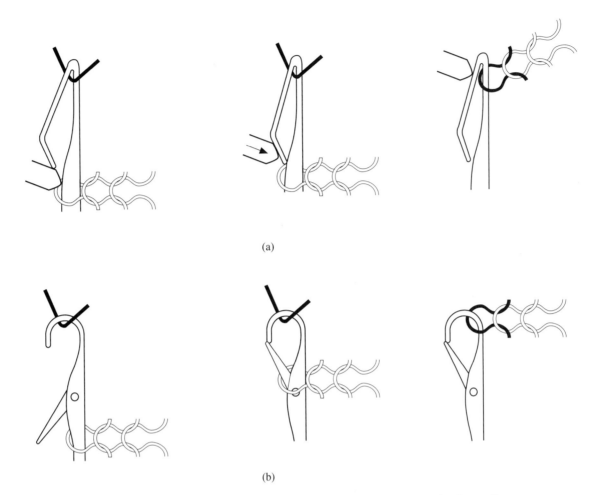

(a)

(b)

Figure 4.45 Formation of stitch with (a) spring beard vs. (b) latch needle.

knitting garments of very expensive yarns (such as camel hair), as there is no cutting waste.

- Fashioning marks will be seen along an edge if stitches have been increased or decreased, e.g., for sleeve shaping in a sweater (see Figure 4.46). However, machines capable of flechage can shape articles without such fashioning marks (see earlier definition of *flechage*).

- As an intermediate method, "blanks" may be knitted roughly to the size of garment pieces and then cut and sewn for the various sizes in a range.

- **Circular knitting** is faster than flat and turns out fabric in tubes, which are often slit open and then treated like any piece goods to make "cut and sew" articles.

There are three **types of single weft knit machines**, with different stitch capabilities:

1. **Plain stitch** is formed with loops drawn always to the back of the fabric, giving the face an appearance of vertical rows (the *shank* or leg of the stitch), while the back shows the *round* or head of the stitch (see Figures 4.43[b] and 4.47 and photos in the *Fabric Glossary*: JERSEY).

This machine is the fastest weft knitting type; since circular machines knit faster than flat, the circular plain stitch machine (also known as the "jersey" machine) is the fastest, often termed the "workhorse" of the (weft) knitting industry.

Plain stitch knits fit the body well, but are the most easily distorted of all knits, and can "run"

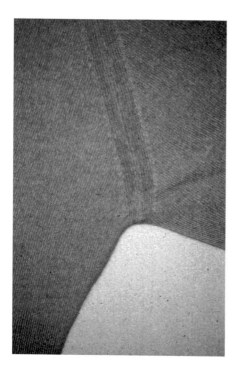

Figure 4.46 Fashioning marks on a sweater sleeve.

(stitches drop, forming a "ladder"), sag, and shrink most readily. The edges curl because of the difference in tension between the face and back.

Fabrics made in plain stitch are jersey, balbriggan, and lisle (see *Fabric Glossary:* JERSEY). Just as plain weave fabrics need not *be* plain, so plain stitch knits can have intricate, knitted-in jacquard patterns (see *Fabric Glossary:* JACQUARD KNIT).

The plain stitch machine is also used and modified to give fabrics with weft insertion or inlay (see *Knitting Action*), e.g., knit fleece, fur-like sliver-knit pile, knit velour, knit plush, and knit terry (see *Fabric Glossary:* FLEECE KNIT; FUR-LIKE SLIVER-KNIT PILE; VELOUR KNIT PILE). Some knit fabrics referred to as "fleece" are more complex; see two-sided weft knit fabrics under *Other Knitted Fabrics and Terms*.

2. **Rib stitch** requires that all the loops of some wales be drawn off to the face and those of other wales to the back. To do this, the machine has two sets of needles, usually set at right angles to each other (rib gating).

Rib knits are described according to the number of stitches drawn to one side by the number to the other, e.g., 2×2, which is read as "two by two." The simplest rib is a 1×1, shown in Figure 4.48.

A rib knit has excellent crosswise stretch and recovery, and so is used for snugness in bands at neck, sleeves, and waist. It also makes a very warm fabric because of the air trapped in its "hill and valley" surface.

Special rib knits are described in *Fabric Glossary:* RIB KNIT, covering accordion, cable, poor boy, and shaker. To knit cable, a group of plain stitches is made to change places with an equal group for some courses, giving a braided, cordlike effect.

3. **Purl stitch** draws loops to the back of the fabric on one course and to the face on the next course (see Figure 4.49 and photo in *Fabric Glossary:* JERSEY). To knit this stitch, some machines use a

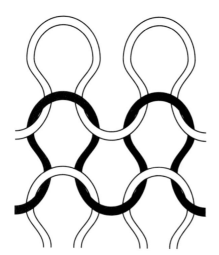

Figure 4.47 Plain stitch technical back.

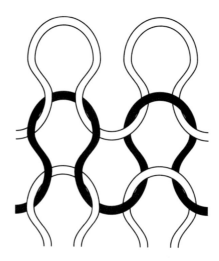

Figure 4.48 A 1×1 rib knit.

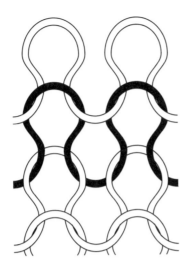

Figure 4.49 Purl stitch.

double-headed latch needle; these machines may be called *links and links* (from the German word for *left,* from the direction of travel of the carriage). Many modern machines accomplish this stitch using a V-bed carriage, with two needle beds set at an angle to one another; this type is shown in Figure 4.50. Such a machine can also produce a sweater front, for instance, not only fashioned, but with collar, pocket, and buttonhole knitted in (flechage). This can effect significant savings in labor costs of assembling a gar-

ment (once the capital investment in the machine has been made!).

Computer-assisted design and manufacturing (CAD/CAM) is shown in Figure 4.51 with a computer design system that can operate this V-bed knitting machine. Intricate designs can be "drawn" on the computer screen and translated directly into control that produces jacquard-knitted patterns in whatever size or color combination is desired.

Machines that knit the purl stitch are the slowest of the three weft knit types, but can also knit plain and rib stitches; this means they are the most versatile. A combination of plain, rib, and purl knitting in one article could come from this type of machine only (see Figure 4.52).

Fabric in purl stitch has good stretch, especially lengthwise, and does not curl.

Doubleknits. Doubleknits are weft knits produced on circular rib machines (using latch needles) by using two yarn feeds, knitting now on one set of needles, now on the other to form a tube of two fabrics knitted together (see Figure 4.53). Doubleknits, therefore, cannot be *fashioned.*

Interlock is the simplest form, a fine double 1 × 1 rib, with the needle gating such that stitches on one side are set right behind those on the other side; Figure 4.54 shows this arrangement of stitches, seen as

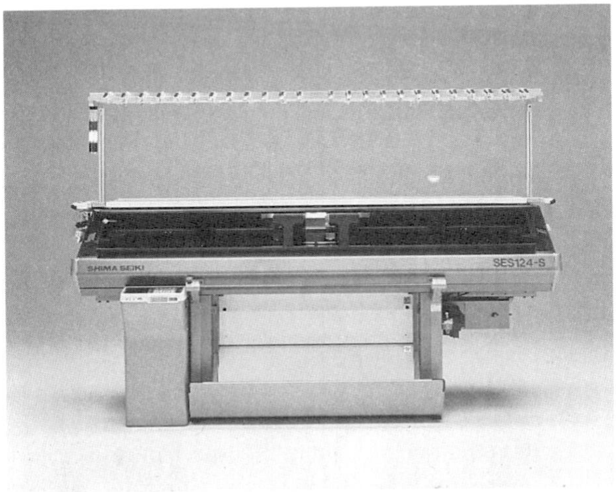

Figure 4.50 Electronically controlled flat weft V-bed knitting machine can knit the purl stitch (and plain and rib as well). (Courtesy of Shima Seiki U.S.A. Inc.)

Figure 4.51 Designs created by "drawing" on the computer screen can be knitted directly into fabric on this V-bed machine with this electronic control system. (Courtesy of Shima Seiki U.S.A. Inc.)

Figure 4.52 Machines that knit the purl stitch are the only ones that can knit all three weft stitches: plain and rib as well as purl, as seen in this knit fabric.

(a)

(b)

Figure 4.53 (a) Circular rib knitting machine that can produce doubleknits, since in this machine, two sets of needles work at right angles. (b) Close-up of the knitting elements of this circular rib machine. (Courtesy of Speizman Industries, Inc. for Jumberca, S.A.)

if the fabric were viewed from an end with the loops spread open. *Both* sides of the fabric *look like* the face of plain stitch single knit and jersey is the best-known fabric in that stitch, so interlock is often called "double jersey," especially when it is knit of filament yarn rather than cotton (see *Fabric Glossary:* INTERLOCK).

What we commonly call a **doubleknit** may be of various stitches. One with a kind of honeycomb stitch is called double piqué, and another is ponte di Roma. Bourrelet is a doubleknit having a corded effect on the surface. Doubleknits of textured set filament polyester yarn have been known as *crimpknits.*

The two sides of a doubleknit can look and feel similar, although if there is a jacquard pattern knitted in, it will be clear on the face and will often have what is called a *birdseye* look on the back. Alternatively, the face may be puffed or otherwise separated from the back, since there are really two fabrics knitted together. These two looks are shown in *Fabric Glossary:* DOUBLEKNIT.

Variations. Some basic variations on weft knit stitches are:

Float or miss stitch occurs when one or more needles do not form a stitch, and the yarn floats across the back of the fabric (see Figure 4.55).

Tuck stitch occurs when a needle holds the old loop and then gets a new yarn, so both stay in the needle hook. This stitch shows as an inverted V on the back of the fabric (see Figure 4.56).

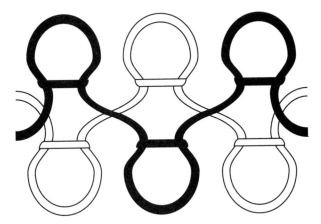

Figure 4.54 Interlock structure shown as if the loops were spread open as the fabric is viewed from an end.

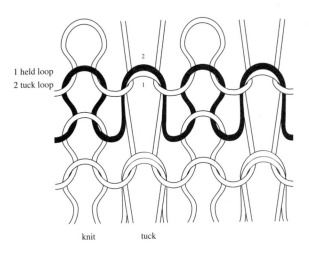

Figure 4.56 Half cardigan stitch (alternate knit and tuck), fabric back.

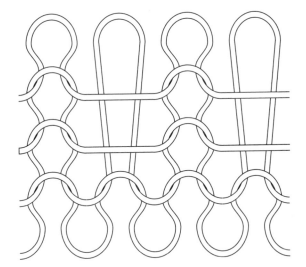

Figure 4.55 Float or miss stitch, fabric back.

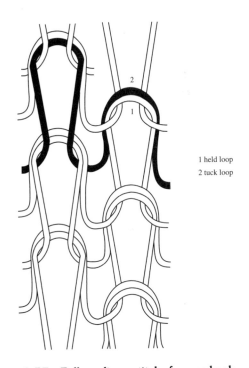

Figure 4.57 Full cardigan stitch, face or back.

Half cardigan stitch has only one set of needles knitting and tucking on the face or back on alternate courses. The construction on the face is the reverse of the back (see Figure 4.56).

Full cardigan stitch is produced in *rib knits* by alternately knitting and tucking on the two sets of needles, then tucking and knitting on the next course, producing a thicker, bulky fabric. The fabric has the same look on both sides (see Figure 4.57).

Rack stitch is a variation of the half cardigan that gives a herringbone pattern on the face.

Warp Knitting

This form of knitting is very different from standard hand knitting; the earliest warp knitting machine was Crane's tricot machine (England), built about 1775. In warp knitting, a yarn is fed to each needle from the lengthwise direction. A bar guiding the yarns to the needles can move from side to side, or to the front or back of the needle, so that the loops can be interlocked in a zigzag pattern. Very wide (over 400 cm, nearly 170 in.), flat fabric can be produced by warp knitting, at speeds in the order of 1,000 courses per minute, giving almost 3 m²/min (3.6 sq. yds./min). The two main machine (fabric) types are **tricot** and **raschel.**

Tricot. Tricot is a machine with one needle bar (spring beard type) and one to three guide bars (most are two-bar or three-bar) (see Figure 4.58). The spring beard needle, accepting mainly filament yarns, has limited the depth of texture that can be achieved in tricot fabrics; some fine spun tricot, produced on machines with hybrid needles, was introduced many years ago, but does not seem to have taken hold in the marketplace.

Figure 4.59 shows a tricot fabric. It can be seen from this photo why a simple tricot is often called "jersey"; the face *looks like* weft plain stitch face, although the back has a different and distinctive look—like chevrons on their sides (>>>>>>>)—because of the zigzag path of the yarns. This *technical back* of tricot is often used as the "right side," as it is smoother, e.g., for printing, and the yarns are more available for brushing or sanding. Moreover, if there are variously colored yarns in the tricot, they meet in a lengthwise stripe much more cleanly on the technical back (see Figure 4.59 and *Fabric Glossary:* TRICOT).

(a)

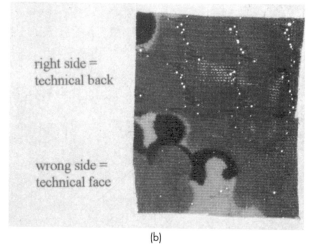

right side = technical back

wrong side = technical face

(b)

Figure 4.59 (a) Tricot technical face (top) looks like plain stitch (jersey), while technical back has crosswise lines of chevrons on their sides and is often more smooth and lustrous. (b) This side (technical back) is often the right side of a tricot, smoother for printing and showing a contrast yarn more cleanly.

Tricot does not ravel, can curl somewhat, and has almost no stretch or "give" lengthwise but a little crosswise.

Note: It may be confusing for French-speaking people to find the word *tricot* meaning, in the English language, the product of this specific warp knitting machine, when in French, *un tricot* means "a knit" and *tricoter* means "to knit."

Raschel. Raschel is the other main warp knitting machine. Fabric from these machines may be of any weight or thickness from lace to carpet; the one fea-

Figure 4.58 Tricot warp knitting machine. Yarns from warp beams are led to each needle from the end, rather than single yarn feeds from the side, as in weft knitting.

ture they share is a *pillar-and-inlay* effect: wales like hand crochet chains forming the "pillar" (see Figure 4.60), with other yarns laid in to form patterns or the main body of the fabric, usually making up the right side (see *Fabric Glossary*: RASCHEL).

Raschel machines have one or two needle bars (usually latch, but may be spring beard), set horizontally on wide or narrow machines with 1 to over 30 *guide bars*. The multiguide bar types are used mostly for laces (see *Fabric Glossary*: LACE, KNIT); most of our moderate-priced laces are knit on this type of machine. They do not have the depth of texture that the twisted Leavers laces or the embroidered Schiffli laces have. Powernet, knit on the raschel machine, incorporates elastomeric yarn to give one- or two-way power stretch for contour fashion (see *Fabric Glossary*: STRETCH, POWER).

Variations on raschel-type machines include **crochet, ketten raschel,** and **Cidega** machines. The latter, similar to raschel, can knit various fabrics side by side, and so is used for many narrow trims called "braids," such as gimp (see *Fabric Glossary*: GIMP "BRAID") and ball fringe.

Minor Warp Knits. **Simplex** is a machine with two horizontal needle bars and two guide bars, producing a double tricot type of warp knit in a fine gauge, with two threads to each loop. The needles in one bar are directly behind those in the other, in much the same way that needles in the weft knit interlock are aligned;

like interlock, simplex *looks like* plain-stitch jersey on *both sides*. The fabric is very firm and stable, used for its greater firmness in loungewear, uniforms, and gloves (see *Fabric Glossary*: TRICOT).

Milanese is a machine with one needle bar, one guide bar, and two sets of threads; one forms the face of the fabric, the other the back. Yarns are carried diagonally all the way across the fabric. Milanese is knit flat (spring beard needles) or circular (latch needles).

Other Knitted Fabrics and Terms
Jacquard knitting control uses punched cards, electronic tape, or direct computer control to produce intricate knitted-in patterns, usually multicolored (see Figure 4.51). A yarn not looping on the face floats across or is caught into the back (see *Fabric Glossary*: JACQUARD KNIT).

Fair Isle is one well-loved design from hand knitting reproduced by machine with jacquard control. The design is named from the southernmost of the group of Shetland and Orkney Islands, northeast of Scotland. Patterns are horizontal bands of colored geometric and floral designs on a contrasting ground. Figure 4.61 contrasts the face of the knit, showing the clear intricate pattern, with the back, where other colored yarns are carried when they are not part of the pattern.

Intarsia (from Italian meaning "inlaid") is usually knit on a flat V-bed machine. The yarn knits only where the design (usually a geometric motif) is formed,

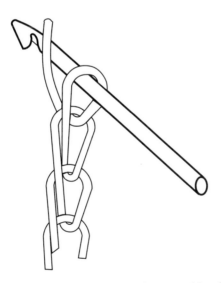

Figure 4.60 Hand crochet stitch is very like the formation of warp knit loops.

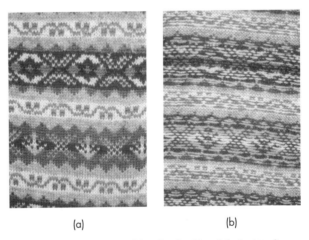

(a)   (b)

Figure 4.61 Face and back of a Fair Isle knitted pattern, typical of jacquard control in machine-knit goods. Where a yarn does not loop on the face, it is carried in the back. (Courtesy of Seneca College Fashion Resource Centre)

so the back of the knit design is the same solid color as the face, giving a sharper, cleaner definition to the pattern. **Argyle** is one classic pattern that looks best when intarsia knit. This knitting method, especially when isolated motifs are shown on a garment, requires careful planning and precise control, and so is usually expensive. A garment with an intarsia motif usually exhibits other features of high-quality knitwear: fashioning, with looping of seams, so the inside of the garment is finished almost as well as the outside, as in Figure 4.62.

Pointelle is a pattern of holes in a knit (see Figure 4.63).

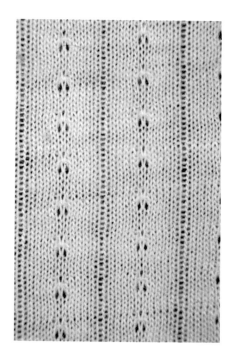

Figure 4.63 Pointelle is a pattern of holes in a knit.

(a)

(b)

Figure 4.62 (a) Sweater with Argyle intarsia pattern; (b) the back of the pattern (inside the sweater) is the same solid color as on the outside. This quality garment shows a clean finish on the inside, as well as the clear intarsia pattern. (Courtesy of Parkhurst Knits, Dorothea Knitting Mills Ltd.)

Knit **pile** fabrics can be produced with extra yarns knitted into either weft or warp knits, left with uncut loops for knit terry or sheared if a plush surface is desired, as with knit velour or knit plush (see *Fabric Glossary:* VELOUR KNIT PILE).

Another method, most often used to give deep pile, fur-like fabrics, catches tufts of sliver in the loop of a plain knit stitch (see Figure 4.64 and *Fabric Glossary:* FUR-LIKE—SLIVER-KNIT). In this area of designing, a thorough knowledge of machine technology is required; Figure 4.64(b) shows the right and wrong side (technical back and face) of such sliver-knit pile imitating one of the endangered spotted cat furs. It would be hard from the wrong side to guess the look or the impact of the right side.

Two-sided weft knit fabrics are well known; a simple knit fleece, for instance, would qualify as two-sided, since it has a very different look and hand on the face and back. However, some knit fabrics have been highly developed so that each side can give optimum performance for a specific purpose. This is called BiPolar Technology™ in a number of series of POLARTEC® fabrics from Malden Mills. The differences between the sides may be achieved by use of different yarns, knitting, and finishing on one side

(a)

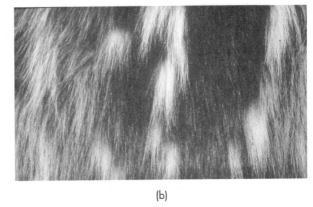

(b)

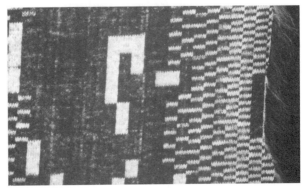

(c)

Figure 4.64 (a) Sliver-knit machine produces circular plain stitch knit with fiber from sliver caught into the round of the stitch at the back (inside the knit tube). (b) Deep-pile, sliver-knit, fur-like fabric. The right side is the technical back, while the wrong side is the technical face of the plain stitch.

compared to the other. In this way, Series 100, meant to be worn next to the skin, has a soft, raised surface on the inside to trap body heat and help the fabric wick perspiration to outer layers, and is treated with an antimicrobial finish (see Section 5). The outer side of Series 100 fabric is finished flat to prevent drag on layers worn over it, to facilitate moisture dissipation and to reduce pilling. Series 200/300 are intended for intermediate layers of garments or as multipurpose outer layer fabrics. They have a high pile velour on the inside for insulation and a tightly knit low pile with water repellent on the outside for better wear and wind resistance. Figure 4.65 shows a logo and hangtag for POLARTEC® fabrics with BiPolar Technology™ (by Malden Mills).

Knitting with Weft or Warp Insertion

Some knitting machines can lay in yarns crosswise (**weft insertion**) or lengthwise (**warp insertion**); a woven appearance plus better stability and resistance to distortion are the advantages.

(a)

(b)

Figure 4.65 (a) Logo for POLARTEC® fabrics, designed by MALDEN MILLS® to deliver BiPolar Technology™, with each side of the fabric developed for optimum performance in different end uses. (b) Hangtag for POLARTEC® with BiPolar Technology™. (Courtesy of Malden Mills Industries, Inc.)

Other Construction Methods Using Yarns

Twisting (Knotting)

Twisting, looping, or tying yarn upon itself is involved when making net and lace by hand. Since yarns must be moved three-dimensionally, machines to make net or lace by twisting are the most complicated and massive in textile manufacturing, notably the Leavers machine, which makes "Nottingham" lace.

A machine with a bobbin Barmen mechanism intertwines threads to give narrow widths of fairly heavy trimming lace, such as Cluny or Torchon (see *Fabric Glossary:* LACE, TWISTED—*Lace Types*).

Net

Net is probably the most ancient textile structure, having been used for hunting (snares) and fishing from prehistory. Net is an openwork fabric formed of yarns twisted to form four-sided or six-sided holes. Some well-known names are illusion, point d'esprit, and tulle—types and characteristics are discussed in the *Fabric Glossary:* NET. Net fabrics can also be warp knitted: tricot or raschel.

Construction of **bobbinet,** a six-sided (hexagonal) hole net, was developed by John Heathcoat in the area of Nottingham, England, in 1808 (see Figure 4.66). Yarns on brass bobbins can be twisted around warp threads in the machine to form the hexagonal hole of bobbinet; see *Fabric Glossary:* NET. This invention paved the way for development of the more complex Leavers lace machine; in the interim, "lace" was produced by hand embroidering on the machine-made net.

Lace

Lace is an openwork fabric with a pattern or design in it.

Machine-Made Lace Types

Knit Lace. Virtually all the lace used today is machine-made, and most is produced on raschel or similar warp knitting machines. This method gives little depth of design, but is much less expensive than the other methods (see *Fabric Glossary:* LACE, KNIT).

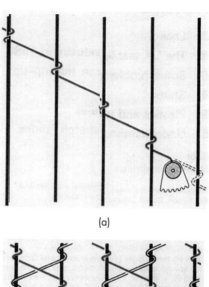

(a)

(b)

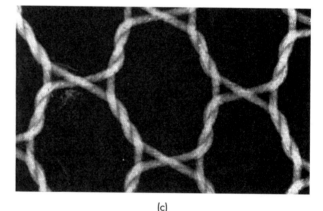

(c)

Figure 4.66 Bobbinet construction: Yarn on a brass bobbin is twisted around each warp yarn in turn (a). There is a bobbin for every second warp end (dark yarns, b), and another set is added, which moves across the other diagonal (white yarns, b). Bobbinet has a hexagonal hole (c). (Courtesy of the Textile Institute)

Schiffli Lace. With this type a lace is achieved by embroidering a pattern on fabric and then dissolving the ground. This method is expensive, but reproduces well some of the needlepoint lace types with great depth of design and no mesh background that go under the rather general name today of Guipure (see *Some Other Handmade Lace Types* and *Fabric Glossary:* LACE, EMBROIDERED).

Twisted—Leavers (Levers) or Nottingham Lace. This is produced by twisting yarns, as described in the opening discussion of twisting (see also *Fabric Glossary:* LACE, TWISTED). The **Leavers machine** is the most complex used in the textile industry, very large in size, with over 30,000 parts, many finely engineered. There are warp or *beam* yarns set up in the machine, and the complex intertwisting is done by yarns carried on paper-thin bobbins that can move in and out among the warp yarns *in any direction,* controlled by a jacquard mechanism (see Figure 4.67).

This machine most nearly duplicates the movement of hands in making lace and can reproduce closely the "look" of many of the grand handmade laces, a few of which are described in the *Fabric*

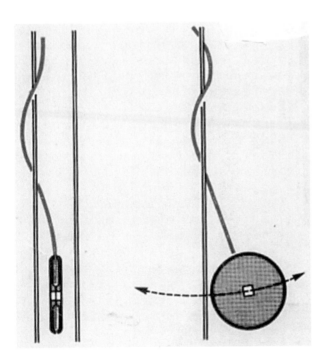

Figure 4.67 In the Leavers lace machine, thin brass bobbins twist thread around warp yarns. (Courtesy of the Textile Institute)

Glossary: LACE, *All Types.* A brief review of these follows, to help us understand (a little!) when we might call a machine-made lace by one of the handmade lace names, which carry such an aura of elegance and refinement into our modern world.

Handmade Lace Types

According to *Ciba Review*,[12] the main divisions of handmade laces evolved from very simple treatments of:

- **Seams,** embellished by drawn-thread work, as in hem-stitching or *fagoting* (shown in Figure 4.70[c]) this gradually led, through cutwork on a larger scale (*reticella*), to **needlepoint lace.**

- **Warp yarns,** which must be cut when woven material is taken off a loom; twisting and tying of these yarns (as in *macramé*) led to **bobbin lace.**

Needlepoint. Needlepoint was the first real lace, derived from embroidery done on parchment, which was later cut away to leave the lace free (*punti in aria:* "stitches in air"). This art/craft began in Italy in the late 15th century, centered in the Venetian Republic; by the late 16th century, lace-making of various kinds was widespread in Europe.

The parts of lace often have special names (many are French). The pattern (*toilé*) is connected with and set off by the ground (*fond*), which may be a mesh ground (*réseau:* net, or *fond simple,* a six-sided mesh), or just tie bars (*brides*). There may be loops from the edges or surface of the design (*picots* or *bead edge*). All this is worked with needle and thread, in stitches derived from embroidery. Often these laces have (naturally) a buttonhole-stitch look.

Some famous needlepoint laces are shown and/or defined briefly in the *Fabric Glossary:* LACE, *All Types,* such as Alençon, rosepoint, Venetian point, gros point, point de neige, point plat, coralline, point de gaze.

The best machine-made versions of a lace such as Alençon come from the Leavers machine, which can make the mesh ground and the designs with their heavy outlining thread (*cordonnet*). When such a cordonnet is applied by hand, often not just a yarn but a special decorative trim like sequin strips, the lace is

[12]Marie Schuette, "Techniques and Origins of Lace," *Ciba Review,* 73 (April, 1949): 2675–2684.

called *re-embroidered* and is usually *very* expensive; Figure 4.68 shows re-embroidered lace of both these types.

Guipure lace typically has no mesh ground; the thick patterns are build up with buttonhole stitches joined by tie bars; it is well reproduced by machines that embroider (Schiffli) and is shown in the *Fabric Glossary:* LACE, EMBROIDERED. The name *Guipure* comes from *guipe,* a cord base around which silk is wrapped to create a spiral yarn, as used in gimp (guimpe) "braid" (see *Fabric Glossary:* GIMP [GUIMPE] "BRAID").

Bobbin or Pillow Lace. This type is formed by threads fed from many bobbins; the work of intertwining the threads is done over a pattern on a bolster or pillow, the threads held by pins. The bobbins are often weighted where the ends hang down.

This type of lace has a "clothy" or woven look in the more solid pattern areas; the Leavers machine can produce this look well. Some famous bobbin laces are shown and/or defined briefly in the *Fabric Glossary:* LACE, *All Types* and LACE, TWISTED— such as Binche, Valenciennes (Val), Mechlin or Malines, Bruges, Chantilly, Cluny, duchesse, and torchon (beggar's). Honiton was a later English type.

When pattern and net are all made of the same (fine) thread, it is called *fil continu* (French, "continuous thread"); made by hand, this method gives relatively narrow lace, an example being Valenciennes or Val.

Some Other Handmade Lace Types. **Appliqué** lace has a pattern of lawn or cambric appliquéed to a net ground, then the net cut away from behind the appliqué. An example is Irish Carrickmacross.

Filet or darned lace, with a square mesh, is made by working thread in and out of a square mesh net.

Tenerife, Paraguay, South American, spider, nanduti, and Tucuman are all associated with similar patterns of *ruedas* (Spanish, "wheel") or *sol* (Spanish "sun"), and often look like a spider web. These were developed from drawnwork, made in Spain, South America, Mexico, and (still) the Canary Islands (Tenerife), where rosettes of cotton thread are made within a frame.

Battenburg lace is one of the "renaissance" laces popular as a craft at the end of the 19th century, following a renewed interest in ancient Italian designs. The design is outlined with ready-made tape held together by loose brides (see Figure 4.69). A Honiton tape lace was made in Devon, England.

Tatting gives delicate laces made of fine, hightwist yarn, using a small, flat, shuttle-like carrier, helped by use of a hook like a crochet hook.

Crochet lace, made with a crochet hook in looped chains of stitches (see Figure 4.60), is well reproduced on the raschel knitting machine (see *Fabric Glossary:* LACE, KNIT).

Lace-like fabrics can also be produced by weaving, weft knitting, and tricot warp knitting.

Lace Forms and Terminology

As well as the terms already discussed, the "vocabulary" of lace also includes names for special forms—

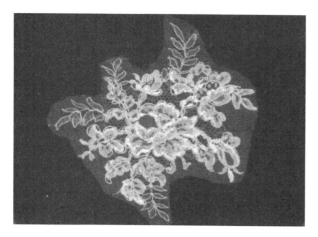

(a)

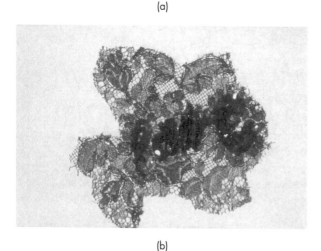

(b)

Figure 4.68 Re-embroidered lace is usually very expensive, with hand-guided application of (a) heavy cordonnet, or other embellishment such as (b) sequins.

Figure 4.69 Battenburg (tape) lace.

the sizes and edge finishes in which lace can be selected for particular purposes.[13] Many of these apply to any trim, including braids and embroidered fabrics.

allover. Pattern all over the surface of the fabric, cut and used like any piece goods; 100 cm (36 in.) or other normal fabric width.

galloon. Both edges scalloped or indented irregularly; up to 50 cm (18 in.) wide.

flouncing. One edge only scalloped, used for ruffles, flounces; 50–100 cm (18–36 in.) wide.

edging. One edge only scalloped, used for edging; usually quite narrow, maximum 50 cm (18 in.) wide. Some examples of this form are seen in the *Fabric Glossary:* LACE, TWISTED.

insertion. Narrow, both edges relatively straight, used between two pieces of fabric or as edge trim (Figure 4.70[a]); picots (loops) on edges.

beading (often insertion form). Has slots in it, through which ribbon can be threaded; in cheaper versions of beading, ribbon may be simply stitched behind the slots, or the effect of ribbon

[13]Most of these lace forms are listed in *Textile Fabrics and Their Selection*, 8th Edition, Isabel B. Wingate and June F. Mohler, printed here courtesy of Prentice Hall Inc., Englewood Cliffs, N.J., 1984.

through slots may be incorporated during manufacture of knitted beading (Figure 4.70[b]).

medallion. Single design or motif used for appliqué, usually Guipure type or other joined by brides, not mesh (see *Fabric Glossary:* LACE, EMBROIDERED).

fagoting. Drawn-thread latticed effect or "ladder" work; threads drawn out of woven fabric, the remaining threads bound with buttonhole stitch (Figure 4.70[c] illustrates drawn-thread work).

Tufting

Tufting creates a pile fabric by inserting yarns, carried by needles, into a base fabric (called the *primary backing* in a carpet), and usually woven (see Figure 4.71). This is like the method used for hand-hooked

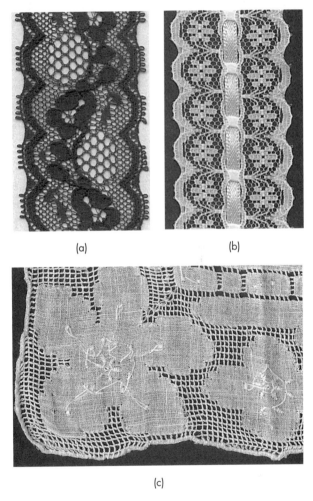

Figure 4.70 Some lace forms and terminology.

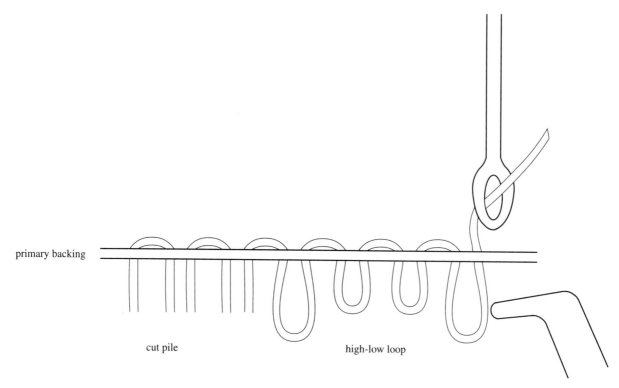

primary backing

cut pile

high-low loop

Figure 4.71 Action of a tufting machine. Yarn, carried by needles, is inserted into a primary backing fabric; loops may be of varying height and may be cut or left uncut.

rugs, but with many needles working, each supplied with yarn. The loops can be of varying height, cut or left uncut, and the process can be electronically controlled. These pile fabrics are used for carpets, rugs and mats, upholstery, and bedspreads (candlewick). Figure 4.72(a) shows a full-width tufting machine for "broadloom" carpet, with primary backing woven of split-film polypropylene. Figure 4.72(b) and (c) gives a closer look in a sample-sized tufting machine, with yarns brought to the multiple needles through narrow tubes from the back of the machine.

Floorcovering (carpet) is probably the heaviest fabric in consumer use. Over 95 percent of this today is tufted, the primary backing made traditionally of jute but increasingly of polypropylene woven of fibrillated or split-film yarn (see Figure 4.73 and *Fabric Glossary:* SPLIT-FILM YARN; also TUFTED). The tufted fabric for carpets (also for mats and upholstery) is coated on the back to hold the pile tufts (see Figure 4.74).

An impervious polyethylene backing was introduced by Solutia in WEAR-DATED® PET-AGREE®

carpet lines. This prevents liquids (especially from pets' "accidents") from seeping through carpet onto padding and floor; when the carpet is cleaned, odor-causing liquids will not remain behind. The PET-AGREE logo is shown in Figure 6.11(c).

Much carpet also has an additional *secondary backing* or a *foam backing for self-underlay* that conceals the tufted structure. Figure 4.75(a) shows two backings made of polypropylene; at left an anti-static primary backing, POLYBAC®/AS (by Amoco), woven of split-film yarn, at right a leno-woven secondary backing, ACTIONBAC® (by Amoco). Such a secondary backing gives superior performance compared to traditional jute-woven fabric and at reasonable cost (see Figure 4.75[b]).

Candlewick or chenille is one of the few tufted fabrics that has no coating on the back; as explained in *Fabric Glossary:* TUFTED, a "blooming" or untwisting of the thicker, soft-twist cotton pile yarns, along with shrinkage of the base fabric in wet finishing, holds the tufts in place.

(a)

(c)

(b)

Figure 4.72 (a) Full-size tufting machine for broad-loom carpet. Primary backing fabric here is woven of split-film polypropylene. (Courtesy of Dominion Textile Inc.). (b),(c) Sample-sized tufting machine at the Woolmark (formerly IWS) Research and Development Centre, Ilkley, W. Yorkshire, U.K.

Figure 4.73 Face and back of carpet tufted into a primary backing woven of split-film polypropylene yarn.

Figure 4.74 Slip-resistant coating on the back of a tufted carpet.

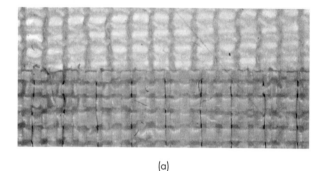

(a)

Jute Backing   All Synthetic ActionBac®

(b)

Figure 4.75 (a) At left, POLYBAC®/AS antistatic primary backing for tufted carpet, woven of split-film polypropylene; at right, ACTIONBAC® secondary backing for tufted carpet, leno-woven of polypropylene. (b) A traditional woven jute (burlap or crash) backing for tufted carpet is subject to rot, mildew, odor, staining, and stretching or shrinkage. ACTIONBAC® fabric for tufted carpet secondary backing is free from these hazards. (Courtesy of Amoco Fabrics and Fibers Company)

Braiding

Braided fabrics are formed when yarns are plaited or interlaced diagonally. Braiding produces narrow, flexible, flat or circular fabrics; variety and uses are shown and discussed in the *Fabric Glossary:* BRAID.

Braid is also a general term for narrow trims, such as ball fringe or gimp "braid" (see *Fabric Glossary:* GIMP "BRAID"), made not by braiding but usually by warp knitting. *Passementerie* is an even more general term that includes beads, cord, and narrow lace trims.

Stitch-Knit

Stitch-knit, knit-sew, loop-bonded, and stitch-bonded are names applied to a method that produces fabric very quickly on machines using a warp knit type of looping to hold together components such as yarns, fiber batt, or foam layers.

Mali fabrics are one family of stitch-knits made on machines from Malimo Maschinenbau GmbH, now part of Mayer Textile Machinery (see Figure 4.76 and *Fabric Glossary:* STITCH-KNIT).

- **Malimo** is made up entirely of yarns in a flat, often open, semisheer fabric much used in curtaining. The **Schusspol** type gives one-sided pile fabrics suitable for carpet, upholstery, or terry fabrics.

- **Malipol** has a one-sided loop pile stitched into a base fabric (woven, knitted, nonwoven, or stitch-knit).

- **Malifol** is a type where flat film is slit and stretched to form yarn, which is then held together by stitch-bonding.

- **Maliwatt** has a base of fiber batt held together with the lengthwise rows of yarn loops, giving a corded effect.

The process to give Malimo is shown in Figure 4.77: horizontal needles carry yarn for the knit looping or stitch-bonding, brought through guides; this looping yarn is usually fine, as shown here, so that it is often hard to see in the completed fabric. Vertical (warp) yarns and yarns like weft, but laid at slight angles to the horizontal, are stitch-knitted together to emerge as Malimo fabric.

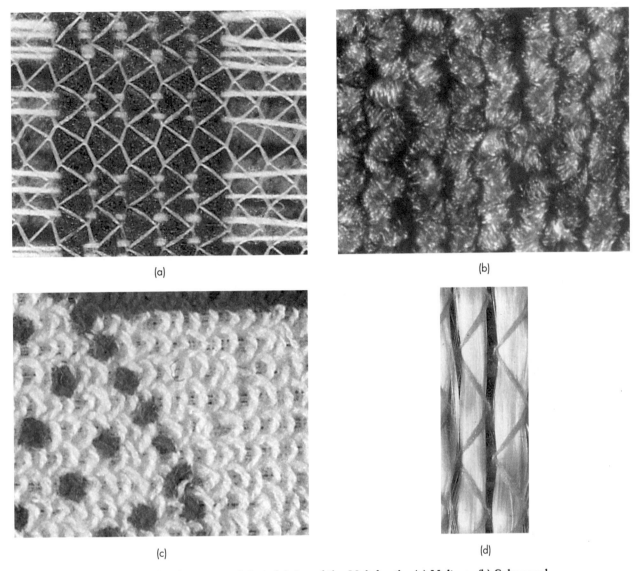

Figure 4.76 Various stitch-knit fabrics of the Mali family. (a) Malimo, (b) Schusspol, (c) Malipol, (d) Malifol. (Courtesy of Malimo Maschinenbau GmbH)

Stitch-knit fabric does not have the inherent elasticity of a true knit, unless elastomeric yarns are incorporated.

A number of machines of the Malimo company do not use yarns at all, but take a web of fibers and, in effect, form some into stitches to hold the web together; these are described under the following heading, *Fabrics without Yarns*.

Fabrics without Yarns

Felt

Felt is a fabric formed by the felting of wool or hair fibers. When a mass of fibers containing about 50 percent wool is agitated with heat, moisture, and pressure, the surface scales allow the wool fibers to move only in the direction of their root ends; eventually the

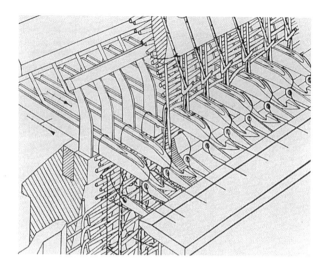

Figure 4.77 Stitch-knit process to give Malimo fabric (all yarns). Fine yarns, carried by guide bars to horizontal needles, loop together a layer of horizontal yarns with vertical (warp) yarns. (Courtesy of Malimo Maschinenbau GmbH)

mass of fibers shrinks together, interlocks, and mats into a fabric—felt (see *Fabric Glossary:* FELT).

There should be about 50 percent of wool to form felt if nonfelting fibers such as cotton or rayon are used with it in a blend; an all-wool felt will be much the strongest, and the best grades may use the short *noils* removed in combing during worsted yarn spinning of high-grade wools, or lustrous undercoat fur fibers such as beaver.

A *web* or *batt* of fibers is prepared, *steamed,* and *pounded* until a sheet of fabric is formed. Felt is made in many thicknesses, used for gaskets, boot insoles, padding, and of course, hats. "Numdah" rugs are felted. Fur felt uses the underfur of certain animals, with beaver giving superb quality and rabbit lower grades; fur fibers give luster, resilience, and water repellency.

Nonwoven

Nonwoven is the term applied to fabrics made directly from fibers, but not by the felting of wool or hair fibers; it has also been called *formed fabric* (see *Fabric Glossary:* NONWOVEN). There are a number of categories, but today they may be combined with one another, or with a process such as stitch-knit.[14]

[14]K. L. Floyd, Shirley Institute, "Nonwovens," *Textiles,* 12/3, 1983: 67.

Bonded Fiber Web.

Fiber webs may be laid at random, crosswise, or lengthwise, and may be bonded using adhesives or heat. Interfacings such as those made by Freudenberg are of this type and come in a wide variety of weights and thicknesses, some carrying dots of material of lower heat-softening point to make them *fusible;* Figure 4.78(a) shows interfacings used to build and hold shape in tailored shirts, and Figure 4.78(b) reveals some that will be hidden by lining in tailored jackets and coats. (Since 1995, the Freudenberg company uses one trademark name, VILENE®, in marketing worldwide to the clothing industry. Others of its trademark names, such as PELLON® or VILEDA®, may be used still in retailing its products.)

ALMOST® is a nonwoven of 100 percent nylon

(a)

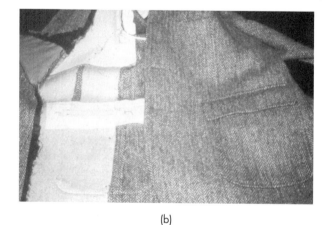

(b)

Figure 4.78 (a) Nonwovens used for interfacings in shirts. (Courtesy of Dominion Textile Inc.) (b) Nonwoven interfacing hidden in tailored clothing.

laid down in a three-directional axis to make a leather-like fabric that is tear- and puncture-resistant and air permeable.

Fiber webs can be held together without yarns by tangling some of the fibers in the web using needles. One type is called simply "needled"; the other is one of the Malimo stitch-knit type.

Needled. Needled (needle-punched, needle-woven, "needle felt") fabric involves inserting fine barbed needles into a fiber batt or web and tangling some of the fibers as the needles go in and out (see Figure 4.79).

One of the early needled products given a trademark name was Fiberwoven (by Chatham) blankets and another was the Ozite feltlike "indoor-outdoor"

(a)

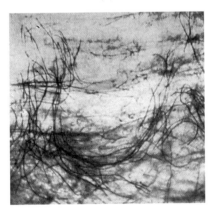

(b)

Figure 4.79 (a) Sample-sized needling machine; (b) section through needled fabric. (Courtesy of *Ciba Review*)

carpet. SUPAC® (by Phillips) is needled, and a type of miniature needling apparatus is used to hold layers of nonwoven fabric together to make shoulder pads.

Very realistic suedelike fabrics can be produced by needling, in a high-tech process that leaves ultra-microfibers on the nonwoven fabric surface, giving the soft hand of real suede (which is created by the naturally formed fibrils of the flesh side of a skin). A web of bicomponent matrix/fibril (islands-in-the-sea) fibers is needled to give an entangled nonwoven fabric. This is impregnated with polyurethane, then the matrix is dissolved with a solvent that does not affect the fibrils, leaving these ultra-microfibers (which can be well below 0.1 dtex) in place, giving the very soft surface. This can be sanded for the ultimate suedelike surface. If the fiber web is given a coating of polyurethane, it can also be embossed to give a leatherlike surface.

The best-known suedelike was created by Toray, Japan, under the name ECSAINE®, licensed as ALCANTARA® in Italy or ULTRASUEDE® in the United States (by Skinner Division of Springs Mills). Other trademark names are FACILE® (by Toray; MOSSO® in Europe, FACILMO® in the United States); BELLESEIME® (by Kanebo, licensed as SUEDE 21®, and using the ultra-microfiber BELIMA X®, illustrated under Microfibers—Suedelike fabrics, Section 2), SUEDEMARK I, II, III; CLARINO AMARETTA® or AMARA®, and a leatherlike version, CLARINO SOFRINA® (all by Kuraray).

Stitch-Knit No Yarns. Various stitch-knit or stitch-bonded processes were described earlier that use yarns in a warp knit looping to hold other components together into a fabric. A number of machines of the Malimo company do not use yarns at all. A web of fibers is stitch-bonded by forming the fibers into stitches to hold the web together as described under needled, except the needles are quite different, and the possibilities for fabric character are much wider (see Figure 4.80). A web formed into half stitches that show on one side only is called Malivlies. A deep pile fabric is made by the Voltex type of machine, while the Kunit type forms plush fabric (see Figures 4.81, 4.82). Malimo machines can take Kunit fleece and feed it to a Multiknit machine, which will knit a fleece on the other side to give a double-sided fabric (see Figure 4.83). This may be taken to move these materials into a third construction category—see Compound

Figure 4.80 Web-forming machine delivers fibrous fleece to a Kunit machine to be stitch-knit into a plush fabric containing no yarns. (Courtesy of Malimo Maschinenbau GmbH)

Fabrics—and offers the possibility of constructing and/or finishing one side of the fabric differently from the other. This has been developed as "BiPolar Technology" on standard knitted fabrics by Malden Mills with POLARTEC®, discussed under Knitting.

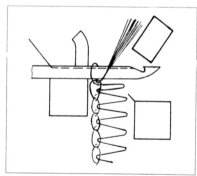

Working position in the KUNIT process

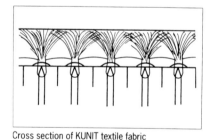

Cross section of KUNIT textile fabric

Figure 4.81 Diagrams of the Kunit process for stitch-bonding a fiber web into plush fabric. (Courtesy of Malimo Maschinenbau GmbH)

Figure 4.82 Kunit plush fabric, stitch-knit with no yarns. (Courtesy of Malimo Maschinenbau GmbH)

Spunbonded. Spunbonding involves holding filaments together just after extrusion from a spinneret; trademark names are ACCORD® (by Kimberley Clark), REEMAY® polyester, TYVEK® high-density polyethylene, and TYPAR® polypropylene (by DuPont). Nonwovens have been spunbonded by the action of heat on bicomponent filaments; the "skin" of the filaments has a lower softening point than the core, so when heat is applied, they fuse to form a fabric. This method was used by ICI to make Cambrelle, of heterofil bicomponent nylon.

Spunlaced. Spunlaced fabrics are formed by tangling filaments after extrusion, using jets of water to form a soft, unbonded structure that can have a repeating pattern. DURALACE® (by Johnson & Johnson), HYDROLACE (by CEL, part of Acordis), and SONTARA® (by DuPont) are of this type, the latter used extensively as an interfacing (see Figure 4.84). MIRATEC (by Polymer Group) is made by a special design- or hole-forming technique, using the Apex system.

Microfiber fabrics are produced on the HYDROLACE (by CEL [Acordis]) system by separating petal-shaped bicomponent filaments as the web is being formed, making a superfine non-woven fabric.

Kunit nonwoven (cross section)

(a)

Multiknit double-side nonwoven (cross section)

(b)

Plain knit surface

Opposite inner fibre orientation

Plain knit surface

(c)

Figure 4.83 Multiknit double-sided nonwoven formed by bonding of two Kunit fleece fabrics. (Courtesy of Malimo Maschinenbau GmbH)

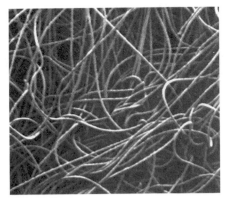

Figure 4.84 SONTARA® is a spunlaced nonwoven fabric extensively used for garment interfacings. (Courtesy of the DuPont Company)

Natural Fabrics

Animal skin can be looked on as a **"natural fabric,"** once the skin has been chemically stabilized to prevent rot (this is called *tanning* for leather, *dressing* for the skin of fur). Used with the hair left on we call it *fur;* with hair removed, we may use the outer side, called *grain* or *top grain leather,* or the flesh side, called *suede;* the middle layer is called the *corium* (see Figure 4.85, Figure 4.86).

Leather

Leather is composed of a very complex protein, *collagen,* classified as a triple alpha helix (see Figure 4.87, which shows only the axes of the polypeptide

Figure 4.85 Cross section through leather (scanning electron microscope). The grain (skin side) layer is at the top, the middle is the corium, and the inside (flesh side) is suede. (Courtesy of SATRA Footwear Technology Centre)

Figure 4.87 Collagen protein of leather—polypeptide chains form a triple α-helix. (Courtesy of the Textile Institute)

LEATHER TERMS

belly

shoulder
head
bend

side
side

Hide: Cow, Steer, Buffalo, Horse

grain

skin side

flesh side

suede (buffed)

cross-section of leather
(variations in density)

Skin: Calf, Pig, Sheep, Goat

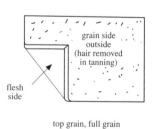

grain side outside (hair removed in tanning)

flesh side

top grain, full grain

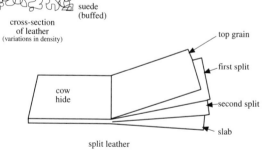

cow hide

top grain

first split

second split

slab

split leather

Figure 4.86 Leather terminology. (Adapted from *Apparel Anatomy*, with permission of Mary Humphries)

chains; the spaces between are packed with groups present on each amino acid residue). This is more complex even than the alpha-helix form of wool protein, keratin (see Figure 2.22). It shares many reactions with protein fibers; for instance, it can be molded with steam.

Leather from a smaller animal is called a *skin;* from a larger animal, a *hide;* so we have *pigskin* but *cowhide.* Half a hide is called a *side.* A thick hide can be *split* into thinner sheets, but an *inside split* will have no top grain and so will be less able to withstand wear; these terms are illustrated in Figure 4.86. "Chamois," as used for coat interlining, is an inside split suede sewn into *plates;* the same is done with fur (see Figure 4.88). (See also *Fabric Glossary:* LEATHER and see *plates* in the *Glossary of Fur Terms* under *Fur.*) Leather is still sold by the square foot, an odd practice in a mostly metric world, and there is no sign that this is about to change. A sheepskin is about 5–8 sq. ft.; a lambskin about 4 sq. ft.; and a cowhide side, 20–30 sq. ft.

Sources of Leather

If it has a skin in the animal world, it has probably been made into leather by humans! Common sources of leather include:

Domestic animals. Sheep (and lamb), goat (and kid, although all goatskin may be called kid), pig, cow (and calf), horse (and pony), deer (and doe)—ranched in New Zealand, buffalo.

Other animals. Kangaroo, rhinoceros, elephant, hippopotamus, etc.

Nonmammals. Snake, alligator—endangered (crocodile), lizard, frog, eel, fish (salmon), birds (see *Plumage—Feathers, Down,* Section 2).

Tanning

Tanning of leather preserves the skin, which has earlier been *cured* in salt (brine). The skin, then, is first *soaked* in a rotating drum to remove the salt, then *fleshing* cleans the inside of the skin of any flesh. *Liming* or *unhairing* uses alkaline chemicals (e.g., calcium hydroxide or lime) or enzymes to remove hair and roots. *Bating* is a final cleaning before the actual tanning.

Vegetable tanning uses chemicals from bark (notably oak, spruce, hemlock), sumac, or wattle; it takes several weeks to stabilize the skin, but the process is still used. Much modern leather, however, is **chrome tanned,** taking only 4–6 hours. First the skin is *pickled* to bring it to the right acidity so that the tanning agents will be soluble. Then chemicals, mainly chromium salts, accomplish the tanning. There is also a combination **vegetable/chrome tanning** process. Chrome-tanned leather has good resistance to moisture, perspiration, and heat.

"Wash leather" of sheep- or lambskin (chamois, or shammy) is treated with halibut oil to preserve it in a particularly soft state.

Hides are next *wrung* to squeeze out excess moisture, and then go through *splitting* and *shaving* to adjust and give uniform thickness. Some will have a *retan* with different compounds, and *coloring* can be done with dyestuffs (aniline finish) or pigments.

Fat liquoring is an oiling process (often using fish oils) that governs how soft or firm the leather will be. *Setting out* stretches and smooths the leather before it is dried. *Drying* affects the look of the leather; the hides may be hung, vacuum dried, or pasted on large plates. After drying, the leather is *conditioned* to introduce some moisture. *Staking* is done on a machine that stretches and flexes the leather in all directions; seeing a motion picture of this machine at work, one is reminded that leather can be chewed to soften it, an action reproduced by the staking machine!

Buffing is a kind of sanding that smooths the grain surface of leather, readying it for further finishing treatments; if it is not buffed, it is called *full grain*. *Finishing* contributes some stain and wear resistance to the leather surface, and usually color as well. It is simplest for the best skins with the fewest imperfections; these may be colored, but receive little surface "cover-up," and are left feeling soft and "buttery." Less perfect skins or hides may receive pigment or other *coating, glazing, metallic laminating,* as well as *embossing, tooling* (pushing out from the back), *antiquing,* etc., all of which can cover or change the surface and even give the look of other leather grains, such as snakeskin. *Plating* is the application of great pressure to smooth the surface.

Leather Properties

Leather is strong, resistant to punctures, and has "give" and flexibility. It is windproof, and if it is dry, it insulates well; however, it absorbs moisture, and if damp will not keep a person warm (see Section 7). Leather is permeable to moisture vapor and so allows

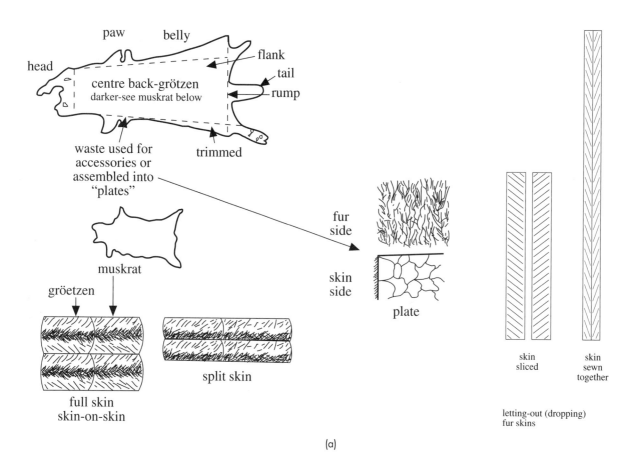

(a)

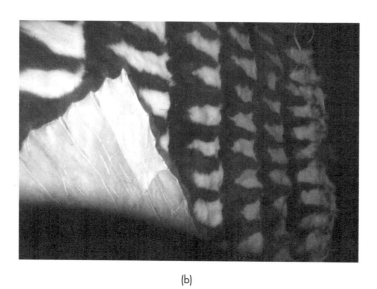

(b)

Figure 4.88 (a) Fur terminology. (b) Fur plate, face and back. (Adapted from *Apparel Anatomy*, with permission of Mary Humphries)

perspiration to pass through, and its absorbency means more comfort in shoes when feet perspire. If coated (as for patent leather) or made truly waterproof, this permeability is usually lost. Leather can be shaped (molded) and will hold a form. Care and storage of leather are discussed in Section 6.

Fur

Fur as a fashion fabric has been criticized for some time by animal rights activists. It is covered in this *Reference* because furs from animals that are either in what is termed "abundant supply" or raised for the purpose (ranched) are certainly still being used as a fabric. It is a very special, usually relatively expensive fashion material on which information is sparse. In the United States, the Fur Products Labeling Act (1952, amended 1980) requires that the animal be identified by a true name in English, and that dyeing or other alteration be specified along with country of origin.

Fur Quality/Price

Fur is not an investment in the sense that it would be expected to appreciate in value; it is an investment in beauty, glamor, and comfort.

Quality of any one type of fur is affected by weather (the best are taken in the coldest climates or weather), the condition of the animal, and its genetic background. Good-quality fur will be lustrous; feel soft and silky; and have soft, pliable leather. The guardhairs will be uniform in length and silky, and the underfur should be dense; check this by blowing the fur lightly on the edge of the garment fronts—it should spring back quickly and fully. Pelts from a female are smaller, with finer, silkier hair and lighter skin than those from a male.

Durability, however, depends on the type of fur (see Table 4.2) as well as its quality, and on the care it receives (see Section 6). Water animals, such as mink, need a coat that protects them all over, and so the skin and hair covering is much the same on the belly

Table 4.2   Fur Durability in Wear

Name of Fur	Durability of Hair	Durability of Skin	Name of Fur	Durability of Hair	Durability of Skin
Rodent Family:			Weasel Family:		
Beaver	E	E	Badger	VG	VG
Chinchilla	F	F	China mink	F	G
Hamster	F	G	Ermine—winter	FG	F
Marmot	FG	VG	Fisher	E	E
Muskrat—natural	VG	F	Fitch (polecat)—natural	VG	VG
Muskrat—dyed	VG	F	Fitch—dyed	G	G
Nutria	E	G	Kolinsky (Russian mink)— dyed	F	G
Rabbit—longhaired	F (sheds)	G	Kolinsky—sheared	F	VG
Rabbit—sheared	G	G	Marten—baum	FG	G
Squirrel, Canadian	F	F	Marten—stone	G	G
Squirrel, Russian	G	G	Marten, Canadian	G	G
Seal Family:			Mink	E	VG
Hair—natural	G	E	Otter, Canadian	E	E
Hair—dyed	E	E	Otter, South American river	E	VG
Hair—Norwegian	G	E	Sable	E	VG
Hair—white coat	FG	G	Skunk	E	E
Fur—Alaska	E	G	Plantigrade (Flat-Footed) Family:		
Fur—Cape, South-West Africa	G	G			
Fur—Russia	E	G			
Fur—Uruguay	G	FG			

continued

Table 4.2 Continued

Name of Fur	Durability of Hair	Durability of Skin	Name of Fur	Durability of Hair	Durability of Skin
Bassarisk (Ringtail cat)	VG	VG	Feline Family:†		
Raccoon—natural	E	E	Genet	FP	G
Raccoon—sheared	VG	E	Lynx	G	E
Raccoon, Asian	F	G	Lynx cat (wildcat)	FG	VG
Hoofed Family:			Lynx cat (Peludo)	G	G
American broadtail sheep	FG	G	Canine Family:		
Borega (jumbo	VG	VG	Fox, Asian red	FP	G
broadtail sheep)—			Fox, Australian red	F	F
South America			Fox—blue	FG	VG
Broadtail, Russian*—	F	F	Fox—cross	FG	VG
natural			Fox—kit	F	G
Broadtail, Russian*—dyed	FP	FP	Fox—red	FG	VG
Broadtail, South-West Africa	FP	FP	Fox—silver	E	E
Calf	G	E	Fox—white	FG	VG
Kalgan lamb	F	F	Wolf	G/E	E
Kidskin	FP (sheds)	FG	Marsupial Family:		
Mongolian lamb	F	F	Kangaroo	F	G
Persian lamb—natural	E	E	Opossum—United States	F	G
Persian lamb—dyed	G/E	F/VG	Opossum—Australia,	G	G
Pony	F	E	New Zealand		
Spanish lamb	VG	E	Miscellaneous:		
Swakara** (Karakul lamb)	G	G	Mole	F	FP
Zebra	G	E	Monkey	F	G

E = excellent   VG = very good   G = good   FG = fairly good   F = fair   FP = fairly poor   P = poor
*Russian broadtail fur comes from still-born lambs of the fat-tailed Bokhara ("broadtail") sheep.
**Swakara is a TM of the South West African government Karakul sheep breeders.
†Others of this family are considered endangered (listed in the Red Book of the International Union for the Conservation of Nature: leopard, ocelot, etc.).

as on the back; not so with a longer-legged land animal such as the fox, where the hair on the underside is more sparse and the skin much thinner.

Longhaired furs in general do not wear well, since the guardhairs tend to break and/or shed; one longhaired fur that does wear well, however, is raccoon.

Change of color is another aspect of wear. A dyed color can, of course, change more readily than a natural shade (bred in the animal), but all furs develop some yellowing with age; this will be less noticeable if the original color has a bluish overtone rather than a reddish.

Price is affected by quality, supply and demand, style, and the amount of labor a garment requires. Furriers tend to use pelts that are reasonable in price, and these, as a rule, will be the most plentiful.

The best buy in a fur would be a good quality of a type with good durability, which was not the most popular or in demand that season!

Furs are sorted and graded by human hand and eye for color, size, and quality, although there are electronic sorting machines for color (see *matching* under *Glossary of Fur Terms*). Enough skins to make a garment are put into and sold by *bundles*.

Construction of Fur Garments

A muslin *toile* is first made so that any adjustments of fit or cut can be made on it at this stage; one does not experiment with fur. The shape is then translated into heavy paper pattern pieces. Furs are matched and placed on the pattern in order, then given to the cutter.

Cutting will be by one of four methods; from least to most expensive, they are: skin-on-skin (full skin), split skin, semi-let-out, or fully let-out (see Figure 4.88[a] and *Glossary of Fur Terms*). With any of these, skins must be cut so that each part matches the color and pattern of the fur next to it.

The cut skins are carefully marked and handed in groups to the sewer, who stitches them together on a special machine, taking care not to catch any of the fur hairs into the special overlock seam (for more detail, see *letting-out* under *Glossary of Fur Terms*).

A fur coat cannot be pressed, as cloth coats can, to make seams straight and the coat hang properly. Instead, as it comes from the sewer, it is dampened and stretched to fit a chalked pattern on a large wooden board. It is then nailed on the board with the leather side out and left to dry. In let-out garments, every seam for the length of the garment is nailed firmly in place to assure a good hang, using thousands of nails.

After the fur is dry and removed from the board, it may be glazed; edges are closed and taped, lining sewn in, and buttons and other trim put on.

A slight scalloped effect at the hem of a fur coat is a good sign; it indicates that the skins were not stretched taut.

Glossary of Fur Terms

bleaching. Lightening of the natural color of a fur by a chemical process; most furs are bleached before being dyed to fashion colors.

boa. A rounded, plain fur neckpiece.

carving. Cutting away or sculpturing fur in parts to make a pattern.

cutting. Done by highly skilled fur craftspeople, using only a knife like a razor blade in a handle. For most intricate cutting, see *letting-out*.

damaging out. Cutting out poorer sections and replacing with better; shows on the inside as tiny, jagged joins.

down. See underfur.

dressing. The treatment of skins to preserve them, comparable to tanning of leather, except that in dressing, the hair is not removed.

feathering. Tipping fur with a dye to make the fur lustrous; a chemical spray gives sheen; water followed by pressing makes the fur smooth.

grötzen or groetzen. The line of darker color down the center of the back of furs. (See Figure 4.88[a]).

guardhairs. Outer hairs that protect the animal from weather; flat furs such as Persian lamb have no guardhairs. Guardhairs are shaved down in shearing.

hair-up. The process of reversing a skin so the rump end of the fur is at the top of the coat. The hair falls away from the body to look fuller.

hide-out. A special technique to make an unlined fur coat reversible.

knitting. Most fur "yarn" for knitting is made of narrow strips of fur sewn together; in a very few cases, yarn may be spun of fur.

leathering. Strips of leather, suede, or ribbon inserted into longhaired furs, such as fox, to make the coat lighter and less bulky.

letting-out, letting-down, dropping. The most skilled method of joining skins. Most skins are too short to be used for the full length of even short garments. The easiest way to join skins is *full skin* or *skin-on-skin,* which does not give much length. Letting-out is a much costlier method, which involves lengthening the skin into a single, longer, narrower strip. *Fully let-out* means that each skin, possibly combined with one or two others, runs the length of the garment; *semi-let-out* merely increases the length of each skin somewhat.

To let-out or drop skins, each is split along the grötzen, matched with one or two others, then each half skin is cut on the diagonal into strips 3 mm (⅛ in.) to less than 1 cm (no more than ⅜ in.) wide; as noted under *cutting,* this takes great skill. Another expert worker sews the strips together, with the edge of one placed a short distance below the previous, to extend the length. This is done on a special seaming machine, holding the two edges of the leather side together and keeping the hairs on the other side out of the way; this makes a flat seam like the overseam used on leather gloves. The result is that the area of the fur has been used, but the *shape* has been changed (*see* Figure 4.88[a]).

matching. Done by a skilled person to match furs that are to lie next to each other, considering length and texture of the hair and fur, color, markings, and the size of the skins. An electronic color shade sorting machine was developed by the Hudson's Bay fur auction house in London, England (no longer any connection with the Canadian firm).

nailing. Nailing dampened garment sections, leather side out, to a board to dry to shape.

oxidization. Natural aging—fading or yellowing—caused by light and air.

peltry, pelt. A raw, undressed skin.

plates. Small waste pieces of fur (paws, tails, neck [gills], flank [sides], etc.), stitched together into a "patchwork" which is then used in the same way cloth would be; the term is also used with leather scraps (Figure 4.88[a] and [b]).

plucking. Removing guardhairs to improve the texture of the fur or when the fur is to be sheared (*see shearing*).

pointing. Coloring the tips of the guardhairs.

scarf. Fur used in its original shape, with head, paws, and tail attached.

shearing. Cutting the fur (plucked or unplucked) to an *even*, velvety texture; this should be done only where the underfur is strong enough. Shearing does not affect warmth, but makes the fur lighter.

skin-on-skin (full skin, brick, chinchilla, or square cut). A method of joining pelts one below the other, giving a pattern of horizontal marks in the garment (Figure 4.88[a]). Seams between the pelts may be straight (weakest), wavy, or zigzag (strongest).

split skin. A method of joining skins in which each skin is split down the center and the halves turned on end, to run side by side, giving narrower dark stripes. For short garments, this method is much less costly than letting-out. (Figure 4.88[a]).

stenciling. Printing on fur, e.g., to get zebra stripes or leopard spots.

stole. A short fur cape extending in long panels down the front.

sweep. The circumference of the skirt at the hem.

toile. A garment made up in muslin to check the cut and fit before translating into fur.

underfur, "down." The soft, fine, downy underhair of furs that also carry guardhairs. Usually more dense and lighter in color than guardhair.

whole skins. A few peltries that are large enough to be used from neckline to hem, e.g., some lambskins.

Fabrics without Fibers

Film

Film is a structureless polymer sheet (no fibers, no yarns), commonly used for shower curtains, inexpensive rainwear, and wrappings. Thickness is identified by *gauge* number. Common materials are vinyon (what we call *vinyl*), saran, polyethylene, and polypropylene; viscose rayon film is used in packaging (*cellophane*).

Supported film involves a polymer coating on a fabric backing, such as vinyl- or urethane-coated leather-likes; see Section 5 and *Fabric Glossary:* COATED.

Microporous film has come to the forefront of development of clothing for inclement weather, with the first and best known an essential part of GORE-TEX® fabrics. Gore Fabric Technologies now has two components in this membrane: an expanded polytetrafluoroethylene (ePTFE) film ("expanded" indicating its microporous state), plus an oleophobic substance, polyalkylene oxide polyurethane-urea, which prevents contamination of the film by oily materials, such as cosmetics, food, or insect repellent. Since Gore fabrics are laminated constructions, they are described further in *Compound Fabrics*, this section, as well as in the *Fabric Glossary:* COMPOUND; WATERPROOF. A version of the film (PACLITE™) has raised dots all over the membrane, which protect against abrasion when it is used, so a substantial fabric liner is not needed (see Figure 4.89 and *Fabric Glossary:* WATERPROOF).

Reflective film is used as a safety marker on clothing and accessories in SCOTCHLITE™ (by 3M).

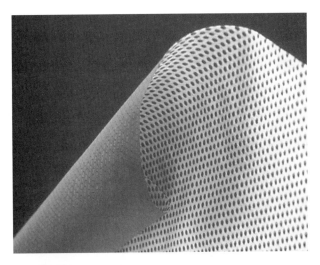

Figure 4.89 Raised dots on special film used in Gore-Tex PACLITE™ fabrics protect against abrasion, allowing a lighter assembly without liner. (Courtesy of W. L. Gore & Associates, Inc.

Tiny reflective beads are incorporated into film, the product designed to be highly reflective and durable, so as to increase visibility by day or night, or in dense smoke (for firefighters).

Film carrying a bar code and able to withstand the chemicals and high temperatures of textile processing has been used to help automatic production of fabric; the nylon film KAPTON has been used in Germany.

Foam

Foam in sheets is used as interlining, padding, or cushioning, usually laminated to another material (see Figure 4.90); it is not a strong structure. Its uses are discussed in the *Fabric Glossary:* FILM, FOAM.

There is a flammability hazard with foam-padded clothing if left hot in a pile after tumble drying (see Section 6).

Compound Fabrics

Compound fabrics (also called multicomponent, multilayer, multiplex, layered/joined) are made of different layers, held together by various means and used as one (see *Fabric Glossary:* COMPOUND). The components may be joined *all over* by **bonding, fusing,** or **laminating,** using adhesive, by heat, or by polyurethane foam made sticky with flame heat (see Figure 4.90).

Stitching holds layers together *intermittently,* as in **quilting** with thread. Trademark systems such as CHEMSTITCH® or PINSONIC® use chemicals or heat (from ultrasonic vibrations—*ultrasonic sewing*) to "**spot fuse**" fabrics together in a stitch effect.

Foam may be used on both sides of a lightweight nylon fabric (scrim) core, with flocked fiber on the surfaces; VELLUX® (by West-Point Pepperell) is a fabric of this construction, discussed further under *Flocking,* Section 5.

Figure 4.90 Tricot bonded to foam by heat, used for lining and cushioning in footwear.

Stitch-knit can give a nonwoven compound fabric, called multiknit (see Figure 4.83).

Vapor-Permeable/Moisture-Resistant (VPMR) Fabrics

Compound fabric configuration is very much in the news with accelerating developments in clothing that is not just high performance (durable) plus water- and windproof, but also comfortable because it is "breathable," i.e., water vapor (perspiration) permeable (VPWR).

Two main approaches have been taken, recorded in the *Fabric Glossary:* WATERPROOF, both involving microporous materials:

1. A coating (see Section 5 and *Fabric Glossary:* COATED).
2. A film laminated to other fabric(s). This is the method used for the original of this type, GORE-TEX® fabric, and its construction has been a model for many others, as well as the beginning of a number of other fabrics from Gore Fabric Technologies.

The basis for GORE-TEX fabric is the very thin, microporous membrane described under *Film*, this section. This is expanded polytetrafluoroethylene (ePTFE) or TEFLON® (by DuPont), having about 1.4 billion pores per cm² (about 9 billion per sq. in.) (see Figure 4.91). The pores are too small for water drops to penetrate but allow water vapor (perspiration) to pass through, ensuring comfort for the person wearing a fabric "system" incorporating this film. In the "second generation" GORE-TEX film, the membrane is combined by Gore with a compound that resists oily substances (body oils, cosmetics, and insect repellents) that might contaminate the film and make it less resistant to water as explained under *Film*; this compound renders the membrane windproof.

In biology, a film such as ePTFE is called a semipermeable membrane, and indeed, the thin film feels eerily like a natural membrane, e.g., the inside of an eggshell. However, most people never see or feel this crucial part of a GORE-TEX fabric, as it is laminated to an outer fabric, often a taffeta or poplin, and, in the three-layer laminate, to a liner such as tricot (see Figure 4.92[a]). The membrane used in PACLITE™ fabrics, as explained under *Microporous Film*, allows fabric laminates that are 15 percent lighter than an

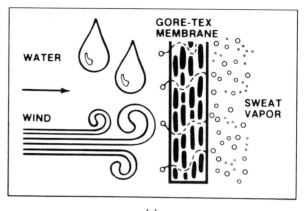

(a)

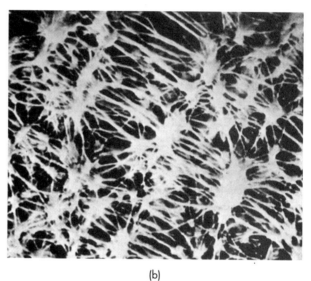

(b)

Figure 4.91 (a) Action of GORE-TEX® membrane; (b) tiny pores shown at 5000× magnification. (Courtesy of W. L. Gore & Associates, Inc.)

equivalent 3-ply GORE-TEX® article (see Figure 4.89). See the special note on care of GORE-TEX fabrics under *Care of Special Items* in Section 6.

So this film provides the magic total—vapor permeable/moisture resistant (VPMR) plus windproof—needed for body comfort outdoors in inclement weather; Figure 4.92(b) shows the action of a GORE-TEX fabric. In addition, the company will guarantee durability, plus quality of the finished article made with this fabric by licensed manufacturers only (see Section 6, *Private Sector Labeling*).

Other fabrics from Gore offer differing performance balanced with benefits for specific activities or

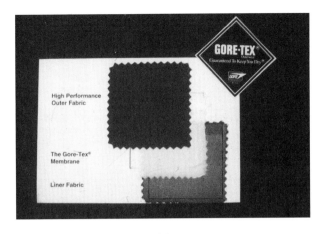

(a)

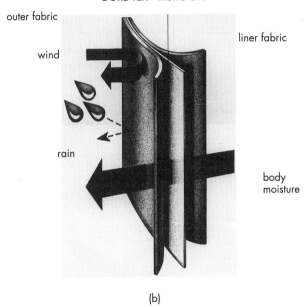

(b)

Figure 4.92 (a) Three-layer laminate of GORE-TEX® fabric, with appropriate logo. (b) Action of GORE-TEX® fabric, which allows body moisture vapor to pass outward through the fabrics and membrane, but blocks water drops or wind. (Courtesy of W. L. Gore & Associates, Inc.)

conditions, presented as a "Comfort Solutions" line-up. All are windproof. GORE-TEX® fabric is also rated waterproof and very breathable. DRYLOFT™ fabric is rated water resistant, rather than waterproof, but is extremely breathable; it was engineered to protect high-loft insulations. ACTIVENT™ fabric is water resistant and the most breathable of all; it is intended for wear during highly aerobic activities. WINDSTOPPER® fabric has no water resistance but is extremely breathable, and will give warmth with comfort in windy conditions; WINDSTOPPER fleece is slightly less breathable, about like the original GORE-TEX material (see Figure 7.6). From Gore also are OCEAN TECHNOLOGY® garments for windy conditions on saltwater, with improved seam sealing, and IMMERSION® fabric, for dry suits and fishing waders.

In combination with Milliken, Gore developed DURATHERM™ material specifically for footwear, one of the hardest parts of the body to protect *and* keep comfortable in bad weather. A GORE-TEX bootie ensures that footwear is waterproof (see Figure 7.4), while another footwear liner developed by Milliken is also a high-performance fabric: 100 percent polyester, with VISA® treatment to enhance wicking, MILLIGUARD® for a bacteriostatic effect (see *Other Special Finishes* in Section 5).

Some of the other systems are AQUAGUARD®, DARLEXX® (described as nylon/spandex stretch fabric with microporous film), CELTECH® (by Unitika, Wind River), and GAMEX® (polyurethane-silicone laminate). SYMPATEX® (by Akzo Nobel) is a very thin membrane (0.01 mm); joined to a microfiber material it is called, SYMPATEX MICROLINER®. See also its use with STOMATEX, Figure 4.93. THERMOCLAD® (by Descente) uses the ENTRANT® system with a very thin coating on the outer shell to shed water, plus an insulating layer of polyester, TEIJINCONEX (by Teijin) aramid and wool, and a lining either of brushed tricot or mesh coated with reflective aluminum. HYDROFLO® (by Doubletex), is a waterproof, breathable film that can be laminated to other fabrics. With a liner of H2OUT® (by Doubletex) the activewear system absorbs and disperses perspiration through the waterproof outer layer.

The outer layer WINDBLOC® series of POLARTEC® fabrics (by Malden Mills) also incorporates a windproof but vapor permeable membrane between two knit pile fabrics similar in weight to POLARTEC® SERIES 200 fabrics, including a water repellent on the outside.

Some trademark fabrics are hard to place in one category, such as the MICROFT® (by Teijin) polyester series; one seems to be coated, another uses a film, while Super-MICROFT, made of ultrafine, crimped polyester fibers, is described as windproof, highly water repellent, and permeable, but not waterproof.

Another approach to providing VPWR performance with comfort is the combination of two complementary layers into an advanced activewear fabric. SYMPATEX® (by Akzo Nobel), a nonporous, waterproof, stretchy membrane, is combined with STOMATEX® (by Micro Thermal Systems), described as a "smart" material, which helps dissipate heat through water vapor (sweat) in response to body activity (see Figure 4.93). Stomatex uses neoprene sheets in various gauges, with a series of convex domes vented by a tiny hole at the top of each dome. Said to mimic the passing of water vapor (transpiration) through the stomata of a leaf, STOMATEX responds to the physical activity of the wearer. It pumps faster when the person is active and more heat is produced, less when the wearer is at rest, thus controlling the release of moisture vapor.

Other trademarked fabrics will be found in Section 5, under the discussion of coatings.

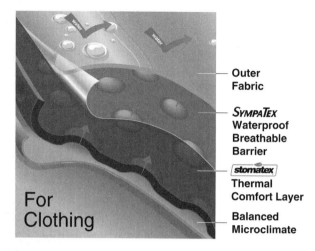

Figure 4.93 "Biometric" fabric of SYMPATEX MEMBRANE in combination with STOMATEX gives waterproof fabric with comfort in wearing. (Courtesy of Micro Thermal Systems and Akzo Nobel)

SECTION FIVE

*F*INISHING OF *F*ABRICS

Role of Fabric Finishing

Greige or gray goods refers to fabric as it comes off the loom (loom state), knitting machine, or whatever machine made it. It is usually rather unattractive, may be soiled, is often a creamy or dull shade of off-white (unless fibers or yarns have been dyed), and has developed little of its potential beauty or character of surface. You would not usually be able to buy fabric "in the greige," but compare unbleached sheeting with finished to see what a great difference bleaching (see Figure 5.1), dyeing, or printing can make. Finishes such as glazing or embossing, which also produce a marked effect on the fabric surface, bring about even more startling changes (see *Fabric Glossary:* CHINTZ; EMBOSSED). Unbleached muslin (the fabric osnaburg) is close to being an example of greige goods, although it is certainly scoured (washed) (see *Fabric Glossary:* SHEETING, APPAREL).

Differences can be even greater in wool family fabrics, e.g., a blanket or coating cloth, in which fulling and napping in finishing totally change the character of the cloth (see *Wool: Fulling* and *Fabric Glossary:* DUVETYN; FLEECE; MELTON).

Finishing is done in special plants called *converters,* which are usually separate from the textile mill that manufactured the cloth; only large manufacturers are vertically integrated to perform almost all functions (short of producing MF fibers), including finishing.

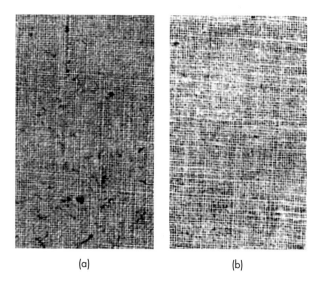

(a)   (b)

Figure 5.1 **(a) Greige fabric; (b) scoured and bleached, most trash and motes removed.**

Finishing the Natural Fibers

Certain finishing procedures have been developed over the centuries, as human skill—art and craft—created superlative fabrics of each of the "big four" natural fibers: wool, silk, cotton, and flax.

Wool

Wool, a protein fiber, is not sensitive to acids but is to alkalies and chlorine bleach; this affects the choice of chemicals in finishing.

Scouring. Scouring (washing), done with low-alkali agents, removes up to 50 percent of the original weight of the fleece: soil, *suint* (perspiration), wool grease (more properly called "wool wax"), and some vegetable matter caught in the fleece. In order to prevent the wool grease from going rancid and to get rid of a lot of dirt, wool is generally scoured in its loose state, pushed by rakes through successive bowls of a scouring machine and passed through wringers between each bowl and the next.

Refined wool grease is *lanolin,* reclaimed for pharmaceutical and cosmetics use, as it goes into human skin with less feeling of greasiness than ordinary animal fats.

Bleaching. Bleaching must be with mild oxidizing agents or reducing bleaches, the types used in household "bleach for the unbleachables." (See *Bleaches* under *Laundering* in Section 6.)

Carbonizing. This is a process unique to wool, whereby any residual plant matter caught in the fleece is removed; this includes twigs or leaves, but especially burrs. The wool is treated with dilute sulfuric acid, then heated, which concentrates the acid, charring the plant material (turning the cellulose to carbon) so that it can be shaken out.

Fulling. Fulling is the controlled felting of surface wool fibers, producing a dense, compact surface and a thicker fabric. Nearly every fabric of wool receives some fulling in finishing. Fulling is accomplished by squeezing or pounding the fabric in a soap solution, and is closely related to **milling.** Fulling is usually done most vigorously on wool fabric of spun (carded only) yarns, especially thick (winter) coat fabrics. Melton has almost completely felted surfaces on both sides. Figure 5.2 shows the dramatic change fulling can make, often in combination with *napping* (see *Other General and Basic Finishes* and *Fabric Glossary:* MELTON). A combination of fulling and napping can even produce a curly or wavy surface, as on chinchilla cloth (see *Fabric Glossary:* FLEECE WOVEN). A thick, knit wool fabric in plain stitch, often with inlay, very heavily fulled produces the comfortable coat fabric Boiled Wool (see *Fabric Glossary:* FLEECE KNIT).

Decating and Crabbing. Decating is a special steaming process for wool fabrics; crabbing is a treatment in boiling water to remove strains that might result in shrinkage or creases later (see also the discussion of London shrinking under *Other Special Finishes—Dimensional Stability*).

Mothproofing. Mothproofing of wool makes the protein of hair fibers indigestible, or kills the larvae. Most agents have been insecticides, and today such a finish is not usually identified by a trademark name, as it once was, since the cost of application has gone down. A principal use is for wool carpet. Such a compound has to be safe for all concerned and resistant to removal by the conditions of care. For more details on attack on wool by insect larvae, see Section 6, *Storage of Textile Articles.*

Silk

Silk undergoes specialized processes, the most significant being *degumming* of raw silk (see Figure 5.3); the stage at which to perform this essential process to give the best-quality product already discussed in Section 2 under *Silk Production.* Wild silk has gum that cannot be entirely removed. The other silk finishing terms mentioned in Section 2 are *weighting, pure dye silk,* and *scroop.* Weighting of silk has been

(a)

(b)

Figure 5.3 (a) Raw silk fabric before degumming; (b) degumming reveals the white, drapable silk fabric.

Figure 5.2 Melton fabric in the greige (loom state) (top), after fulling (lower right) and finished (left). (Courtesy of the Woolmark Company, formerly IWS)

done to increase the body of these expensive fabrics; it is not common any longer. Metallic salts are used, often tin salts. Weighted silk is not as strong as fabric without weighting; weighted fabrics are more stiff, can crack more easily, are more readily attacked by perspiration and light, and show water-spotting, which unweighted silk will not. See *Other General and Basic Finishes* for a discussion of *mill washing* of silk.

Cotton

Cotton, a cellulose fiber, is not sensitive to alkali or chlorine bleach but is to acid, especially mineral acids.

Scouring. Scouring of cotton is done near the boil, in a kier, with high-alkalinity built detergents ("heavy-duty" detergents; see Section 6).

Bleaching. Bleaching of cotton is safe with strong oxidizing agents; the types most familiar to consumers are sodium hypochlorite (liquid "chlorine" bleach) and calcium hypochlorite (solid type). Scouring and bleaching of cotton also remove the last of the plant impurities called *trash* or *motes* (see Figure 5.1). Sometimes this "natural" look is retained on purpose, when fabrics such as osnaburg become fashionable (see *Fabric Glossary:* SHEETING, APPAREL).

Mercerizing. Mercerizing of cotton is a permanent alteration accomplished by treatment with the strong alkali sodium hydroxide (NaOH, also called caustic soda or lye). The material is usually held under tension, or it will shrink up; **slack mercerization** (without tension) gives a degree of "stretch" to woven cotton (see *Fabric Glossary:* STRETCH, COMFORT). The cotton fibers swell, losing their twisted ribbon shape, to revert to a nearly cylindrical form (see drawings of typical features of fibers seen through the microscope, Section 2 and Figure 5.4[a]). They are smoother and more lustrous, and also get stronger and more absorbent. Goods that are mercerized are usually high quality, i.e., made of long-staple cotton fibers in combed yarns; typical fabrics as indexed to *Fabric Glossary* Files for mercerized cotton are BATISTE (some); BROADCLOTH (COTTON); CHINO; and lisle under JERSEY (see Figure 5.4[b]). Mercerizing is also used for good-quality cotton sewing thread (see *Thread* in Section 3).

Flax (Linen)

Flax, although a cellulose fiber like cotton, is given specialized finishing procedures.

Bleaching. For the best-quality linen, bleaching is done by somewhat milder methods than for cotton, including *dew or grass bleaching,* in which the fabric is spread on grass fields to allow the moisture of dew and the natural oxidation of light to bleach it. Chlorine bleach must be used with more care on flax because this bast fiber is composed of many cells (rather than a single cell like cotton); if the waxes and pectins holding these cells together are attacked, as by strong bleach, the fiber can be weakened.

Beetling. Beetling is applied to table linens such as damask (see *Fabric Glossary:* DAMASK) or to cottons to give a linen-like finish. The fabric is hammered by wooden blocks for up to 60 hours, flattening yarns permanently and closing the weave to give a soft hand and luster.

Other General and Basic Finishes

Napping (Raising). Fiber ends are teased out of loosely spun yarns and brushed so they stand up on the surface of the fabric. Fine bent wires are used to nap most fabrics. Figure 5.5 shows how a nap covers the weave structure; the change of shape of the square check pattern to a rectangle reflects the lengthwise pull on the fabric during heavy napping.

A few fabrics of very fine wool, notably wool broadcloth (see *Fabric Glossary:* FLEECE WOVEN) or cashmere, are napped with natural teasel burrs; in Yorkshire and the Scottish borders, these are also called "mousers," suggestive of cats' claws. Because these burr barbs will break before the delicate fibers do and the burrs have to be replaced frequently, imitation "burrs" of nylon have been tried for this purpose. For other wool family fabrics with an obvious napped surface see *Fabric Glossary:* DUVETYN, FLANNEL (and the cheaper FLANNELETTE), and MACKINAC.

When fiber ends are worked out of some cotton fabric, such as denim, it is termed **brushed,** rather than napped.

Emerizing (Sanding). Emerizing with emery- or sandpaper-surfaced rollers produces a brushed or

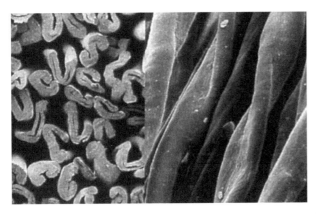

(a)

(b)

Figure 5.4 (a) Cotton fibers (left) are made smoother (right) by mercerizing. (Courtesy of Morrison Textile Machinery Company) (b) Lisle, knit of mercerized cotton.

suedelike finish. Emerizing has long been used for fabric such as tricot, to break the filaments and leave a soft surface (see *Fabric Glossary:* SUEDED). A sophisticated version gives the suede-like polyester fabric from Spain, ALCATRAZ® (T.G.I. Fabrics).

Shearing (Cropping). Shearing is applied to much napped and pile fabric, by passing it over a cylinder with blades like a giant hand lawnmower; in fact, this machine was the inspiration for the lawnmower (see Figure 5.6). The fabric may then be brushed to remove cut bits of fiber, or brushed and steamed to lay a nap or pile in one direction; **brushing** here is done with bristles set in a cylinder, not wires or an emery surface. (See *Fabric Glossary:* VELOUR KNIT.)

Singeing or Gassing. This is the process of passing a fabric quickly over a gas flame to burn off any protruding fibers. It is done to give a smooth surface, as in lisle (see *Fabric Glossary:* JERSEY). Singeing can also help prevent pilling, for instance, in polyester suitings, by fusing any protruding fiber ends.

Calendering. Calendering is mill pressing, done by passing fabric between huge, heavy, heated rollers so that heat and pressure polish the cloth. Ciré, today usually a nylon taffeta for sportswear (see *Fabric Glossary:* CIRÉ), has the shiny surface given by calendering on thermoplastic fabrics. The *Schreiner calender,* engraved with many very fine lines, gives a satinlike luster; this is often applied to tricot used for lingerie,

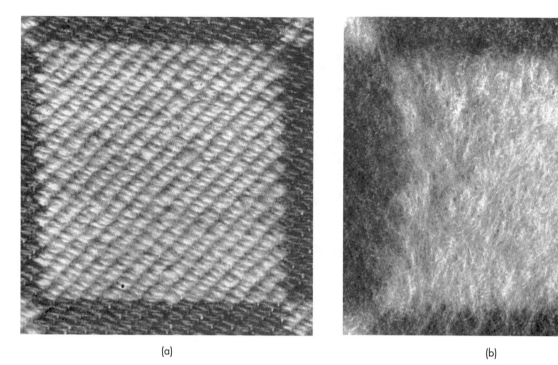

(a)   (b)

Figure 5.5 Effect of napping on a ⅓ weft-face twill check. (a) Before napping; (b) note extension in length of the check after napping. (Courtesy of the Woolmark Company, formerly IWS.)

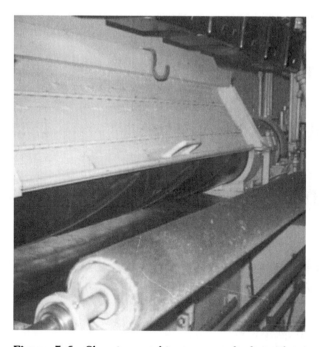

Figure 5.6 Shearing machine uses a cylinder with a blade like a giant hand lawnmower.

referred to as satinized or given a name like satinesque.

Creping. Creping gives the pebbly surface associated with crepe fabrics as traditionally produced by using very high twist yarns containing a fiber that will swell in water. When the fabric is immersed in the creping bath, the fibers swell; held tightly in the high-twist yarn, they form little bumps on the fabric surface or, in a more complex weave, the bark-like wrinkle of crepon (see *Fabric Glossary:* CREPON, BARK CREPE). A crepe effect can also be obtained by using textured set filament yarns that will shrink up in wet finishing to give a crepey surface. The *Fabric Glossary:* CREPE, ALL TYPES lists all ways of achieving a crepe, then concentrates on crepe given by crepe weave.

Crinkle Sheeting. This is achieved by shrinking high-twist yarns to give a bark crepe effect (see *Fabric Glossary:* SHEETING, APPAREL).

Stiff or Crisp Finish. Stiff or crisp finishes may be durable or not. Nondurable types are given by sizings or fillers such as starch or natural gums; a durable crisp finish can be given by resins. A permanent crisp finish is given to organdy by the action of acid on cotton cellulose; a similar process on other fabrics or paper is called *parchmentizing:* the acid turns some of the cellulose to a jelly, which hardens, leaving the fabric thinner and permanently crisp. This process takes great skill, and such organdy will be expensive (see *Fabric Glossary:* ORGANDY). Other examples of crisp or stiff fabrics are discussed in *Fabric Glossary* Files: ORGANZA regarding organza and mousseline de soie; GAUZE regarding buckram, book muslin, and tarlatan; and TAFFETA regarding taffeta.

Softeners. Softeners very similar to those sold for home use are often applied to goods in manufacture to give a pleasing hand and more fullness. They will also take up moisture from the air to help dissipate static, but have only a temporary effect, and most can cause yellowing. However, more durable, high-quality softeners have been developed, with the most promise for cottons coming from polysiloxane compounds.[1] Lightweight, washable wool fabrics demand high-performance softeners, and SOFTLAINE SLW (by Stephenson Thompson), a silicone-based microemulsion, is said to give a cashmere-like hand, last through washings, and improve sewability of woven goods.[2]

Mill Washing. Mill washing or prewashing of cotton fabrics has grown greatly in popularity; it gives a "relaxed," worn look, popular for some time with denim in jeans and other garments. **Stone washing** is applied mainly to blue denim, and consists of wet tumbling with *pumice*—small lava rocks found in areas with recent active volcanos,[3] which are much less dense (lighter) than regular stones (see Figure 5.7).

Other denim finishes give a worn appearance variously called, depending on the effect, **frosted, distressed** or **abused,** and indeed, this tough fabric has been attacked with buckshot or even sandblasting

Figure 5.7 Denim stone-washed with pumice.

so that the most fashionable and highest-priced jeans can look to be in the worst condition! Some effects called "sandblasted" spray the material with sand, but others use less abrasive solid material or powdered color remover. Other finishes have achieved the well-used look by methods with little relation to the name given them: **Acid-washed** employs an oxidizing chemical to take out color, either chlorine (wet process) or permanganate (dry), while **mud-washed** usually gets its effect from prewashing and overdyeing. The processes have been refined in recent years to give the effect with much less actual damage to the fabric (or to the environment—see Section 7). For instance, **enzyme-washed** uses *cellulases*—enzymes that attack the cellulose—instead of or along with stone washing. This process removes any surface fuzz on cotton fabrics to prevent or reduce pilling in use; one such process was given a trademark name, BIO-POLISHING™ (by Nuovo Nordisk, U.K.), but *biopolishing* has become a general term for the process. Cellulase treatment has been found to reduce fibrillation in lyocell fabrics. A combination of enzyme treatment and stone-washing is called *biostoning*, and requires less stone or pumice to give the worn look.[4]

[1] I. Holme, "Challenge and Change in Functional Finishes for Cotton," *Textile Horizons*, February/March, 1997: 17–23.

[2] "Tomorrow's World," *Textile Horizons*, September, 1998: 18.

[3] Jerry M. Hoffner, "Identifying Acid Wash, Stone Wash Pumice," *Textile Chemist & Colorist*, 25/2, February 1993: 13.

[4] In Holme, "Challenge and Change," 17–23.

With linen, a term used for mill-washed flax yarns is *delavé*.[5]

This worn look is in demand even for silk, but what is called *sand-washed silk* might better be called *sanded washable silk;* there seems to be confusion here between terms such as *stone-washed* used with denim and **sanding**, the dry process already discussed, in which fabric is passed over emery-covered rollers that break surface filaments to give a soft, matte surface (see *Fabric Glossary:* SUEDED). Some sources report that silks are tumbled in sandpaper-lined drums, but other sources suggest they are washed with sand to roughen the filament surface.

Other Regular Finishing Processes. The *tenter* or *stenter* frame holds fabric as it goes through various processes, such as coating and drying. Whether pins or clips are used along the edges of the material, tenter holes are left along the selvage of woven goods or the waleswise edge of flat knit fabrics or circular knits slit open to handle flat in finishing. These holes are usually smaller on the face of the fabric (see *Fabric Glossary:* SELVAGE).

Weft straighteners can be sophisticated machines used with tenters to prevent *off-grain* wovens, in which the weft is not lying at a 90-degree angle to the warp; these are termed *bowed* if the weft is curved, or *skewed* if the fabric, held up along a weft, does not fall straight.

Fabrics with slight flaws can be reclaimed by careful hand **mending** in a textiles mill, and most fabrics have any loose ends clipped off in **burling**, usually done along with mending. **Final inspection** or **perching** is carried out as fabric is passed over a raised, lighted frame, and today this process usually provides computer-controlled tracking of faults for quality control.

"Added Value" and Special-Purpose Finishes

Most finishes that can be classified as **"added value"** or **special-purpose** are chemical and additive, but are not always detectable by look or hand; many do carry trademark names, and for the outstanding ones, these are a virtual performance guarantee.

[5]"World News: Spinning Eastwards," *Textile Horizons,* August/September 1997: 7.

Coatings

Coatings have become increasingly complex, and the line between coating and compound (multilayer) fabric grows increasingly hard to draw, so refer also to *Compound Fabrics,* Section 4.

Coatings of "vinyl" (polyvinyl chloride or PVC), rubber (latex), resin (one incorporates dimethylformamide or DMF), polyurethane (PU), nylon, polyester, foam, or metallic particles (usually aluminum) in a resin may be applied. Of these more common coatings, PU has the considerable advantage for rainwear of being dry-cleanable, which vinyl and rubber are not.

Leather-like fabrics very often incorporate a coating, often an "expanded" foam layer with a somewhat spongy feel to imitate the hand and construction of actual skins (see Figure 5.8 and *Fabric Glossary:* COATED).

Pile fabrics (tufted, sliver-knit, fur-like pile and upholstery materials such as frisé) usually have a coating on the back to bind the pile to the fabric; latex (rubber) is often applied. **Drapes** may have a foam backing to make them opaque for room darkening, and for added insulation. Latex coatings on drapes or tufted mats and carpets can either dry and crumble or turn to sticky goo with heat and age.

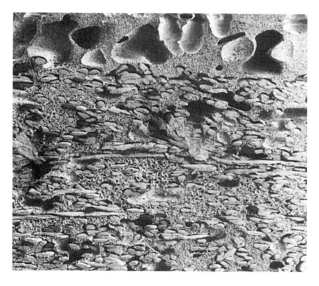

Figure 5.8   Cross section through a leatherlike fabric. A coating of foam provides the outer layer (like leather grain); a nonwoven fabric acts like the leather corium layer (scanning electron microscope). (Courtesy of SATRA Footwear Technology Centre)

Impermeable. When a coating is impermeable, it is virtually a film supported by a fabric, useful in such applications as upholstery but, in most cases, less so in clothing (see *Fabric Glossary:* COATED). However, some **hydrophilic coatings** have been developed to create a film that, even though impermeable to water vapor, can carry moisture away by diffusion. Research, for instance at the Shirley Institute, the United Kingdom, has combined hydrophilic materials with nonporous PU films to give this effect.

Microporous. Microporous (permeable, "breathable") coatings are a rapidly growing group of finishes, usually part of a fabric "system" of a number of layers (which takes many into the area of compound fabrics, as noted earlier).

In most clothing applications, microporous coatings are intended to give protection against inclement weather, particularly wet conditions, while keeping the wearer comfortable. The importance to comfort of moisture vapor (perspiration) being allowed to escape was discussed in Section 4 under *Compound Fabrics.* Microporous coatings can do this because they are permeable to the vapor form of "insensible perspiration." These are discussed here with trademark names.

Microporous polyurethane (PU) is one type, which is used on the inside of rainwear to make DERMOFLEX® (by Consoltex); see Figure 5.9. Another trademark name for this type is NAUTEX (by Nautica).

A microporous coating is also part of CYCLONE (by Carrington) fabric and ENTRANT (by Toray), a system that includes a very thin coating on the outside to shed water. THERMOCLAD (by Descente) uses the Entrant system, but is many-layered, and so is described under *Compound Fabrics,* Section 4.

Others that use a very thin microporous coating are EXELTECH, KKOTE (by K-Way), HELLY-TECH (by Helly-Hansen), H2NO (by Patagonia), HOKUS POKUS, MICROTEC, OMNI-TECH, PERMIA, and ULTREX.

THINTECH™ (by 3M) is a fabric impregnated with PU, to draw moisture away from the body.

Reflective. Reflective coatings have been used to create "Space Age" high-performance textiles, to conserve body heat in very light fabrics. One such trademark name is SOLARSILK, which incorporates an aluminized layer with ULTRAFIL siliconed hollow-fiber insulation in various constructions.

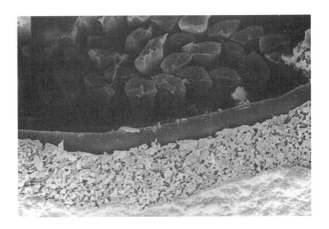

(b)

Figure 5.9 (a) DERMOFLEX® microporous polyurethane coating on the inside of rainwear allows perspiration vapor to escape but stops water. (b) DERMOFLEX logo. (Courtesy of Consoltex Inc.)

Metallized lining fabrics (Milium® [by Milliken] was a well known name some years ago) are no longer much used in clothing, but a wider use for a metallized coating is on the back of drapes for insulation and/or room darkening. HIPORA-TM is a fabric coated with DMF and aluminum.

Carbon/Ceramic Particles. Carbon or ceramic particles in a coating are also used to retain body heat. THINSULATE™ CERAMIC is based on THINSULATE microfiber insulation and also adds ceramic particles, as does HIPORA-CR, the latter coated with DMF and ceramic particles.

Photoluminescent. Photoluminescent coatings are applied to clothing as well as structures to glow in the dark or in smoke, a boon for fire and other rescue service personnel. PERMALIGHT is a nonradioactive material that is also incorporated into paints. Another approach to making highly visible safety material is SCOTCHLITE™ reflective fabric (by 3M); see *Film,* Section 4.

Microthermal (formerly called Phase Change Materials or PCMs). Microthermal materials applied in microcapsules as a coating on textiles (see Figure 5.10[a]) provide clothing that can protect the body against cold by reducing heat loss. In general terms this can be described as a *heat-flow barrier,* also termed *temperature regulation* (see Figure 5.10[c]) and *comfort management.* MicroPCMs can be incorporated into fibers, and so could belong in Section 2 under *Additions to Manufactured Fibers before Spinning.* They can also be incorporated into layers of foam.

The PCMs melt at about skin temperature; when these are incorporated into a garment worn outdoors in cold weather (or in a commercial cold room), excess heat generated by the body is absorbed into the OUTLAST layer and distributed throughout, reducing cold spots. Stored heat is released back to the body as needed, and will not be lost to the outside until the PCMs are all in a liquid state, and then more slowly than through a fabric without the PCMs. Once liquid, the PCMs will again solidify in the cold, giving off heat (see Figure 5.10[c]).

With selection of different microthermal materials, various temperature ranges can be targeted, e.g., protection for firefighters, although the original research was applied to protection from cold. OUTLAST was developed under research for NASA and the U.S. Air Force, with the original use in space gloves, to give nonlofted insulation that did not depend on air entrapment. OUTLAST articles are not only less bulky, but if they do get wet, unlike air-trapping insulation, the insulating value is not lost. Wetness from perspiration is less of a problem, since overheating is deferred. In shoes, PCMs provide foot cooling.

In work on microthermal materials by other companies, an earlier compound used, ethylene glycol, has not proven as satisfactory as the purified waxes (paraffinic hydrocarbons) now used, either synthetic or obtained from petroleum.

Other Encapsulation Technology. Other finishes use microencapsulation to apply anything from fragrance to insecticide to a fabric surface, to be released during wear.

The NEXTEC process (by Nextec Applications) allows individual fibers in a fabric to be encapsulated with an ultrathin sheet of polymer to give a wide variety of possible additions to the material, from water repellency to chemical or biochemical active agents.[6]

[6]In Holme, "Challenge and Change," 17–23.

(a)

(b)

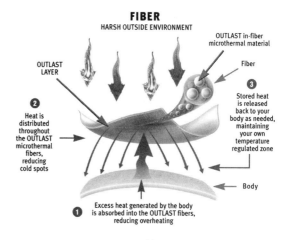

(c)

Figure 5.10 (a) OUTLAST® temperature regulation fabric is coated with microthermal material, which acts as a heat flow barrier. (b) OUTLAST logo. (c) Temperature regulation in a cold outside environment. (Courtesy of Outlast Technologies, Inc.)

Other Special Finishes

Water Repellent. Water-repellent (showerproof) finishes commonly use resins or (more effective) silicone-containing compounds such as SYL-MER or, on leather goods, SYLFLEX (by Dow). In the 1990s, wax finishes on cotton and linen fashion fabrics became popular (see *Fabric Glossary:* WATER REPELLENT). Such finishes will hold off a light fall of rain (shower), but are *not* waterproof.

Stain Resistant/Soil Resistant. **Stain-resistant** finishes must go a step further than the water repellent and repel oily as well as water-borne stains; this is done by **fluorocarbon** finishes, such as SCOTCH-GARD™ (by 3M), TEFLON® (by DuPont), ZONYL® 8070 (by DuPont, jointly with Ciba-Geigy). **Soil-resistant** carpets can combine a number of approaches: use of a soil-hiding, voided fiber modification, with fluorochemical finish plus **blocking of staining.** This latter involves saturating the carpet fiber with a colorless acid dye, since most staining agents in food and drink are acid-dye-type colors. A problem has arisen that is being researched: that of a reduction in stain resistance in stain-blocker-treated nylon with protracted exposure to ultraviolet light. Some major trademark names of these soil-resistant carpets are STAINMASTER®, SPILLBLOCK® (by DuPont), all WEAR DATED® carpet lines (by Solutia), and ANSO V WORRY FREE® (by Allied). (Discussion of how to clean such a carpet is given in Section 6.)

Soil Release. **Soil-release** finishes are used where items get a lot of soiling and are washed often, especially if made of polyester. (They therefore serve a different purpose from stain repellents, which are most helpful on items such as home furnishings, which are difficult to clean.) Well-known trademark names of soil release finishes are CELISA® (by Celanese), REPEL-O-TEX® PSR (by Rhodia), SCOTCHGARD™ STAIN RELEASE or SCOTCH-RELEASE™ (by 3M), VISA® (by Milliken), and ZELCON® (by DuPont). These finishes are also promoted as giving polyester better absorbency, which will contribute to comfort in wearing but also means that stains held in a more absorbent surface can be washed away during laundering. (See Figure 5.11.)

Permanent Hydrophilic Treatment. Finishes can be applied to fabrics of cellulose or other fibers to increase moisture transport. INTERA® (by Intera Technologies) is one process that promises a permanent bonding of hydrophilic material to the surface of materials made of a variety of fibers, including nylon, polyester, acrylic, and aramid. This gives the benefits of wicking and allowing for evaporation of perspiration away from the skin so important in activewear. It means the material will release soil more easily (as discussed under *Soil-Release* finishes). Evidence shows that fabrics with this treatment that remain damp are not as liable to bacteria growth as untreated, damp fabrics. Figure 5.12 gives results of a standard

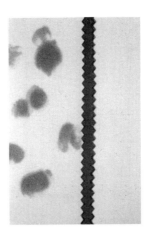

Figure 5.11 Polyester fabric with REPEL-O-TEX™ PSR soil-release finish (right) comes clean much better than untreated polyester (left). (Courtesy of Rhodia, formerly Rhône-Poulenc)

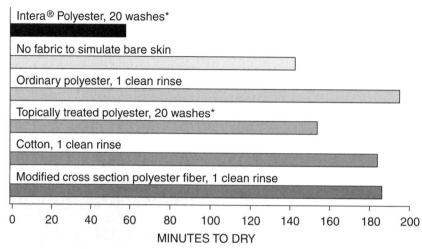

Drying time for .77 grams of water (sweat) to evaporate through a piece of fabric.

Intera® Polyester, 20 washes*

No fabric to simulate bare skin

Ordinary polyester, 1 clean rinse

Topically treated polyester, 20 washes*

Cotton, 1 clean rinse

Modified cross section polyester fiber, 1 clean rinse

MINUTES TO DRY

Figure 5.12 Standard test of drying time of knit fabric treated with INTERA® compared to others. (Courtesy of Intera Corporation)

* Refers to Standard Absorbancy Wash Test. All other moisture transport technologies begin to wash off after the first wash and after as little as ten washes are half as effective as when new. Intera® technology is permanent.

test of drying time of knit polyester treated with INTERA (after 20 standard washes) compared to that of a similar knit fabric with another treatment on polyester after 20 washes; cotton; a modified cross section polyester; and no fabric to simulate bare skin. A test kit is available to demonstrate this fabric treatment (see *References and Resources, Teaching Aids*).

Flame Retardant. Flame-retardant finishes can be applied to fabrics of cellulose or other highly flammable fibers, but generally these give poor aesthetic qualities, e.g., a harsh hand. An improved type made of lyocell and polyester was developed for Carrington Career and Workwear Fabrics under the name FURY®. Approaches to conferring flame resistance, other than by finishes (such as fabric construction and garment design), were discussed in Section 2 under *Burning Behavior.*

Bacteriostatic Agents. These inhibit growth of bacteria in an attempt to prevent unpleasant odors from developing in textiles (discussed in Section 2 under *Additions to Manufactured Fibers before Spinning*). Some trademark names of finishes are DAISY FRESH, MILLIGUARD (by Milliken), and STERI-SEPTIC.

Wrinkle Resistant or Crease Recovery. Such a finish is needed with cellulose fiber fabrics. A durable finish will last for the life of the article under normal wear and care, but will soften or lose some of its effectiveness over that time. "Wash and Wear" fabric will have this property. With washable silk of great interest, research has been done to counteract the wrinkling of silk when it is wet, due to its low wet resiliency. Application of one of the polycarboxylic acids (butanetetracarboxylic acid or BTCA) as a cross-linking agent is one such treatment of silk. **Crush resistance** is a special finish applied usually to rayon velvet.

Durable Press. Durable Press (often called "perma-press" or some such term falsely suggesting permanence) gives the completed article a set shape and size and a pressed or finished look. Cotton family fabrics are often a blend with polyester; in such a blend, a **resin** finish holds the cotton, while the **heat** to cure the resin holds the polyester. With such a blend and finish, a durable rather than permanent set results. Well-known Durable Press trademark names are KORATRON (by Koret) and SANFORIZE-PLUS 2 (by Cluett, Peabody). To set a Durable Press on 100 percent cotton fabrics, a liquid ammonia process is used, e.g., SANFORSET (by Cluett, Peabody), and FIBER-SET (by Kleinewefers). There has also been nonformaldehyde finishing of all-cotton fabrics, applied to such a major trademark name as Levi's jeans.

Manufacturers and retailers had to clarify promotions that used the terms "Wrinkle Free" (as in HAG-GAR® WRINKLE-FREE™) or "0% Wrinkles" rather than Durable Press. These terms can be quite misleading to many consumers; they mean "wrinkle-free—(warm) from the dryer," not that wrinkles will never occur *during wear.* For care procedures to get the best performance (including no wrinkles) from Durable Press, see Section 6.

Dimensional Stability, including Shrinkage Control.

When a fabric will not shrink or stretch during use and care, it is dimensionally stable. **Heat setting** of nylon, polyester, or triacetate fabrics can accomplish this.

Shrinkage control may involve counteracting relaxation shrinkage in fabrics of almost any other fiber, as well as felting shrinkage, specific to wool and hair fibers.

Felting shrinkage of wool must be counteracted by an **antifelting** treatment to prevent this special kind of matting and thickening, which results in shrinking (see Figure 5.13). The best (trademark) finishes make wool fabrics machine washable and, if the article allows, machine dryable, with no matting or shrinking. This is achieved by chemical alteration of the fiber surface, or by coating it with a very thin layer of polymer to make the scale surface smoother, as shown in Figure 5.14(a). Treatments by the latter method and backed by the Woolmark Company are identified by the logos for MACHINE WASHABLE WOOL, for TOTAL EASY CARE WOOL, Figure 5.14(b), and Figure 5.14(c) (see Section 6, *Dimensional Stability, including Shrinkage Control* for laundering such machine washable wool).

Relaxation shrinkage is possible in a fabric of any fiber content, if there are tensions in the material that can **relax** when strains are released in wet treatment or washing and (especially) tumble drying (see Figure 5.13 [middle photo]).

Shrinkage-controlled cotton or rayon fabric may have a **resin** finish, which will give at best a durable shrinkage control.

For a more permanent treatment, woven goods are given a **compressive preshrinking;** SAN-FORIZE® (by Cluett, Peabody) is a very well-known

Figure 5.13 Shrinkage control may have to counteract relaxation shrinkage or, in wool fabrics, felting shrinkage. (Courtesy of the Woolmark Company, formerly IWS)

trademark name for such a treatment. Before the process, each fabric is tested to determine possible shrinkage and then forced to shrink that much. (Figures 5.15 and 5.16 show the effect of the process.) This is accomplished by passing the wet fabric, sticking tightly to a compressible felt or rubber blanket, first over a convex curve where the blanket is extended, then through a concave curve, so that the material is compressed and dried in this form by a steam-heated Palmer cylinder (see Figure 5.17). The guarantee is that there will be no more than 1 percent residual shrinkage (if the article is pressed). SANFORKNIT and PAK-NIT are trademark preshrink processes for weft knit goods, also promising no more than 1 percent residual shrinkage (see Figure 5.18). It is generally much harder to stabilize weft knits than wovens. For additional comments on shrinkage and fit, see Section 8.

London shrinking is a special process used for fine worsteds: Tensions are released by allowing fabric to lie between cold, wet blankets, then after slow drying, fabric is subjected to great pressure in flat presses.

Erosion.

Erosion (denier-reduction) is removal of some of the substance of polyester filaments to make

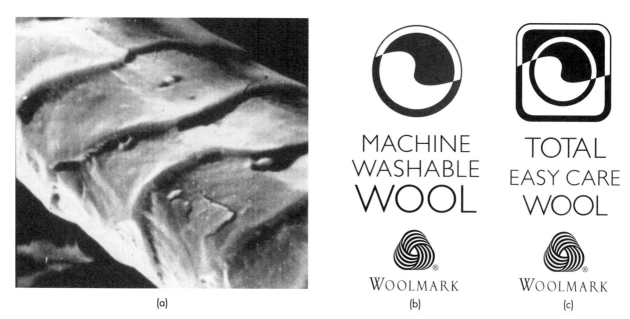

(a)   (b)   (c)

MACHINE WASHABLE WOOL

TOTAL EASY CARE WOOL

WOOLMARK

WOOLMARK

Figure 5.14 (a) Wool fiber with scales coated to prevent felting. Logos for (b) MACHINE WASHABLE WOOL with WOOLMARK® and (c) TOTAL EASY CARE WOOL (machine washable and dryable) with WOOLMARK®, treatments that offer easy-care wool. (Courtesy of the Woolmark Company, formerly IWS)

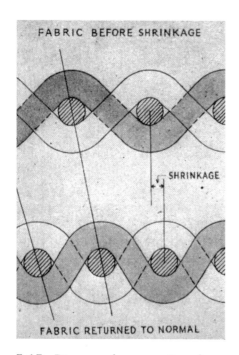

FABRIC BEFORE SHRINKAGE

SHRINKAGE

FABRIC RETURNED TO NORMAL

Figure 5.15 Diagram of cross section of woven fabric before and after controlled compressive shrinkage. (Courtesy of the Sanforized Company division of Cluett, Peabody & Co., Inc.)

Figure 5.16 Woven fabric before and after a controlled compressive shrinkage process. (Courtesy of the Sanforized Company division of Cluett, Peabody & Co., Inc.)

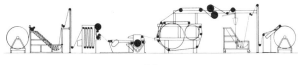

(a)

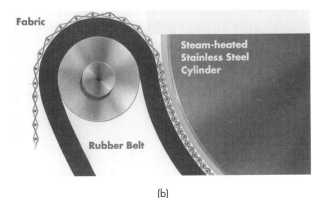

Fabric

Steam-heated
Stainless Steel
Cylinder

Rubber Belt

(b)

Figure 5.17 **(a) Controlled compressive shrinking process: overview, with (b) enlarged diagram of area in which controlled shrinkage takes place. (Courtesy of Morrison Textile Machinery Company)**

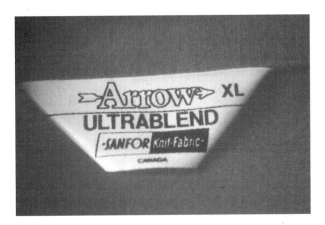

Figure 5.18 SANFORKNIT® label on preshrunk knit goods.

them more silk-like, imitating the effect of degumming, which confers lively drape as silk fibers lose substance (gum). Erosion is done by treatment in hot caustic soda, which also etches the fiber surface, giving more of the hand and scroop of silk and somewhat better absorbency. In Japan, as much as 50 percent of the fiber weight is removed in the erosion process; in the United States, it is more often under 20 percent.[7]

[7]Herman B. Goldstein, "Mechanical and Chemical Finishing of Microfabrics," *Textile Chemist and Colorist,* 25/2, February 1993: 17.

Carpet Shading Prevention. Shading is an optical effect that results when carpet pile leans in different directions. This is, of course, more noticeable with a plain shade, cut-pile carpet, but with pressure from crushing during manufacturing or shipping, or from foot traffic when it is first laid, can become permanent. Technologists at WRONZ Developments in New Zealand have came up with a TRUTRAC treatment to set the natural pile lay so that it will not be disturbed in use.[8]

Application of Color—Dyeing and Printing

What Is Color?

For all of our poetic, romantic, or sentimental references, color is actually a sensation in the eye from absorption (or reflection) of light by an object. Electromagnetic wavelengths are measured in Ångstrom units ($1\text{Å} = 10^{-10}$m), or in SI metric, in nanometers (1 nm = 10^{-9}m); by comparison, the diameter of fibers is measured in millionths of a meter with microns or, in S1 metrics, in micrometres, with $1\mu\text{m} = 10^{-6}$ m). The wavelengths of light to which the human eye can respond are in a *very* narrow band of the total range of electromagnetic radiation, the rest being absorbed but not seen.

The range is as follows:

- gamma-rays (shortest, highest energy), in the order of 10^{-13} m)
- x-rays, from below 10^{-11} m, midpoint 10^{-10} m (1 Å), to 10^{-9} m (1 nm)
- ultraviolet rays, from 1 nm, midpoint 10 nm, to over 100 nm, tanning rays 280–400 nm
- visible light rays, from about 400 nm to 700 nm
- infrared heat rays, from 1000 nm to 10^{-3} m (0.001 m)
- radio waves, from "short wave" to longest— 0.001 m to 100 m

A beam of white light breaks into the visible *spectrum* of colors in order as violet, blue, green, yellow, orange, and red, representing increasing wavelengths

[8]"Carpet Machinery: Beating Shading," *Textile Month,* June 1998: 33.

as noted. This is the separation that takes place when we see a rainbow or when we see light passed through a prism. What color an object will appear to us is determined by which wavelengths of light falling on it are absorbed; we see the color of the wavelengths that are reflected. If all wavelengths are absorbed, the object appears black. If the object absorbs wavelengths outside the visible range, or if all light is reflected, it will appear white.

As we all know, different people see colors differently. Some cannot distinguish red from green—what we call "color blindness"—and anyone can see color differently depending on what is placed next to it, or in what kind of light it is viewed. When a color looks different when viewed in daylight compared to artificial (incandescent or tungsten-filament bulb) light, the phenomenon is called *metamerism*, which can also affect perception of a color in an older person compared to a younger, due to changes in the eye. It is important when matching trim to a main fabric, for example, to view it in both daylight and artificial light. Another significant aspect of the subjectiveness of color vision is the way a color can look different when placed next to another.

Hue is the word used to signify one color distinct from another (red, blue-green, brown, etc.). *Value* is the degree of lightness (tint) or darkness (shade) the color shows. *Intensity* or *chroma* represents how strong or saturated the color is, how intense; with low intensity, colors are dull rather than bright.

Application of Color to Textiles

As in most of the aspects of textile processing discussed to this point, electronic controls govern the action and timing of application of color in the most modern methods. This can be especially noteworthy in areas that have involved a good deal of art and craft. One of these is dye formulation and shade matching, where use of a computer color-control system, which includes a spectrophotometer, can dramatically improve the speed and accuracy of both formulation and color matching (see Figure 5.19). NEOCHROME is the trademark name for COURT-ELLE® (by Acordis) acrylic fiber dyed by a computer-controlled dyeing process that offers over 12,000 shades, with close matching and reproduction of each.

Preparing color pastes for top-quality screen printing might be thought to be a handcraft opera-

Figure 5.19 Color-control system includes Datacolor International's CHROMASENSOR® CS-5® spectrophotometer. (Courtesy of Hafner Fabrics)

tion, but even here, mechanisms have been evolved to replace hand-mixed pots of print paste with a computer-controlled machine that delivers the mixture automatically (see Figure 5.20). However, in both of these cases, the human eye usually remains the final judge of color, pattern, or total result.

Printing is taken to be the application of a pattern to the *surface* of a fabric, whereas **dyeing** involves *penetration* of the material.

Dyeing

Dyeing is usually carried out in a water bath (dye liquor), though there are other methods, such as solvent and molten metal dyeing.

- A dye, therefore, is defined first of all as being able to be *dissolved in water,* as opposed to a pigment, which cannot be dissolved. One type of dye—disperse—is only slightly soluble in water, but it is still classified as a dye.

- A dye (in most cases) appears to the eye as a *color,* although reference to colorless dyes will be made.

- Many dyes are *substantive to the material* being dyed—that is, they are taken up by it without a *mordant,* or material that binds the dye to the fiber (from French *mordre* meaning to bite, that is, to hold the dye). Other dyes are changed or actually created within the fiber, usually to give better wetfastness, but there *are* methods to get them in there, and so they qualify as dyes.

(a)

(b)

Figure 5.20 (a) Print paste hand-mixed—Ratti print-works, Italy, 1986. (b) Computer-controlled print paste mixing—Ratti printworks, Italy, 1988.

Two exceptions to any definition of a dye are included in this discussion, pigment "dyeing" and solution "dyeing."

Different fiber generics accept only specific types or classes of dyestuffs, as discussed under *Dyes and Colorfastness,* Section 6.

Types (Classes) of Dyes

As noted, **substantive** dyes are taken up or adsorbed by a fiber, but need specific treatment if they are not to have only fair-to-poor wetfastness; that is, if in water (e.g., in washing) they are not to come out of the fiber as readily as they went in. The various classes of dyes accomplish this in varying degrees and various ways.

Acid Dyes. These are salts of color acids, substantive to wool, silk, and nylon, and can be applied to special forms of acrylic and polyester. They give bright shades, usually have good fastness to light, but are seldom of good wetfastness.

Chrome or Mordant Dyes. Historically, oxides of a number of metals (aluminum, chromium, copper, iron, tin) have been used as mordants and give different shades with the same acid dye. Today, chromium salts are nearly the only mordant used to hold acid dyes to wool or nylon, and so the type is called a **chrome dye.** The addition of metal dulls the shade but greatly improves wetfastness. The mordant may be applied before, during, or after dyeing with acid dyes.

Acid Metallized, Premetallized, or Metal-Complex Dyes. These are very much like chrome dye, but the metal is incorporated as the dye is manufactured. These dyes are applied either in a strongly acid bath (acid metallized) or a nearly neutral one (premetallized), in an operation considerably simpler than chrome dyeing. They offer muted shades of excellent fastness.

Basic, Cationic Dyes. These are salts of color bases, and so are *cationic* (see Section 8). They are substantive to silk; the first synthetic dye ("Perkin's mauve," 1856) was a basic dye used for silk. These older silk dyes have poor wet- and lightfastness. It was found that these dyes are also substantive to acrylic, and with the need for better fastness for this synthetic fiber, superior dyes of the basic group were developed and given the name *cationic.* They may be used on special forms of nylon and polyester as well as acrylic.

Disperse Dyes. Disperse dyes are very finely ground colors, almost insoluble in water, that are *dispersed* in a detergent solution to be taken up into the fiber. They dye the less-absorbent fibers that do not swell or allow the soluble types of dyes to enter. They are used most on polyester, acetate, triacetate, and for lighter shades on filament nylon (see the discussion of nylon in *Dyes and Colorfastness* in Section 6); they are also used on acrylic and even olefin.

Direct Dyes. Direct dyes are substantive on all cellulose fibers, but need special *fixing* treatments to prevent them from coming right off again; i.e., to give them better wetfastness.

Direct Developed Dyes. These have better wetfastness, because after the direct dye is applied, it is *diazotized and developed,* creating a larger and less soluble dye in the fiber; this is, of course, a longer method. These dyes are not fast to chlorine bleach.

Reactive (also called Fiber-Reactive) Dyes. Reactive dyes are different from any other dye type, since they form a chemical union with the fiber. They are used mainly on cellulose fibers, the dyeing can proceed at room temperature (these are the "cold-dyeing" types), and there is a full range of bright colors. However, for deep shades, these dyes are expensive because it takes a good deal of dye to give a full shade. Reactive dyes are also used to a lesser extent on wool, silk, and nylon but are still principally applied to cellulose, and that means mostly cotton, where they show excellent wet- and lightfastness, but are not as fast to chlorine bleach as vat or naphthol dyes.

Naphthol (Azoic) Dyes. These dyes are formed in the fiber from two components added one after the other. A coupling takes place producing the final dye and color inside the fiber (also in the dyebath if excess chemical is there). The process is run very cold, hence they are also called **ice dyes.** Naphthol dyes have excellent fastness even to commercial laundering (very hot water, built detergents, chlorine bleach). Oddly enough, some are not at all fast to dry cleaning.

Vat Dyes. Vat dyes are a group of dyes that are insoluble in water, but they can be reduced, in alkaline conditions, to a form that has little color, or an entirely different one, but is soluble (the *leuco* form). When it has been taken up by the fiber, the dye is oxidized and left in the fiber as an insoluble color. Application of these dyes is long and fairly difficult, but they are substantive to cellulose fibers, give superb wetfastness even with chlorine bleach, and the lightfastness of most is good. This is the one dye type name we are familiar with, from the stamp "vat dyed" on good linen tea towels (dish towels) or interiors material. There is not a complete color range in vat dyes; for instance, they lack a true bright red. Vat dyes are sometimes applied to wool, although, since the bath must be alkaline, conditions must be carefully controlled.

Sulfur Dyes. Sulfur dyes are also insoluble in water, but will dissolve in a solution of sodium sulfide, with or without sodium carbonate. Sodium sulfide reduces the dye to a compound that is substantive to cellulose, and which oxidizes back to the original state. Sulfur dyes are inexpensive and wetfast but not fast to chlorine, and they have only a narrow range of dull shades.

Pigment "Dyes." "Pigment dyeing" is application of color, both pigments and dyes, not really by any dyeing process but by binding the color to the surface of the fabric, much as a print paste is applied, using resins as a rule. This can produce a rather stiff fabric, and while colors may have reasonable wetfastness, they may *crock* (rub off); if the binder is sensitive to solvent, the color could come off in dry cleaning.

Dyeing Stages, Methods, and Effects

In processing fibers to fabric, the earlier the stage at which color is introduced, the better chance there is that it will not be removed in processing, use, or care—that it will be *colorfast.* See *Dyes and Colorfastness* in Section 6 for a discussion of the relationship between the types or classes of dye used on various fibers and colorfastness.

Many design effects are related to a certain stage of dyeing (heathers, checks, etc.). If such an effect is imitated later, by printing, for instance, the pattern will likely be less well defined and of inferior fastness, but it will be considerably cheaper, as a printed compared to a yarn-dyed woven glen check will be (see Figure 5.21 and *Fabric Glossary:* TRANSFER PRINT). In a plain weave, a woven check is also *reversible,* an advantage in garment construction, as

Figure 5.21 **Transfer-printed glen check (left) vs. yarn-dyed woven glen check (right). The more expensive woven check is clearer and more durable.**

with a convertible shirt collar (discussed under *Yarn Dyeing*).

Cost alone, per dyelot or batch, would probably make an early dye application seem less expensive, as it usually involves a large lot; however, there is a general "expense" in applying color at an early stage—you have then made a *color decision*. You are committed to warehouse a distinct coloration, and even more nerve-wracking, as well as potentially expensive, you have "second guessed" a fashion direction! More on this in the discussion of cross-dyeing, but these cost and risk effects underlie the summaries of stages and methods of dyeing that follow, which are listed in order, from the earliest stage of coloration to the latest.

Solution Dyeing. Solution dyeing (giving goods also called *producer-, polymer-, spun-, or dope-dyed*) as suggested in the earlier definition of a dye, does not really qualify as *dyeing,* since in this process, pigment is added to the liquid before an MF fiber is extruded. The color is locked into the fiber, and therefore is completely fast to any condition, from sunlight to water at the boil, that will not actually damage the fiber itself. This method results in a huge batch of each (fairly standard) color, and so is not usually suitable for fashion items, which normally call for a season's specific shade of color. It is used in patterns, such as stripes, checks, or plaids, where a limited number of colors can produce a wide range of pleasing, "classic" combinations; one example is taffeta in a red and green with white, black, and/or gold plaid, which is perennially popular for holiday ribbons and piece goods—very likely solution dyed. Such fabrics are also often used for neckties, ribbons, and less-than-high-fashion umbrellas for the person who wants basic rain protection that will "go with everything," last for many years, and can be left between showers to withstand horrendous exposure "tests" in the back of the car of a person like me. Solution-dyed fiber is called for anywhere exceptional fastness is required, such as dark sliver for a spotted-cat look in a fake fur, which might then be overdyed (at the boil) to give a range of ground shades (see *Fabric Glossary:* FUR-LIKE). Trademark names for solution-dyed fiber are ZEFKROME® and KOLORBON® (by BASF).

Fiber Dyeing. Fiber dyeing (*stock dyeing*) is done at the earliest stage at which a natural fiber can be colored. Loose fiber is dyed either in the bale (a rela-

tively new method) or held in a basket in a dye machine (see Figure 5.22). Using stock-dyed fibers, various colors can be blended to give *heather* or *mixture* effects, adding a misty, indistinct tone to the overall shade, although individual fibers may show quite strongly colored (see Figure 5.23). *Colored nubs* can be introduced into a yarn using stock-dyed fiber. Fibers may also be dyed before spinning in *top* form, when the loose rope formed after combing is wound on perforated cores. *Marl* is a mottled look, usually tone-on-tone rather than multicolor, given by blending *top-dyed* roving in a single yarn, or in at least one

Figure 5.22 Fiber or stock dyeing machine.

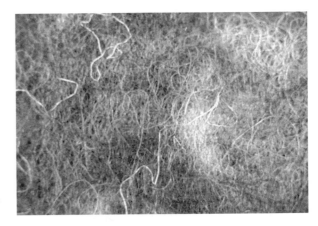

Figure 5.23 Fiber-dyed mix for tweed.

ply of a 2-ply yarn; other names used for this effect are *salt-and-pepper* or *ragg*, the latter originating with *ragg wool*, reclaimed and reworked, but now used for a pleasant "mixey" look no matter what the fiber content. Marl or heather effects and colored nubs are all characteristic of tweeds (see *Fabric Glossary:* TWEED).

Yarn Dyeing. Yarn dyeing requires making sure the yarn does not get tangled as it is dyed; while some soft or bulky yarn is **skein-** or **hank-dyed**, most is **package-dyed**, where it is held more firmly and so is much easier to handle. For package dyeing, yarn is wound on packages, each with a hollow center that allows liquid to flow through it. The packages are stacked on perforated, hollow posts, and liquid is pumped through these and the packages. Package machines are enclosed and can be pressurized, so the dye liquor can reach temperatures above the atmospheric boiling point (100°C or 212°F) for faster dyeing; this is especially helpful in dyeing standard types of polyester in normal batch times, without having to use chemical "carriers." (See Figure 5.24.)

With woven fabrics, for example, shirtings, the term "yarn dyed" is connected with quality: a check woven in with dyed yarns will look sharper, with a clean, well-defined pattern, compared to one printed (see Figure 5.21) and will probably be more colorfast. It is also reversible, as most prints are not, except in the case of the few duplex prints and those on sheer fabrics. This is an advantage in garment construction, as with a convertible shirt collar to be worn closed or open.

Many fabrics have their character derived from dyed yarns; a few are listed here, with their *Fabric Glossary* File name in capitals: CHAMBRAY; a wide variety of wool family, twill weave checks such as houndstooth and glen check under CHECK; DENIM; GINGHAM; HERRINGBONE; MADRAS; TAPESTRY; TARTAN; and TICKING.

When knitted fabric is made with dyed yarn, the color or design is said to be *ingrain,* and almost all jacquard and intarsia knits are ingrain. These two patterned knits can look very similar on the face; they can be distinguished from one another by looking at the back. In a jacquard knit, any color not looping on the face is carried in the back on that course, and can be clearly seen, in both single knits (see Figure 4.61 and *Fabric Glossary:* JACQUARD KNIT) and double knits (see *Fabric Glossary:* DOUBLEKNIT). With

Figure 5.24 Package dyeing machine is used for most yarn dyeing. (Courtesy of American Textile Manufacturers Institute, Inc.)

intarsia, each colored yarn loops only in the area of the motif, so the back shows the same color as the face in that area (see Figure 4.62).

Variable color effects are given when fabric is woven with warp a different color from weft, so that the color changes as the fabric is moved; this effect is variously called chameleon, *changeant,* iridescent, luminescent, pearlescent, and shot (as in taffeta) (see *Fabric Glossary:* COLOR VARIABLE).

A number of distinct effects are achieved by having a pattern in the yarn before the fabric is made; these and others are discussed and illustrated in the *Fabric Glossary:* PATTERN IN YARN.

Space-dyed is the effect of yarn-dyed with more than one color or shade along its length at random intervals (see Figure 5.25). This can be done by injecting packages of yarn with color, or yarn may be knit up into a tube, printed, unraveled or "deknit" to be used as space-dyed.

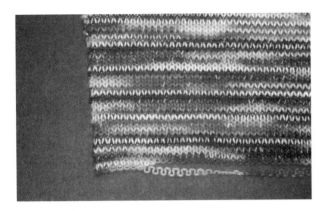

Figure 5.25 Fabric knit of space-dyed yarn.

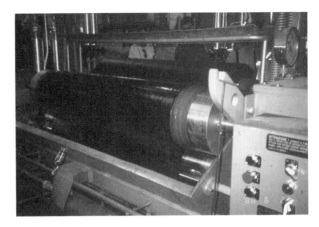

Figure 5.26 In a pad dyeing machine, piece goods are passed from one roller to another through a trough.

Yarns hand dyed by the **tie-dye** method in patterns before weaving give *ikat* designs, which have an indistinct or blurred outline called a *chiné* effect. Designs can be warp or weft ikat, from only warp or only weft yarns tie-dyed, or the astounding *double ikat,* such as patola, in which both warp and weft have been tie-dyed and the design emerges as the cloth is woven. Other color effects in yarns come through printing: warp yarns printed gives a chiné effect and *mélange* is a different printed effect. These are discussed under *Printing Methods and Effects.*

Piece Dyeing. Piece dyeing is done after the fabric is made. The most common method traditionally has been with the **winch** dyeing machine or **beck,** in which goods are sewn into a loop to be dyed as a continuous piece, drawn out of the dye bath over a winch reel or roller, and returned to the bath to continue the cycle. Lengths of fabric are also wound on a **beam,** in a compact machine that is much easier to pressurize than the dye beck and so is useful for polyester fabrics. In the **jet** dyeing machine, goods are forced through a narrow jet but then lie loose as they pass through the machine cycle; this type is especially suited to dyeing knit goods, as there is little strain put on the fabric. In both **pad** and **jig** methods, piece goods are passed from one roller to another through a trough containing much smaller amounts of liquid than is used in the machines discussed so far (see Figure 5.26). The fabric is held at full width, so there is less chance of wrinkling and creasing during dyeing. Padding is also used to apply finishes, as the thick liquids, dye or finish, are pressed into the fabric.

Union-dyed is a term used for achieving a single (solid) color on piece-dyed fabric of differently dyeing fibers. Dyes of different types suitable for each fiber present, and of the same shade, are included in the dyebath. (Home dye tints are made up with such mixtures; see the discussion under *Dyes and Colorfastness* in Section 6.)

Cross-dyed describes the effect of getting a multicolor, tone-on-tone, or heather effect on piece-dyed fabric of differently dyeing fibers (also called **fiber-mix** or **differential dyeing**). A dye bath made up with dyes of different types for the differently dyeing fibers, and those in different colors will give a multicolor dyeing. The fibers may be of different families that take different dye types or may be modifications of the same generic that accept either different dye types or the same type but to a different depth of shade, as with nylon 6, 6 and "deep dye" nylon 6, giving tone-on-tone effects. Dyeing one fiber and leaving the other undyed for heather effect is a good deal less expensive than blending stock-dyed fibers. Cross-dyeing is used mostly for carpets, where it is an advantage to have these huge pieces of fabric on hand undyed but with the possibility built (tufted) in of almost infinite colorations. A customer can select from a sample and *then* the fabric can be piece-dyed. Figure 5.27 shows a cross-dyed sock knit of nylon (dyed) and polyester (undyed).

Product Dyeing. Knit garments such as socks and sweaters are dyed in bags in **paddle machines,** with paddles over or at the side of the machines to move the bags about in the dye bath by bumping them. A type of revolving drum machine, similar to those used

Figure 5.27 Sock cross-dyed, knit of nylon (dyed) and polyester (undyed).

to process and dye leather hides and skins, is also used for product dyeing, while other front-loading drum machines have been developed for the latest wave of product dyeing.

In recent years, dyeing of finished consumer products, especially towels and casual wear garments of woven fabric, has been used to give the "edge" of lower inventory and quick response to orders in times of tight money and intense competition. Dyeing at this last possible stage works only with a fabric that dyes fairly simply and, of course, where compatible thread, trim, etc., have been used; an example would be an all-cotton garment, either woven or knitted, and stitched with cotton thread, although garment dyeing is not limited to these. The hangtag shown in Figure 5.28 warns that in such articles color even-

> **GARMENT DYED**
> **WASH SEPARATELY**
> **BEFORE WEARING**
>
> DUE TO THE SPECIAL NATURE OF GARMENT DYEING SLIGHT VARIATIONS IN COLOUR AND FIT CAN BE FOUND WITH EACH GARMENT. THESE ARE INHERENT CHARACTERISTICS ASSOCIATED WITH THE PROCESS. MAKING EACH ITEM UNIQUE AND RESULTING IN A TRULY VIBRANT COLOURED COMFORT-ABLE GARMENT.

Figure 5.28 Tag from a product-dyed article explaining that color and fit may vary from lot to lot, in a way not tolerated with dyeing at other stages.

ness and garment fit often vary from one dyelot to another.

Printing

Printing is the application of a design, whether colored or not, using dyes or pigments, usually in a thick paste, bound to the surface of a fabric or other substance (paper, leather).

This brings up the distinction between **applied** and **structural** design: Applied design is a pattern put on after the fabric has been made, such as a print or embroidery. This is distinct from structural design, a pattern built into the fabric during construction, such as a dobby birdseye, a jacquard damask, a knit cable, or a doubleknit houndstooth effect; with all these structural designs, the fabric comes off the machine that made it with the pattern already showing.

The combination of colors in a print design is termed the *colorway*. Any design is commonly produced in several colorways.

Printing Methods and Effects

Sliver or Top Printing. Sliver printing or top printing, then spinning, gives mélange yarn, which looks very like heather or marl except that individual fibers may not be entirely colored.

Warp Printing. Warp printing involves printing the warp yarns when they are wound on the warp beam, then weaving the cloth with weft all one (usually dark) color. The result is that the print pattern is slightly disturbed and has a blurred, indistinct outline, as if the colors had "run" or "bled"; this effect is called **chiné** (see *Fabric Glossary*: PATTERN IN YARN).

Roller Printing. Roller printing is still one of the fastest methods of printing and can be relatively inexpensive, *once the rollers are made* (see Figure 5.29). (Other fast methods are rotary screen printing and jet printing.) Engraved rollers, one for each color in the design, each turn in a trough of color paste, which is scraped off with a *doctor blade,* except where it remains in the engraved grooves. This color pattern is applied to the fabric (which is moving over a central drum) as each roller is pressed against it. The length of the pattern (pattern repeat) is limited by the circumference of the (heavy) metal rollers—a maximum of about 45 cm (18 in.)—and the width by

Figure 5.29 Roller printing is fast and, once the rollers are cut, relatively inexpensive. (Courtesy of Cranston Print Works Company)

the width of the rollers—usually not much wider than 1 m (40 in.). Preparation (engraving and chroming for surface protection) of the copper rollers is very expensive. For these reasons, roller printing is most suitable for relatively small designs or pattern repeats, on less-expensive fabrics and/or those of standard, "classic" design, such as calico and many chintzes (see *Fabric Glossary:* CALICO; CHINTZ). It is not used for large, topical, and/or exclusive designs. Figure 5.30 shows the contrast between a typical roller-

Figure 5.30 Size of roller-print pattern repeat (left) compared to that of a screen print (right).

printed repeat of pattern (looking from bottom to top of the fabric, not from side to side) and a screen-printed toile de Jouy drapery fabric (of which we do not see the entire pattern in this segment) (see also *Fabric Glossary:* TOILE DE JOUY).

Screen Printing. Screen printing may be done by two methods:

1. **Flat (silk) screen printing** provides a means of printing large patterns with designs that are exclusive or topical, since the cost of preparation of the screens is much less than for rollers or rotary screens. The design is put on "screens" of a fine, plain-weave fabric, such as filament voile, which today is made of nylon rather than silk (see *Fabric Glossary:* VOILE [*filament*]). One screen is prepared for each color, with areas other than that color's design covered with a substance that will resist the dye paste. When the paste is forced over the screen with a flexible (rubber) blade called a squeegee, the color passes through the screen only in the area of the design for that color. Flat screen printing can be either manual (each register of the screen made, and the screen moved on, by hand) or automated (see Figure 5.31). Figure 5.30 shows a good example of a typical large-scale screen

(a)

(b)

Figure 5.31 (a) Manual screen printing. (b) Automated screen printing. (Courtesy of MASTERS OF LINEN/USA)

Figure 5.32 Rotary screen printing can print multicolor designs on wide fabrics very quickly. (Courtesy of American Textile Manufacturers Institute, Inc.)

print; see comments on repeat of pattern under *Roller Printing* earlier. See also *Fabric Glossary:* TOILE DE JOUY.

2. **Rotary screen printing** is done with thin metal foil "screens" in a cylindrical form with the print paste in the center pulled through by electrostatic force. These screens are tricky and expensive to prepare, but once up and running, can print even very wide fabric, such as sheeting, very quickly (see Figure 5.32). In the United States, this is now the dominant printing method.

Jet Printing. This is a category that covers a number of methods that allow color to be applied from jets positioned above the surface of fabric moving beneath them. A few are discussed here:

Polychromatic printing (or dyeing) is the result when a number of dye jets are set to squirt color over a fabric in a changing, random pattern. The result can be a multicolor pattern or a tie-dye effect using one color.

Ink-jet printing is a development that allows complex designs to be programmed and then printed, with direct control from a computer, onto fabrics or other materials, such as wallcoverings. High resolution in designs and no strain or pressure on the fabric are two advantages of this method.

Transfer Printing. This method gives prints that are very well defined, with a "3-D" look. It is ideal for knits, since the fabric is not under tension, so the design will never be distorted, as it is sometimes when a knit relaxes after being pulled or stretched in other printing methods. Special paper is prepared with the design, which may be in a number of colors. This paper is brought into contact with the material being printed (fabric or other), and the pattern is transferred.

The original type of transfer printing has been called **thermal** or **heat transfer printing (HTP),** as it involves applying heat, which causes the dyestuffs on the paper to *sublime,* or turn from solid to vapor, and so transfer to the fabric. This is also called **sublistatic** or **vapor-phase transfer,** and one of the original companies was named Sublistatic. The machines involved in transfer printing are not expensive, relative to other textile equipment. Printing can also be done on completed garments as well as on piece goods. Designs can be exclusive, and there are many to choose from. Printing of coordinated patterns on materials other than cloth is also possible. An advanced sublimation process, PHOTOFABRIC (by CPL Group), gives full color printing with near-photographic quality.

The Xerox Corporation even offers a means of transferring a color photograph or design to fabric, by means of the XEROX 5775 digital color copier/printer, using a special *AB–X* paper (developed for Xerox by Graffoto Inc. of Vancouver), followed by a heat pressing to the fabric. The much more old-fashioned, pressed-on "transfers" are also used, although they hardly qualify, in durability, to be considered as part of commercial printing.

There are also **wet and melt transfer printing** processes, though the original HTP is still most used, employing wide rolls of paper transferred by heat to piece goods, especially knits. The paper retains a (pleasing) subdued pattern after printing, and this good-quality paper may be used to print from more than once, or is recycled, for example by florists to wrap bouquets. An outline of the present range of types of transfer printing is presented in the *Fabric Glossary:* TRANSFER PRINT; see also Figure 5.21.

Engineered Prints. Engineered prints are those designed to fall in a certain predetermined position on the garment or article to be made of that fabric. These are usually prepared by screen or transfer printing.

Blotch Print. A blotch print is one in which the background, as well as a design motif, has been printed on (not dyed). Unless the fabric is very lightweight, the printed color will not penetrate well enough to show as strongly on the back as the face, and this naturally gives a less solid-looking ground than the much more costly processes of piece dyeing the background, with either resist or discharge methods to provide for the motif areas (see *Resist, Discharge Printing*).

Resist Printing. This involves coating certain areas of a pattern with a substance to *resist* the color; the fabric is then piece-dyed, with the result that the background and pattern areas are equally distinct on the face or back of the fabric. *Fabric Glossary:* PATTERN ON DYED GROUND (DISCHARGE, RESIST) discusses the ancient hand method of **batik** (which involves **resist printing, then dyeing**), **and tie-dye.**

Discharge Printing. This is an expensive method, not much used today, that also involves piece dyeing the fabric. It gives an excellent result when a deep background color with an overprint is desired, as in a traditional challis print (see *Fabric Glossary:* CHALLIS). The background color is then removed chemically (discharged) from the areas that will receive the overprint. This discharge process can damage the fabric if not carefully done and neutralized. *Fabric Glossary:* PATTERN ON DYED GROUND shows how to recognize a discharge print; the ground dye is not taken out on the back of the fabric as "cleanly" as on the face, so some of the ground color can be seen on the back, within the "discharged" and overprinted areas.

Duplex Printing. Duplex printing is achieved by printing both sides of the fabric, either in the same pattern or with different designs on each side; Figure 5.33 shows a right-hand drill fabric printed on the face, over the steep twill line, with a scattered motif, while a denim look has been printed on the back, where the fabric is quite flat, with little of the weave twill line visible.

Block Printing and Stencil Printing. These are methods rooted in handcrafts that are seldom sold commercially but may occasionally be used. A color paste is applied from the projecting pattern created on a *block*, or forced through pattern spaces cut in a card or thin metal *stencil*.

Figure 5.33 Duplex print on white drill; back is printed to resemble denim.

Printing Other than Color

Some applied design methods involve printing, but not application of color.

Burned-Out. Burned-out, etched, or découpé is an effect achieved on a compound woven fabric, with surface yarns made of one fiber type and a ground weave made of another. Some surface yarns are removed, usually by printing on a chemical that will dissolve them without affecting the (usually sheer) background weave. This effect, then, is neither "burning" nor even "cutting" as the name *découpé* suggests; *Fabric Glossary:* BURNED-OUT covers the fabrics coupe de velours, dévoré velvet, façonné velvet, satin découpé, and voile découpé.

Flocking. Flocking involves applying and holding short bits of fiber (*flock*) to a fabric (or wallcovering) by means of adhesive printed on in a pattern. The fibers may be shaken onto the adhesive, or held in an orderly arrangement in an electrostatic field.

Much cheap dotted Swiss has flocked dots, which are likely to come off easily (there are tales of dots coming off as a garment was being sewn), and they make the fabric less flexible than the much more expensive woven-in dots (see *Surface Figure Weaves* in Section 4 and *Fabric Glossary:* DOTTED SWISS). Similarly, less-expensive point d'esprit (dotted veiling) also has flocked rather than worked-in or embroidered dots (see *Fabric Glossary:* FLOCKED, NET).

If adhesive and then flock are applied all over the fabric, a suede-like or pseudo-velvet can be produced. In this form, the stiffness, lack of pliability, and durability are even less appealing than a flocked dot.

Flocked fashion fabrics, then, whether an applied design or an allover effect, are usually associated with cheap, nondurable, and less desirable effects; see Section 6, *TLC or Beware: High-Fashion Specialties.* However, flocking can be very durable if fibers are oriented by electrostatic flocking and a lasting adhesive is chosen; one such sturdy flocked material is VELLUX® (by West-Point Pepperell), described under *Compound Fabrics,* Section 4. See novel marine use (SEALCOAT) under *Third Millennium Problem Solving and Innovations,* Section 7.

Plissé or "Crinkle Crepe." Plissé is a puckered effect that may resemble seersucker or an allover crepe or may have a small pattern showing as a crinkle. Some areas of a cotton fabric are brought in contact with caustic soda (sodium hydroxide, NaOH),

the chemical used for mercerizing; in those areas, the fabric shrinks, and the other parts of the fabric form puckers. This may be accomplished by printing caustic soda onto the cotton or by printing on a resist agent and then immersing the fabric in caustic. The characteristics and uses of plissé are discussed in *Fabric Glossary:* PLISSÉ.

Mechanically Applied Design

Embossing. Embossing is the result of passing fabric between rollers, at least one of which is engraved with a design (see *Fabric Glossary:* EMBOSSED). Most leather-like fabrics have a grain effect embossed on them (as well as some inside split leather!), and coated upholstery fabrics may also be embossed, for instance, with a jacquard weave pattern, such as a brocatelle. Pile fabrics are sometimes embossed, so that part of the pile is pressed flat in a pattern.

Sculptured or Carved Design. This involves considerably more processing: A pile fabric is first embossed, then the pile left upstanding is sheared off, and that which was flattened is brushed up, leaving the sculptured or carved design. Note that these terms are used also for *structural* designs built into pile fabric such as carpet or velvet, which have been tufted or (over-wire method) woven with pile of different heights.

Moiré. Moiré is a random "woodgrain" or "watermark" design. This pattern is produced when plain weave, crosswise-ribbed fabric, such as taffeta or faille, is calendered in a double layer; the ribs in one layer do not lie exactly over those in the other layer, and so flatten these at random, creating the moiré pattern (see *Fabric Glossary:* MOIRÉ). If the fabric is made of thermoplastic fiber and the calender rolls are heated, a durable moiré results. Acetate gives a good-looking, inexpensive moiré, although polyester is now in much the same price range, is more durable, and is easier to care for. Moiré can also be embossed from a roller engraved with the pattern, or the effect can be printed on or woven in.

Two layers of sheer, plain-weave fabric, such as organdy, lying one over the other but with yarns not exactly aligned, will also show the typical woodgrain effect in a visual pattern called *birefringence.*

Embroidery. Embroidery is applied to piece goods by huge machines with hundreds of needles controlled

Figure 5.34 Embroidered fabric.

by punched cards; the Schiffli machine, developed in Switzerland, can embroider elaborate patterns in this way on woven fabric (see Figure 5.34) or net. Eyelet is embroidered fabric with holes cut within the embroidery pattern; see *Fabric Glossary:* EYELET. What is called Schiffli lace is the result of embroidering all over a fabric in a continuous design; the background fabric must be made of a fiber that can be dissolved away by a chemical that will not affect the stitching thread (see *Schiffli Lace,* Section 4 and *Fabric Glossary:* LACE, EMBROIDERED).

Individual motifs are embroidered on garment sections or small pieces of fabric by machines with multiple separate "heads."

Other Stitching. Stitching can give surface results other than embroidery. **Stitching with elastic thread** results in various raised, puckered, and puffed designs. **Stitching with padding,** often involving two or more layers of fabric, can give the decorative result of **trapunto** (backing of the design padded) and **Italian quilting** (padding cord under the stitched-down design lines only), plus regular **quilting,** which also introduces a surface design. Various kinds of gathering, some involving decorative stitching, also serve as applied design: **smocking, ruching, shirring,** even **top-stitching. Appliqué** involves stitching pieces of one fabric (or more) in a motif on another piece of material.

Pleating. Pleating, or pressing fabric into sharp folds or creases, is sometimes done in such a way that it may be considered an applied design. **Form pleating** uses paper forms to hold the fabric as it is pressed (previously called *gauffering* [see Figure 5.35]). Some pleating is accomplished by crushing the fabric, or embossing, and in all cases, use of a resin can give a durable result; use of heat on a thermoplastic material can give a durable or permanent design. **Crushing** is usually taken to mean a kind of unorganized pleating; "broomstick" pleats result from such crushing when fabric, wound around a core, is compressed. **Fluting** is rounded folds, and may result from the fabric structure, as in sheer tricot knit fluted edging, or may be applied.

Miscellaneous Effects. Fabric or lace may be **embellished** with such add-ons as sequins, decorative cord, and the like, on lace called re-embroidered—see Figure 4.68. Other applied design is **painted on,** or like studs, **hammered on.**

Figure 5.35 Pleating with paper.

SECTION SIX

CARE OF FABRICS

Home Care

Where Are the "Knows" of Yesteryear?

Old-fashioned know-how—what used to be called *household science*—has gone down the drain for many consumers, as far as caring for today's fabrics is concerned. Even older people may be no wiser when it comes to washing or pressing or taking a stain out of one of the bewildering array of materials used in our modern clothing and household textiles. The resurgence of interest in fabrics such as silk that *do* require special care just adds another source of problems.

Many people developed a strong feeling over the last quarter of the 20th century that we should turn back to a more conserving attitude toward the resources around us. In the public at large, this definitely lessened in some ways from the days of the "oil crisis" in the late 1970s, but concern over the environment in general has increased to an astounding degree, underlined by government action in many areas, such as pollution prevention. Such a trend need not be at odds with the mainstream of the fashion industry; it does lead us to focus more on **quality for purpose,** and to acquire and apply **knowledge in selection and care.**

An identical consumer focus comes with times of economic hardship, and this, too, in the 1990s, heightened consumers' search for quality in textiles and clothing and for information on proper care. To teachers and communicators, this offers a welcome challenge to provide *new-fashioned know-how— consumer science for the 21st century!*

Because, in addition to caring for contemporary textiles, consumers sometimes want to preserve heirloom items for posterity, rudimentary conservation skills are needed as well.

Fiber Properties and Care

The way a fabric behaves in care is based on the reaction of the fibers to heat, water, mechanical action, and chemicals. This discussion covers the first three as they are encountered in home care, and deals mainly with the major fibers we use.

Heat in Fabric Care

Heat is one of the main factors that must be considered in care of fabrics, in relation to fiber content. Cellulose fibers (such as cotton or rayon) are resistant to heat, and so can stand hot wash water, a hot clothes dryer setting, and even ironing at high settings. Nylon and polyester, being thermoplastic, would melt under a hot iron, but will withstand hot water or a hot (cotton setting) home dryer; for this reason, they are *not* classified as *heat sensitive* in this *Fabric Reference*. However, commercial gas dryers could reach temperatures unsafe for nylon. Ironing or pressing any thermoplastic fiber must be done with care (that includes all major MF fibers except those of reconstituted cellulose, such as rayon).

Acrylic fabrics should be protected from hot drying, or they may become lifeless and feel somehow thinner, although they may not have been otherwise damaged.

Heat-sensitive fibers (defined in Section 2) should not be exposed to heat, as in tumble drying, without great care; in the case of olefin (polypropylene), avoid use of a heated dryer at all. Those expensive ski long johns or sleek cycling pants will dry quickly anyway.

There are other heat hazards for textiles made of heat-sensitive fibers:

- If a fur-like fabric coat is damp, perhaps with snow, do not throw it over a hot **radiator** to hasten drying—this would only hasten the end of its life as a fashion garment.
- There is also the story of a woman checking the progress of a pie baking (very hot **oven**), while she was wearing a wig (modacrylic); the dry, hot air frizzled the locks immediately.

Heat has a harshening and drying effect on wool, silk, leather, and fur; see notes including detailed instructions and cautions for a number of such specific fiber types and fabrics under *Tender, Loving (Home) Care.*

Water and Mechanical Action in Fabric Care

Fiber strength, especially when wet, is significant in home care. Fibers that are weaker when wet need support and TLC (tender, loving care) when they are washed.

Foremost is wool, often made into a bulky article that can absorb a lot of water; the wet garment is heavy. Wool in any article needs careful handling in washing, even if it has an antifelt treatment, because, like our own hair, it is weak when wet. Silk also loses strength when wet, but it is much stronger than wool to begin with, and fabrics made of it are often light.

Standard rayon and acetate both lose a great deal of their strength when wet and have only fair or poor strength to start with, so care is needed. HWM rayon has better dry strength than standard rayon and loses less strength when wet.

Only two fibers, cotton and flax, are significantly stronger when wet—ready for lots of mechanical action in laundering. Lyocell fibers, which are stronger than cotton when dry and do not lose a great deal when wet, can stand laundering procedures well. Synthetics start with good to excellent strength (except for spandex, present in small amounts as a rule) and change strength very little when wet. These types are the best candidates for machine washing care at home. With a Durable Press finish, the strong cellulosic fibers can also offer total easy care.

Easiest Home Care

Easiest home care, for most people, probably means machine washing and drying, with little or no pressing. So, first of all, a procedure to accomplish just that:

Steps for avoiding having to press after laundering (mainly applying to Durable Press items)

1. Do not overload the washer.
2. Avoid "shock cooling" between washing and rinsing, which may produce stubborn wrinkles (going from hot wash to cold rinse).
3. Add fabric softener to the last rinse (or use in dryer) to lubricate fibers and yarns.
4. Use a tumble dryer (we are not dealing here with heat-sensitive fibers); select a lower temperature for thermoplastic fibers, especially acrylic.
5. Take articles out of the dryer *as soon as it stops;* if articles are allowed to cool lying in the dryer, the weight of other items in the load will set wrinkles in heat-softened pieces, even knits.
6. Shake out, smooth, and fold or hang newly dried articles, "finger pressing" edges to shape, closing fasteners, etc., to arrange for the best possible finished look.

In this outline, one of the most significant steps is the tumble drying. Most of our "easy care" fabrics contain thermoplastic fibers and/or resin finishes, and we can use the softening action of heat to help **remove** wrinkles (if misused, however, heat can **set in** or create wrinkles). Promotion of a garment as "Wrinkle Free" really means *as taken out of a (warm) dryer* (discussed in more detail under *Durable Press* in Section 5). Tumble drying is also the best method to allow the self-crimping action of bicomponent fibers.

Tumble drying, then, is virtually essential to easiest care, even though there can be problems with static electricity developing unless an effective fabric softener is included in the wash or dry cycle. A great many people still do not own a dryer, but may have access to one in an apartment building or can use one in a laundromat. What do you do if you do not have access to a dryer at all, or, almost as troublesome, convenient access? This is the case with the large number who use laundromats or are apartment dwellers; they must either lurk in a laundry room for hours, dash there by the clock, or expect wrinkles in a cooled-down dryer load.

Tumble dryers pose fire danger from two sources. One is **lint,** which is highly flammable as a rule, virtually exploding into flame at a spark. It should be cleaned out of the lint trap after *each* drying load; occasionally vacuum out any traps, pipes, or openings you can get at, as well. The other fire hazard is **foam,** used as padding in bras, shoulder pads, and such, or as backing on some small mats. **Do not allow these to get bone dry, nor to lie warm and damp in a load,** in or out of the dryer; enough heat to cause a fire can be generated "spontaneously" in warm foam.

Drip drying is the next best method to tumble drying. You must not wring articles, and it is well to bypass the machine spin-dry, although you could try a gentle salad-spinner extraction (yes, literally) for small items. Now you proceed with drip drying, hanging clothing dripping wet on rustproof hangers, arranging items following step #6. Most people abhor this "drippy" route, and be prepared: with every move away from steps #1–6, you move further from literal *wash and wear* (without pressing).

Tender, Loving (Home) Care (TLC)

Tender, loving care (TLC) is given few textile articles by modern consumers, for it entails hand washing, air drying, careful dampening, and painstaking pressing—

who needs it? It is reserved, by most of us, for items such as cherished table linens or special (expensive) lingerie or blouses. We do not expect "easy care" for these (unless we take them to an expert cleaner— easy care of another kind, but hardly home care).

Discussed in this section are major cautions for home care of silk, linen, cotton, lace, pile fabrics, wool, down, suede, leather, and fur, followed by general care required by some trims and high-fashion creations, plus notes on care of modern special items, such as GORE-TEX® fabrics and stain-blocked carpets. Care of glass fiber fabrics is discussed under *Inorganic Manufactured Fibers, Section 2.*

Silk

Silk garments should be cleansed *soon after they are worn,* to avoid the tendering action of perspiration discussed in Section 2.

Silk articles respond well to hand laundering, if (a) the color is fast; test by pressing an unexposed piece of the material between layers of dampened white tissue or fabric, leave to dry, and examine for any staining; and (b) there is little fear of shrinkage; **heavier (suiting) fabrics** of silk may shrink out of fit, unless they have been preshrunk. In any case, dry cleaning may be preferable for these heavier fabrics, as they may pill less and they may keep their shape better if not softened by washing.

In hand-laundering silk, use wool method #2 under *Wool and Hair Fibers* to give heat and chemical conditions suitable for a protein fiber. There is less worry about agitation while hand-washing silk, for there can be no danger of felting as there is with wool.

Washable silk (washer silk) is expected to be machine washable, but it is imperative that you treat it as silk, not cotton; in particular, do not use built detergents (heavy-duty), or yellowing may result and more color loss than with the milder conditions as outlined for wool. Color on washable silk is often not fast, so get it dry quickly, either by tumble drying or rolling in a towel and pressing at once. (Dry cleaning may be no solution for this silk, as dyes may be more fugitive in dry-cleaning solvent.) Fabric softener is recommended for **"sand-washed" silk,** to prevent stiffening. In my experience one of the main weaknesses in less-expensive silk garments aimed at the middle market is inadequate seam finishing, quite aside from any special care needed for the fiber or fabric; with such smooth yarns, an enclosed seam such as flat felled is necessary to prevent yarn slippage along any seam that takes stress in wear.

Cultivated silk fabric (smooth, silky) should be pressed when slightly damp, on the wrong side, using a dry (not steam) iron set at warm; or use a damp press cloth. Silk may water stain if too damp during pressing. **Wild silk** is better pressed when nearly dry.

If the silk article is printed with more than one color, those colors are probably not fast. If you wash it, *prevent colors from bleeding:* First, remove excess moisture by rolling it in a towel immediately after washing, and then press dry *at once.* Do not leave it lying damp, or colors may "migrate" and bleed.

For storage of silk, see *Storage of Textile Articles.*

Linen

Linen (fabric made from flax fiber) takes vigorous washing well; go easy on chlorine bleach, because linen can be attacked by it sooner than cotton. Linen demands TLC mostly in *ironing* (you could *never* call it just pressing!). Linen articles to be ironed must be thoroughly, evenly damp, yet cannot be left long at room temperature without danger of mildew growth; put dampened articles in the freezer to hold them safely for ironing. Linen calls for a hot (top setting), dry iron, and must be ironed until *completely dry,* or wrinkles form as soon as it is moved. *This* is TLC, and it can be worth it for a favorite linen garment or a splendid damask tablecloth, once in a (long) while. To avoid shine, as with dark linens, iron on the wrong side; for luster, iron on the right side.

For storage of linen, see *Storage of Textile Articles,* but always avoid sharp folds; flax can crack where folded continually.

Cotton

Cotton fabrics, in general, do not call for TLC, unless they are high-fashion items; in fact, "careless care" of **top-quality**, functional articles of cotton is perfectly expressed in the care instructions for TILLEY ENDURABLES®: "Give 'em hell!"

However, to keep colors bright, or dyes from bleeding, use a lower washing temperature; if you wash with cold water, you will not get as efficient cleaning, although it may not be critical if the article is not badly soiled.

Pretreatment of soils will greatly help in removal, especially oily soil at collars and cuffs and any oily spots (see *Home Treatment of Spots and Stains).*

Counter mildew smell with a germicide or a fragrant fabric softener dryer sheet.

Ironing of firm cotton fabrics with **no Durable Press finish** is the same as for linen. **Durable Press finished** cotton and blends of cotton and polyester can be ironed without dampening, dry, with a steam iron.

Lace

Lace can be pinned or sewn into a bag or pillowcase before washing if it is valuable or the openwork vulnerable; use a washing method safe for the fiber content and lace construction.

Press lace with a cloth covering to protect it from the point of the iron; for lace with a raised design, see method for pressing of pile.

Pile Fabrics

Pile fabrics need special care in pressing to prevent the raised (three-dimensional) surface from becoming flattened; this procedure applies not only to pile fabrics such as velvet, velveteen, and corduroy, but to lace with a raised pattern or heavily embroidered fabric. Press face down into a thick terry or velour towel; for **velvet,** use a special needleboard, or lay the fabric face down over a horizontal raised screen (for small areas, over a clean, firm, flat hairbrush); press with a steam iron.

To remove wrinkles, a **velvet** garment may be hung in a steamy bathroom. Brush pile with self-fabric or a soft brush.

Launder washable pile fabrics inside out, to avoid trapping lint in the pile. Remove from the dryer while still slightly damp, to prevent crushing.

Carpet is a pile fabric and requires care different from most pile garment fabrics. Crushing and matting in use may be construed by consumers as wear, but as long as the carpet pile is not worn away, it is considered to have performed satisfactorily, according to a typical carpet guarantee that states something like: "will retain at least 90 percent of its pile for 5 years . . . when properly maintained."

Proper maintenance includes vacuuming often, using a machine with a beater bar, and keeping the carpet clean. Dry powder cleaners and/or application of carpet "shampoo" suds are two other stages of regular carpet care. See also *Care of Special Items* for care of stain-resistant nylon carpet. Vacuuming at least twice weekly is recommended not only to look after

the carpet, but to remove dust and microorganisms, especially where there is little fresh air ventilation. Spills on carpet should be taken up at once; Figure 6.3 under *Home Treatment of Spots and Stains* shows such a procedure.

A good carpet underlay will prevent some crushing, entrance mats can collect dirt before it gets tracked on to a carpet, and more even wear can be encouraged by rearranging furniture from time to time, if possible, so heavy traffic is redistributed.

Wool and Hair Fibers

Wool and hair fibers must be treated as protein fibers, not like cotton, using washing conditions that would be safe for our own skin and hair. Avoid alkali and high temperatures to prevent harshening and yellowing: no heavy-duty (alkaline) detergents, NEVER chlorine bleach, water lukewarm rather than hot. Keeping these cautions in mind, wool articles are laundered either by machine washing (with or without machine drying) or by hand:

1. **Machine washable wool** will carry a label or hangtag announcing some (trademarked) antifelt treatment (see Section 5). Use warm water, a good suds of mild (unbuilt) detergent (ULTRA IVORY SNOW will do), reduce time or agitation, and add fabric softener; if the article is labeled as *Machine washable and dryable*, use a lower dryer temperature. This latter designation is suitable usually for knitwear given an effective antifelt treatment; such is the case with the trademark TOTAL EASY CARE WOOL (includes the WOOLMARK®) (logo Figure 5.14[c]) from the Woolmark Company. Items so labeled are guaranteed not to show felting or relaxation shrinkage, color bleeding, or pilling with machine washing and drying. Articles such as wool trousers, which may be machine washable without felting but should be hung to dry (largely because of components in the garment construction other than the wool fabric), represent a separate category. For this, the Woolmark Company developed the trademark MACHINE WASHABLE WOOL (includes the WOOLMARK®) (logo Figure 5.14[b]). Pressing is part of the procedure for this type of garment (see pressing of wool below).

2. **Hand washable wool (not labeled as machine washable);** articles are possibly not safely washable at all, if color could bleed or "migrate" and

leave the article ruined on this account—especially important if two or more colors are present. Because wool and hair articles not given an antifelt treatment are expected to be dry-cleaned, their dyes have not been selected to be washfast, as they are for machine washable wool. *Test the colorfastness* before proceeding (press an inconspicuous part of the garment between two layers of dampened white tissue or fabric, leave to dry, and examine for any staining). See *Dyes and Colorfastness* for general comments on colorfastness of dyes on wool.

If the color is fast enough for washing, and keeping in mind that wool and hair fibers are weaker when wet, your main concern is prevention of felting. The finer the fiber, the more care is needed, so a very fine wool needs more care than a coarse one, and **cashmere,** for instance, needs extreme care to avoid felting.

Felting is encouraged by any unnecessary agitation, so wool articles should be hand-washed in lots of lukewarm water; have a good suds of mild (unbuilt) detergent (liquid hand dishwashing detergent or shampoo can be used); avoid moving the article about—keep it below the surface, and do not lift it in and out; do not rub—gently work the material to loosen soil or spots, and alternate this gentle hand working with soaking; let the suds run away without lifting the article; give rinses until the water is clear; add fabric softener to the last rinse, using as little water as possible; gently squeeze water from the article; roll in towels to extract excess moisture.

Dry flat on a towel, sweater dryer, or screen. If you wish to block to dry, you must draw an outline of the article before washing, and use rustproof pins to hold it to this outline during drying. Press wool using steam, and never directly on the fabric; use a press cloth; do not press heavily with the iron.

A **blanket** or other large article can be dealt with in a bathtub but is more easily soaked in the tub of a top-loading washing machine (lukewarm suds), given brief rinses and a spin extract, and dried over two parallel clotheslines.

Storage of wool and hair fibers is discussed under *Storage of Textile Articles.*

Down

Down is the under-plumage of water birds and makes a light, soft, air-trapping filling for cold-weather clothing or bedding. Feathers, less desirable with their stiff quills, are often mixed with the scarce and expensive down.

When buying a down-filled item, look for one closely quilted, preferably in more than one direction, to prevent the down from shifting and "clumping," as it tends to do when the down can move up and down long channels. During use, check for, and repair at once, any breaks in the quilting stitching; check especially before cleaning. Fluff down filling from time to time, by hand or by tumbling in a dryer set on low or "air" setting, with something like a couple of clean tennis balls or a clean running shoe to promote the fluffing action.

Do not allow items to get too soiled before cleaning. On the other hand, down duvets in constant use during cold weather usually need washing only about twice a year. Take any duvet larger than twin-size to a laundromat with an oversize machine and an extractor. If the general construction and fabric of the down-filled article allow washing, follow this procedure:

Close Fasteners. Pretreat stains or more-soiled areas with detergent. Use soft water, if possible, and select conditions as outlined for wool method #1 or 2; the action of a front-loading washer is easier on a quilted article than the agitation of a top-loading machine. If using a top-loading washer, let it fill partly, push in the down article, and continue filling. Check during washing and press air out of the fabric from time to time. You can also handle a large item, such as a comforter or sleeping bag, as recommended for a wool blanket. Avoid lifting a wet down-filled article, as it will be very heavy. Rinse well, or residual detergent can cause clumping during drying.

After extracting water, dry in a dryer using low heat, with tennis balls or a clean running shoe and towels to assist fluffing and drying. **Feathers,** which have a hollow quill shaft, will take considerably longer to dry than down.

For storage of down, see *Storage of Textile Articles.*

A down-filled duvet that has gone flat or lumpy may be renovated by a duvet maker—the down washed and blown back into a new cover. These duvet cover fabrics are *very* tightly woven (part of the expense of a down duvet), with thread counts of from 230 to over 300.

Suede and Leather

Suede and leather are "natural fabrics" composed of protein, like wool. While they can give excellent wear, they are specialized items, and do not invite careless handling.

Suede has a soft, velvety surface, made up of tiny fibrils. Light-colored suedes will soil easily, and the buyer must accept the need for more frequent cleaning; since this should be done by an expert cleaner, upkeep of suede can be quite expensive.

"Lamb suede" is a type of lightweight suede with no surface treatment to protect it from stains. Permanent staining can result if a protein-containing stain is allowed to dry and bond to this unfinished suede; wet out such a stain (e.g., egg or milk), seal the article in plastic, and see that it gets to a specialist suede cleaner *before that stain dries out.*

If a new suede article sheds fine particles, brush gently with a dry sponge or damp towel; this will remove loose fibrils, and they will usually not go on shedding long. Brush suede garments frequently, but never with a wire brush; use a bristle brush or dry foam sponge. Avoid cleaning fluids; use an eraser for nonoily spots, and try to prevent stains, for instance, by wearing a scarf to avoid skin oil and makeup staining at the neckline.

We do not depend on leather to give us waterproof footwear, but often cannot avoid exposing it to snow, rain, or slush. If suede or leather gets wet, dry *away from heat or direct sunlight,* hanging a garment so that it does not touch other clothing and stuffing shoes or boots with paper. Press, using heavy brown paper as a "press cloth," at low heat, use no steam, and press lightly on the outside.

Thorough spraying of suede or leather when new, using a stain repeller such as SCOTCHGARD® or those especially intended for the purpose, such as TANA ALL PROTECTOR®, can prevent much soiling, though they will likely be less effective on suede (or not recommended). One of the scourges of freezing weather for leather and suede can be road salt stains. Dried salt should brush off protected articles, and then leather can be given a final wipe with a damp cloth.

Again, suede will probably retain some staining, even with spray protection. White vinegar is recommended to remove salt stains on leather.

Leather should be polished frequently; for some firm leather boots, saddle soap will resist soil and keep them soft, but use with care on fine fashion leathers. Leather can be wiped off with a mild soap on a soft, damp cloth.

For storage of suede and leather, see *Storage of Textile Articles.*

Fur

Fur requires care both for the **skin side**—the same general care in drying as leather, for instance—and for the **hair side**—protection in storage very much like wool. However, since fur garments can be so valuable, commercial "cold storage" over the summer is usually needed; control of humidity is as important as a cool temperature, and is often not available or effective at home. However, if a home is equipped with a good air-conditioning *and dehumidifying* unit, a fur could be safer in home storage than in a poorly maintained commercial storage unit.

In winter, during use, air may be too dry; try to have sufficient humidity in the air. Do not expose a fur to direct heat, such as a radiator or heat vent, nor to direct sunlight for an extended time; heat and light can dry the leather and harshen the hair.

Guidelines for care in use include the following:

- Provide a broad-shouldered, curved, padded hanger for a fur coat or jacket; never hang on a hook.
- Make sure there is good air circulation where the fur article is hung (not crushed into a full closet).
- Shake fur frequently.
- When fur becomes wet or damp, shake off water and hang the article to dry, away from heat, with good ventilation.
- Wear a scarf at the neckline.
- Never put perfume on furs.
- Never pin jewelry on furs.
- When wearing a long fur coat, undo the lower buttons and flip the skirt up when you sit; in a car, undo all the buttons, or take the coat off.
- Do not spray moth repellent on a fur.
- Try not to get road salt on a fur garment, as it can affect the hair and lining.
- If hair becomes matted, for instance, from the friction of a seatbelt, comb the fur lightly with a plastic comb in the direction the hair flows, and *not at all deeply* with longhaired furs. If this does not give instant results, take the fur to a qualified furrier cleaner.

- Have fur cleaned and glazed as needed—not necessarily every year, but according to the amount of wear you give it. Fur picks up a good deal of dirt, and fur cleaning is a specialized process. The garments are tumbled in a drum of sawdust dampened with solvent. The sawdust (and dirt) are shaken and blown out, and the garment finished, with any minor repairs needed.

For storage of fur, see *Storage of Textile Articles.*

TLC or Beware: High Fashion Specialties

Certain areas of high fashion fabrics need really expert care, or they may become "wardrobe gremlins"—a source of trouble and grief to the consumer-owner, the retailer, and probably the dry cleaner. Some of these, and their particular weaknesses, follow.

Lightweight, sheer fabrics such as chiffon, **very crisp materials** such as taffeta, and especially **crisp sheers** such as organza are easy to damage, particularly if the fabric is relatively inexpensive for that type. Some stiffeners shift in water; if you lose that crispness, a less-than-expert dry cleaning process will leave fine "cracks" or hair lines. **Fragile materials** such as lace are usually of limited serviceability by their very construction.

Embossed designs and raised and puffed effects are often characteristics of fabrics that need TLC, such as matelassé, cloqué, moiré, and sculptured surfaces, to prevent distortion of those effects.

Beads, sequins, and such fancy trims may bleed or dissolve in dry cleaning solvent or be heat sensitive. There are also mirror-look plastic trims with solvent-soluble backing. Since such trim is usually applied to garments for special occasions, and these are normally dry-cleaned, the manufacturer should make sure such trim will withstand solvent, and the retailer or consumer had better get some assurance that it will, and pass on any information, such as on a hangtag, to the cleaner.

Surface designs in general are likely to show wear quickly. Sequin and bead trims have been mentioned, but there are also metallic brocades, all kinds of shag, pile, nap, or other three-dimensional surfaces, floating yarns that can snag as in satins, and heavily printed fabrics. **Pigment-colored fabrics** can lose or change color, and this often produces streaks, due to rubbing off (crocking); other prints do this too: gilt, paint, etc. (See Section 8 regarding testing for crocking of color.) A few surface designs are simply **glued on**; if the adhesive is dissolved by dry cleaning solvent, there goes the design! In most cases, these would fare no better in washing.

Unbalanced fabrics can wear easily, those, for instance, with fine yarns in one direction of a weave and much heavier yarns in the other. The fine yarns usually cover the other set and so form the surface, take most of the wear, and can split from strain. Such fabrics can also show yarn or seam slippage: rough or bulky yarns will slip along finer, smooth ones, leaving openings and distortions in the weave at points of strain, including seam stitching. (See Section 8 regarding testing for yarn or seam slippage.) These fabrics include the large family of dressy, silky-surface, plain weave ribbed materials: bengaline, faille, moiré, and others. Fabrics with stiff silk yarns running one way only (usually warp) can become tender from perspiration, and will then split in wear or cleaning.

Suede and leather may cause problems in commercial cleaning unless the consumer is able and willing to take them to a specialist and pay for the service. Restoration of the surface appearance and color of suede, for instance, requires a real expert and a good deal of time, hence the labor cost and high price. Dark leather combined with light fabric can give problems of color loss from the leather.

Crushed velvet-like fabric with a flocked pile surface, as explained in the discussion of flocking under *Printing Other than Color* in Section 5, has given poor wear in fashion fabrics, although manufacturing technology can produce flocked surfaces that give very good wear. When the flock fibers are held by an adhesive that is loosened by the dry cleaning solvent, the material will give trouble, even when cleaned by an expert.

Knits of fine-filament, textured yarns, especially if made of **microfibers,** are easily distorted or snagged; their behavior in use depends first on proper handling in manufacture of the yarn and fabric, and next of the garment, e.g., in laying out. They will always call for TLC in use and care.

Potential Troublemakers in Fabrics and Garments

Some articles taken to a dry cleaner may cause trouble if you pick an inexpert cleaner, but there is a limited category of **unserviceable merchandise** that cannot be satisfactorily cleaned, no matter what the method or skill applied. To avoid stocking these, the retailer must refuse merchandise if the manufacturer cannot provide reasonable care instructions (difficult for any of these), while the consumer should look for a *written* assurance that the article can be cleaned by *some* method. Otherwise, there is risk of returns, complaints, or lost customers for either dry cleaner or retailer. This can happen not only with "low-end" or cheap merchandise but also with high fashion specialties, and the dry cleaner is usually the first suspected of causing trouble when it occurs, because most consumers have a distorted idea of what goes on in a dry cleaning plant.

In the category of unserviceable articles are those with a cloth component that shrinks in wet cleaning, sewn to vinyl-coated trim that will not stand dry cleaning: you ruin it any way you try.

Bonded fabrics, one laminated to another, have caused many complaints in the past, though better techniques have lessened the problems a great deal. Trouble arises if one adhesive is attacked by solvent, while another type will not stand washing. A different method of bonding uses a thin sheet of foam, which, when heated, acts as the adhesive; foam laminates may deteriorate, separate, or turn quite yellow and show through a light-weight face fabric over time.

Buttons or trim, especially some polystyrene, can bleed color, swell, dissolve, melt under heat, crack, or break, creating havoc in a dry cleaning load. Such buttons, for instance, may be either very cheap or costly. You can detect some bad actors by running your finger around the edge of a button; if you feel a slight projection, it is the type to give problems. Elaborate buttons, such as those with rhinestones set in, should always be removed before cleaning, as should any trim of questionable performance (wooden, china, etc.).

Dark-colored interfacings such as black buckram, hidden in a garment, may bleed from a spill or during spotting in dry cleaning.

Care of Special Items

GORE-TEX® fabric was first used in garments intended to be washed, and many items will still be constructed of materials that can be laundered. If you buy an article with care instructions to dry clean, it may also carry special instructions that you should take to the dry cleaner (for instance, to clean in distilled solvent or follow cleaning with several rinses). The microporous film can become clogged with soil, and if this happens, while it will still repel water, it does not allow perspiration vapor through and so will no longer keep the wearer comfortable. Clean solvent will flush out the soil, restoring the film to its full performance. The film used in GORE-TEX fabrics now has a component to resist such contamination (see *Film* in Section 4). Dry cleaning "charge" systems (containing detergent—a wetting agent) can counteract water repellency of an outer fabric, and so a spray treatment may be needed after cleaning for this outer layer, even though no water will get past the film layer beneath it.

Stain-resistant nylon carpet is such a sophisticated product that cautions are given for cleaning, most directed to commercial cleaners but some affecting consumers' home care. Cleaning solutions must not be too alkaline, so do not use ammonia (unless in a procedure followed by a vinegar solution) or heavy-duty (built) detergents on stains. Do not use hot water on such a carpet. Finally, do not put a bacteriocide, antistatic agent, or softener into any cleaning solution; these are probably cationic and negate the stain-blocking ability built into the carpet.

A number of prominent fiber manufacturers give very specific directions regarding both cleaning and what "topical" treatments (surface stain resistants) may be applied, if their guarantee is to hold. ANSO V WORRY-FREE® carpet (by Allied) should have no topical treatment; STAINMASTER® (by DuPont) may have only TEFLON® MF; WEAR-DATED® (by Solutia) allow SCOTCHGARD™ or TEFLON® MF to be applied; carpets with SCOTCHGARD™ STAIN RELEASE (by 3M) may have only SCOTCHGARD™ CARPET PROTECTOR used.

As well as stain-resistant treatment for carpet pile, an impervious backing has been developed by Solutia for its PET-AGREE® carpets. This prevents liquids from seeping into the padding and onto the floor.

Garments insulated with THINSULATE™ (by 3M) *may* be damaged in dry cleaning with the most common solvent, perchloroethylene; shrinkage can occur after processing more than about four minutes, and even cold tumble drying can damage. *Follow the manufacturer's directions;* the article may be hand or machine washable or dry cleanable.

Articles insulated with THINSULATE™ LITE-LOFT (by 3M), such as sleeping bags, carry directions such as these:

- Can be machine-washed cold, gentle cycle, with a mild detergent. Tumble dry low, remove promptly. Do not wring or stretch. DO NOT DRY-CLEAN.
- Store away from heat and never compressed (rolled, or stuffed into a small sack); hang loosely in a large storage sack.
- To revitalize, tumble dry low.

Articles treated by the INTERA® process (by Intera) should be washed at warm setting, using less detergent than usually recommended; no bleach should be used. Fabric softeners should not be used in the wash or as softener dryer sheets. Tumble dry cool, and use a cool iron if needed.

Laundering

Water—The Basic Cleansing Agent

"Getting it clean" in washing fabrics is first of all a matter of using water. Water itself can remove much soil, especially things such as perspiration salts or sugar, which dissolve in it. Water, however, needs help to make things wet! Because of surface tension, we must add substances to water to act as *wetting agents;* we must also counteract problems from minerals or other substances in the water, assist in loosening oily soil, and help keep soil suspended until it is rinsed away.

Water "Hardness." Water hardness is one of the most significant factors in choice, amount used, and effectiveness of fabric washing compounds. Water dissolves mineral salts from rocks and earth. The type that precipitates out of boiling water onto pots and teakettles will not cause trouble in washing (unless you are still using a wash boiler!). The so-called *permanent hardness* minerals are usually salts of calcium and magnesium; these can cause trouble in laundering (and bathing and dishwashing). They combine with soap, replacing its sodium (or potassium) with calcium or magnesium, and create an insoluble (soap) compound that we see as a gray curd or scum. This is what forms a bathtub "ring," or in laundering, settles on fab-

rics to reveal itself as a "tattletale gray" color, a harsh feel, or even an unpleasant odor if it goes rancid.

Water will in general have highest hardness levels where there is limestone rock, which is easily dissolved.

In the United States, this is in the north-central area down to the west part of Texas, plus the Florida peninsula. (There are many exceptions, of course, in such a broad area.) In Canada, the hardest water regions are the midwest (except where the Laurentian Shield curves down from the north into the Prairie Provinces), and around the limestone escarpment (Niagara to Manitoulin Island) and Kingston areas of southern Ontario.

The softest water (most free of minerals) will be rain or melted snow, plus ground water that cannot dissolve anything out of the hardest rock, or where there is not much mineral substance available. On the map these areas are the upper New England states; the East Coast generally in both the United States and Canada; the area draining into the central part of the Gulf of Mexico coast; the West Coast states of Oregon and Washington plus the Canadian West Coast; parts of Alaska and the Yukon; and areas in Canada over the granite of the Laurentian Shield, that is, the Northwest Territories, Nunavut, northern parts of the Prairie Provinces, Northern Ontario, and most of Quebec.

Degree of water hardness has traditionally been given in grains per gallon (gpg), a figure that is converted to parts per million (ppm) by multiplying it by 17.1; water with 1 grain of hardness has 17.1 parts of mineral to every 1,000,000 parts of water (17.1 ppm).

Soft water, then, has up to 3.5 gpg of hardness, or up to 60 ppm; medium-hard water has up to 7 gpg, or 120 ppm; and very hard water has 10.5 gpg, or 180 ppm and up.

Detergent directions for amounts to use will probably be based on medium-hard water.

Iron. Iron in water is another mineral that can cause problems with fabrics, either by staining as rust or by accentuating the action of chlorine bleach, resulting in holes in cotton fabrics; do not use chlorine bleach where rust is present.

Water Softeners. Water-softening (ion exchange) units remove hardness minerals from water by passing water through zeolite, a complex resin that takes out calcium and magnesium, replacing them with sodium. When the zeolite is saturated with calcium and magnesium, it is recharged by passing through it a solution of common salt (sodium chloride), which reverses the combination and puts back sodium ready for another cycle.

Water Pollution. Since the 1970s changes have been enforced or introduced in the agents we use in home laundering, with the aim of maintaining the quality of our water sources—avoiding water pollution. There are different kinds of water pollution.

The most obvious type is **harmful bacteria,** counteracted by primary treatment when sewage is processed.

Next in priority is the presence of any **toxic or unpleasant chemicals.**

A nonharmful but unsightly type of pollution was caused when laundry detergents were not *biodegradable,* that is, when they could not be broken down by bacteria and so persisted, causing unsightly foam buildup. All major manufacturers changed to biodegradable detergents around 1970.

Acid pollution is a result of "acid rain" from air pollution. Acid forms when moisture combines with some chemicals in the air, mostly sulfur dioxide emissions, plus some others such as nitrogen oxides. The long-range effects of acid rain are of great concern to many environmentalists and to citizens with property on lakes where the water has become too acidic to allow many forms of life to survive; such lakes may be unnaturally clear—lifeless.

The most direct link between water pollution and home care of fabrics involves another kind of pollution that is not directly harmful to humans, but does lower water quality—again of concern to cottagers. This chain of events promotes the natural process called **eutrophication,** whereby a body of water changes from one rich in aquatic life to a kind of mud puddle. When water quality is highest—for fishing, swimming, boating, or just looking at—it is not only uncontaminated by germs or chemicals and relatively clear (though not so clear as a too-acidic lake), but has a good supply of oxygen, which supports sport fish such as trout. As eutrophication proceeds, there is less and less oxygen in the water, and life is gradually snuffed out.

This is the process: Algae (one-celled plants) and other aquatic plant growths, when nourished by cer-

tain substances in the water, thrive, eventually die, and rot in the water. Besides being unsightly and smelly, the rotting algae take precious oxygen from the water, affecting first the "highest" forms of fish, such as trout, then on down through other fish, turtles, and various aquatic creatures, until the body of water is "dead"—able to support only the most primitive forms of life (such as mudworms) that need almost no oxygen.

In the ordinary course of nature, the progression of eutrophication takes long ages to accomplish; we are seeing it happen in a frighteningly short time as human activity results in a lot of nutrient material entering the water. Algae, thus encouraged, increase dramatically to form large, often greenish "blooms" that seem to hang in the water.

Phosphate salts in water act as nutrients for algae growth; some of these are among the most effective aids to detergent action ("builders"), but have been virtually eliminated from laundry detergents because of this effect on algae growth; they were limited to 25 percent in 1970 and 5 percent in 1974. By 1978, this phosphate "ban" was credited with lowering phosphate in some municipal water effluents by about 50 percent. In the 1990s, major companies have reduced phosphate content of heavy-duty machine-washing detergents to zero. Of course, phosphates are an essential part of plant fertilizers and so still enter our waters as runoff from farmland, as well as from other sources.

Detergents and Detergency

A detergent helps water cleanse—mainly by helping it make things wet. Water is made up of countless molecules strongly attached to one another by forces that act in all directions. However, on the surface, where there are no forces acting from outside, the molecules are drawn in to reduce the surface area to a minimum: a sphere. The tension in the surface prevents further shrinking. This surface tension prevents water from coming into close contact with the fabric surfaces, or the dirt to be removed; it keeps water from "wetting out" the fabric.

Detergents (soap or synthetic detergents) have a "head and tail" structure; the head is hydrophilic—attracted to water—while the tail is hydrophobic or oleophilic—attracted to oil or grease (Figure 6.1). Detergents reduce the surface tension of water (they are *surfactants*) and so act as wetting agents—breaking the bonds between water molecules at the droplet surface by means of the hydrophobic tails pushing out away from the water. Detergents also help remove soil by loosening it from the fabric (see Figures 6.1 and 6.2) and then helping to hold it suspended or emulsified until it can be rinsed away—the oleophilic tails in the surface of the greasy soil, the hydrophilic heads in the water. Heat and agitation further the process of soil removal.

Soap. Soap is one of the best detergents possible, in both soil removal and suspension, if it is used in *warm, reasonably soft water.* However, it does cause problems with hard water, as was described earlier in the discussion of water "hardness" under *Water.* Soap is the salt of an alkali and a fatty acid from a natural fat (oils as well as animal fats)—a triglyceride. When the alkali is sodium hydroxide, we get a "hard" soap, which needs hot water to dissolve it. When the alkali is potassium, we get "soft" soap, which will dissolve in warm water. Toilet soaps and products such as the original IVORY SNOW (a soap) are made to act in lukewarm water and to have no free (excess) alkali left from the process; even the mildest soaps, however, are slightly alkaline in solution, whereas synthetic detergents are neutral.

Synthetic Detergents. Synthetic detergents or "syndets" have a chemical makeup of the normal hydrophilic head and hydrophobic or oleophilic tail,

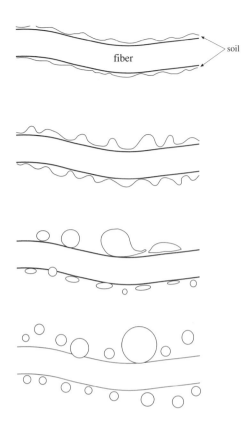

Figure 6.2 Roll-up and removal of soil in laundering.

but they differ from soap in that they cannot react with the calcium and magnesium salts in hard water to form a curd; this means that they will act in cold water, hard water, or even seawater.

Hand dishwashing liquid (which is mild or unbuilt syndet) is "pure" syndet in the same way a toilet soap is "pure" soap—nothing has been added to it. Compounds called *builders* are added to make "heavy-duty" or *built* detergents, suitable for machine-washing heavily soiled fabrics that are usually cottons (**note** that some built detergents are available in liquid form).

None of these built detergents is appropriate for protein fibers because of their alkalinity. By contrast, unbuilt syndet is safe for all fibers, but is a very efficient oil remover and so may take skin oil from the hands of someone doing dishes. For this reason, it may seem "harsh," even though it is chemically neutral. These liquid hand dishwashing detergents provide a safe and inexpensive detergent for hand-washing protein fibers such as wool and silk, or other delicate materials. Shampoo or products such as WOOLITE

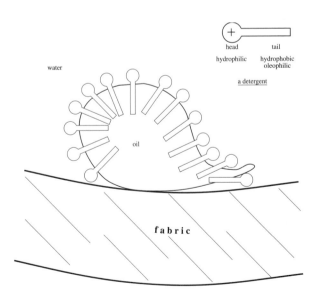

Figure 6.1 Detergents act as wetting agents or surfactants to loosen soil from fabric.

or ZERO may also be used. ULTRA IVORY SNOW detergent has been formulated to be safe for machine-washable wool or silk.

Heavy-duty syndets, such as TIDE or CHEER, are designed for machine washing of clothing and household textiles, especially cottons. Do not confuse a **liquid** heavy-duty syndet such as WISK with dishwashing **liquid** (unbuilt detergent).

By the late 1990s, built detergents were marketed more in formulations from which much "filler"—material such as Glauber's salt (sodium sulfate) with no active washing properties—was removed, so that the consumer got used to using less than a third of the amount formerly measured out.

Other Laundry Agents

Water Softeners. Water-softening agents have traditionally been added along with soap, to wash in hard water. Washing soda (sodium carbonate), sodium silicate, borax (sodium tetraborate), and ammonia are agents well known for this use. If soap alone is used in hard water to wash fabrics, the soap will be used up until it "softens" the water, i.e., reacts with all the calcium and magnesium; only then will soap form suds and perform its detergent functions. More hard water curd can be formed in the rinse water too, as its minerals react with soap carried over in the fabrics. Today, it is usually easier and more effective, when using hard water with soap, to add a **water conditioner or softener** such as CALGON to both wash and rinse waters. It *sequesters* or hangs on to the hardness minerals, so that soap will not react with them. Such a product helps whenever soap and hard water are used, e.g., in the bath.

Builders. Builders are alkaline salts added to help detergents disperse soil and hold it in suspension until it is rinsed away; they are added to give heavy-duty washing products. Syndets are very efficient at loosening dirt and do not cause the troubles with hard water that soap does; for these reasons, there is no soap used for home machine-washing products, although some of today's well-known names were once soap-based heavy-duty products, such as RINSO. Syndets, however, are *not* as good as soap at the "holding in suspension" function of washing, and so need builders even more than soap did. Since phosphate salts have been drastically reduced in amount used, old-fashioned agents such as borax, as well as nitrogen salts, are used as builders.

Bleaches. Bleaches may be added to detergent compounds or used separately.

"Oxygen bleaches" are the mildest type and include sodium perborate, monosodium persulfate, and the liquid hydrogen peroxide; one, BLEACH FOR UNBLEACHABLES®, is a powdered oxygen bleach. These are the only type safe for protein fibers like wool and silk (or human hair), or for many colored materials. Oxygen bleaches are introduced more as lower wash-water temperatures are used, since these are less effective in removing soil.

"Chlorine bleach," so-called, is used for stronger whitening action, stain removal, or disinfecting action on cellulose fibers: the liquid, sodium hypochlorite (JAVEX, CLOROX) or the solid, calcium hypochlorite. These should always be used *with care;* it is noteworthy that the Canadian care symbols have no Green (go) triangle representing chlorine bleach, only Amber (caution). It should always be added to the water before the clothes are added—never poured undiluted over a load already in the washer; never used on dyed goods without first checking the colorfastness (see *Dyes and Colorfastness*); NEVER, ever, used on wool or silk; can harm rubber; will yellow spandex.

Reducing bleaches are compounds used for removing or "stripping" dyes, or for treating certain stains. The **color remover** sold with home dyeing products such as RIT or TINTEX is of this type, as is sodium hydrosulfite. If a stain or discoloration does not come out with an oxygen bleach, then a reducing bleach might be tried; use a rustproof pan, and follow the procedure for whitening nylon under *Dyes and Colorfastness.*

Optical bleaches—whiteners or fluorescers—are fluorescent dyes that convert light that would be invisible (at the ultraviolet end of the spectrum) to visible light; they therefore *do* make fabric "whiter than white" or "brighter than bright." The type included in detergents "takes up" on cellulosic fibers, so the whiteness of cottons is renewed with each washing, as long as chlorine bleach is not also used; this bleach destroys the fluorescent. See the discussion of brighteners under *Dyes and Colorfastness* for notes on optical bleaches on fibers other than cotton.

Disinfectants. When someone has an infection, or when laundering articles such as diapers, it is often desirable to make sure bacteria will be killed during laundering. Very hot water and the process of washing will do quite a good job, but wash boilers are not part of 21st-century home laundries, and today we may lower the temperature of wash water from normal hot (about 60°C [140°F]) to cool to save energy. Chlorine bleach would disinfect, but is often undesirable for its effect on color, protein fibers, rubber, spandex, etc. Quaternary ammonium compounds, which do not harm fabrics and have no odor, are very suitable, or phenolic disinfectants may be used.

Enzymes. Enzymes in presoak or prespray compounds are of the *proteinase* (protein "digesting") type, effective in lukewarm water, to break down stains such as egg, meat juice, blood, milk, and milk products. They are knocked out in hot water, can irritate skin, and should not be used for soaking wool and silk (protein fibers).

Home machine washing compounds, then, contain a variety of agents to assist in cleaning fabrics, aimed mostly at cotton (cellulose fiber). All that advertising of "X is better than Y" is not entirely "suds in your eye"—there are other special additives, such as metal protectors to prevent corrosion in the washing machine, suds suppressors to prevent excessive foaming, fragrance, fillers to keep a powder running freely, and so on. Consumers should keep in mind that all wash loads do not need a "total" complex built detergent; if the wash is made up of colored or dark fabrics, a detergent with a bleach incorporated is not necessary.

Fabric Softeners. Fabric softeners (not to be confused with water softeners, discussed earlier) deposit a waxy or fatty lubricant on fabrics to give a number of advantages. Most are cationic (positively charged, usually quaternary ammonium compounds) that cling to the surface of (usually negatively charged) fabrics, making them softer, fluffier, and easier to iron (or need less ironing). Because the softener absorbs moisture, static is conducted away. Some leave a fragrance in the fabric. There can be yellowing of some fabrics, and some loss of absorbency has been reported, although tests do not agree on this latter point.

Some softeners are designed to be used in the tumble dryer; this is a boon to those who have no means of conveniently adding liquid softener to the last rinse in washing. Dryer manufacturers have warned against any that give a noticeable buildup on the inside of the dryer drum. Another problem that seems related to the use of fabric softeners in the dryer is the occasional development of darker spots or splotches, usually on a plain polyester fabric in a solid, light color (no "camouflage"). These spots can usually be removed by treating with an oil- or grease-lifting agent and rewashing; avoid drying with the same type of softener sheet. If the marks are small, round, darker spots, and you used too much softener in the wash rinse, they may have been driven into the fabric at the tub holes during the water extraction spin. Light spots, by the same token, are usually from lint, produced on the fabric in the same way. One dryer softener sheet maker has developed a product intended to add stain resistance to fabrics being dried with it; the claim is that over a number of dryings, the articles gradually acquire stain resistance. There is a recommendation to give any oily spots that may develop much the same treatment as outlined above for any marks attributable to softener.

Home Treatment of Spots and Stains

Home treatment of spots and stains, usually called (optimistically) *stain removal,* is presented in a very condensed format, beginning with a set of dos and don'ts:

DO decide first whether you can safely and effectively apply home treatment; it will be safe for most washable articles.

DON'T use complicated or strong home "recipes." Commercial cleaners are often faced with a worse stain when someone has first tried Great-Aunt Agatha's sure-fire mixture.

DO attend to spots and spills *at once,* though not necessarily at home! Stains treated early will not become set, they are still at the surface of the material, and you usually know what caused them. Figure 6.3 shows such treatment with a carpet, in this case inherently stain-resistant because it is made of CORTERRA® PTT polyester. A stain left for a time can concentrate, until an otherwise harmless substance such as lemon juice can attack

Figure 6.3 Prompt treatment works well for spills on this inherently stain-resistant carpet of CORTERRA® PTT polyester. (Courtesy of PTT Polymers)

a fiber or color; time also allows oils to oxidize and darken.

Permanent stains can be caused by alkali, age, or heat. Following are the three worst "scenarios" in staining:

1. **Tannin** becomes set with alkali, if left too long, or if exposed to heat. Tannins are the coloring matter in most plants and in most foods (except beets) and drinks, from wine to ginger ale, and including tea and coffee.

2. **Oil oxidizes** if left too long or heated. It turns darker (think of the color of old salad oil); from being almost invisible, it becomes a noticeable stain, impossible to remove. Oil can be from food/cooking oil or it can be skin oil (*sebum*), which gives "ring around the collar." Oily stains are very troublesome on polyester/cotton Durable Press fabrics, since both polyester and the resins in most Durable Press cotton finishes hold oily soil. When oil is not removed, not only is a stain left, but bacterial action on residual oil can develop clinging, unpleasant odors. Treatment is

described in the Stain Treatment Procedures Chart (Figure 6.4).

3. **Sugar caramelizes** with application of heat; it turns brown—the change we see when we toast a marshmallow or make caramel or butterscotch. Again, a spot that was invisible (dissolved white sugar) becomes noticeable and permanent. There may be sugar in drinks that do not have much color, such as tonic water; this is one main reason for the warning against pressing over a spill before the spot is removed. It is also why we should mark and identify a spill for a dry cleaner so it will get a prespotting treatment; otherwise, the article will go through solvent cleaning, which does not remove sugar well, and a spot like this can caramelize from the heat in subsequent drying and pressing.

"First aid" for treatment of stains on washable fabrics:

DO remove excess material—blot up excess liquid (do not rub into the fabric) OR absorb with powder (cornstarch, talcum) and let the paste

Stain Treatment Procedures

Follow steps in the order given

Stain Type	Key #	Stain Type	Key #	Stain Type	Key #
adhesive tape	1, 6, 9	hair tint	DC	water based	2, 9
asphalt (see *tar*)		ice cream	2, 6, 9	(must be still	
beer	3, 9	ink:		wet)	
berries	3, 9 + 7a	ballpoint	6, 5a, 9	pencil	soft eraser
blood	2, 8, 9	marker,	6, DC	perspiration	5a, 8, 9
butter (see *grease*)		permanent;		rubber cement	2, 5a, 6, 9
carbon paper	5a, 9	India		rubber heel marks	5a, 6, 9
chocolate	1, 8, 9 + 7a	washable	7a, 9	rust	7c, 9
coffee	3, 9 + 7a	iodine	6c, 7b	salad dressing,	3, 8, 9 + 7a
cold wave	DC	ketchup	3, 7a, 9	cooked	
(permanent)		lard (see *grease*)		salad dressing, oil	3, 5a, 6, 9
cosmetics:		lipstick (see *cosmetics*)		salt, road	2, 9
foundation	6, 9, DC	margarine (see *grease*)		scorch	7a, 9
lipstick	6, 9, DC	mascara (see *cosmetics*)		shoe polish	5a, 6, 9
mascara	6, 9	mayonnaise	3, 7a, 8, 9	shortening (see *grease*)	
other	5a, 9, DC	meat juice	2, 8, 9	soft drink	3, 9 + 7a
crayon (see *wax*)		medicines	7a	softener, fabric	5a, 9
cream	2, 6, 9	mildew	7a, 9	sugar solution	2, 9
deodorant	5a, 9	milk	2, 6, 8, 9	tar	5a, 6, 9
egg	2, 8, 9	mucus	8, 9 + 7a	tea	3, 9 + 7a
excrement (feces)	4b, 4a, 8, 9 + 7a	mud	5b, 9	tobacco	3, 9 + 7a
fruit juice	3, 7a, 9	mustard	3, 5a, 7b, 9	tomato sauce	3, 7a, 9
glue (except	DC	nail polish	6d	urine	4a, 3, 8, 9
rubber cement)		oil:		varnish	6d
grass	6c, 9	cooking	5a, 6, 9	vegetable juice	3, 7a, 9
gravy	6, 8, 9	motor	5a, 6, 9	vomit	4b, 4a, 8, 9 + 7a
grease: auto	5a, 6, 9	skin; hair	5a, 6, 9	wax	1, 6c, 9
food	5a, 6, 9	paint:		wine	11, 3, 9 + 7a
gum, chewing	1, 6, 9	oil based	6d, 9		

Figure 6.4 Stain Treatment Procedures Chart.

dry; gently scrape off solids with a spatula, spoon or dull knife (except those that call for chilling, which is #1 in the *Stain Treatment Procedures Chart*); try not to rub into the fabric.

DON'T use alkaline agents as a first aid treatment, without consulting the *Stain Treatment Procedures Chart*; alkaline agents include heavy-duty machine-washing agents, ammonia, borax, washing soda, and even soap.

DO treat protein-containing spots and stains at once, avoiding heat, and if possible soaking in or applying a product containing an enzyme, usually a protein-digesting type (*proteinase*).

DON'T use such protein-digesting products in treating wool or silk (protein fibers). Stains containing protein include those from any animal material (blood, secretions, meat, egg, dairy products in any form, and products made using dairy products or egg, such as mayonnaise), so the range is wide. Enzymes are inactivated by hot water.

DON'T press over a stained area, especially if it is nearly invisible when dry, as is a stain containing dissolved sugar.

Dry-cleanable articles or any you are unsure of treating at home:

DO take to a reputable cleaner.

DO pin on a note stating the nature and location of the stain (especially important if it is nearly invisible), plus information on anything you have already tried on it.

Figure 6.4 gives a Stain Treatment Procedures Chart; below is the key to the procedures. These procedures avoid hot water or alkali until the final wash, except for #4a and #4b, which are rarely applied. Try to *test first* on an unexposed area. Following is the **method for stain treatment:** With spot laid *face down* into white absorbent cloth or paper (tissues or towels), drop the solvent agent through the fabric (a dropper bottle works well). *Do not rub;* use a dabbing or patting action, working from the outside of the stain to the center; you are pulling the stain out and into the absorbent material by capillary action. As the stain is taken up, move to a clean area of the absorbent material, being careful not to transfer any staining back from the absorbent material.

Key to Procedures

DC = Take to an expert dry cleaner.

#1   Chill by application of ice, or put in a freezer.

#2   Cold water; soak if possible; if not, sponge.

#3   Cool water + 5 mL/250 mL (1 tsp./cup) *each* of liquid hand dishwashing detergent and white vinegar; this is on the acid side.

#4a   Cool water + 5 ml/250 mL (1 tsp./cup) *each* of liquid hand dishwashing detergent and ammonia; this is slightly alkaline.

#4b   Dry baking soda; this is also alkaline.

#5a   Work liquid detergent (undiluted) into the stain to penetrate and lift oil.

#5b   Make a paste of liquid detergent and powdered (mild) bleach suitable for all fabrics.

#6   Solvent; may be any of #6a, 6b, 6c, or 6d.

#6a   Gasoline type: lighter fluid, wood floor cleaner (VARSOL); this type is *flammable*—use with special **CARE.***

#6b   Nonflammable type: perchloroethylene—use with special **CARE.***

#6c   Rubbing alcohol or other colorless alcohol; *flammable*—use with special **CARE.***

#6d   Special or specific solvent, such as nail polish remover, paint thinner, (for paint, varnish, etc.), or manufacturer's recommendation; *flammable*—use with special **CARE.***

#7   Bleach or other special chemical; **use with care;** if in doubt, take the article to an expert dry cleaner (DC in chart).

#7a   Chlorine or oxygen bleach as safe for fabric or color; oxygen bleach in as hot water as is safe. **Note:** Do not mix chlorine bleach with, for instance, ammonia or vinegar. See #7.

#7b   Reducing bleach or color remover; see #7.

#7c   For rust only (see #7):

Oxalic acid crystals; use **with care,** wear rubber gloves.

Lemon juice, white vinegar, or citric acid crystals, with salt: cool water + 5 mL/250 mL (1 tsp./cup) of each.

Commercial rust remover.

*****CARE:** Do not breathe solvent more than necessary, use with good ventilation; watch sparks or flame with flammable types; never use with electrical appliances; watch any heat source near solvents, as vapors will form that may be toxic.

7c continued: On carpet: after application, rinse well, dab up excess moisture, then (if rust is gone) hold a steam iron over the area for a few minutes.

#8 Enzyme presoak or *enzyme detergent*, 5 ml/250 mL water (1 tsp./cup), or make a paste with water.

#9 Wash as appropriate; #<u>9</u> Water as **hot** as is safe.

#10 White absorbent substance such as talcum, cornstarch, chalk (on suede: ground, uncooked oatmeal).

#11 Shake salt on a wine spill, then shake salt off with absorbed stain, or vacuum.

Commercial Cleaning

Fabric care is important—that is not just a selling line for commercial cleaners. Soil can *harm* fibers and fabrics, either physically (tiny specks of grit cut and abrade fibers), or chemically (action of stains, or even moisture and sunlight reacting with certain dyestuffs). An advertisement (for EUREKA vacuum cleaners) says that a clean-looking carpet can hold 1.5 times its own weight in *hidden* dirt—about 90 pounds for a 9 ft. ×12 ft. carpet (40 kg for 275 × 365 cm). A carpet can hold more dirt than most other fabric articles we use, it is true, but all fabrics can hide a certain amount—something to think about. If the consumer cannot or will not undertake cleaning at home, then a commercial cleaner should be found. Commercial cleaning, until the mid-1990s, was taken to mean dry cleaning or commercial laundering; the latter does not come into the scope of *Fabric Reference*, except to define it as being applied mainly to cotton fabrics, using very hot water, and built detergents (plus chlorine bleach). To these we now add **commercial wet cleaning**, but will discuss dry cleaning first.

"Dry" Cleaning?

There is a credibility gap between consumers or even retailers and dry cleaners. The public does not understand what dry cleaners can and *cannot* do, or how various fabrics can and cannot be cleaned or handled. Possibly most bewildering of all, the name does not make sense to the literal minded: "They call it *dry cleaning* when you can *see* your clothes sloshing around in some kind of liquid!"

What happens in a dry cleaning plant?

Basically this: Clothes are cleaned in a liquid solvent other than water (hence the "dry"); in comparison with home laundering, such solvents remove oily and greasy soil better, take out some soils or stains that are a challenge to budge in water, minimize shrinkage from fiber swelling, and minimize disturbance of colors and finishes, as well as keeping the garment's original shape and tailoring details which will be disturbed more in water, requiring restoration in finishing beyond the skills of the consumer using home equipment. However, some commercial wet cleaners have successfully developed machines, special detergents, and protective and finishing agents so they can manage using water rather than solvent for most articles except furs and some items of rayon (see *Wet Cleaning*).

Most plants use solvents in what is called a *charge system;* in this a small amount (1 to 2 percent) of detergent is added to the solvent to carry some moisture needed to dissolve out some kinds of soil, such as perspiration. Some cleaners will use this only for a batch that is very heavily soiled, such as seldom-cleaned trench coats. Tumble drying at up to 70°C (160°F) evaporates off the solvent, and cleaning is followed by steam pressing or steam-air finishing.

Dry Cleaning Solvents

Two main kinds of organic solvents are used in dry cleaning, referred to as **petroleum** and **synthetic,** and there are some choices within these types. It is significant to realize that dry cleaning machines are designed to operate with one specific solvent; it is well to understand the characteristics of solvents, and then find what type is used by the cleaner you are considering.

Petroleum Solvent
Petroleum solvent is related to gasoline; hence it is flammable. **Stoddard solvent** is the name of the petroleum type most used in North American dry cleaning; in the United Kingdom, it is called *white spirit*; in Europe it is referred to as *hydrocarbon*. This solvent type must be used only in plants where fire regulations can be met; it will *not* be used by a cleaner in a corner plaza. A new version of petroleum solvent has been tried in Europe that is less flammable and may be safe for use in shopping malls or plazas. A report at an International Aqueous/Nonaqueous

Conference by Dr. Josef Kurz of the Hohenstein Research Institute in Germany recorded 5,000 perc (see below) machines in Germany, 1,000 using petroleum solvent, and 1,000 for wet cleaning, but new installations in Germany were running 90 percent petroleum, 10 percent perc, because of the low toxicity of the petroleum solvent.[1]

Despite its disadvantage of flammability, petroleum solvent has the advantage of being easier on some materials that are adversely affected by solvent, notably rubber (e.g., a latex-coated fabric used in a swamp coat or as the bottom outside layer of a sleeping bag) and vinyl (film or coated materials such as a leather-like). Such materials will eventually be deteriorated by any solvent, but would be relatively unharmed by a few cleanings in petroleum solvent; this is known in the trade as having *less solvent power.*

Synthetic Solvent

Chlorinated. Chlorinated solvent is used in a majority of plants in North America, and the particular solvent is perchloroethylene (PCE or tetrachloroethylene, also called perchlorethylene, and much shortened to "per" or "perc"). In Europe, trichloroethylene is also used.

Chlorinated solvent is nonflammable and therefore suitable for use in the many neighborhood, on-the-spot cleaners, as it meets fire regulations. It has, however, the disadvantage of great solvent power, so that an article made with rubber or vinyl, for instance, will be ruined by one cleaning in perc. Its fumes are toxic if inhaled in large amounts, but even small amounts accumulate in the body. The U.S. Environmental Protection Agency, with the industries involved, has been exploring alternative cleaning agents without this health hazard.

Coin-operated dry cleaning machines use perc; these are not common, but there is a caution to give: When an article such as a sleeping bag has been cleaned in a self-service dry cleaning outlet, the consumer should make sure that the item is *thoroughly dried* (solvent all evaporated off) and *well aired* before using it. This is no place to save a bit of money on drying time! This kind of machine will use chlorinated solvent, and if the fumes from these are inhaled in

massive doses, the result can be fatal. Such tragic accidents have been rare—in fact it may be hard to locate a coin-op dry cleaning machine—and use of these solvents in commercial cleaning plants is stringently controlled (further discussion on this follows).

Fluorinated. Fluorinated is a second type of synthetic solvent that has had minor use in dry cleaning. It was tried for dry cleaning since, like perc, it was nonflammable, yet like Stoddard solvent, had moderate solvent power; in addition, it evaporated at a lower temperature than either of the older solvents, which meant shorter drying times—more gentle conditions for delicate articles. After it was classified as a chlorofluorocarbon (CFC) contributing to depletion of the ozone layer, its production was banned in parts of Europe and in the United Kingdom. This led to the letter *F* being removed from the circle that represents dry cleaning in the ISO care symbol system (see Figure 6.9[a]). Fluorinated solvent has gone under the trademark name of Valclene (by DuPont) and was known as *R11* (trichlorofluoroethane) or *R113* (trichlorotrifluoroethane) in the United Kingdom.

Ultrasonic Cleaning

Ultrasonic waves were worked with in the 1980s to clean garments by shaking soil loose in a very short time; because soil was so thoroughly removed, with a fluffing out of the fibers, it was said that little pressing was needed in comparison with traditional processes, "dry" or wet. Little progress had been made by 1994, when a system was tested by Garment Care, Kansas City, which involved passing garments, held between pieces of mesh, through water, where an ultrasonic process shook the soil loose. Because garments were constrained, it was felt that shrinkage and the need for pressing were minimized. The process was aimed to be efficient and yet good for the environment, but still has not made much impact in the commercial cleaning field.

Commercial Wet Cleaning

Commercial fabric cleaning or *fabricare* went through a dramatic refocusing at the end of the 1990s, with stringent governmental controls of some solvents used in dry cleaning, and much more acceptance of commercial wet cleaning. Water, in specially designed machines, was first successfully used in the mid-1990s

---

[1]Marcia Todd, "Putting Wet Cleaning in Perspective," *Fabricare Canada*, September/October 1996: 20.

to clean some leather and vinyl-and-leather garments; Suede Life developed a process called "Clean & Green," so-named for being more environmentally "friendly" than dry cleaning.[2] Special wet cleaning machines also were shown at exhibitions such as the Texcare Exhibition in Frankfurt, Germany. This pointed up that not just any machine could be used for wet cleaning leather, since a load of leather garments is very heavy compared to fabric; one dry cleaner tried to duplicate the water process in an ordinary machine and had an explosion![3] Special cleaning additives as well as specially engineered machines were found to be needed in this revolutionary approach to leather cleaning. It was found that leather garments with wool in them or those with cotton backings could not be cleaned in water because of shrinkage. Garments had to be hung to dry (which took a lot of room), and then finished on hot head presses.

By the end of the 1990s, machines and process additives had been developed so that some plants were able to wet clean from 60 to 96 percent of all garments left for commercial cleaning, not just leather. Wet cleaning has become a legitimate adjunct to or alternative to dry cleaning. The most advanced equipment such as that developed by the German machine maker Miehle can give super-gentle action, as slow as 2 seconds of agitation followed by a 28-second pause, for articles such as mohair or angora garments. Sizing or softener can be added during cleaning. A low speed extractor removes all but about 35 percent of moisture. Drying may be completed with garments hanging in a warm air drying cabinet. Special finishing techniques have been developed for wet-cleaned garments.[4]

How to Rate Cleaning

The range of prices, especially in dry cleaning, roughly parallels the quality of expertise or service, from self-service (coin-operated machines—not many of these around), through economy "clean and steam" processes, to much-higher-priced service by expert "professional" operators. In between the last two, of course, may be the plant that advertises what is apparently complete service but which cuts corners with inexperienced staff or poor equipment maintenance/ quality control.

To budget cleaning for best value, you must know:

- How to recognize a trained cleaner for treasured articles.
- What you can satisfactorily clean in economy processing.

Quality Checklist. The best cleaning will give you:

- Articles tagged; any buttons or trim removed that might be damaged; materials sorted, so that fabrics of similar weight and color are put together; fragile articles bagged. (Note: if you are dealing with any but the best [most expensive] service, *you* should take care to check and clean out pockets, and to brush out cuffs.)
- Articles put through clean solvent; articles resized if fabric had stiffening in it; solvent removed—no trace of "cleaning odor" left; colors bright and (within reason) stains removed. If a stain is not removed, a note should inform you of this defect.
- Garments well pressed; pleats and creases sharp (and in the right place!); no old wrinkles or creases left around seams, buttons, crotch, or underarms; no fabric shine; lint brushed out from cuffs and pockets.
- Minor repairs taken care of, e.g., standard buttons replaced, tears mended.
- Special services, by many plants, include mothproofing, showerproofing, suede and leather cleaning. Rug, drape, or fur cleaning may also be handled, as well as shirt laundering.
- Note that this quality checklist will be the same for any commercial cleaner, including those using wet cleaning. Also, if any article you are having commercially cleaned is part of an outfit, e.g., a dress and jacket, or a suit, both parts should be cleaned each time to keep each piece the same color.

When You Need the Best Cleaning

In the quality checklist are tucked the two most important reasons to take some articles to the best cleaner

[2]*Canadian Cleaner and Launderer*, March/April 1994: 4, 6, 8.

[3]*Canadian Cleaner and Launderer*, January/February 1994: 42.

[4]Nathan Schiff, "Profile of a Dedicated Wet Cleaning Plant," *Fabricare Canada*, January/February 1999: 16.

you can find: (1) removal of tough spots and (2) expert finishing.

Tough Stain Removal. Removal of spots and stains in many cases requires different solvents or chemicals from either dry cleaning solvent or water. It takes a special kind of wizard to make an educated guess at what treatment will do the job for a particular stain (often unidentified) on a fabric of a certain fiber content (known only if the label is still with the article), with dyes or finish that may not react kindly to the manipulation needed to deal with the stain; and often involving interlining, buttons, trim, or other decorations that might bleed or melt during this tricky operation. This hair-raising procedure is known, perhaps unfortunately, as *spotting.*

It is very important to the treatment of some stains that they be *prespotted,* that is, done *before* the article goes through cleaning, after which it is dried. Heat can develop stains of tannin, oil, or sugar so that they darken and may be impossible to remove. Tag a garment or other article to show where a spill has dried, especially when it leaves little mark, identify the substance, and record any treatment you tried yourself.

Finishing. Finishing is the second significant service given by a commercial cleaner. You can put bulky sweaters, sleeping bags, blankets, children's play coats, or snowsuits through solvent cleaning in even a self-service, coin-operated machine, for none requires careful steaming and pressing.

Articles that *do* require careful finishing will look "like rags" until they receive it. Such items generally fall in the class of tailored clothing, such as suits.

Dry cleaners' presses are many and specialized. Two of them are **form finishers,** which bring the garment to shape with steam, and special **puff presses.** Even these methods will not restore "as new" the finish given a custom-tailored suit, involving hand pounding and pressing. However, the cleaner with a high-quality standard will do a good job on finely or elaborately constructed apparel. With wet cleaning, finishing is even more important, and units such as steamers with tensioning for trouser legs have been developed. Other cleaners give a soft, partly hand-pressed finish.

The "bottom line" is that both expert spotting and careful finishing can cost a good deal; the consumer must decide when this is well worth it.

How to Select a Dependable Cleaner

Choice of a dependable cleaner can be important to a retailer (of ready-to-wear or piece goods) as well as to consumers. To the uninitiated, most dry cleaning plants look equally impressive if the equipment is located right there (on the spot), or equally mysterious if you deal with a branch store of a company with a central plant or with a small store that acts as an intermediary only, sending cleaning to a large wholesale plant that serves many separate companies or stores.

Among all these are some cleaners you can depend on to give you quality cleaning and even good advice when you need it. To locate one of these, you should look first for identification of the cleaner's membership in one of the trade associations that inform their members of the best way to handle new or difficult fabrics. Many cleaners in the United States and Canada belong to a long-established organization, the International Fabricare Institute (IFI), 12251 Tech Road, Silver Spring, MD 20904. A national group was re-formed in Canada in 1994 under the name Canadian Fabricare Association, P.O. Box 24026, Kitchener, ON N2M 5P1.

Having identified a cleaner as a member of a trade association, make a personal survey: Pick a special garment, perhaps a good-quality suit, an all-weather coat, or an evening gown. Take it to several cleaners near you. Ask some basic questions:

- Do you run your own plant?
- Where is the cleaning done?
- What is your cleaning charge for this specific garment?

Of course, you will find some cleaners more expert than others, even within the membership of a trade association, and the final "proof" is the quality of the actual cleaning job. The price charged, as with many consumer items, is a rough guide—up to a point. With a rock-bottom price, some of the points of quality cleaning will almost certainly be scanted on or missed.

Beyond a certain point, you pay for super, "custom" cleaning, which, you will remember, includes finishing. This may be well worth it for a suede suit, an elaborate cocktail dress, a fine knit outfit, a good fur- or suede-like fabric coat; it may also be worth it for a retailer to have a top-notch cleaner deal with a customer's article if there is a question or problem to do with cleaning high fashion merchandise from your department or store.

For many simply constructed garments or straightforward materials with no difficult stains, you do not really need the most expensive cleaning service.

When cleaning costs are budgeted over the range from most expert cleaner (expensive) to lowest price or even to coin-op loads, a consumer can receive better value and feel less resentful about the cost of cleaning care.

Dyes and Colorfastness

Colorfastness is a term used for the degree to which a dye holds "fast" to the fiber or fabric. A high or good fastness means that the dye does not fade in light, *bleed* or run in washing, *crock* or rub off in wear. Colorfastness is also measured to perspiration, seawater, pool water (containing chlorine), dry cleaning, weathering, various types of washing, fume fading, as well as finishing processes such as milling, decating, and others. A *fugitive dye or tint* is one that is easily removed; sometimes one is applied to identify a particular construction, e.g., for easy identification while it is being processed in a mill (British: *sighting colour*).

What Can We Deduce about Colorfastness?

Textiles texts written for fashion or consumer studies programs invariably discuss dyestuffs according to type or class, e.g., vat, direct, acid, etc., outlined in Section 5. While it is *necessary* to have some familiarity with these names, it is almost *never* significant to the consumer or retailer to be told how or to what fiber each type is applied. This is because none, with the exception of vat dyes, is ever identified as such when articles are sold, and *that* is when we wish to know something of what colorfastness to expect.

This anomaly in all available texts gradually dawned on me as I began teaching textiles to fashion students at Seneca College in 1968. Most of my working life before that was spent running a testing and development laboratory that served textile mills. Our greatest single effort was the development of formulas (recipes) for dyeing almost every fiber and combination. Putting that "inside information" to work, I

have arrived at some generalizations we can make concerning the colorfastness to be expected of various fabrics: We do *not* know whether an article has been dyed with chrome, disperse, reactive, or whatever dye; we *do* know:

- of what fibers it is made.
- the character of its color (bright, dull, deep, pale).
- the price range of the fabric or article (cheap, expensive).

Here is what you can deduce from this, working from the *fiber.*

Acetate

Acetate gives no trouble in dry cleaning, and most fabrics of acetate are dry-cleaned. It has only fair to poor fastness to washing; the hotter the water, the worse the fastness. *Fume fading* is a problem met with dyed shades on acetate: certain blue shades (or blue-containing, such as green or purple *plus* gray or beige) show a change to pink when exposed to the fumes formed when many fuels are burned (nitrous oxide fumes).

Dyes used are disperse, and while there are fume-fading-resistant members of this dye type, they are more expensive and are not generally used on acetate, since consumers' expectation of performance has been generally lower for acetate.

Acrylic

Acrylic shows good general fastness to care, including washing and light, no matter what the brightness or depth of shade. The cationic dyes used give bright, fast shades on acrylics, and other fast dye types are used as well.

Cellulose Fibers

Cellulose fibers (cotton, flax [linen], ramie, lyocell, viscose, cuprammonium, rayon, hemp) will all take the same types of dyes. In general, fastness is closely linked to price and quality.

Inexpensive products made of cellulose fibers, if made in a wide range of colors, will likely have only fair to poor fastness to wet conditions or to light, and very low fastness to chlorine bleach; they were probably dyed with direct dyes, which are not fast. I do not know of any effective home treatment to "fix" such dyes to make them fast, in spite of many "old wives' tales." Some inexpensive articles in limited and rather dull shades may show good fastness to washing and light, but will not stand up to chlorine bleach; these would have been dyed with sulfur dyes.

Deep shades (navy, burgundy) on moderate-priced articles could be fast to warm water washing, but not to hot water nor to chlorine bleaching; this will be the case if they have been dyed with direct developed dyes, which are more costly and faster than the simpler direct dyeing process.

More expensive articles of these fibers should have significantly better fastness. There are, for instance, direct dyes of very high fastness, but these cost more than those used on cheap items.

Highest fastness, though, comes only with dyes and/or dyeing methods that are very expensive; with these you get excellent fastness to even hot water washing, including heavy-duty detergent, and to chlorine bleach and light. These will be dyed using vat, naphthol, or reactive dyes.

Consumers may be suspicious of tags on some (usually cotton) articles, declaring the need to "wash separately," or "wash before use"; however, either is probably a reassuring direction, because deep shades on good-quality items such as cotton terry towels *can* exhibit a washing off of surface dye, as a result of complicated methods of application. If washed with like colors a few times, the excess dye will be removed, and the dye in the fibers will show its good fastness from then on (see Figure 6.5).

These top-notch dyes are vat and naphthol, with long and complex methods of application, plus reactive, which are expensive to buy, call for a lot of dye, and are tricky to apply. Reactive dyes are not quite as fast to chlorine bleach as vat or naphthol. Where highest fastness to chlorine bleach is needed (such as vat dyes can give), naphthol dyes may also be needed, for instance, to give a deep, "true" red, which does not exist in the vat dye range. Note the anomaly that some dyes of top washfastness bleed in dry cleaning solvent—naphthol bright red is one!

Although indigo, traditionally used to dye the blue warp yarns of denim, is a vat dye, as most of us know, excess color does come off new items; a practical consumer's tip is to wash faded denim with a new blue denim article—that is, unless one *wants* the faded look.

Nylon

Nylon articles divide into two groups, pastel shades or deep colors, from which there are different expectations of colorfastness.

Pastel or light shades on nylon articles made of filament fiber, such as stockings and lingerie, will have only fair washfastness in anything but lukewarm water, no matter how expensive the garment. Disperse dyes must be used for pale shades on filament nylon to ensure level dyeing (no streaks or *barré*). Other, faster types can be used for deeper colors.

Deep shades may be quite washfast *if* they have been "fixed" on the fiber; you can expect this with

100% COTTON/COTON/ALGODÓN

MADE IN U.S.A.
FABRIQUÉ AUX ÉTATS-UNIS
HECHO EN E.U.A.
©SPRINGS INDUSTRIES, INC.
FORT MILL, SC 29716

TWIN/JUMEAU/INDIVIDUAL
FOR 39 IN X 76 IN MATTRESS
POUR 99 CM X 193 CM MATELAS
PARA 99 CM X 193 CM COLCHÓN

WASH BEFORE USE. WASH WARM, DARK
COLORS SEPARATELY. NO BLEACH.
TUMBLE DRY, LOW. REMOVE PROMPTLY.

LAVABLE AVANT USAGE. LAVABLE TIÈDE,
LES COULEURS FONCÉES SÉPARÉMENT,
NE PAS BLANCHIR. SÉCHAGE PAR
CULBUTAGE, BASSE TEMPÉRATURE.
RETIRER IMMÉDIATEMENT.

LAVAR ANTES DE USAR. LAVAR A
TEMPERATURA MEDIA, COLORES
OSCUROS SEPARADAMENTE. NO USAR
BLANQUEADORES. SECADO A
TEMPERATURA BAJA. REMOVER
RÁPIDAMENTE.

(a)   (b)

Figure 6.5 (a) U.S. care label with phrases in English, including warning to wash dark colors separately. (b) U.S. content/care label, in English, French, and Spanish.

good-quality articles and *may* get it even in cheap ones. TACTEL COLOURSAFE (by DuPont and Dy-Star) has high washfastness from changes in the nylon polymer and the reactive dye range.

Whereas it is difficult to build up deep shades on nylon, the fiber takes up small amounts of dye very quickly. This leads to what is called "scavenging" of *dis*-coloring matter from wash water; pale or white nylon articles should be washed separately to keep a distinctive shade or bright white. Further, all parts of a set of nylon nightwear, e.g., gown and peignoir, should be washed together (the same number of times) to keep the shade the same in each.

If nylon becomes stained or dull-looking, it is probably from this taking up of color from other articles. Use the color remover sold with home dyes such as RIT or TINTEX to strip color (use a rustproof pan and wear rubber gloves); then apply a brightener (see *Brighteners*).

Polyester

Polyester dyed articles will not bleed, and do not pick up dye stains easily (but tend to hold oily stains).

Polyester is very difficult to get dyes into, unless it is a special, more dyeable form. Dyeing of standard polyester is accomplished in a reasonable time either by (a) using *carriers*—chemicals to swell the fibers—dangerous and unpleasant to work with, and largely phased out in the 1990s, or (b) dyeing in pressurized machines above the temperature of atmospheric boil reached by open machines (100°C or 212°F); at a temperature of 120°C (248°F), for instance, dye penetration is greatly speeded up. With polyester, then, once in the fiber, dyes will not come out easily.

Do not confuse dyed fabrics with printed; pigment prints on polyester may show rubbing off (crocking) of color.

Silk

Silk articles are generally expensive, but unfortunately there is no established connection between price and good wet- or lightfastness of dyes used on silk. Colors on silk give no trouble in dry cleaning. Now that more medium-price silk garments are marketed, usually as being washable, we may see a better level of fastness to washing, perspiration, water spotting, and light. Fast dyes for silk are available, but some old-fashioned basic dyes that have poor wet- or light-fastness are still used.

Triacetate

Triacetate (fiber little used now) usually shows good fastness to washing as well as to dry cleaning. Disperse dyes are used on triacetate, as on acetate, but since the consumer *expects* to wash triacetate articles, dyes of better fastness (to fume fading, e.g.) are chosen from this group, or the more expensive disperse developed dyes are used.

Wool and Specialty Hair Fibers

Dyes on wool and specialty hair fibers (cashmere, mohair, angora, camel, et al.) show good fastness in dry cleaning, so tailored apparel and many other high-quality articles of these fibers are usually thought of as "dry clean only." Pale and/or very bright shades on wool are likely to have poor fastness to light; beware a shade such as aqua, for instance, in wool carpet or an upholstered furniture suite that will be exposed to direct sunlight!

If a wool item carries a "machine washable" label, you can assume that the dyes will be washfast *under conditions suitable to wool washing.* If there is no such label, you *cannot* assume that the dyes will be washfast, so even if you know how to hand-wash wool without felting, you must take care to test the color, as indicated under *Tender, Loving (Home) Care* for wool. Good wetfastness on wool can be achieved by moderate-priced dyes in dull shades: metallized or chrome (mordant) dyes. In bright shades, expensive dyes must be used: specially selected acid dyes, reactive, or even vat dyes. An added difficulty with pale, bright shades on wool is that the naturally creamy fiber must first be (carefully) bleached.

Home Dyes

Home "dyes" such as RIT or TINTEX are mixtures of dye types (probably direct, acid, and disperse) able to cover cellulose fibers, wool, silk, nylon, and acetate, to roughly the shade shown on the package (*union dyeing*). These products will not dye acrylic, standard polyester, or olefin.

"Dyeing" at home presents a choice: get the color on fairly levelly by using a washing machine and the hottest water from the tap (not hot enough for fastness, even if these home dyes would give it), or dye in a pan on the stove, where you get the heat necessary for good dye penetration, but will probably find uneven shading from "hot spots," where the material settles to the bottom of the pan. A *baffle* (like a trivet) placed in the bottom of the pan can help reduce this hot spotting.

Brighteners: What to Expect of "Whiter than White"

The glaring white on many textiles today is achieved by an *optical bleach* (see *Other Laundry Agents* regarding bleaches). Here is the fastness you can expect on various fibers:

Cellulose fibers. Satisfactory and renewed with detergent washing.

Acrylic, polyester. Do not take up brightener in detergents, but those put on in manufacture of the fibers have good fastness to washing and light.

Nylon. Will not take up the brightener in detergents, but special products are sold as nylon brighteners.

Wool. Fluorescents available have poor lightfastness. If a wool article has one of these brighteners on it, the dye will break down after a relatively short exposure to sunlight, giving yellowing. This dye residue has to be removed before whiteness can be restored. Better to cultivate a taste for naturally creamy or less than glaring white wool!

Care Labeling

Many countries have developed systems for labeling textile products to denote care, in some cases mandatory, in many others voluntary, but with a specific system available. In most, symbols are used to represent various aspects of cleaning and maintenance of fabrics, as a means of offering information without the use of language. But the question then is, do consumers readily understand the label directions? The debate goes on.

U.S. Care Labeling Rule

The *Care Labeling Rule,* drawn up by the United States Federal Trade Commission, was first passed in 1972, revised in 1984, especially as to the *Glossary of Standard Terms,* with alternative Care Symbols in place by 1999.[5] The rule requires that textile clothing

[5]*Writing a Care Label,* an FTC Manual for Business, from Federal Trade Commission, Sixth and Pennsylvania Avenue NW, Washington, DC 20580.

carry a permanent label giving one method of care safe for that article. There is no requirement to give all safe methods nor to warn about procedures that may not be safe (unless the product cannot be cleaned by any procedure). The Care Labeling Rule thus requires instructions either for home washing *or* commercial cleaning but may be modified to require both, so that consumers would know if they could choose between these cleaning methods. Certainly commercial cleaners would prefer that both be shown if the article can be cleaned either way. Care information is also required for certain piece goods. If a product can be cleaned by all of the most severe methods, it does not have to carry a regular permanent care label, but should be marked "wash or dry clean, any normal method."

A glossary of short phrases to convey care instructions with an agreed-on meaning was developed. Labels are required to be in English (see Figure 6.5[a]), although the addition of other languages is allowed. This has become more significant under the North American Free Trade Agreement, which includes countries using French and Spanish as well as English (see Figure 6.5[b]). The revised rule and the glossary did address some of the misunderstandings that arose with earlier phrases, such as "no iron," which could certainly be taken to mean "needs no ironing" but which was intended to convey "do not iron." There is no national standard, inspection, or testing for how the label care instruction terms are used. The system developed by the American Society for Testing and Materials (ASTM) D5489–96c, Standard Guide for Care Symbols for Care Instructions on Textile Products, may be used instead of words or combined with words (see Figure 6.6). The manufacturer or importer is responsible for labeling with an appropriate wording or symbol choice. No other symbol system may be used in the United States.

A discussion of just what these **symbols** mean should help clarify many aspects of systems used in many other countries as well (shown under Figure 6.7 and Figure 6.9[a]). The five basic symbols represent **wash, bleach, dry, iron,** and **dry clean,** and any that are used on a label must appear *in that order.* In all cases, a warning appears as the **symbol with a X over it**, to indicate DO NOT do that.

The **washtub symbol** (for washing) may seem archaic, since most of its references are to machine washing, but it is used because it is very difficult to devise a symbol that looks like a washing machine

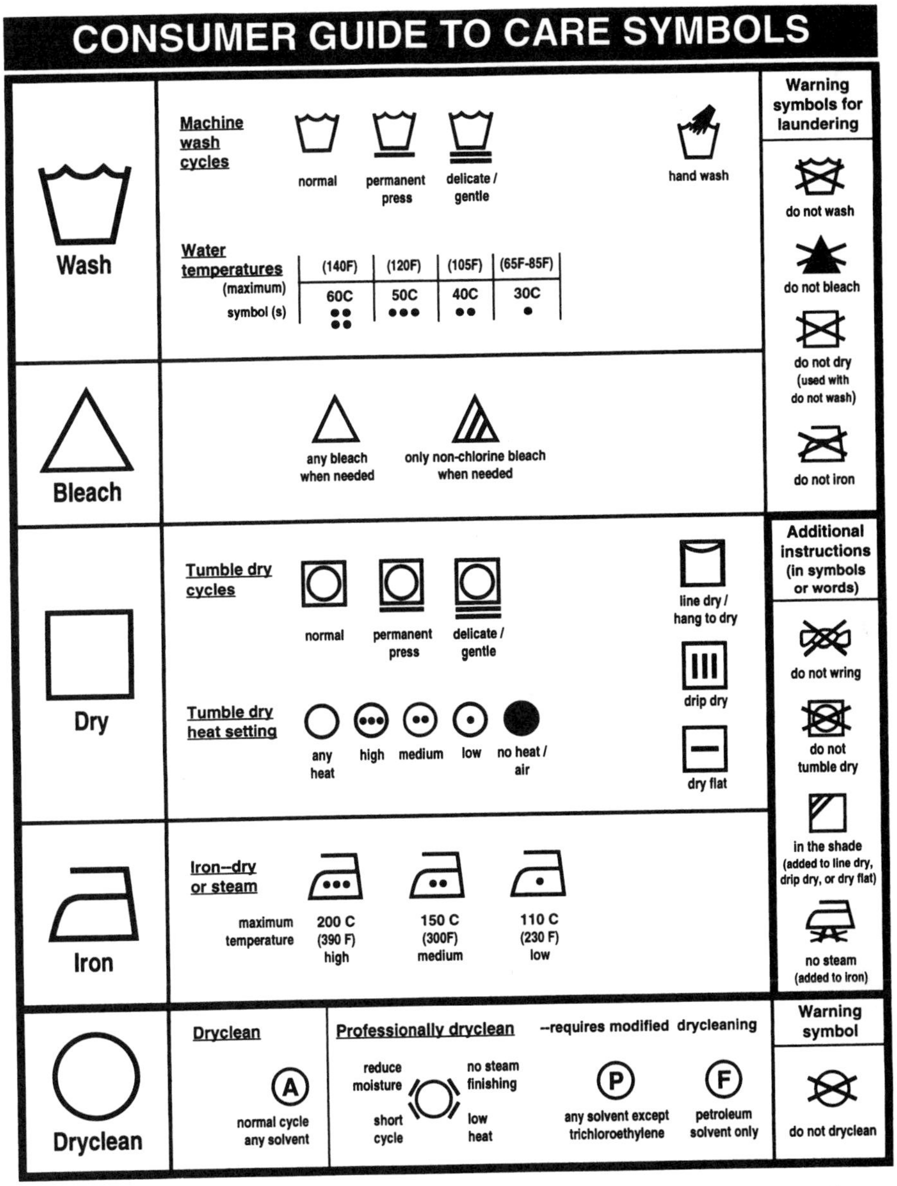

CONSUMER GUIDE TO CARE SYMBOLS

Wash

Machine wash cycles: normal, permanent press, delicate / gentle, hand wash

Water temperatures (maximum)

(140F)	(120F)	(105F)	(65F-85F)
60C	50C	40C	30C

symbol (s)

Warning symbols for laundering

do not wash

do not bleach

do not dry (used with do not wash)

do not iron

Bleach

any bleach when needed

only non-chlorine bleach when needed

Dry

Tumble dry cycles: normal, permanent press, delicate / gentle

Tumble dry heat setting: any heat, high, medium, low, no heat / air

line dry / hang to dry

drip dry

dry flat

Additional instructions (in symbols or words)

do not wring

do not tumble dry

in the shade (added to line dry, drip dry, or dry flat)

no steam (added to iron)

Iron

Iron—dry or steam

	200 C (390 F) high	150 C (300F) medium	110 C (230 F) low
maximum temperature			

Dryclean

Dryclean: normal cycle any solvent (A)

Professionally dryclean: reduce moisture, short cycle, no steam finishing, low heat

--requires modified drycleaning: any solvent except trichloroethylene (P), petroleum solvent only (F)

Warning symbol

do not dryclean

Note: This Figure illustrates the symbols used for laundering and drycleaning instructions. As a minimum, laundering instructions include, in order, four symbols: washing, bleaching, drying, and ironing; and, drycleaning instructions include one symbol. Additional symbols or words may be used to clarify the instruction

Figure 6.6 U.S. Care Symbol chart (Copyright American Society for Testing and Materials, 100 Barr Harbor Drive, West Conshohocken, PA 19428-2959).

(some are front-loading) but is distinguishable from a tumble dryer. **Wash cycles** for machine are indicated by no line under the tub (normal), one line (permanent press), or two lines (delicate or gentle); a hand in the tub means hand wash. **Water temperature** is given by dots inside: from 1 (cool), through 2 (lukewarm), 3 (hand hot), 4 (hot), 5 (very hot for home wash) to 6 (commercial laundry water temperature).

Bleach is indicated by a **triangle**, indicating any bleach when needed, unless there are two lines through it, warning to use only nonchlorine bleach.

A **square** represents drying. The symbol for drying the most fragile materials represents **drying flat,** plus symbols for **drip dry, hang to dry. Tumble drying agitation** is given by no line under the square (normal), one line (permanent press), or two lines (delicate or gentle cycle). **Tumble dry temperature** is indicated in the circle representing the dryer door by no dot (any heat), dark circle (no heat/air dry), one dot (low), two dots (medium), and three dots (high).

Additional instructions may be added using either the symbols developed for this ASTM guide, or words: *do not wring,* and *dry in the shade.*

Ironing is indicated by a hand-iron-shaped symbol. Dry or steam **ironing heat** is shown as one dot (low), two dots (medium), and three dots (high) in the same way as on an electric heating pad switch. Addition below the iron of two jets and an X indicates *do not use steam* (no steam).

A **circle** represents dry cleaning, normal cycle, with **letters** inside as to which **solvent** is safe: *A* for any solvent; *P* for any solvent except trichloroethylene; *F* for petroleum solvent only. (It may be confusing to have this letter used in North American care symbols with a different meaning from that formerly used in Europe, as noted under *Fluorinated Solvent.*) Additional instructions as to dry cleaning are given by lines in any one of four positions around the circle.

Canadian Standard Care Labeling

Canada developed a National Standard for Care Labelling of Textiles (see Figure 6.7), similar in many respects to the symbol systems used by other countries. The Canadian system is voluntary; manufacturers are not required by law to give care instructions. So the system may be freely used, as long as provisions in the standard (CAN2–86.1–M79) are followed; being a national standard, the symbols are trademarks of Canada. Administration is the responsibility of Industry Canada (formerly Consumer and Corporate Affairs Canada).[6]

Canada's system is different from all others in one aspect: the symbols appear in one of the three "traffic light" **colors: green, amber, and red.** This addition of color adds an extra dimension and can convey a good deal of significant additional information, much more specific than a simple "go ahead,"

[6]*Guide to the Canadian Care Labelling Program,* from Industry Canada, 50 Victoria Street, Hull, QC KIA OC9.

"be careful," or "stop." The amber color, for instance, is used to indicate reduced agitation in washing (the U.S. and ISO systems use a line under the symbol). The **warning** in this system is not only an X over the symbol but the color red. See the preceding discussion of the symbols, their meaning and order.

Wash water temperatures are in four steps, and since they are given in °C and few people are familiar with how water feels at a specific temperature, some benchmark is needed to be able to "translate" temperature readings to practical meaning when looking at a label in a garment, with no handy chart or key for reference. The Canadian standard now uses degrees Celsius, but the Fahrenheit temperatures previously used are included here as well. The lowest is cool water, 30°C (85°F), indicated as well by a hand in the tub for hand washing. Next is lukewarm, and for machine washing, the equivalent of lukewarm is 40°C (105°F), just above body temperature. The next setting is called "warm" on the chart, but "hand hot" is a more useful term, and this is 50°C (120°F); few of us can keep our hands in water this hot, although my mother and grandmother could! Hot is 70°C (160°F), which is hotter than most home water heaters will deliver to a washing machine. While two labels may carry the same washing symbol temperature, one may be in amber, calling for lower speed of agitation, and the other green, meaning vigorous agitation.

The only symbol that recommends use of chlorine bleach is an amber **triangle with *Cl*** inside it; there is no green triangle. Amber here means "use as directed"—according to manufacturer's directions.

A **square** represents drying, and the Canadian system was adapted with minor changes for the ISO system; Japan and the United States also have symbols for drying. Amber indicates a low tumble dry temperature.

Iron settings in the Canadian system may be given by temperatures, puzzling to North American consumers, since no such setting appears on irons. If confronted with one of these, think oven temperatures, in which most of us are conversant with °F. At these high temperatures, Celsuis degrees can be taken to be about half of Fahrenheit; this gives 110°C close to 220°F or low, 150°C close to 300°F or medium, and 200°C close to 400°F or high. The more sensible alternative, which the Canadian system offers, is one, two, or three dots for low, medium, and high, as noted for the U.S. system.

Follow the Signs

These symbols tell you which procedures to use or avoid when washing, drying, ironing and dry cleaning.

	Stop	Be careful	Go ahead
Washing	Do not wash	Hand wash in cool water; Machine wash in cool water at a gentle setting—reduced agitation (30°C); Machine wash in lukewarm water at a gentle setting—reduced agitation (40°C); Machine wash in warm water at a gentle setting—reduced agitation (50°C)	Machine wash in warm water at a normal setting (50°C); Machine wash in hot water at a normal setting (70°C)
Bleaching	Do not use chlorine bleach	Use chlorine bleach with care	
Drying		Dry flat; Tumble dry at low temperature	Tumble dry at medium to high temperature; Hang to dry; Drip dry
Ironing	Do not iron	Iron at low setting (110°C); Iron at medium setting (150°C)	Iron at high setting (200°C)
Dry Cleaning	Do not dry clean	Dry clean—with caution	Dry clean

Industry Canada   Industrie Canada   Recycled paper   Canada

Figure 6.7 Canadian standard for care labeling. (Courtesy of Industry Canada)

The **circle** representing dry cleaning has no letter choice in the Canadian system. When the system was worked out by a consensus committee of consumers, professional cleaners and launderers, machinery manufacturers, and federal government experts, it was decided that an article classified as dry cleanable must be safe in any solvent used commercially. Amber here means care with heat applied, not what solvent is used.

One important aspect of the system often not understood is the number of symbols that must be used. There must be enough to enable the article to be restored to acceptable, usable condition. If bleaching, for instance, would damage an article, the label must give this warning. On the other hand, a warning should *not* be given just to be "on the safe side"— what is called *"low labeling"* or *"underlabeling."* This is a tendency to give care instructions for the mildest treatment (safest for the manufacturer to promise fastness), but not necesarily easiest for the consumer and still safe for the article; it can lead to those "hand wash" labels on children's play clothes!

Optional care information may be given in words (English and French) near or on the symbol label, e.g., "wash separately/laver seul."

Standards and test specifications have been worked out for each combination of symbol and color, so information is very specific for colorfastness and shrinkage or stretch, if textile articles are cleaned in the way the symbols recommend. However, these do not suggest or guarantee a standard for any other aspect of wearability, quality, or performance. The symbols refer to the whole article, including findings, trim, belt, etc. The system no longer applies to yarns.

Care Labeling—International Symbols

Care labels giving instructions by means of symbols are found on textile articles from many countries. These are all very similar to those in a system proposed by the ISO (International Organization for Standardization). This system (see Figure 6.9[a]) has been formulated (and is owned as a trademark) by GINETEX—the International Association for Textile Care Labelling, which licenses use of it to members. These symbols are included in *ISO#3758: Care Labelling Code Using Symbols,* published in 1991. The trademark logos used by ISO and GINETEX are shown in Figure 6.8.

Symbols are printed in black only; a symbol with an X through it means: "Do not use this procedure."

All systems use an open washtub to represent washing (hand or machine), and when there is a hand inside the washtub, it means do not machine wash, use hand washing (with much less agitation). Wash water heat is indicated in degrees Celsius.

A triangle with *Cl* inside stands for chlorine (hypochlorite) bleaching.

The series of symbols within a square developed by Canada to represent drying has been added to the ISO proposed system, with minor changes. The circle in the square is to touch all sides, to distinguish it from a front-loading washing machine. Dots indicate dryer temperature: two for normal drying, one for lower temperature setting.

A hand-iron-shaped symbol represents ironing or pressing, the one in the ISO proposal having an open handle. The iron shape varies in different countries,

(a)

(b)

Figure 6.8 (a) Trademark logo for ISO, the International Organization for Standardization. (Courtesy of ISO) (b) Trademark logo for GINETEX, the International Association for Care Labelling. (Courtesy of GINETEX)

although they are all recognizably irons (compare with Canada's symbol). Heats low, medium, and high are given with one, two, or three dots.

A circle indicates dry cleaning, and has a letter in it to indicate the type of solvent that may safely be used. Many countries in Europe and elsewhere that use these symbol care labels also carry a letter in the circle, but for them there will no longer be the circle carrying an *F* for the treatment with least solvent power; this especially referred to fluorinated solvent, which has been banned from many European countries as a contributor to global warming. There will be only *A* for any solvent and *P* for perc or petroleum type, with a bar under a circle with *P* to warn of some limitation in the cleaning process. (Note U.S. use of F.)

In addition, the symbols are arranged horizontally on labels from most countries (see Figure 6.9[b]), although some may show them vertically.

There is also a GINCODE for information of the textile and garment industry; numerals represent the symbols, with a zero corresponding to "do not use." An example is shown (left) in Figure 6.9(b), with the equivalent GINETEX symbol label (right).

Care Labeling in the United Kingdom— HLCC System

The HLCC—Home Laundering Consultative Council—is a British trade association that helped develop, through the British Standards Institute, a

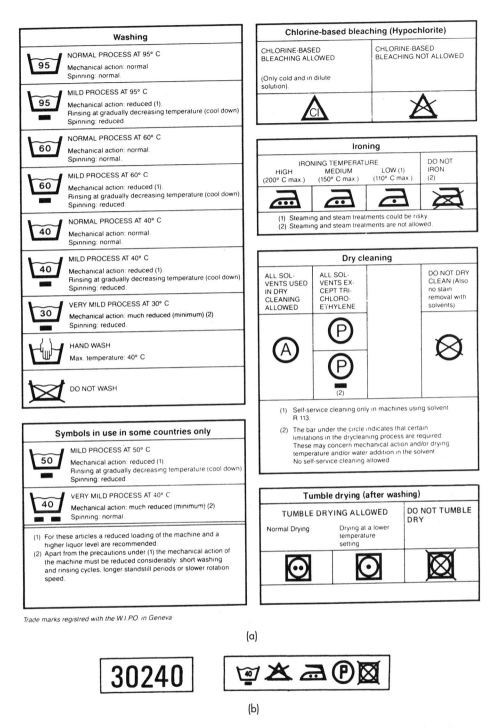

Figure 6.9 (a) International symbols for care of textiles labeling, registered to the nonprofit organization GINETEX. (Courtesy of GINETEX) (b) GINCODE (left) is a cipher code indicating care treatments for use in the textile and garment industry. The numbers correspond to the symbols (on right), with a zero equivalent to "do not use."

system to indicate washing methods, using numbered symbols along with words. The numbers had appeared inside the washtub, but work to develop an ISO standard led to a compromise, whereby the numbers are used only in additional information, which includes directions in English, very like the phrases used in the U.S. care system. See Figure 6.10.

Private Sector Labeling with Implications for Care

Trade Associations

A number of labeling schemes have been established by trade associations or interest groups in the private sector, as distinct from government-backed or

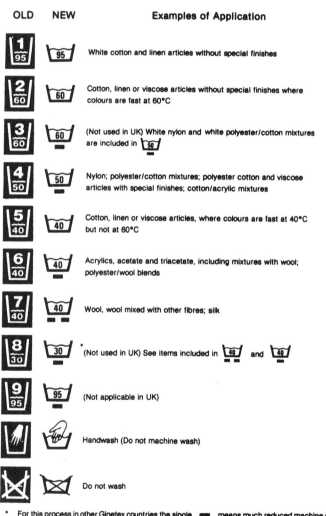

In 1986 HLCC changed from the Old to the New Washing Processes Symbols as shown below:

OLD	NEW	Examples of Application
1/95	95	White cotton and linen articles without special finishes
2/60	60	Cotton, linen or viscose articles without special finishes where colours are fast at 60°C
3/60	60	(Not used in UK) White nylon and white polyester/cotton mixtures are included in 50
4/50	50	Nylon; polyester/cotton mixtures; polyester cotton and viscose articles with special finishes; cotton/acrylic mixtures
5/40	40	Cotton, linen or viscose articles, where colours are fast at 40°C but not at 60°C
6/40	40	Acrylics, acetate and triacetate, including mixtures with wool; polyester/wool blends
7/40	40	Wool, wool mixed with other fibres; silk
8/30	30	*(Not used in UK) See items included in 40 and 40
9/95	95	(Not applicable in UK)
(handwash)	(handwash)	Handwash (Do not machine wash)
(do not wash)	(do not wash)	Do not wash

* For this process in other Ginetex countries the single ▬ means much reduced machine action.

Figure 6.10 Symbols used for washing methods by HLCC, the Home Laundering Consultative Council, United Kingdom. (Courtesy of the HLCC)

-imposed systems. Among the most recognized and trusted are the WOOLMARK® and WOOLBLEND-MARK®, backed by the Woolmark Company. Symbols associated with the use of cotton do not have such a clear basis of quality, but are known by many, especially that of Cotton Incorporated, which promotes, as well, NATURAL BLEND®, which is 60 percent or more of cotton in a blend, often with polyester.

Individual Companies

Private companies give many specific promises relating to textile performance, with development, quality control, and promotion done on their own. In fact, a great many trademark names can be taken to represent just this, since they are often not applied for retailing until the quality standards of the owner of the trademark have been met (see Section 2, *What Is a Trademark Name?*). Fibers and special yarns from all the major producers, such as BASF, Bayer, and DuPont, implicitly carry this type of assurance.

Probably the most ambitious system is the warranty program by Solutia for WEAR DATED® brand products. It was developed (by Monsanto) before government care labeling, and involves setting and applying standards and test methods for each product category. One fiber type alone, their ACRILAN® acrylic, can be used in socks, sweaters, blankets, carpet, etc.—each with a different wear life, so this involves a significant effort. Figure 6.11 shows labels for warranties of (a) 18 months (children's wear) and (b) 5 years (upholstery). All of the Solutia lines of WEAR-DATED nylon carpet carry a 5-year warranty. ACRILAN® PLUS acrylic carpet is also WEAR-DATED. Solutia also offers the PET-AGREE® backing with any of these lines—described under *Tufted*, Section 4, logo shown in Figure 6.11(c).

Another company with a long record of delivering satisfactory performance along with their trademarks is Cluett, Peabody, with SANFORIZED®, SANFOR-SET®, and other well-known finishes by the Sanforized Company division.

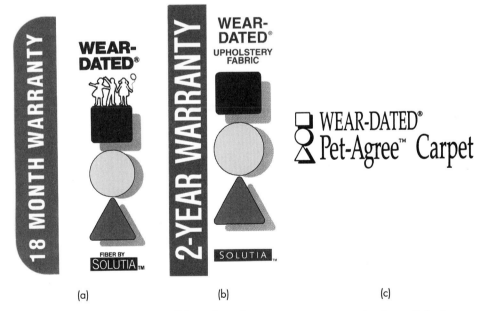

(a)   (b)   (c)

Figure 6.11 WEAR-DATED® brand products carry a warranty to give satisfactory service in normal wear for a specified time. Two tags and a logo for these products are shown here: (a) 18-month warranty typical for children's wear, (b) 2-year warranty on upholstery fabric (there is also a 5-year warranty), (c) logo for WEAR-DATED® PET-AGREE™ (now ®) carpet with an impervious polyethylene backing that prevents liquids soaking through—discussed under *Tufting*, Section 4. (Courtesy of Solutia Inc., formerly Monsanto Fibers)

A leader in advanced performance textiles, W. L. Gore, has a total guarantee: "If you are not satisfied with the performance of your GORE-TEX® outerwear, send it back to us, and we will either replace it, repair it, or refund your purchase price." Backing such a warranty means establishing a quality control program for all manufacturers using the GORE-TEX® fabric component—a sweeping commitment (for more on Gore materials, see *Compound Fabrics* in Section 4).

An interesting guarantee has been developed by 3M for sleeping bags containing their trademark THINSULATE LITELOFT™ insulation. The "Sleep Warm Warranty" is on a special TYVEK® (by DuPont) label, permanently attached to each bag; it carries care instructions *plus* a toll-free telephone number whereby a customer service representative will deal with any dissatisfaction about comfort or warmth, including replacing a sleeping bag with a warmer one—that's quite a warranty!

And then there is *beyond care*—BASF led with the 6ix AGAIN™ program to recycle any carpet made of their ZEFTRON® brand nylon 6, manufactured to meet their requirements after February 1, 1994 (see Figure 6.12). There is a toll-free number for this program as well; more on this under *Recycling* in Section 7.

Figure 6.12 Qualified commercial carpet made of ZEFTRON® nylon 6 can be reclaimed for use as virgin fiber by calling a toll-free number. The logo for this long-range recycling program, 6ix Again™, is shown here. (Courtesy of BASF Canada Inc.)

Storage of Textile Articles

In most storage conditions, natural fibers and leather are acted on by many forces of dissolution: microorganisms, insects, chemicals, oxidation (light and weather). Few fabrics, therefore, are of great antiquity, much less in good condition. Some have been preserved by unusual chemical conditions (such as tar deposits) or by virtue of the dyestuff used on them. Aside from these, the best examples of preservation of ancient textiles have come from Egyptian tombs or certain caves. Conditions in these were ideal:

> Dry cool clean dark dustfree (sealed)
> Home storage, especially of winter articles in a climate of cold winter/hot summer, almost never provides this optimum combination. The article can be cleaned, it is true, and can be stored sealed, away from light. However, in most homes in summer, the only **dry** place would be an attic (who has one anymore?) and this would be hot, while in any **cool** place the air is usually fairly damp, especially in a basement. An unheated garage or cottage offers textiles a wildly varying "climate."[7]

Commercial "cold storage" offers controlled humidity as well as a low temperature (dry *and* cool) that makes it essential for valuable articles. However, there *is* a home procedure that will give at least essential protection for any textile article, though commercial storage is recommended for expensive items such as furs, or for heirlooms or antiques (more on these under *Storing Vintage Textiles*).

Basic Home Storage Procedure

The following steps make up a basic home storage procedure:

> Choose as **dry** and **cool** a location as possible.
> **Clean.** Never store any article that is soiled; wash or have it commercially cleaned (unless it is an heirloom or vintage textile that should have spe-

---

[7]Esther Mété, "Conservation Notes: Preserving Your Child's Heirloom Garments," *Rotunda: The magazine of the Royal Ontario Museum*, Fall/Winter 1998: 41.

cial conservation procedures). Stains can concentrate with time and attack fiber or color. Insect larvae will eat any fiber with a protein stain on it.

Opaque container. Keep light out, or store in a **dark** place. Plastic film should not be used, as it is not moisture vapor permeable.

Protective fumes. Inside, at the top of the container, hang a perforated holder with moth crystals (paradichlorobenzene), which are much better than mothballs (naphthalene). The fumes from these crystals are heavier than air, so they drift down through the stored material. It is safer not to sprinkle the crystals directly among the articles, as some materials (e.g., vinyl) and dyes may be damaged. Fumes also prevent mildew. *Do not trust cedar* to keep hair fibers or fur safe from moths; aromatic cedar has a reassuring odor when fresh, but is *not* an insect repellent; red cedar has never been claimed as a moth killer. Cedar chests generally gave an airtight container—all to the good, but not "mothproof." *Roll linens* or other items such as quilts rather than folding them for storage. It is good to pad folds in any article if it is not rolled.

Seal. Seal the storage container to hold the fumes in and keep out dust and dirt. If even after airing, the odor of moth crystals or mothballs persists when articles are removed from home storage, try a commercial cleaner who deals with fire insurance claims (smoke damage) or has an ozone generator (try drapery cleaners). There are not many, and the service may be costly.

(a)

(b)

Figure 6.13 Larvae of the webbing clothes moth (a) and carpet beetle (b) do great damage eating protein fibers such as wool and fur. (Courtesy of Merrow Publishing Co. Ltd.)

Major Hazards to Textiles

Major hazards to textiles are listed here, with illustrations of the insect hazards (Figures 6.13, 6.14, 6.15); the numbers serve as the key to the Principal Storage Hazards Chart in Figure 6.16, in relation to specific fibers.

1. **Mildew** or other fungus growth thrives in damp, especially warm and damp, conditions. It can stain fibers, leave a musty odor, and will eventually rot materials. Cellulose is especially liable to fungal attack, but leather is also often ruined by mildew. Cotton towels left damp in warm conditions quickly develop a sour or musty odor. To avoid mildew, dampened linen can be held in a

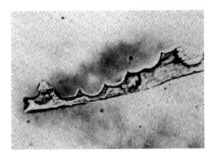

Figure 6.14 A wool fiber showing mandible marks of the larva of a black carpet beetle. (Courtesy of Merrow Publishing Co. Ltd.)

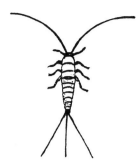

Figure 6.15 Silverfish eat what moth and carpet beetle larvae do not: starch and cellulose.

refrigerator or (if for longer than a few hours) freezer before ironing.

Bacterial rot is much less of a hazard in temperate climates than in tropical or subtropical areas. Again, microorganisms grow best at body temperatures.

Principal Storage Hazards (in order of importance)

(Use the preceding numbered list as the key)

Fiber	Key #
silk	6, 4, 5
wool, hair fibers	2, 5, 4
leather, suede	1, 5, 4 (to color)
fur	2, 1, 5, 4
down	5, 1
rubber	5, oxygen, oil
nylon	4
other synthetics	none if clean
cellulose fibers	1, 8, 3, 4, 5
flax (linen)	also 7*
acetate	none (to fiber) if clean; fumes (to colors)**

*Store unstarched; pad folds, roll, or hang over a rod to prevent cracking.

**Fumes from burning fuels (furnace, gas stove) will cause fume fading; i.e., a change in many blue or blue-containing colors to a pinkish tone. Keep acetate away from such fumes (e.g., from heat vents) in storage or when hung in closets.

Figure 6.16

2. **Clothes moth and carpet beetle larvae** eat protein, even tiny bits such as nail parings or whisker clippings. Larvae of the webbing clothes moth and various types of carpet beetle do millions of dollars of damage to valuable fibers and fabrics of wool and hair fibers plus furs. If a sample of yarn at a hole can be examined before cleaning, such "chomped" fibers provide definite identification of the reason for the hole! (See Figures 6.14 and 6.15.) Good "first aid" for an item found infested with moths, carpet beetles, or their wool-eating larvae is freezing—seal in a zipper plastic bag and put in a freezer for simple and effective eradication.[8]

3. **Silverfish and firebrats** are primitive insects that feed on cellulose or starch. They live a surprisingly long time (several years) and like undisturbed, dark places; silverfish prefer those that are damp, such as basements, firebrats those that are warm, such as furnace rooms or a bakery (yum! starch *and* heat!). These insects eat cotton, linen, rayon, and other cellulose fibers, as well as paper; with wallpaper, they can enjoy both the paper and the starch paste. However, they are not nearly as great a commercial hazard as the protein-eating larvae. (See Figure 6.16.)

4. **Light** can oxidize some materials till they fall to powder. Two of the strongest fibers, silk and nylon, are *tendered* by prolonged exposure to light, although light-resistant nylon can be produced. Light will also yellow fibers and fade dyestuffs.

5. **Heat** will harshen and stiffen materials by drying them out, especially protein fibers and leather. Heat can also develop and concentrate stains.

6. **Perspiration,** if allowed to age, first changes from slightly acid to slightly alkaline, and will then concentrate so that it can attack some materials, notably silk.

7. **Sharp folds** can cause a stiff fiber such as flax (linen) to crack. Repeated sharp folds in the same place can lead to splitting in tablecloths and napkins.

8. **Acid** attacks cellulose fibers, especially over time. Ordinary paper, cardboard, and unsealed wood

[8]"Moths, Shoes and Home Freezers," *Footnotes: The Quarterly Newsletter of the Bata Shoe Museum,* 2/2, Fall 1996: 7.

are all acidic. For lengthy storage of special cellulose fiber articles, pad folds or line boxes drawers, etc., with washed sheeting or acid-free paper, or use acid-free cardboard or olefin plastic boxes (obtain acid-free products from a museum or art supply company).

Storing Vintage Textiles

The handling of vintage or antique textiles in a museum is, of course, much more elaborate than the steps a consumer might take to preserve an heirloom fabric article at home.[9] However, there are basics that are in keeping with professional conservation, and so if you have much-prized textiles and want to keep them for future generations you should follow carefully the home procedure already outlined for storage, particularly the steps to avoid the major hazards to fabrics. If the article is truly rare and valuable perhaps you should consider whether home storage can provide suitable conditions at all, since, as discusssed earlier,

great changes in the "environment," normal for homes, are harmful.

If you are dealing with a vintage item at home, first make sure there is nothing on it that can rust, such as pins, paper clips, metal backings on covered buttons, and such. The next step with many such items is vacuuming—this should be done with the fabric supported and shielded by nylon screening. Use a hand tool such as an upholstery brush and reduce the vacuum suction as when vacuuming drapery. Even after checking colorfastness, think well before embarking on washing an old fabric article; commercial wet cleaning may be far safer since the physical conditions and agents used are much closer to what professional conservators would use. However, if you do go ahead, support the article on nylon screening (with fragile pieces, stitch between two layers of the screening), and arrange a soak-wash in a large sink or a bathtub. Conditions should be the same as outlined in this section for hand washing of wool, and soft water should be used if at all possible. Keep the fabric supported during rinsing and drying. Depending on bulk, shape, and fragility, store the item flat or on a (padded) hanger; if hung, cover with well-washed sheeting, *not* plastic.

[9]Michael L. Ryder, "The Conservation of Textiles," *Textiles Magazine*, 3, 1996: 15–20.

SECTION SEVEN

*F*ABRICS AND *E*COLOGY

Clothing as Environment

For many of us in developed countries, by the third quarter of the 20th century clothing had come to have little functional relationship to our surroundings; we might even have to put on a sweater in air-conditioned buildings in hot weather, and have little need for protection in cold weather, going from centrally heated homes, offices, and schools via heated transport to closed-in shopping malls or other complexes. Design and construction of seasonal clothing became much less a part of fashion aimed at the ordinary urbanite's wardrobe. It was no longer gingham and voile only for hot weather, tweed and velvet for cold!

Two developments in lifestyle in the last quarter of the century led back to the design and production of clothing to serve special functions, as well as be fashionable: the "energy crisis" in the late 1970s and the "participaction" or fitness drive. The concern about oil supplies also led to a heightened environmental awareness—conservation of natural resources. Through the 1990s, this all developed into a strong trend toward **fashionable, quality, protective, insulating activewear,** plus renewed and much broader concern about the environment and our relationship to it, in other words, **ecology.** Let us follow these developments, beginning with the idea of clothing as our most immediate environment.

Comfort in Clothing

This *Reference* opened with the question: "What do we want in clothing?" The answer was, "We want clothing to make us look and feel good." More and more, consumers are responding to textile products that have been produced with the environment in mind; more discussion on this appears at the end of this section. We have also discovered anew that looking good will *not* necessarily result in our feeling good, and designers have finally teamed with technologists to make this connection.

Two kinds of comfort, psychological and physiological, must be recognized. *Psychological* comfort drives the *eco-friendly* developments that make us "feel good"; it has also been the core motivator of fashion—clothing with consumer acceptance and/or the individual appeal that makes you "feel good" because you "look good." Clothing that delivers *physiological* comfort, on the other hand, has either to follow traditional, tried and true forms, or consciously take into account how the body functions in the particular end use for which the garment is intended. To do that, basic research must be done.

Basic research into functional design until nearly the 1980s was carried on largely by research groups developing workwear or military clothing, clothing that was anything but good looking! By now, though, fashion design has addressed itself with avidity to making special-purpose apparel appealing, using many technological developments that seem to spring up everywhere, including those that derive from research for the U.S. space program. The basic research still goes on, but more often now it is done from the beginning with consumer apparel and other textile products in view.

As with the "chicken or egg" question—which brings on which? It does seem that changes in consumer lifestyles have been crucial to the growing interest in making functional clothing fashionable. The basics of insulation in cold weather, for instance, have been well documented for decades, particularly by researchers for defense specialists for far northern countries who often studied the clothing of our Arctic peoples—the Inuit. In the 1950s, insulated garments were produced for the military at considerable expense, but there was no chance of getting these garments for even interested consumers until there was (a) more consumer demand and (b) acceptance of their look in fashion, or (c) new ways to achieve the result with a more acceptable fashion look, such as occurred when less-bulky quilted clothing was possible with THINSULATE™ instead of down.

Laboratories other than defense or space research institutes, but usually government backed, develop clothing (often protective) for specific occupations, such as fishing, mining, or firefighting. Such basic research still goes on, monitoring the effectiveness of specialized materials in clothing. This may be done on real people, or by means of a "skin model," which can be computer directed.

Some of the complexities of measuring and recording clothing comfort with real people are involved in the testing shown in Figure 7.1. The bike-like machine is called an *ergometer,* and the wear comfort of an absorbent acrylic fiber in clothing is being tested in a climate-controlled room (temperature, relative humidity, and air speed are all controlled). A test subject "works" and rests for alternate

Figure 7.1 Ergometer testing of wear comfort of absorbent acrylic fiber in top worn by test subject. (Courtesy of Bayer AG)

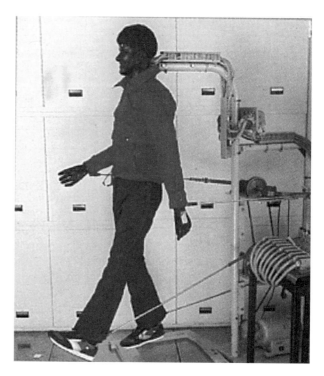

Figure 7.2 "Copperman Charlie"—instrumented mannequin—testing wear comfort of GORE-TEX® fabrics in clothing, Hohenstein Institute, Germany. (Courtesy of W. L. Gore & Associates, Inc.)

periods. The person can record subjective feelings of heat and cold, of dampness of the test garment, scratchiness on the skin, etc.; the climatic, machine, and physiological data are automatically registered. The latter include pulse, skin temperature, humidity between skin and textile, skin conductivity as an indicator of perspiration, heat flow density to help indicate excess perspiration on the skin, and body radiation.[1] The test shown in Figure 7.1 was done with Dunova absorbent acrylic, since discontinued by Bayer AG.

Tests using a "skin model" may be done with a complex instrumented mannequin like the one called "Copperman Charlie," used at the Hohenstein Institute in Germany (see Figure 7.2). In this case, clothing of GORE-TEX® fabrics is being tested in much the same way as outlined for a live test subject. The "climate" in the room for "Copperman Charlie" dressed in a GORE-TEX® fabric outfit will probably be more severe: cold, windy, and rainy, no doubt.

"Charlie" will not be alone after the year 2000. A joint effort headed by the Swiss Federal Laboratories for Materials Testing is developing a "SAM"—a sweating and fully-articulated mannequin—to measure transport of heat and vapor through garments. Par-

ticipating members come from Belgium, Finland, Germany, and the United Kingdom.[2]

Basic Principles of Physiological Comfort in Clothing

Permeability to Water Vapor. This is now commonly recognized as a vital element of comfort in clothing that is worn for any extended period. Perspiration is essential to our temperature-regulating system; clothing must allow this moisture to be dissipated. (More on perspiration and its importance under *Warm Weather Tactics*). We throw off about a liter (quart) a day of *insensible* perspiration as vapor, diffused through the skin from the blood vessels; we never notice it until heat loss must be increased and we get drops gathering on our skin from the activity of the sweat glands.[3] If we are outdoors in the cold

[1]Dr. W. Körner, "New Results on the Wear Comfort of the Absorbent Acrylic Fibre Dunova," translated from *Chemiefasern/Textilindustrie*, 31/83, February 1981: 112–116.

[2]"Innovations: Europe to Develop Sweaty Man," *Textiles Magazine*, 4, 1997: 5.

[3]H. M. Taylor, "Textiles for Indoor Thermal Comfort, Part 1—Clothing," *Textiles*, 11/3, 1982: 66.

and fabric is not permeable, perspiration will condense on the inside.

In some specialized conditions, there is a need to prevent any penetration of clothing by water: very heavy rain, waves hitting a small fishing vessel, water under high pressure from a fire hose. Fabric for articles worn in these conditions has traditionally been made waterproof but **impermeable,** e.g., oilskin or rubber-coated fabric. This kind of fabric is not all-purpose, however; it cannot be worn for long, or the wearer will be soaking wet, not from water coming from outside, but from perspiration inside! Many exciting developments have occurred in the category of fabric that can act as a layer **permeable to vapor (perspiration) but not to liquid.**

For outdoor activewear, it is especially important to have water vapor permeability in areas of greatest concentration of sweat glands: head, hands, and feet (see Figure 7.3). A design for footwear that is waterproof, insulating, and water vapor permeable is shown in Figure 7.4.

Insulation. Insulation prevents body heat loss when the surrounding air is cooler than body temperature. It is hard not to think in terms of "keeping the cold out," but there is no such thing as "coolth"—only absence of warmth! One of the most effective insulators known is **still air;** it is what we use in thermal windows (double- or triple-pane, with air between) or fluffy wall insulation. In windless conditions, clothing that traps air, such as a thick sweater, will prevent loss of body heat; if wind blows, a barrier must be present or heat will dissipate rapidly. We even call one such garment a windbreaker (see the windchill chart in

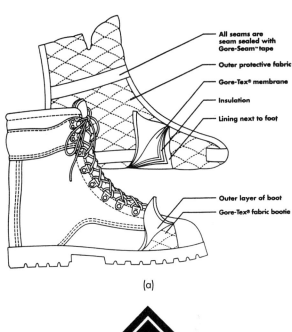

(a)

(b)

Figure 7.4 Design of footwear that is waterproof, insulating, and water vapor permeable, with appropriate GORE-TEX® footwear logo. (Courtesy of W. L. Gore & Associates, Inc.)

Figure 7.5). WINDSTOPPER® (by Gore) fabrics were developed to provide insulation and wind protection in one light, vapor-permeable layer (see Figure 7.6). A truly "Space Age" approach to insulation is the heat-flow barrier (see *Microthermal* under *Added Value Finishes* in Section 5)

Water Conducts Heat. Water conducts heat some 27 times faster than air;[4] when fabrics get wet or

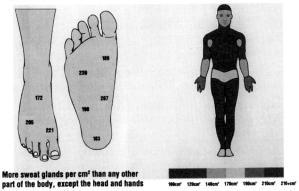

Feet Sweat

More sweat glands per cm² than any other part of the body, except the head and hands

Figure 7.3 Concentration of sweat glands. (Courtesy of W. L. Gore & Associates, Inc.)

[4]C. J. Brooks, "Ship/Rig Personnel Abandonment and Helicopter Crew/Passenger Immersion Suits: The Requirements in the North Atlantic," *Aviation, Space, and Environmental Medicine,* March 1986: 276.

Fabrics and Ecology **233**

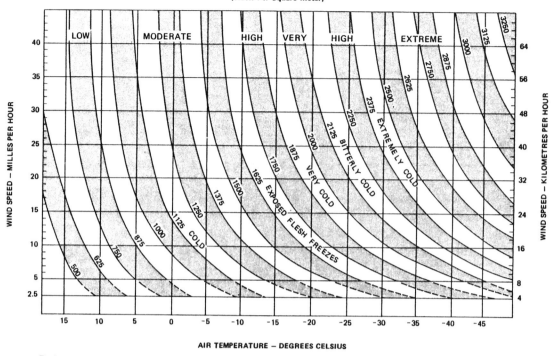

WIND CHILL COOLING RATES *
(Watts Per Square Meter)

To determine the *wind chill factor* follow the temperature across and the wind speed up until the two lines intersect. The value of the wind chill factor can be interpolated using the labeled wind chill factor curves.

Chart courtesy of Atmospheric Environment Service, Environment Canada.

For example, at −10°C with a wind speed of 20 miles per hour the point of intersection lies between 1500 and 1625, or approximately 1570.

It is not recommended that wind chill factors be calculated for wind speeds below 5 miles an hour, since it is difficult to determine wind chill factors at these wind speeds and because other factors such as relative humidity become important.

Figure 7.5 Windchill chart.

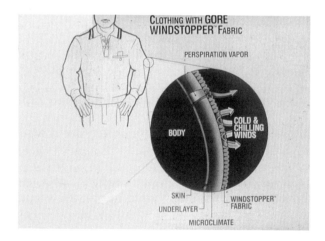

Figure 7.6 Action of WINDSTOPPER® fabric to protect the body's "microclimate." (Courtesy of W. L. Gore & Associates, Inc.)

damp, water replaces air, and the material can chill us quickly. We must guard against this.

Heated Air Rises. Air warmed by the body also rises and will escape from waist, neck, and head areas if the person is standing. A person lying down will allow even more heat to escape.

Head and Hands. These are two critical parts of the body in considering heat loss. It is relatively easy to prevent heat loss from the trunk, harder for the limbs, hardest for face and hands yet much heat can be lost from the uncovered face and hands, by radiation, convection, and evaporation.[5] If you are one of

[5]D. M. Kerslake, "Physiological Aspects of Comfort," *Textiles For Comfort*, papers from the Third International Seminar, Shirley Institute, Manchester, U.K., 1971.

those who goes without a hat in cold weather, consider this: Heat loss from your unprotected head can be half or more of your body's heat production at a temperature of −15°C (5°F); in less chilly conditions, with even a light wind blowing, if your head is not covered and dry, you can still lose a quarter of your body's heat production.[6] See Figure 7.13.

Circulation of Blood. Blood circulation must not be impeded; what keeps us warm is our blood, and whether we wish to conserve heat or disperse it, clothing must not be too tight. Constricting clothing also squeezes out insulating air.

Density. Density is significant; a fiber of low specific gravity will be lofty, allowing warm fabric with little weight.

Fashion and Energy

When we ignore clothing as environment and if we wish to keep comfortable indoors, we put more emphasis on heating and cooling (air-conditioning), using energy to accomplish both. This energy is derived largely from nonrenewable fossil fuels, especially for heating systems. While some energy sources are renewable or huge in supply, such as hydroelectric, tidal, wind, nuclear, solar, wood-burning, wood alcohol, and hydrogen power, it seems unlikely that we will be able to ignore the basic questions about our use of energy that were raised during the "oil crisis" of the late 1970s.

Technology has allowed us to ignore climate in cities, but it has also allowed us to develop remarkably functional special-purpose clothing (discussed in Sections 2, 4, and 5). These have served to counter the rigors of climate for any of us, and also provide space suits, armed forces clothing, all kinds of special workwear, and active sportswear. Most of these advanced, highly engineered materials are made of synthetic fibers. In case you recall that they, too, need fossil fuels in their manufacture, the small amount involved was noted in Section 1. Figures consistently quoted into the 1980s assigned only about 5 percent of oil used worldwide to making chemicals, plastics, and fibers, with the most being used for fuel. Figures for the United States indicated that synthetic fiber manufacture

accounted for only 1 percent of the petroleum used and only half of that for actual *feedstock* or raw material, while the whole U.S. chemical industry used only 5 percent of the total. These percentages did not change markedly in the 1990s. Most hydrocarbon fuel in the United States is used to heat homes, offices, and factories (the 1980s figure was 40 percent); the amount is undoubtedly higher in Canada.

Cold Weather Tactics

To conserve body heat indoors in cold weather and so reduce a hefty fuel consumption, we can therefore investigate the efficient use of clothing and furnishing fabrics to help insulate ourselves or a room. It is worthwhile to emphasize cold weather tactics, since the benefits of conservation in cooler climates can be great; steps to take to keep cooler and save energy in warmer climates or warm weather are discussed later in this section.

It helps if the home is well insulated and tightly built. If so, turning a thermostat down three Celsius degrees (five Fahrenheit degrees) overnight should reduce fuel consumption by about 5 percent; setting it back six Celsius degrees (ten Fahrenheit degrees) should cut fuel consumption by about 8 percent. If you also turn the home thermostat down during workday hours, a three Celsius (five Fahrenheit) degree reduction should net about an 11 percent fuel cut, and a six Celsius (ten Fahrenheit) degree downturn should give about a 15 percent lowering of fuel consumption. A tight, well-insulated house may not even cool this much while the thermostat is lowered. However, with an old, underinsulated, leaky house, the thermostat could be turned down more, as the inside temperature will drop much faster.

A **note of caution:** When dealing with babies or the elderly, we should be aware of the dangers of *hypothermia,* body temperature too low for safety. Elderly people can suffer hypothermia at a room temperature that would seem just uncomfortably cool to others: between 10°C (50°F) and 18°C (65°F). This reminds me of the first bath I gave my daughter, when she turned blue—the surroundings were just not warm enough for a baby. If you go in for this fuel-saving effort, you will certainly have to change what you wear at home to stay comfortable, and change what you wear when you *come* home from frequently overheated offices, schools, or shopping malls.

Another aspect of energy savings comes with laundry care of fabrics (washing, drying, pressing); a

[6]"Warming Trends," *Newscience*, Ontario Science Centre, 10/5, Winter 1985: 1.

revealing chart can probably be obtained from your electric or gas company recording energy use and approximate monthly cost for various home appliances. Some programs will test and rate appliances according to efficiency in energy use, with a labeling system to inform the consumer at point of sale (see Figure 7.7). Water heaters are a major energy user; there are many ways to cut hot water usage (and bills), from repairing leaking hot water taps to installing water-savers on taps or shower heads. It is also of significant help to insulate the first 1–2 m (yd.) of hot water pipe from your water heater. A main step is to lower the temperature control setting; this is usually all to the good, except for having less of a disinfecting action in the washing machine. A water level control on a clothes washer can save water and energy. A clothes dryer that shuts off automatically as soon as the load is dry will save energy and your clothes.

Putting the emphasis for saving energy on clothing for cold weather, let us apply the basic principles already outlined. In searching for practical designs

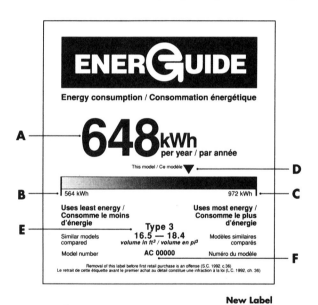

LEGEND

A Annual energy consumption of the appliance model in kilowatt (kWh) hours.

B Annual energy consumption of the most energy-efficient appliance model compared to others that fall within the same class (type and capacity) as the model tested.

Figure 7.7 EnerGuide program, Canada.

Figure 7.8 Basic items of traditional Inuit clothing.

that test these principles to the ultimate, we look first at clothing that has kept people warm, living full-time and for much of the year in very cold conditions, over some 20,000 years, and which still rivals our modern technology! These are the Inuit (the name agreed upon at the 1977 Circumpolar Conference in Barrow, Alaska, to replace the word "Eskimo"), with present world population approximately as follows: Siberia, 1,600; Alaska, 50,600 (10,300 urban); Yukon, NWT, Nunavut, 32,400; Kalallit Nunaat (Greenland), 51,650.[7]

Traditional Inuit Clothing. The sketches shown in Figure 7.8 give the general layout of traditional Inuit garb (the terms given to the parts of clothing will in many cases be those commonly used by the rest of the population of the United States and Canada—the appropriate ethnic terms will be found with an accurate description, tremendously detailed and well illustrated, in the footnote #7). Just how simplified these sketches are from the "real thing" is apparent from the photo of the main parts of an actual outfit (Figure 7.9), and especially from the detailed pattern drawings of how it was cut!

The parka sketched in Figure 7.8 is for a man and in many cases also has an extension at the back, like a shirttail, to give a sitting pad, shown in the pattern in Figure 7.9. A woman's parka (*amauti*) differs at the back hood to accommodate a baby; there is an

[7]Betty Kobayashi Issenman, *Sinews of Survival: The Living Legacy of Inuit Clothing*, Vancouver Press, 1997.

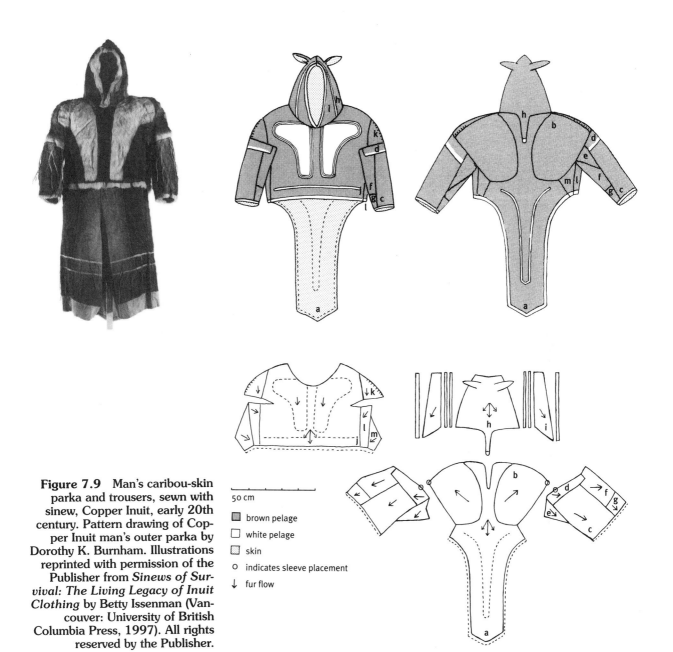

Figure 7.9 Man's caribou-skin parka and trousers, sewn with sinew, Copper Inuit, early 20th century. Pattern drawing of Copper Inuit man's outer parka by Dorothy K. Burnham. Illustrations reprinted with permission of the Publisher from *Sinews of Survival: The Living Legacy of Inuit Clothing* by Betty Issenman (Vancouver: University of British Columbia Press, 1997). All rights reserved by the Publisher.

50 cm

▨ brown pelage
☐ white pelage
▧ skin
○ indicates sleeve placement
↓ fur flow

apronlike front flap, and her boots or mukluks (kamiks) are much higher, with the pants shorter. In such clothing, individuals are reported to have survived alone, without heat or shelter, through an Arctic blizzard. The parka for winter wear is traditionally a double one of caribou skin, a layer fur side out and a layer fur side in. The skins are scraped to become quite permeable to water vapor yet still wind resistant. This is helped by the unusual nature of caribou hair: It flattens down in the wind, and each hair has a cellular, air-trapping

core, providing more insulation. No underwear is worn traditionally—the person is naked under the pants and parka.

The genuine Inuit cut of the hood has no seam at the neck; the hood curves up to form an elflike peak in the back, then comes down in a perpendicular line in one piece with the back. The face opening is just large enough to allow the hood to be pushed back from the head in calm weather. The parka ruff is of rare wolverine fur because, better than any other fur, it sheds the frost formed by condensation of breath; this was found to be because wolverine guardhairs are thick, strong, smooth, long, and uneven. Soft fur of even hair length such as fox turns into solid ice if covered with vapor from the breath.

The traditional Inuit hood is cut so that it fits closely around the face, and although styles do vary across the Arctic, there is usually no front body opening. The rising heated air can be trapped at the waist and chin. The arrangement at neck and head is vital; it is called the *air-capture principle.* The sleeves on the Inuit parka are long enough to cover the hands and close enough to prevent cold winds from entering if the person is moving. (Some of this effect is seen in a traditional coat without a hood, developed in North China, with a close-fitting collar, overlapping front opening, and extra-long sleeves—see Figure 7.10.)

The pants of the Inuit ensemble have no front opening, but there is a drawstring or toggle/loop closing at the waist and perhaps at the legs; these and the stockings are double layered for winter, like the parka. Mitts and mukluks complete the clothing, which weighs only 4.6 kg (10 lb.).

Besides making careful choice and use of specific skins and parts of skins, Inuit women tailor and fit these garments, using darts, gussets, and easing, and

Figure 7.10 **Traditional coat for cold weather, North China.**

sewing waterproof seams with caribou sinew (*ivalu*), with exquisite technique (see Figure 7.11). All this produces what the author of *Sinews of Survival* called in an earlier article "the most appropriate, efficient, sophisticated, and elegant clothing" to meet the extreme weather conditions in which the Inuit live a good part of the year, clothing that takes "great skill to make, repair, use, and maintain."

A person caught without shelter in a blizzard could literally "sit it out," pulling arms inside the parka—the warm air would not escape *down* the sleeves. One can sleep an hour at a time hunched forward, sitting up, but if you lie flat in cold surroundings, retained air will escape so fast the chill will waken you in minutes.

On the other hand, a person wearing such an outfit while moving, or when it is not so cold, can easily let warm air escape (periodic ventilation) by pulling the garment forward at the front of the throat, or pushing back the hood, and by loosening the closure at the waist.

When Europeans came into the Arctic, most made changes that greatly reduced the efficiency of this clothing: Hoods were made large enough to go over a fur cap, making gaps that let warm air escape; front openings were made in the parka, a fly opening was made in the pants, and so on.

When we depart from the basic principles of cold weather dressing now, there are no drastic results in most cases, since we do not have to survive a blizzard in our clothing, but it is well to understand the super-efficient clothing system developed by the Inuit.

Clothing for Cold Weather. **The air-trapping principle** can be applied to everyday, indoor clothing both in materials used and in clothing design or selection. Heat can be kept from escaping at the neck with a turtleneck or a convertible type of collar that can be worn open or closed; blouson tops and drawn-in pants are available in lounge- and sportswear; sleeves can be long or have a turn-back cuff. Warm slippers lined with cozy pile or foam are available. It is hard, though, to keep hands warm in a cool room—great-great-grandmother's fingerless gloves, anyone?

Several layers of light fabric can be more flexible, and so more comfortable, than one thick layer, and will trap air between layers, especially if made of resilient fibers. A light, long-sleeved sweater has been estimated to add about 1 C degree (0.6 F degree); a heavy sweater can add 2 C degrees (1.2 F degrees),

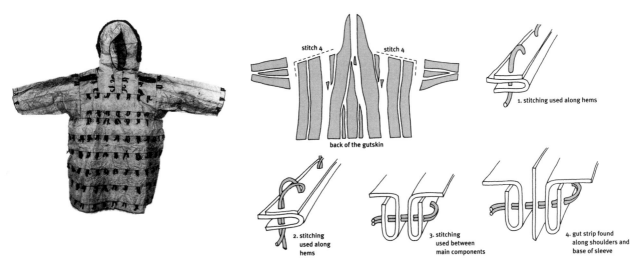

Figure 7.11 Gutskin (waterproof overgarment), walrus intestine, auklet beaks, and feathers, sewn with sinew. Collected at Sivuqaq, Alaska, by Henry Collins in 1930. Drawings show pattern, seams, and stitches for similar garments. Illustrations reprinted with permission of the Publisher from *Sinews of Survival: The Living Legacy of Inuit Clothing* by Betty Issenman (Vancouver: University of British Columbia Press, 1997). All rights reserved by the Publisher.

and two light sweaters about 2.5–3 C degrees (1.4–1.7 F degrees).

Air spaces in fabrics provide insulation, and we incorporate them using constructions such as foam, cellular knits or weaves, napping, pile (double faced even better than single), double woven or doubleknit fabrics, or batts of loose fiber quilted or otherwise held to other layer(s).

To maintain air spaces created in napped, pile, or quilted fabrics, we use materials that are **resilient** (springy). Fortunately, most of these are also of low density or specific gravity, so we can have a lot of air-trapping volume with little mass—these are lofty materials that give us warmth with little weight: protein (wool and other hairs, silk, down), acrylic, and polyester. Special forms of some fibers have air-trapping channels to improve the insulating ability of a given amount; see *Modifications of Manufactured Fibers*, Section 2. See also the explanation of insulating value measures under *Metric in Textiles Study,* Section 9.

The general guide in fabrics for warmth has been that insulating value varies directly with the **thickness** of a fabric, unless a very thick material is also very open in construction. This guide has been true because fibers do not keep us warm—they simply trap the still air that can. This rule is no longer valid when some new factors are introduced, such as **microfibers,** which have tremendous surface area and so have increased air-trapping power; this is made even more effective when the microfibers are olefin (polypropylene), the lightest fiber we have, used in THINSULATE™ (by 3M). This gives so much fiber surface with so little mass that a relatively thin layer will provide insulation equivalent to a down layer nearly twice as thick.

Stretchy fabric should not be put over insulating (air-trapping) layers, as it will compress them and reduce insulation. If it is a power-stretch fabric, it will also reduce blood circulation.

Wind has to be taken into account when selecting or designing apparel and accessories for use outdoors in cold weather; see the windchill chart in Figure 7.5. Unless air is still, we need an **outer wind-resistant layer,** since wind blowing against "thermal" materials will reduce or destroy the air-space insulation. Such a layer should still be permeable to water vapor, whether or not it is water resistant or waterproof; hence a non-water-resistant fabric developed by Gore to preserve warmth in windy but not wet conditions: WINDSTOPPER®. Less high tech but more traditional, closely woven fabrics have also been used as windbreakers: Gabardine (twill weave) and satin have been used, since in these weaves, yarns can be packed closely together. Microfibers have been used here to give an exceptionally wind- and water-resistant fabric with no special finish at all (see Figure 2.86).

Inner layers need to be **permeable** and either be **absorbent or wick** to let vapor through and to take up sweat from the skin.

Plain weave is regularly used for ski- and rain-wear, because it is strong for its mass; taffeta in a tough fiber such as nylon or polyester can be calendered using heat and pressure to flatten and close up the yarns—giving ciré. Since such a thin fabric, even of tough nylon, can tear, it is often made in a "rip-stop" form, with occasional heavier yarns in a cross-bar effect (see *Fabric Glossary:* CIRÉ). With some cotton fabrics, e.g., Shirley Cloth (developed by the Shirley Institute), the swelling action of the cotton fibers when the cloth is wet is counted on to close up the pores in the fabric.

Other approaches to keep the elements out, for fabrics of cotton or its blends, are to apply **water-repellent finishes** to, for instance, poplin, or to apply a **permeable coating** such as microporous polyurethane. These and other fabric systems for inclement weather are discussed in Sections 4 and 5.

A traditional "natural fabric" for winter outdoor wear is **fur,** although for maximum insulation, we should wear it with the permeable and wind-resistant skin side out and the air-trapping hair inside.

A wind-resistant outer fabric shell with a removable insulating liner such as pile is a good textile combination. A highly fashionable but accurately designed garment that goes a step further is Linda Lundström's LAPARKA® (see Figure 7.12); a water-repellent, machine-washable nylon shell may be worn by itself as a windbreaker or over the wool duffel coat, which may also be worn by itself.

Head protection is vital, as outlined under *Basic Principles of Physiological Comfort.* Yet so many people do nothing about headgear in even the coldest weather, due in many cases to peer pressure to be "cool"—and they will be (see Figure 7.13).

Fasteners for cold-weather clothing, if they will be close to the skin, should be plastic, not metal. If metal is used, there should be a covering placket, fastened outside with buttons or toggles. Zippers (especially for children's wear) should be large for outdoor use, when fingers may be clumsy with cold; on a long jacket, a two-way zipper should be used to allow the wearer to sit or bend without the jacket riding up.

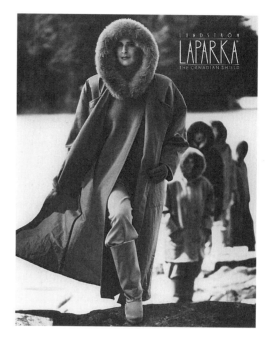

Figure 7.12 LAPARKA® features two layers, worn separately or together: a wind- and water-repellent, machine-washable nylon shell and a wool duffel coat. (Courtesy of Linda Lundström Ltd.)

VELCRO® is also a very good fastener for cold-weather outdoor wear.

Furnishings to Retain Warmth. Foam-lined drapes keep drafts out; carpet with foam, cellular, or fibrous underlay (unless one has in-floor heating), draft-inhibiting rugs, and other window and doorsill guards are all helpful. Wing-sided chairs keep one cozy—remember the basic principles—you will feel chilly faster if you stretch out on the couch. Articles that might be classified as either home furnishings or clothing are air-entrapping wraps and throws such as afghans. In cold parts of the country in the late 1970s, the "Snug Sack" was offered, a quilted comforter-*cum*-wrap. It was a great help, but the upper half was not well designed. Every few years some form of this gets reinvented; in 1996 it was a blanket called "The Warmer" which allowed snap-conversion into a sack with a shawllike upper section.

Warm Weather Tactics

Regulation of Body Temperature. Keeping cool in hot weather is difficult, especially when it is humid

Figure 7.13 When it's "cool" to wear no hat. (FOR BETTER OR FOR WORSE©. Distributed by United Feature Syndicate. Reprinted by Permission.)

with no breeze, because an essential cooling mechanism of the body is evaporation of perspiration, taking care of about a quarter of body heat. When body heat and perspiration cannot be lost, we feel both hot and sticky! We lose about a liter (quart) a day of perspiration as vapor, without even knowing it; it is only when more heat must be lost that sweat glands give off drops of moisture on the skin, and we are aware of sweating. This regulation of body temperature takes place at our skin, from perspiration formed mainly by the two to five million eccrine glands deep in the skin, taken to the outside openings (pores) by coiled tubes. Of course, when one perspires a lot, salt should be replaced.

Clothing for Warm Weather. Besides the cooling comfort bathing gives, we can choose clothing that helps: absorbent and porous fabrics, in garments that are loose to let air circulate, especially where perspiration glands are concentrated—on the back, the front of the chest, forehead, palms of hands, soles of feet, underarms. To keep these areas open for evaporation, we should draw hair back from the forehead and up off the neck; select garments with a low-cut neckline, no sleeves, and no belt; and make sure our hands

and feet are bare—not all possible at the office! There can be a "bellows effect" to help cool the body if air can be pumped across the back when the arms are moved. An air vent near the small of the back area will allow air to be pulled in there during movement and the upward movement of warm air will push it out at the neck. This is explained by Dr. Keith Slater in a report on development of surgical gowns that need to be comfortable as well as protective,[8] but it could be applied to consumer summer wear.

Fabrics, as well as being absorbent, light, and porous, should also be crisp and of spun yarn, so as not to cling. A good deal of research has been done to achieve coolness in other than traditional informal summer wear. COOL WOOL® and LIGHT WOOL® (by The Woolmark Company) apply basic principles and carefully tested specifications to articles before these brand names may be used. See Section 2 and *Fabric Glossary*: TROPICAL WORSTED.

With summer wear, we often have to balance comfort against ease of care. Fibers such as cotton, flax, viscose, and lyocell, with good absorbency, can

[8]Keith Slater, "Textile Use in Surgical Gown Design," *Canadian Textile Journal*, July/August 1998: 17.

wrinkle badly. They either take a lot of thorough iron-ing, or, if a Durable Press finish with resin has been applied, they lose absorbency and can lose strength. Some newer finishes leave cotton soft while giving it wrinkle resistance; see Section 5 for more detail. An easy-care fiber like polyester absorbs little in its stan-dard form, although some do wick, and more absorbent forms have been developed.

Sun Hazards. Hot weather hazards come from both the heat of the sun and ultraviolet (UV) light rays. In general, we are warned to protect skin from the sun's UV rays with hats, light-weight clothing cover, sun-screen cosmetics, and even parasols. A sunscreen should be applied about 15 minutes before you go outside and renewed after swimming or sweating. We should especially protect the head from the sun's heat when we are outdoors in hot weather, but other protective clothing is needed; *watch infants and the elderly* especially carefully—in fact children in gener-al, because they have more skin area in relation to body weight, thinner skin, and three times the annual sun exposure of adults. Babies are especially at risk, since, regardless of how fair or dark their skin, they are not born with a developed skin protection sys-tem. Also, they cannot tell us if they are in trouble with the sun, nor can they get themselves into the shade. Avoid exposure to sun when the rays are strongest, between 11 A.M. and 4 P.M., as much as possible. Sun can penetrate light cloud cover, fog, and haze; it is reflected off sand, snow, and water. Use lots of sunscreen with an SPF (see below) of 15 or more, and reapply every 2 hours if you are working or play-ing outdoors.

The sun's ultraviolet rays are divided according to three ranges of wavelengths: UV-C are the shortest (100–280 nm), and do not reach us; UV-B (consid-ered the most damaging) are medium in wavelength (280–315 nm) and cause delayed tanning, burning, and aging of the skin; UV-A are the longest (315–400 nm) and cause immediate tanning, as well as aging and wrinkling of the skin. Holes in the ozone layer allow more UV radiation to reach earth. It is estimated that *every 1 percent drop in stratospheric ozone will increase the rate of skin cancer by as much as 2 to 3 percent.*

Research goes on investigating whether and how textiles can protect skin against UV. A good deal of this research has been done by a textile scientist from Australia, M. Pailthorpe, who has equated fabric properties to penetration by light to develop an Ultra-violet Protection Factor (UPF) and relate this to a sun-protective factor (SPF) that can be assigned to clothing as well as sunscreen lotions. Many aspects of a textile affect its UPF: cover, fiber type, yarn and fabric construction, finishing and dyeing procedures, and UVR absorbers. Professor Pailthorpe ranks **fab-ric cover** as by far the most important,[9] and this is involved also when a fabric is stretched (less cover) or wet. With water in the interstices of a fabric, there is less scattering of light than when the material is dry (air in the spaces) and more UV is transmitted. (It is the same optical effect that can make a wet T-shirt see-through.) Dermatologists recommend a minimum SPF of 15 wet or dry for hot weather clothing; when clothing gets wet or damp, the SPF factor is reduced by more than half. This can happen from perspira-tion, which also washes away sunscreens applied to the skin.

A line of sun-protective clothing made of fabrics developed in Australia is claimed to provide 100+ SPF protection, whether the fabric is wet or dry, and without application of chemicals to accomplish this. C-TEX™ is a tricot knit of 88 percent nylon and 12 percent LYCRA® spandex, while C-TEX™ SPORT is a cotton/LYCRA® spandex blend; both are very close fabric structures. In contrast, an ordinary cotton T-shirt has an SPF of only 15 dry and 5 when wet! C-Shirt Canada of Victoria, BC, has the North American license to make and market C-TEX products (shown in Figure 1.6 as well as in Figures 7.14 and 7.15).

The UV Index™ has been developed as a trade-mark by Environment Canada and is commonly broadcast across that country with weather reports in hot weather and for holiday destinations. This turns out to be another matter needing world stan-dardization, however. Should the scale be 1–10 (as with the UV Index) or 1–15? Is the midday reading taken at solar noon or averaged over the hour from 11:30 A.M. to 12:30 P.M.? Without cloud cover or with consideration of some cloud? Using easy-to-burn (light, untanned) skin as the base for measure or gear-ing the scale to a median type of skin in the popula-tion? It will take some years to work all this out, and in the meantime, reports given in the United States as to how long a person would be safe in the sun from burning will not coincide with those coming from

---

[9]M. Pailthorpe, "Sun-Protective Clothing," *Textile Hori-zons,* October/November 1996: 11–14.

(a)

(b)

Figure 7.14 (a) This mother has protected her child and herself from UV rays with outfits of C-TEX™ fabric, developed in Australia. It gives a sun protection factor (SPF) of 100+ wet or dry. (b) C-SHIRT logo. (Courtesy of C-Shirt Canada)

Figure 7.15 These children are protected from UV rays with T-shirts of C-TEX™ SPORT fabric and swimsuits of C-TEX™, promising an SPF of 100+ wet or dry. (Courtesy of C-Shirt Canada)

Light colors worn outdoors are better than deep ones, because light bounces off paler shades but is absorbed by darker ones. Never underestimate the power of psychology with summer clothing and furnishings; some colors such as red and orange are "warm," while others such as blue and green are "cool." However, if you have to avoid bugs, wear khaki rather than blue, which attracts the pests.

Furnishings to Keep Out the Heat. Remember grandmother's cool summer parlor (maybe that was *great*-grandmother's)? If the air is cooler in early evening, open windows and doors to let the house cool all it can overnight. Close windows and blinds and draw drapes early in the morning. Sun-control film can be of great help on east- or west-facing windows that receive sun when it is lower in the sky and are hard to block with awnings; awnings are better for south windows. These films reflect heat, to help in cold weather, too.

Textiles and the Environment— How Green?

Eco Concerns

Having explored and recorded the contribution of textiles to human comfort, we must take a much wider

Canada, which can thoroughly confuse those living near the (long) border between.[10]

On the UV Index, over 9 indicates extremely strong UV, with sunburn time less than 15 minutes; 7–9 is high UV, burning in about 20 minutes; 4–7 is moderate UV, burning in about 30 minutes; 0–4 is low UV, over an hour before burning. Typical summer midday values are: tropics, 10; Washington, D.C., 8.8; Toronto, Ontario, 8; Edmonton, Alberta, 7; North Pole, 2.3.

[10]Stephen Strauss, "When You're Hot in Windsor, You're Not in Detroit," *The Globe and Mail*, October 15, 1994: D8.

focus to trace our continuing concern with *ecology,* defined as "the totality or pattern of relations between organisms and their environment." Interest in all things labeled "Green" has been both brought on and followed by the appearance of a myriad of products and services of varying validity, sincerity, and effectiveness! At the beginning of the 1990s it was said that the environment would be the single most important influence on consumer behavior during the decade,[11] and this held true, affecting everything from fashion color selection to the design of buildings.

"Eco concerns" were pushed first by warnings of danger to all of us if there were not concerted action to protect the environment, then pulled by the developing consumer acceptance that these predictions were legitimate and must be heeded. Next, action has been strongly propelled by government legislation in many jurisdictions, eventually impacting on both consumer and business activities in this verdant field of action. Space views of earth's beauty contributed!

One landmark in worldwide notice came with the Brundtland Report in the spring of 1987; this was the work of the United Nations–sponsored Commission on Environment and Development, headed by then–Norwegian Prime Minister Gro Brundtland. It concurred with the many voices from the scientific community that said the earth could not sustain the industrial and population growth we were imposing, and that we did not have much time to make changes. Air pollution, deforestation, gradual warming of the planet, destruction of the ozone layer that shields us from ultraviolet radiation, acid rain—many of these problems need action on a global scale, and we are seeing that taking place.[12] (See *Third Millennium Problem Solving and Innovations.*)

As we passed from the 1980s through the 1990s, the pace of "greening" picked up, with the realization by more and more firms that this adapted very well to enlightened self-interest, or as others have suggested less kindly, market opportunism: "It pays to be altruistic." The consumer of the new millennium can be seen as the mature 1960s idealist, applying a lot more experience and influence to this later-in-life cause of planet Earth, and we have seen business responding

to this deep consumer reaction many times and in many ways.

An outstanding textile development coincided with these interests—TENCEL®, the lyocell CMF introduced by Courtaulds (now by Acordis). As well as the fiber being both absorbent and strong, the process uses a solvent for cellulose that is of low toxicity and virtually all recovered, so the fiber, made from a natural, renewable material (cellulose from trees), is genuinely "environmentally friendly." Renewed interest in hemp fiber is also related to its growth with little or no need for pesticides or agrochemicals. (However, others insist that nothing we consume can be looked on as good for the environment. "There's no such thing as an environmentally friendly consumer. Everything we use has an environmental price."[13])

Energy production can be a major polluter, yet both consumers and industry need more and more power as a country develops. An interesting example of concerted action began in 1992 with an "E7" industry group formed among the large energy producers of the G7 countries (United States, Canada, United Kingdom, Germany, France, Italy, Japan), to advise and train their counterparts in developing countries in technologies that will pollute least. Coal-burning power plants are among the greatest contributors to air pollution that results in acid rain.

The Commission for Environmental Co-Operation, whose members are the United States, Mexico, and Canada, was set up to monitor governments' conformance to their own antipollution laws. Begun in the summer of 1994 as a spin-off of NAFTA, the commission provides a means of rationalizing standards, technology, antipollution rules, and other matters of environmental concern shared by the three countries.

Fashion color directions can be influenced by the consumer focus on the environment. As an indication of this, 1996 contract colors for corporate customers were seen in that year to relate to the economy, ecology, and the environment, according to the Color Marketing Group, an association of design and color professionals based in Virginia.

A much more significant link between color and the environment can be found in articles made of cotton fiber colored naturally, as it grows. Instead of

[11]Peter F. Greenwood, "Any Color You Like as Long as It's Green," *Textiles*, 19/2, 1990: 51.

[12]James A. Morrisey, "Washington: More Attention to Environment," *Textile World*, February 1998: 61.

[13]Michael Bloomfield, quoted in "Earthly Goods," *Canadian Consumer*, 7, 8, 1990: 17.

bleaching out this natural color, in the 1990s it was celebrated, thanks to the cross-breeding experiments of Sally Fox, growing the results in Arizona and Texas. She branded it FOXFIBRE® (see Figure 7.16), and since these colors grow best without applying chemicals, she calls it COLOUR BY NATURE. The most frequent shades are various browns and a kind of celery green, soft tones that originate in wild cottons, which are shorter and weaker than standard upland varieties; in 1994 naturally colored cotton varieties represented less than 0.3 percent of the total U.S. crop.[14] However, the program continues and the colored cottons are being improved to meet modern spinning technologies. Naturally colored cotton has been used in a variey of products; Figure 7.17 shows some of the coordinated line of home fashions called ECO-ORDINATES™ offered by Park B. Smith. To make these, naturally colored cottons are used with some that are dyed, but with natural dyestuffs such as natural indigo, acacia bark, madder root, onion skins, and pomegranate rinds.

A long focus on our dilemma with the environment came from a professor who has been studying garbage landfills for over twenty-five years. William Rathje, director of the University of Arizona's Garbage Project, along with his students, has been applying his archeological and anthropological knowledge to what our garbage reveals. He decided (in 1994) that we have the marks of a decadent period, as other civilizations have shown (Roman, Mayan), and that "the key is for us to get very efficient before we're forced to. Because when we're forced, it's already too late. The cycle of rise and fall is getting faster and faster."[15]

Textiles and Pollution

Wastewater

In North America, for most of the few hundred years of settlement from Europe, lakes and rivers have been used as convenient sewers (as has the ocean, but most of us do not get our drinking water from the salt seas). The Great Lakes, shared by the United States and Canada, hold one-fifth of the freshwater on earth and

Figure 7.16 Label indicating use of FOXFIBRE® naturally colored cotton.

Figure 7.17 Home fashions made with FOXFIBRE® cotton in natural colors or cotton dyed with natural dyes. (Courtesy of Park B. Smith)

[14]Philip Burnett, Executive Vice President, National Cotton Council, "Cotton, Naturally," *Textile Horizons*, February 1995: 36–38.

[15]Bill Marvel, "When Garbage Becomes Archeology," *The Toronto Star*, September 17, 1994, E5.

four-fifths of all the freshwater in North America, so the early settlers could be forgiven for thinking nothing could pollute them. However, we have succeeded in doing that thoroughly, making fish and other water life unfit for consumption and water unfit for swimming. Reports to the International Joint Commission on the Great Lakes reveal high levels of toxic chemicals in the "smaller" of these natural marvels we have taken for granted. Dr. David Suzuki, a passionate and informed proponent of guarding the environment, reminds us of the eternal cycling of natural materials *of which we are a part.* We are made up of over 70 percent water, which could have been at one time part of an ocean, a rainforest, or the Serengeti plains.[16] We cannot lay all the responsibility of water pollution on the textiles industry, but it does use a great deal of water, and in 1993, the U.S. Environmental Protection Agency ranked it seventh among industrial water polluters.[17]

The textiles industry focused early on cleaning up wastewater (effluent) from mills in general and converters in particular, which use so much in finishing—scouring, all that stone washing and other prewashing, and traditional water bath dyeing. Various levels of treatment are necessary, very much like municipal water treatment: primarily, to clarify wastewater by removing suspended material and dissolved compounds, then secondarily, to get rid of microbial pollution.

In textiles operations, besides the possibility of toxic chemicals in the waste from wet processing, there is offensive residual color from dyelots. One fascinating paper dealt with this particular problem at a 1992 AATCC Symposium on "Environmental Awareness: Targeting the Textile Industry." A research team at North Carolina State University successfully used *chitin* (see Section 2) and a derivative *chitosan,* both obtained from ground-up crab shells. Chitin is the most abundant organic compound next to cellulose, which it resembles greatly in structure, as a polymer based on a sugarlike unit (compare Figure 2.61 with Figure 2.60). These compounds, and especially chitosan, removed dyebath residual color completely and quickly, for all types of dyes except basic![18]

A similar conference in the United Kingdom reviewed a number of ways to remove color from wastewater; ozone treatment was found to be very effective.[19]

Dyes that leave little or no undesirable residue in the wastewater are termed low-impact dyes, but it is very difficult to relate this to certain dye types (classes), much less to natural versus synthetic dyes.[20]

A method of applying mothproofing to wool for carpets to qualify for the WOOLMARK® has been developed that eliminates effluent, which would otherwise contain mothproofing chemicals, some of which are toxic to invertebrates on which fish feed.[21]

For end users of textiles—consumers—major efforts to reduce water pollution come with what goes out with the wash water, and large detergent companies have taken *all* phosphates out of heavy-duty detergent compounds. Phosphate is still a major agent in machine dishwasher powder detergents, unless no-phosphate products are sought out, e.g., in health food stores.

Air Pollution

Some dyeing and finishing departments or plants must address air as well as water pollution; many still have coal-fired boilers, contributing to emission of sulfur dioxide into the atmosphere, and so to the formation of **acid rain.** Burning any fossil fuels also produces carbon dioxide, the main **"greenhouse gas"** responsible for holding the sun's heat in the atmosphere, leading to gradual climate warming.

Solvents other than water are used, not so much in production but in care of textiles. The chlorinated and fluorinated hydrocarbon solvents were discussed in Section 6, and of late years, choices for dry cleaners have been reduced while regulations for safer use of the solvents have multiplied. This is in line with the general drive to reduce or eliminate chlorofluorocarbons (**CFCs**), which can destroy the ozone layer in the stratosphere, which protects us from very harmful effects of ultraviolet radiation in the sun's rays. Substitutes have been and are being found that will not have this effect and that can be used in refrigera-

[16]David Suzuki, "Paying Attention to the Warning Signals of Nature," *The Toronto Star,* March 24, 1990: A2.

[17]Sarah Hone, "The Greening of the Textile and Clothing Industry," *Textiles Magazine,* Spring 1994: 18.

[18]Brent Smith and Sam Hudson, "A Novel Decolorization Method for Textile Wastewater Using Crabshell Waste," AATCC Symposium, March 19–20, 1992, Charleston, S.C.

[19]Peter F. Greenwood, "Textile Finishers and Environmental Solutions," *Textiles,* 22/4, 1993: 18.

[20]Brian Glover, "Are Natural Colorants Good for Your Health? Are Synthetic Ones Better?" *Textile Chemist and Colorist,* 27/4 April 1995: 17.

[21]"Carpets: Mothproofing the Ecology-Safe Way," *Canadian Textile Journal,* Dec. 1994/Jan. 1995: 28.

tion systems, for instance, or in dry cleaning. By taking chlorine out or by adding hydrogen into the compounds, less harmful products have been worked with.

Chlorine again figures as a villain with polyvinyl chloride (PVC or vinyl), more common as a coating or film in textiles than as fiber (vinyon). It is seen as the largest source of **dioxin,** an especially long-lasting and toxic compound created as the vinyl is being made or even when finally disposed of, as in a landfill. Concern with chlorine, connected to the formation of dioxin or just on its own, brings us back again to water; chlorine use is being reduced or eliminated, for instance, in the treatment of pulp and paper, in efforts to improve water quality; this has been a thrust of the International Joint Commission.

Recycling

Many of the most positive developments coming from environmental concerns have been in recycling of everything from chemicals, through fiber waste, to creative reuse of finished textile products. A complex flowchart of the many routes and forms that recycling can take was constructed at the University of Central Michigan, with discussion of possibilities.[22] Only a few of these paths will be reported here. Perhaps because recycling can be so upbeat, logos are everywhere, celebrating the rebirth of useful products from cast-offs.

One major player insists that "Recycling doesn't pay—it saves." Wellman, Inc., is the largest recycler of consumer plastics and specializes in PET (polyester) beverage bottles plus HDPE milk and water jugs, both polyester; Wellman calls its heavy-denier recycled staple polyester fiber FORTREL® ECO-SPUN, and the company is a major U.S. polyester carpet fiber producer. Luggage and footwear take a good deal of this fiber, but lighter apparel fabrics are also made, especially fleece, which features in the creation of the Master-Apprentice Collection. This collection, created by leading designers in collaboration with fashion students, shows garments from evening dresses to outerwear. Such fabrics may be more expensive than "virgin" fiber, but consumers seem willing to pay to help the environment.

TREVIRA® TWO (by Trevira) has been used in the United States by Malden Mills for a number of

[22]Tanya Domina, Katy Koch, "The Textile Waste Lifecycle," *Clothing and Textiles Research Journal*, 15/2, 1997: 96–102.

their branded POLARTEC® Recycled Series, made at least 50 percent of the recycled polyester. Malden calculates that an average-size jacket will keep some 25 large 2L (2 qt.) beverage bottles out of landfills.

One company that has begun at the beginning of processing is 3M, with its 3P program: Pollution Prevention Pays. As well as changing the way it does things to be less polluting, it also concentrates on recycling wastes.

An individual spearheaded reclamation of textile waste from the cotton field on through yarn spinning. Judy Heifetz, of Niagara-on-the-Lake, Ontario, found that a great deal of waste occurred in the production of cotton consumer goods in North America. She and her husband began a small company and set out to develop such waste products. They turned them into textiles using no harmful processes—and it worked. The result was Eco Fibre Canada Inc., and the fabrics resulting from this "post-industrial cotton waste" have been made up by the company into consumer goods such as T-shirts, knit shorts, sports caps, and lunch bags, in fabrics such as jersey, fleece, and various wovens (see Figure 7.18). The company had two

Figure 7.18 Products made from ECO FIBRE™ recycled cotton waste. (Courtesy of Eco Fibre Canada Inc.)

shades only at first, natural and Eco-white, then added "ash" by mixing a small percentage of recycled black polyester to the natural cotton. The same recycling approach can be taken with waste in processing fibers other than cotton, such as wool or acrylic, and some headway has been made here as well.

A firm that waded in with this "recycle any and all fibers" set up an upscale boutique in Montreal called C.A.L.I.CO, with trendy designer apparel and accessories coming from recycled fibers. Used material, torn apart back to the fiber stage (garnetted), can be respun and rewoven or reknitted into sturdy fabric called **shoddy,** which did not originally carry the stigma we now associate with the name. This version is definitely upscale, with color provided by the original tones of the materials, sorted into lots before recycling. As well as recycled wool or synthetics, the boutique uses virgin hemp in its fabric blends, as an environmentally friendly fiber. Kenaf is another bast fiber, grown in the U.S. Southwest, that is used for webbing by a firm also engaged in recycling—PlesGlas Corporation of Williamsport, Indiana. The company recycles many materials into nonwoven webbing for a variety of uses and sees the secret as finding markets and applications for these recycled materials. A similar effort has been made by Polywert Faserrecycling GmbH, of Bobingen, Germany, turning all kinds of textile residues into products such as insulating panels (see Figure 7.19).

Figure 7.19 Textile waste recycled into insulating panels. (Courtesy of Polywert Faserrecycling GmbH and *Techtextil Telegramm*)

U.S. Roads has made shoes with soles from recycled tires, making a dent in the huge volume of auto tires that are dumped as waste. Wine cork wastage can be made into floor tiles. A Manchester firm that recycles clothing is called REEF—for Recycled, Environmental and Ecological Fashion Co-operative. Sounds more and more like the 1960s, but there has been a difference, and that is in the hard technological basis of action that developed through the 1990s.

Carpet is another giant source of material for recycling, and the BASF program 6IX AGAIN™ was mentioned under *Private Sector Labeling* in Section 6. Qualified commercial carpets made from ZEFTRON® nylon 6 fiber can be recycled by calling the BASF information number, 1–800–477–8147. This is a carefully thought-out program and could account for large volumes of material. When nylon 6 (caprolactam) has been repolymerized, it can be used as if it were virgin fiber. Partnership for Carpet Reclamation, which DuPont Canada has been instrumental in forming, collects and recycles carpet made of various fibers from homes and commercial buildings. The material can be used in a variety of products, or even as fuel for generation of power. A "Green House," featured in a National Home Show in Toronto in September 1991, was made largely of recycled products; the carpet underpad came 50 percent from recycled tires, the carpet (polyester) came from recycled bottles, and the floors were finished with recycled vinyl.

Automotive interior fabrics are another huge pool of material, but have proved to be very difficult to recycle in the most-used form: a compound material held together by lamination with polyurethane foam. Separation of this assembly seems impossible, so research is directed at developing 100 percent nonwoven polyester fabrics that will do the job and would be recyclable.

A battle has gone on between disposable and cloth diapers, since this is a large market, and arguments can be made on either side as to impact on the environment. As to convenience, cloth diapers have been redesigned, and there are diaper services to see to laundering. However, disposables have held their own in this marketing struggle. The ultimate in "cradle to grave" is the arrangement by the Crib Diaper Service of Plymouth, Minnesota, to donate the lint it gathers from laundering a quarter million diapers a week to a casket manufacturer for use in stuffing pillows.

Third Millennium Problem Solving and Innovations

A global-warming treaty signed in December 1997 by the United States and 163 other countries calls for U.S. industries for their part to reduce air emissions that contribute to the "greenhouse effect" or warming to 7 percent below 1990 levels. Other pressures come from the Maximum Achievable Control Technology standard proposed by the Environmental Control Agency going into effect by 2003.

E3 (Encouraging Environmental Excellence) is a program of the American Textile Manufacturers Institute. Since its inception, over 50 companies have qualified as members, including many major fabric producers. Each company makes a top management commitment to preserving the environment, including having plant facilities examined (with safety and health audits as well) and setting goals for pollution prevention. Education of employees, suppliers, customers, and the community at large is part of the program, and members may use the registered certification mark logo (see Figure 7.20[a]).

The eco-tex® consortium is an initiative of worldwide companies in production and related areas of the textile industry. To reach the consortium's standards for producing "ecologically optimized textiles" and earn certification, fabrics are audited at all stages, including recycling and final disposal; such products may be labeled with the logo shown in Figure 7.20(b). These far-reaching programs provide a pattern for taking companies into the next millennium.

Many other efforts, less organized or comprehensive, are on the track of environmental awareness. One of these was created by John Edmonds, owner of a lawn maintenance firm in Halifax and Dartmouth, Nova Scotia. He decided to change from all the artificial things done to produce a lawn and work with natural products and procedures. Although this does not relate to textiles, his comments are significant: "Environmentalism is going to be the biggest change since the Industrial Revolution. It's going to affect every aspect of our lives, and business had better get ready for it."[23]

Those in business who agree see a great need to educate and train people in waste minimization and

[23]Daniel Stoffman, "Companies that Care," *Canadian Living*, December 1, 1990: 40.

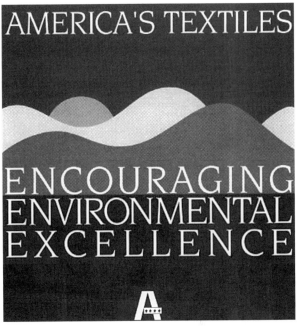

AMERICAN TEXTILE MANUFACTURERS INSTITUTE

(a)

(b)

Figure 7.20 Certification logos: (a) The E3 program of A.T.M.I. (Courtesy of American Textile Manufacturers Institute, Inc.); (b) the eco-tex® consortium. (Courtesy of eco-tex)

hope for economic incentives that will encourage participation. One concept is that of "duty of care" on the part of the seller of goods, to be sure that they come from sources that are environmentally responsible. Otherwise, domestic manufacturers bear an unfair load of responsibility that may be avoided by foreign suppliers.

One environmental problem with a different twist is that of water, not polluted, but disappearing. In many parts of the world, a process called *desertification* is proceeding, a terrifying inroad on the small percentage of the earth's land that produces food. One example linked to textiles is the shrinking of the

Aral Sea in Uzbekistan, which was the world's fourth largest lake, and which may disappear in another 20 years. Water was diverted from two rivers that used to flow into the Aral for irrigation of cotton farms in what was then part of the U.S.S.R., but suggestions to reduce cotton crops to help the Aral meet considerable resistance. The lake's changed state is blamed for climatic changes, such as windstorms, and some say it could affect the climate of the world.

One notable development of the 1990s rooted in textiles will certainly reverberate in the 21st century: the first-time cloning of a mammal from a cell from an adult animal—a sheep, with progeny named Dolly. This research, carried out at the Roslin Institute, Edinburgh, is hoped eventually to lead to breakthroughs in curing genetic diseases such as cystic fibrosis, besides the obvious applications to wool production. When Dolly was shorn for the first time in May 1997, the fleece was donated to the Cystic Fibrosis Trust to raise funds. The Trust ran a competition among schoolchildren for a sweater design (British: *jumper*) to be knit of the history-making wool. The fleece was turned over to the School of Textile Industries at the University of Leeds to process. It was a challenge to produce sufficient yarn and have it soft enough from only 2.5 kg of fibers that were relatively coarse. The winning design was by 11-year-old Holly Wharton, and now Leeds faced the final hurdle: match the colors the first time as there could be no second dyelot! The sweater is now on permanent display in the Science Museum in London, and Holly received a sample of Dolly's fleece (see Figure 7.21).

Two lines of biotechnological research pursued by DuPont involve more lowly creatures than sheep, yet can produce fibers unlike any so far known. In one, the extraordinary capacity of spider silk to absorb energy of impact could help create stronger, lighter ballistic protection such as bullet-proof vests. Variants of DuPont's aramid fiber KEVLAR® may eventually incorporate some of the processes and chemistry of the spider. Although KEVLAR has outstanding strength, spider silk has more than four times the capacity to absorb impact energy than any synthetic fiber yet produced—think of a large bug hitting a spider web.[24] The other research by DuPont is much closer to commercial use—creation of the basic chemicals for fiber synthesis, not from petroleum by-

Figure 7.21 The first fleece shorn from Dolly, the cloned sheep, went to make a prize-winning sweater designed by Holly Wharton, who wears it here. With her are actress Jenny Agutter, and Steve Melia and Barry Greenwood of the School of Textile Industries, University of Leeds, where the historic lamb's wool was processed. (Courtesy of School of Textile Industries, University of Leeds)

products, but from materials such as corn starch and glucose. This genetic engineering can also give completely new polymers and fibers, described as "natural synthetics," from agricultural crops.[25]

An electroconductive carbonized textile (ECT), GORIX® (by Gorix) has taken the electrical conductivity of carbon fibers into a wider application. The basic fiber is first baked, then woven and subjected to further heat; the highly conductive material can be incorporated into a compound fabric. GORIX can be used as a heating or temperature control element in clothing for extreme conditions (e.g., an undersuit for divers), heated blankets for humans or horses, car seats, or carpets. It can also be used as a temperature sensor.

Light has been brought into and through textiles in a number of developments, from fashion show-stoppers to serious medical applications.[26] Fiber optic cables in bedding bring therapeutic blue light to jaun-

[24]"Tomorrow's World: Web of Intrigue at DuPont," *Textile Horizons,* December 1998/January 1999: 16.

[25]Derek Ward, "Equipment Makers React to Contemporary Conditions," *Textile Month,* January 1999: 21–26.
[26]"Tomorrow's World: Let There Be Light," *Textile Horizons*, October 1998: 17.

diced infants, and hospitals investigate the relaxing effect of light. In theater and fashion, a number of light-emitting or -changing properties give fascinating effects—see ANGELINA under Bicomponent Fibers, Section 2, and Holograms under COLOR VARIABLE in *Fabric Glossary*.

Success with flocking fibers to boat hulls or marine installations obviates use of (usually) toxic paints to prevent growth of barnacles and other marine life. The moving fibers act like the coat of a seal, hence the company's name SealCoat, of Athens, Greece.[27]

Development of a technology called *electro spinning* that can produce fibers much finer than any microfibers on the market is based on work done at the University of Akron, Ohio.[28] Professor Darrell Reneker explained that a liquid in a tube subjected to a high voltage will be projected out in jets by the electrical forces overcoming surface tension, and that the jets split into finer and finer filaments, down to diameters of about 3 nanometers (0.0000001 dtex) (about a single molecule wide), compared to ultra-microfibers down to 3 micrometers or 0.1 dtex). This would give enormous surface area and covering power at very low weight.

Of all the other new thrusts of technology and rebirths of traditional values and approaches, this section has discussed a number with staying power into the new millennium. Recycling should gain momentum. Use of naturally colored fiber, especially cotton, and of other renewable fabric components including natural dyes seem to hold a strong appeal. Applications of the slipperiness of TEFLON® filament yarn in consumer goods, to reduce friction or resist water or oils, could be varied. Use of the plentiful complex chitin from shellfish offers intriguing possibilities in creating new textile products. Sun-protective clothing is in its infancy and there should be intriguing developments in the next decades. Microencapsulation presents a myriad of possibilities not yet explored. Here's to fabrics of the 21st century!

[27]"Flocking: A Niche of Niches," John W. McCurry, *Textile World*, February 1999: 94.

[28]"Tomorrow's World: Single Molecule Fibres," *Textile Horizons*, October 1998: 18.

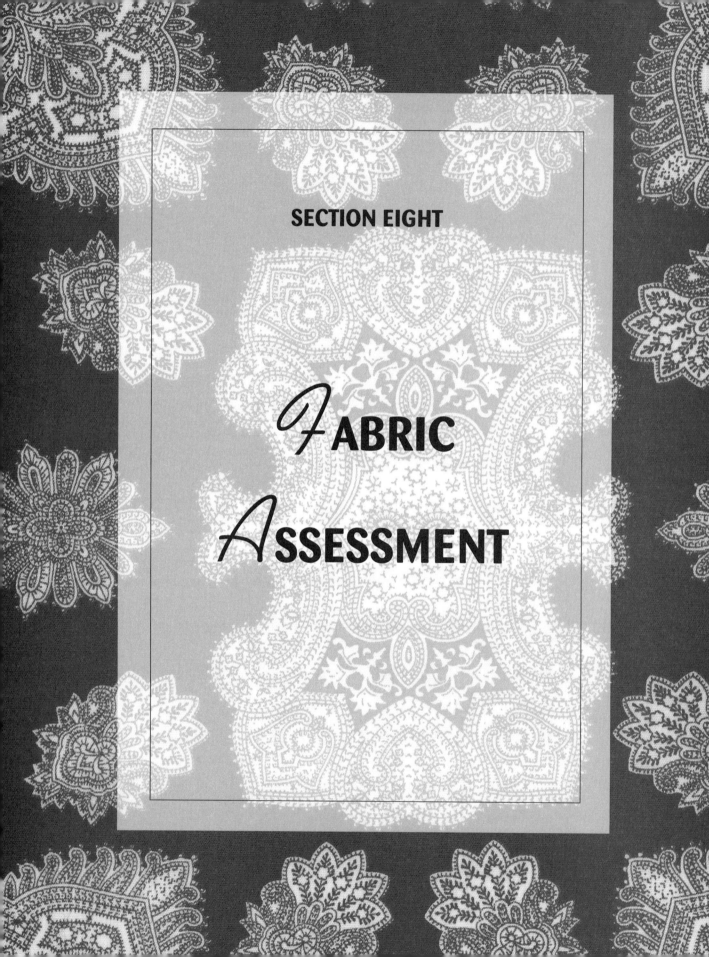

SECTION EIGHT

Fabric Assessment

Fabric Assessment—How It's Done

An experienced technical specialist in textiles once said, "Fashion is not enough!"[1] What he implied was that fabrics and clothing must perform adequately in use and care. Textile engineering is as important as design to the consumer, and with the burgeoning interest in and awareness of functional apparel, the results of technology have become a part of everyone's life.

Various factors are involved in deciding whether an article will do a good job for a certain purpose. Factual information about the makeup of a fabric may be obtained from the manufacturer's label and/or from testing and analysis. Designers or home sewers may wish to keep a record for a particular fabric of its makeup and the way it behaves: a Fabric Case History record is included in this section, in case it is of interest to some. Some amateur consumer tests are also suggested. Basic information that a testing facility might gather includes such things as fabric construction and composition, strength, resistance to abrasion, wrinkle recovery, and colorfastness. For particular end uses, there may be special tests, such as water repellency for a raincoat, resistance to fading and tendering by sunlight for drapes, or (see Figure 8.1) slip resistance of shoe soles to floor surfaces. Furthermore, in many cases, particularly contract interior design, specifications must be met for fabric performance, usually related to standard tests.

Standard methods must be followed for any fabric assessment by testing to be fully meaningful. For example, after testing, you might want to convey to someone in another company that the dye in a jacket lining comes off on clothing worn under it. Without a standard test method, you would have to resort to phrases such as, "it bleeds a bit in perspiration" or "quite a lot of color rubbed off." With a standard test, there will be a valid sampling technique; the person who runs the test must, of course, know exactly how to do it and record the results carefully; finally, that result will be given a rating according to a standard (see Figure 8.2 for a rating standard). Textile testing in the United States follows many methods set down by the AATCC (American Association of Textile Chemists and Colorists) and the ASTM (American

[1](The late) Fred Fortess, then (August 1968) Research Director, American Celanese, later Chairman, Department of Textiles, Philadelphia College of Technology and Science.

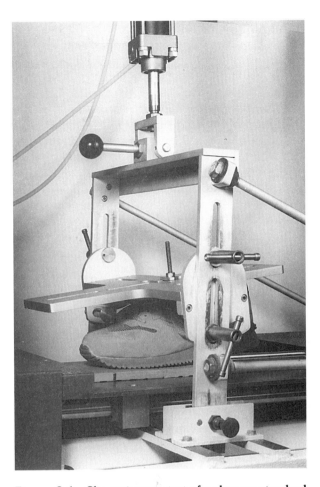

Figure 8.1 Slip resistance test of a shoe on standard quarry tile surface. (Courtesy SATRA Footwear Technology Centre)

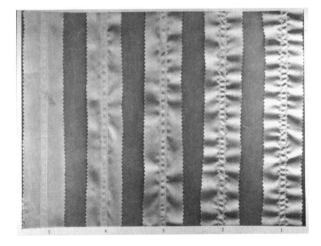

Figure 8.2 AATCC standard for rating seam puckering.

Society for Testing and Materials). In Canada, the CGSB (Canadian General Standards Board) methods are also used, and the United Kingdom has methods set by the British Standards Institute. A test result might be given as: Fastness to Perspiration: Grade 3, AATCC Test #15 + revision year. Such a result can be understandable to anyone, anywhere.

Unfortunately, no laboratory or accelerated test can duplicate actual wear. Therefore, wear trials or tests in use can provide the most revealing information about a fabric, but they take much longer to complete and are often difficult to assess. Individual differences introduce even more specialized wear that cannot be fully taken into account, e.g., carrying a heavy handbag or working at a rough desk.

Any information gathered from testing must be evaluated, and on this basis we decide whether the article will do a good job in its intended area of use and care. Any experienced manufacturer, retail buyer, or consumer has built in a very complicated assessment procedure over many years of observing how various factors affect performance in different situations. What the garment maker, the retailer, and of course, the consumer expects of the fabric is crucial in this process; someone buying materials for theatrical costumes, for instance, will look for characteristics very different from those appropriate for sportswear.

Selection of the right fabric for each use requires the application of both art *and* science; "fashion is not enough."

Standard Tests and Rating

Standard textile tests require a specially equipped laboratory and must be applied at a standard temperature and humidity if the results are to be strictly comparable to those from other test agencies. However, if you wish to make comparisons within a group of fabrics, you can run an approximation of these tests, since even such nonstandard attempts can yield helpful information, just as those strictly amateur ones outlined in this section can. They can also serve as a striking demonstration of fabric behavior for students or staff.

Standard textile testing methods may be obtained from the groups previously mentioned:

AATCC Technical Manual, updated annually, from the American Association of Textile

Chemists and Colorists (see *Resources, Associations* at the back of this text for address).

ASTM methods, updated annually from the American Society for Testing and Materials (see *Resources, Associations* for address).

CGSB Standard Test Methods CAN2–4.2–M77 from the Canadian General Standards Board, 222 Queen Street, Ste. 1402, Ottawa ON K1A 0G6.

Recorded here are some key items of information to do with standard tests and ratings that I have been asked for, especially by high school teachers.

Measurement of **pH** is an important step in many aspects of textiles testing. The pH of a solution measures whether it is acid, alkaline, or neutral. The scale is from 0 to 14; very acid substances register at the lower end of the scale (e.g., battery acid 1, lemon juice 2, tomato juice 4); water is virtually neutral at about pH 7—neither acid nor alkaline; and very alkaline substances register at the high end (household ammonia 12, strong lye solution [NaOH or caustic soda] reaches pH 13). Machine-wash water would have a pH around 12, face soap about 8.

The measure is inversely related to the concentration of hydrogen ions and can be registered very accurately electronically. (An **ion** is an atom carrying an electrical charge; if positive, it is a **cation,** if negative, an **anion.** A substance may be defined as an **acid** if it releases positive hydrogen ions in water; an **alkali** [**base**] releases negative OH ions in solution.) For less stringent tests there are **indicator papers;** the simplest is **litmus,** which simply indicates acid or alkaline, but others have a range, with a change to a specific color at a certain pH. One must be careful in storing such papers to protect them from fumes that could change or destroy their reaction; the older such papers are, the more chance there is that they have been affected. Indicator papers can be obtained from laboratory supply houses.

Colorfastness Tests and Ratings. Samples given any colorfastness tests can be rated for staining of white cloth or for color change. Scales of standard rating evaluation greatly help consistency and are not expensive. They may be obtained from the AATCC; the Color Transference Chart (showing staining) is particularly useful (color change is officially rated using a separate Gray Scale, that may not be very helpful to the uninitiated).

Following is the AATCC Grade Number rating for colorfastness tests (except to light), with the equivalent degree of staining or color change represented:

Grade #	Staining or Color Change (except to light*)
1	severe (poor fastness)
2	strong (fair to poor fastness)
3	moderate (fair fastness)
4	slight (good fastness)
5	negligible or none (excellent fastness)

*Lightfastness is rated from Grade 1 (poor) to Grade 8 (excellent).

Multifiber cloth, used for fiber identification, is a useful part of colorfastness testing. It is woven with repeats of narrow strips of different fibers, used to register possible staining of those various fibers when a dye bleeds in a care procedure (see Figure 8.3). For example, color from a blouse fabric damp with perspiration might stain a nylon slip but not a rayon lining or a wool jacket; this would show in a single test with the basic "6-fiber cloth." Multifiber cloth can be obtained from Testfabrics, Inc., 415 Delaware Avenue, West Pittston, PA 18643, (717) 603-0432, fax (717) 603-0433; or Textile Innovators Corp., P.O. Box 8, 101 Forest Street, Windsor NC 27983, (252) 794-9703, fax (252) 794-9704.

Fume-fading of blue (or blue-containing) shades on acetate can be demonstrated by hanging the fabric over a solution that releases nitrous oxide fumes. To a 2-g/L solution of sodium nitrite add 2.5 g/L sul-

furic acid; for 100 mL you can use 20 mL of 1 percent solution of sodium nitrite, make up to 100 mL, add 18 mL of a 1 percent solution of 75 percent sulfuric acid; use distilled water for solutions. (Note: use **caution** when handling strong sulfuric acid.)

Colorfastness to perspiration tests require making up two solutions, since perspiration when fresh is slightly acid and when acted on by skin bacteria becomes slightly alkaline. The "recipes" outlined for AATCC Test #15 are:

Acid Solution	Alkaline Solution
10 g sodium chloride	Make up the same as the
1 g disodium orthophosphate anhydrous	acid solution, except that instead of lactic acid, use 4 g ammonium
1 g lactic acid, USP 85%	carbonate USP.

(If obtainable, add to either solution 0.25 g histidine monohydrochloride—to reproduce the effect of natural perspiration on some dyes.) Make up to 1 liter with distilled water.

Wet out samples of colored fabric about 10 cm × 5 cm (4 in. × 2 in.), each having a similar piece of white (multifiber) cloth to back it (see Figure 8.4); roll in paper towels to extract moisture. If the standard apparatus (Perspirometer) is not available, roll test samples and insert to dry in narrow tubes or vials, with the end of the sample protruding about 2 cm (1 in.); when dry, rate Grade #1 to 5 (see the previous chart) for either staining of the white multifiber cloth or change of shade of the colored samples.

Absorbency or Wicking. This can be demonstrated using an approximation of the Weirick test (Sears Roebuck). Cut identical strips of various fabrics about 25 cm × 2.5 cm (10 in. × 1 in.); suspend over containers of water so that the strips will be under the surface about 2.5 cm (1 in.). Enter all strips at the same time, and note the rise of water on each strip after one minute (easier to see if coloring is added) and after five minutes, and record when the water reaches the top of the strip, if it does so in 30 minutes.

Thermophysiological Comfort. Standard tests for thermophysiological comfort of clothing are being applied. Three factors cited in *Textiles*[2] as measurable

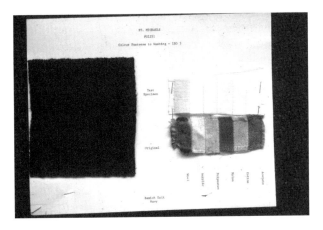

Figure 8.3 Multifiber cloth used in colorfastness test.

[2]British Textile Technology Group (BTTG) activity, reported in *Textiles*, 1992/3: 5.

Figure 8.4 Standard colorfastness to perspiration test.

and significant are thermal insulation, permeability to vapor (perspiration), and wicking ability of fabric next to the skin. Clothing comfort is discussed in Section 7.

Nontechnical Fabric Tests

You can make some very revealing tests on fabrics without laboratory equipment or training.

Not Requiring a Sample

Crease Resistance, Wrinkle Recovery. Simply crush the fabric in your hand, then release; if it creases sharply and there is no immediate sign of the creases coming out, the fabric will likely wrinkle badly in wear. You can also tie a knot in the material (or in a sleeve or pant leg), leave it for a given length of time, untie and observe. Creases tend to show up most on light, solid-colored materials; there is a camouflaging effect with dark color and surface designs such as prints.

Appearance, Drapability. Hold the fabric in different ways, gather it in your hand, and note how it falls; does the pattern look better going one way than another? Would you cut it on the bias? Drape lining along with garment fabric to see how they combine.

Closeness of Construction. The closeness of fabric construction can often be checked by holding it up to the light. The base fabric of terry towels, for instance, can be examined in this way; a sleazy, open ground weave will not give good wear no matter how dense a structure the pile loops seem to give.

Wind Resistance. Compare the resistance of fabrics of cold-weather sportswear as you blow through them. Hold the fabric taut and right up to your mouth. A closer construction will offer more resistance to your breath, as well as to the cold wind on a ski slope or at a bus stop.

Stretch and Recovery. Stretch wovens can be pulled out in the direction(s) of "give," and you can assess their tendency to snap back when that tension is released. Where stretch is vital in a knitted garment, a pattern will often include a "gauge" against which you can check the extensibility and recovery of the fabric; see the Fabric Case History record for such a gauge, with the interpretation of the result. To test stretch this way, with the fabric held over the measure given in the gauge, grasp the material firmly at the two points, held in the direction you want to test stretch (lengthwise or crosswise); pull out firmly and measure the percentage increase in length.

Colorfastness to Crocking or Rubbing Off of Color. Rub the fabric with a white cloth or tissue held over a finger. Try this test two ways: (a) using a dry cloth or tissue and (b) using a cloth or tissue moistened slightly. You can also try rubbing with a clean eraser. Figure 8.5 shows a laboratory crocking test.

Seam Slippage. Give a good pull across seams to make sure there is no marked tendency for the yarns to slip and part along the seams. Seam slippage is a real problem with many moderate-price silk garments,

Figure 8.5 Colorfastness to crocking or rubbing off of color.

where only a simple seam, such as overlock, rather than a stitched-down or enclosed one has been used.

Seam Stretch. In garments made of stretch materials, pull a seam in the direction of the stretch, to make sure the seam has been sewn to give sufficiently with the fabric; otherwise there can be stitching breaks during wear.

Napped Wool Fabrics. Insert a straight pin through the nap only, and try to life the fabric; the pin should not pull easily out of the nap. The fibers in the nap should be matted closely enough to support the weight of the fabric.

Quality of Felt. Pull on the felt, and scrape the surface with a hard object to see if the fibers hold together.

Requiring a Sample to Do the Test

Make such tests *before* making up your fabric. If you are assessing a ready-made article, take a small bit of fabric from a "nonvital" and inconspicuous part before using the item (seam allowance or self-facing), although not much information may result from a tiny piece.

Colorfastness to Cleaning. Test the colorfastness to the method of cleaning you expect to apply:

- **To washing.** Using white thread, stitch the swatch of material to a large piece of white fabric similar in type. Try to duplicate actual washing conditions, without putting the test piece in a real wash load in case it does bleed. Use the water temperature and type of detergent you would normally use, and after test washing or soaking and rinsing, roll and squeeze out most of the moisture and let the swatch dry on the white fabric. Check for bleeding or transfer of color to the white fabric, and note any change of shade in the washed sample compared to the original.

- **To dry cleaning.** Follow the washing test procedure for making up the test swatch, and take it to a dry cleaner who uses perchloroethylene (perc); a dry cleaner will usually be glad to put a test swatch through a process suitable for that fabric. After dry cleaning, you will be looking mainly for shade change or color loss.

If you may wish sometimes to wash the article and other times to dry clean it, be sure to test for colorfastness to *both* procedures.

Shrinkage. Mark a measured length and width on as large a piece of fabric as you can spare; a meter (yard) is best, because results will be very inaccurate with a small sample. Mark preferably with thread, and make at least three marks each way. Wet the sample thoroughly; you may need a very small amount of hand dishwashing liquid or shampoo to help wetting out. After wetting the sample, squeeze and roll out excess water and tumble dry completely. Smooth out the sample and remeasure. If the fabric is badly wrinkled, first tamp press using a steam iron, avoiding any pushing of the fabric as you press.

Shrinkage of 3 to 5 percent in all but *easy-fitting* garments would probably result in loss of fit, and would be quite noticeable in drapes. Unstable fabrics can shrink over 7 percent, which would shorten a pant leg of 80 cm (32 in.) over 5 cm (2 in.).

It is advisable to buy preshrunk material with a guarantee of no more than 1 to 2 percent residual shrinkage. If you plan to tumble dry cotton knit goods that do not have a "preshrunk" or "Durable Press" label, buy the article at least one size larger than usual. Garments with a good-quality Durable Press finish do not require such precautions—they are designed so that tumble drying can replace ironing; see Section 6 for procedures to ensure the least need for pressing.

If you plan to use a garment *without ironing,* allow for some take-up in size by "wrinkle shrinkage," even for goods such as SANFORIZED® that will not shrink more than 1 percent *if ironed.*

Seam Raveling. Ravel a fabric to the straight of grain crosswise, and cut up along the selvage as well; pull yarns away to see how easily they ravel off in either direction. If a fabric you are going to use in a garment ravels easily, use some kind of stitched-down or enclosed seam, such as French or flat-felled. If you are testing a ready-made garment, check whether any seam edges are unfinished; if seams are well finished, you should not have to worry about raveling.

Seam Slippage. With piece goods, use an appropriate needle, thread, and stitch size to make short test seams both lengthwise and crosswise. Give a good pull across the seams. If the fabric tends to slip readily along a seam, again follow a stitched-down or enclosed seaming method to distribute strain.

Sagging, Bagging. Secure a sample of fabric over the neck or top of something such as a flask, bottle, or jar, using a heavy rubberband. Leave for a specified time, then remove the band and rate the degree of distortion, and time how long the fabric takes to recover.

Snag Resistance. Stroke the fabric sample with a FABRI-COMB® (sold to remove pills), the rough (barbed) side of VELCRO® tape, or a small grater; note the degree of snagging given by a specified number of strokes *or* count the number of strokes to produce snagging. Figure 8.6 shows a laboratory "Mace" test for snagging.

Figure 8.6 Snag test using "Mace."

Fabric Case History

Fabric Name _____

Purchase Data:

Source _____

Width _____ cm (yd)

Price $ _____ /m (yd)

Date _____

Manufacturer _____

☐ regular retail

☐ sale

☐ wholesale

☐ mfr. old stock

Special fiber
or yarn type? _____

Fiber Content _____

Finish or care info. given POS? _____

Fabric Construction _____

Sample: See back for sample mount.
Intended use: See back for sketch, pattern picture, or description.
Degree of stretch (stretch gauge on back):

☐ stable (< 10% stretch)

☐ moderate (20–30% stretch)

☐ high (35–80% stretch)

☐ power (30–50% stretch, 95% recovery)

Was the pattern adjusted for stretch fabric? If so, specify on back.

Layout: Specify any special matching, e.g., nap, pile, one-way design

_____

Cutting problems? _____

Trim, findings _____

Construction: Record any special techniques, seam finishes, facings, hems, etc.

_____

Pressing problems? _____

Expected care method _____

Behavior in use and care (notes to be made after garment is in use):

Effectiveness re: design or pattern (line, drape, etc.) _____

_____

Looks retention (sagging, pilling, etc.?) _____

Behavior in (circle applicable) home laundering / dry cleaning:

Color bleed, fade, rub off, change? Shrinkage, stretching? Lose body?

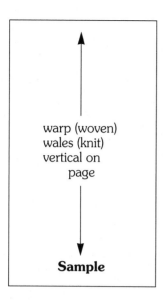

warp (woven)
wales (knit)
vertical on
page

Sample

Sketch or other illustration of garment
(indicate placement of warp <u>with arrow</u>)

Samples and identification of trims, findings

Stretch Gauge for Knits (adapted from Butterick pattern gauge)

original length   10%   33%   50%   80%   100%

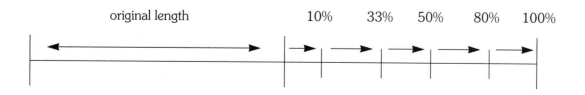

SECTION NINE

METRIC IN TEXTILES USE

As we enter the 21st century virtually all countries in the world, including the United States, are committed to metric conversion, although a few still officially use inch-pound measures (English or Imperial system). Within a number of countries, however, there are still "islands" in the "metric sea," and the garment industry, in both the United States and Canada, is definitely one of them. Official metric conversion went a long way in Canada, but withered after a change of government in September 1984. However, this *Reference* presents metric units used in textiles, clothing, and interior design work and study, as an essential basis for the global economics that affect everyone today.

Origin of Metric Measurement

The earliest measures were derived from parts of the body (in fact, metric still carries over that base, since decimals probably relate to our 10 fingers and toes, when mathematically, we would be better off with a base 12). The metric system, on the other hand, started in France with a proposal in 1670, finalized in 1791, that the unit of length should be the **metre** (from the Greek *metron* meaning "measure"), which is one ten-millionth of a meridian of longitude between the North Pole and the equator. The decimal relationship was accepted, and a cubic centimetre of water became the unit of mass, called a **gram.**

In the same way, each metric unit has been firmly based scientifically and rationally developed. When the length of the standard metre was finally determined, along the meridian that goes through Paris, the work had gone all through the French Revolution and its aftermath; when the standard metre was presented to Napoleon in 1810, he said, "Conquests pass, but such works remain." This standard metre was long a physical entity, but has now been redefined in terms of the speed of light[1]—insubstantial but much more accurate as a reference. So the science and technology of measurement (*metrology*) changed in the 20th century. Metrology, for any trading country, must have reference to internationally accepted standards, and these are expressed in metric terms.

SI Usage

There are choices to make even within metric systems, and **SI** is one particular set of metric measures and units. The letters stand for the French *Système International d'Unités*. SI has been stipulated as the accepted metric system and terminology for the United States, it was the one chosen for use in Canada in 1960, and it was followed in preparation of this *Reference* section. For this reason, too, spelling of *metre* and *litre* follows international rather than American spelling in this section. A unified American National Standard for use of SI was developed (1997) by the American Society for Testing and Materials and has replaced previous SI standards of ASTM and ANSI/IEEE.[2]

For temperature degrees (weather, cooking), SI uses the **Celsius** scale, the same scale as centigrade, with the same symbol, C; water freezes at 0°C and boils at 100°C, whichever name you give to the scale. However, in France, a *centigrade* is 1/100 of an angle (*grade*), so to avoid confusion internationally, the temperature scale was given the name of its inventor, Anders Celsius.

Similarly, in yarn count, there is denier, which is metric based, but the SI unit is **tex.**

Because SI is an international measurement language, it has very carefully defined rules of usage, set down to avoid ambiguity or confusion. It is important for communicators to understand these rules. One basic principle is that with SI, we are using symbols, not abbreviations, and so neither a period nor plurals are needed (e.g., gram and grams are shortened to the symbol g, not gm. or gms.).

Further, prefixes can modify base or supplementary units to provide a range of dimensions:

Prefix	Symbol	Factor	Multiplier
giga	G	10^9	1000000000
mega	M	10^6	1000000
kilo	k	10^3	1000
deca	da	10	10
deci	d	10^{-1}	0.1

---

[1]"Canada's National Standard System," film from the Canadian General Standards Board.

[2]IEEE/ASTM SI-10, a 72-page document (1997), may be obtained from ASTM (see *Associations* under *References and Resources* for address; for quote call (610) 832-9685.

Prefix	Symbol	Factor	Multiplier
centi	c	10^{-2}	0.01
milli	m	10^{-3}	0.001
micro	μ	10^{-6}	0.000001
nano	n	10^{-9}	0.000000001

Some other major rules are outlined here:

- Where there is a prefix, accent the first syllable in pronouncing the measure; thus, one drives so many *kilo*metres.

- A measure such as fabric weight (mass), in order to be understood in any language, is expressed as g/m^2, not g per sq. m.

- A space is left between the quantity and the symbol, *unless* the first character of the symbol is not a letter, as is the case with temperature degrees (e.g., 37 m but 37°C).

- Symbols derived from a proper name are written as a capital, as C for (Anders) Celsius. Kilogram is therefore k, as K is the symbol for kelvin, the base unit of temperature, from the name of William Thomson, Lord Kelvin, British physicist and inventor.

- In some countries a comma is used as a decimal; Canada decided to continue marking a decimal with a period. Fabric lengths, then, would be written as 2.90 m (not 2,90 m as in Europe). You will also see body height recorded on European patterns as, for instance, Misses: 1,65 to 1,68 m; in Canada, height would be recorded in centimetres as, for instance, Misses: 165 to 168 cm.

Metric in Home Sewing

In Canada, conversion to metric of retailing of textiles to home sewers was officially observed with an "M" Day on July 1, 1978. Because of extensive preparation, the transition was for the most part painless, except where a small segment of retailers resisted it. (Because a metre is about 1/10 longer than a yard, the price per metre is more than the price per yard of the same fabric.) A major holdout on metric conversion came from carpet retailing, where the price difference for the "larger" metre is accentuated because you're dealing with square units.

Most of the problems were those of perception; a person will use the same amount of fabric and pay the same amount to make the same article, whether it is measured in metres or yards. Furthermore, there is much less complication in any calculation in metric. However, the process of total conversion got side-tracked in Canada, and has not happened in the United States. To this day, then, fabric (in Canada) is measured at retail by the metre, but may well be asked for and priced by the yard! In the garment industry in both countries, it may be bought by the metre, if the supplier is not in the United States, but everything from pattern-making on will probably be discussed in inches, feet, or yards.

Piece Goods (rather than "yard goods"). Length in metres and decimals, e.g., 1.75 m (not 1 m 75 cm and certainly not 1¾ m); width in centimetres (fabric over 30 cm wide); narrow fabrics (trim, elastic less than 30 cm wide) in millimetres.

Following is a piece goods width comparison of metric to the English equivalent:

Metric	70	90	115	140	150	165	cm
English	27	36	45	54	60	66	in.

Sewing Machine Needle Sizes. Metric size is termed "Nm" (numérometrique or metric number). The diameter of the blade or shaft (the part just above the eye) is expressed in hundredths of a millimetre. Numbers 80 and 90 are the most commonly used needle sizes; see Table 9.1.

Besides the right size of sewing machine needle, you should select the right type: a pointed tip (set point or cloth point) or a ballpoint needle will sew about 90 percent of fabrics; the ball point (rounded tip) avoids damage when sewing fine or light knit goods, especially synthetics (see Figures 9.1 and 9.2). Use a triangular point or denim needle for close, tough fabrics and a wedge point or leather needle for leather and leather-likes. Replace the needle often if sewing tough synthetics.

Stitch Length. This is measured in millimetres; a larger number equals a longer stitch. (The system on some machines of stitches per inch means that a larger number equals a shorter stitch.)

Seam Allowance. This is given in centimetres and decimals; a throat plate sticker can be made for some

Table 9.1 Sewing Machine Needle Sizes

Needle Size		Appropriate Fabrics
Metric	Older (British)	
60–70	8–10	sheer, delicate fabrics: chiffon, voile, organdy, lace
80	12	light fabrics: crepe, taffeta, lining
90	14	medium fabrics: sheeting, velvet, light suiting, vinyl, sail cloth
100	16	heavier suitings, denims, coatings, drapes
110–120	18–19	extra heavy or tough fabrics: awnings, upholstery

Figure 9.2 Ballpoint needle for sewing jersey knit. (Courtesy of the Textile Institute)

sewing machines that don't have the markings already on, when you are working in metric.

Following is a seam allowance comparison of metric to the English equivalent:

Sewing Thread Length. This is given in metres per spool; if sold by mass, see yarn ball sizes.

Metric	0.3	0.6	1.0	1.2	1.5	1.8	cm
English	⅛	¼	⅜	½	⅝	¾	in.

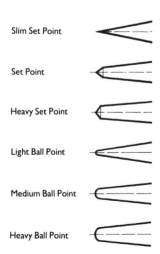

Slim Set Point

Set Point

Heavy Set Point

Light Ball Point

Medium Ball Point

Heavy Ball Point

Figure 9.1 Tip shapes of needles. (Courtesy of Coats Patons)

Thread Size. Cotton thread marking is still based on the count of cotton yarn (English number or Ne), where a larger number is a finer thread; the relationship is: #10 = 59 tex; #50 = 12 tex. Sewing thread made of synthetics may be marked in metric count (Nm) for spun yarn and denier for filament, but these figures are rounded off and do not correspond closely to standard units. Tex Count = 1,000/Nm.

The **ticket number system** (related to Ne, Nm, and denier) describes approximately the thread thickness. A synthetic thread ticket number multiplied by 0.6 is equivalent to a cotton number; e.g., a Ticket No. 60 synthetic thread would be equivalent to a Ticket No. 36 cotton thread (this compares size only, not strength).[3]

Measuring Tapes. These are marked in centimetres and millimetres; a tape at least 150 cm long is needed for body measurements.

Hem Markers, Gauges, Scissors, Blades. These are marked in centimetres.

Slide Fasteners (Zippers, Coil Fasteners). Length is measured in centimetres, width in millimetres. Following is a slide fastener length comparison of metric to the English equivalent:

Metric	12	18	22	30	40	50	60	cm
English	5	7	9	12	16	20	24	in.

[3]"What's in a Thread?" *The Technology of Thread and Seams,* J & P Coats Ltd., Glasgow.

Buttons. Diameter is measured in millimetres (formerly by the *line,* which equaled 0.025 in. or 0.635 mm).

Craft Yarn (Knitting, Needlework, etc.) .The length of the ball or skein is measured in metres, the weight (mass) in grams. Following is a ball or skein weight comparison of metric to the English equivalent:

Metric	25	50	100	250	500	g
English	1	2	4	8	16	oz.

Patterns for knitting or crocheting often give the metric conversion for the number of balls of yarn needed, stitch density, needle size, and so on. Old patterns will doubtless be treasured, however, so keep old needle sizers and such references, even when or if you are working more in metric.

Stitch density is given in rows per centimetre and stitches per centimetre.

Knitting Needle, Crochet Hook Sizes. These are marked in international or "continental" metric sizes, given in detail in Tables 9.2 and 9.3 from Patons & Baldwins.

Metric in Home Furnishings

Metric measurement and calculation of drapery fabric, for example, is so simple in a coordinated decimal system, and more so with areas, as with carpet, where the inch-pound system has figures such as 1,296 sq. in./sq. yd.! Tufted broadloom carpet width is given in centimetres until machines are built to tuft even 3- or 4-metre widths; lengths are given in metres.

Bedding (sheets, pillowcases, blankets, bedspreads) as well as table linens, towels, and blinds are "sized" according to use in many cases (e.g., "twin bed sheets" or "bath towels"). Fitted sheets for extra-thick mattresses use a term such as "deep pocket" to identify this sizing. Where dimensions are given, they are in centimetres.

Metric in Miscellaneous Textile Articles

Other textile articles are generally sized as follows:

Twine, cord, rope, surgical dressings. Length in metres; weight (mass) in grams; linear density in tex; width (bandages) in millimetres.

Tents. Length and width in metres and decimals; weight in g/m².

Awnings, tarpaulins, canvas goods. Any one dimension more than 250 cm (8 ft.) in metres; dimensions less than 250 cm in centimetres.

Sleeping bags, recreational, sports, and outdoor equipment. Dimensions in centimetres.

Table 9.2 Knitting Needle Suggested Equivalent Chart

Canadian	000	00	0	1		2	3	4	5		6	7		8	9	10		11	12	13		14	15
American		15	13	12	11		10 ½	10	9	8		7	6		5	4	3		2	1	0		00	000
Continental (mm)	10	9	8	7 ½	7		6 ½	6	5 ½	5		4 ½	4	3 ¾	3 ¼	3		2 ¾	2 ¼	2		1 ¾

Table 9.3 Crochet Hook Suggested Equivalent Chart

Milward Disc (Canadian and British)	000		00		0 2		4		5		6		7		8		9		11		12		14				
Milward Steel																			2/0		1/0		1		2	3	4
Plastic (American)					10 ½ 10 or K or J		9 or I		8 or H		6 or G		5 or F		4 or E or C		2 or B		1								
International (mm)	10.00	9.00	8.00	7.00	6.00	5.50	5.00	4.50	4.00	3.50	3.00	2.50	2.00	1.75	1.25	1.00											

Metric in Home Maintenance of Textile Articles

Washing Machines. **Outside dimensions** of washers (and dryers) may eventually conform to metric building modules. Washers generally have a **capacity** of 50 L (approximately 12 gal.). The amount of **detergent** is measured using dry ingredient cooking measures; use 125 mL for ½ cup and 50 mL for just under ¼ cup.

The "benchmarks" for water **temperatures** are the intervals in degrees Celsius used on U.S. and Canadian Standard care labels for cool, lukewarm, warm, and hot water; see Table 9.4 (see also discussion under Canadian Standard Care Labeling in Section 6).

The Canadian Home Economics Association (CHEA) Metric Committee worked out a **washing machine load** description and procedure that describes laundry loads by volume and *not* by weight (mass). Materials must have room for efficient agitation, and it is the bulkiness, not the weight, that is important. CHEA suggestions for load description and procedure were as follows:

Top-loading washing machine: Pour the required amount of detergent into the wash tub/basket before or as the machine begins to fill. Load the washer with dry, unfolded articles of various sizes, starting with large, bulky items. On top of these drop small items, one at a time. Then place medium-size articles on top; do not pack down any of the load items. The layering of the load will help prevent clothes from slipping over the top of the wash tub/basket during the spin. For a maximum load, fill to a level about 5 cm from the top of the tub/basket, or to the top of the agitator vanes.

Front-loading washing machine: For a maximum load, add dry, unfolded articles loosely to the top of the door opening.

Pressing and Ironing. Following are the temperatures that correspond to the care symbols given on U.S. and Canadian Standard care labels:

Optional Care Symbols	Iron Setting	°C	°F
1 dot	low	110	230
2 dots	medium	150	300
3 dots	high	200	390

Home Tinting. Packages of dye are labeled in grams; water volume is given in litres.

Metric in Textiles Study

Students of textiles will encounter all the metric units mentioned previously, plus a number of specialized ones.

Staple Fiber Length. This is given in millimetres. The shortest spinnable fiber (some cotton) is about 12 mm long (½ in.); the longest staple fiber (some flax) would be about 500 mm long (20 in.). (The length of cotton hairs is still given in thirty-seconds of an inch.)

Filament Fiber Length. This is given in kilometres.

Table 9.4 Fabric Wash Water Temperatures

Water Temperature Description	°C*	°F*	Relationship to Water Heater Output
Cool	30	85	
Lukewarm/hand wash	40	105	
Warm (hand hot)	50	120	
Hot	60	140	As from hot tap in many homes.
Very hot	70	160	Very hot for home.
Very, very hot	85	185	Commercial laundry.
Boiling	100	212	Wash boiler, anyone?

*Temperature conversion: °C × 1.8 + 32 = °F; °F − 32 ÷ 1.8 = °C

Fiber "Thickness" (Diameter). This is measured in micrometres (μm). Note that *micro-* is a prefix to indicate multiplying by 10^{-6} and its symbol is μ; this symbol in SI *of itself,* then, does not represent a *micron* or one millionth of a metre (1/1,000,000 m) as it does in the inch-pound system.

Fiber Bale Weight (Mass). This is measured in tonnes (t), or 10^3 kg (1 tonne = 2,200 lb. or 1 ton [2,000 lb] = 907 kg). In spoken English, it may be clearer to speak of a "metric ton."

Fiber Tenacity (Tensile Strength). This is given as newtons per tex (N/tex); centinewtons per decitex (cN/dtex) is often a more convenient measure and is close to the familiar grams per denier figure. The newton is a derived unit of force in the SI system, used instead of the gram since it will not vary according to gravitational force on a body.[4] To convert g/denier to cN/tex, multiply by 8.83, or to cN/dtex, multiply by 0.883.

Linear Density of Fibers (Hair Weight per Centimetre). This is given in mg/cm $\times 10^5$. For notation of fibers in the tex system, the small unit of millitex (mtex) can be used (equal to mg/1,000 m).

Yarn Linear Density (Yarn Count). This is based on tex (g/1,000 m); tex = denier $\times$ 0.111 (or dtex = denier $\times$ 1.11). Some relationships with familiar or traditional examples follow:

59 tex	= cotton count 10	16.5 dtex	= 15 denier
7.5 tex	= cotton count 80	33 dtex	= 30 denier
15 tex	= worsted count 60	111 dtex	= 100 denier

An emphasis in fashion on fine, flexible yarns composed of many very fine filaments has brought into the fashion media the use of the technical notation of both the total yarn size (linear density) and the number of individual filaments that make it up. Denier per filament is discussed under *Microfibers and Very Fine Fibers* (filament) in Section 2 and *Yarn Notation* in Section 3.

Yarn or Fabric Thickness. This is given in millimetres.

[4]J. E. Ford, "Textile Units for Fibres and Yarns," *Textiles,* 14/1, 1985: 17–20.

Woven Fabric Thread Count. Warp count is given as ends per centimetre; filling as picks per centimetre (possibly per 10 centimetres for a coarse fabric).

Knitted Fabric Stitch Density. This is given as wales per centimetre or courses per centimetre. **Note:** Two knitting terms in common use are difficult to convert to metric: *cut* and *gauge*. The metric unit suggested is needles per one hundred millimetres.

Fabric Area. Conversion factors between metric and English systems are as follows:

$1 \text{ m}^2 = 1.196 \text{ sq. yd.}$
$1 \text{ sq. yd.} = 0.836 \text{ m}^2$

Fabric Weight (Mass). This is given in grams per square metre (g/m²) or per running metre (g/m). Note the distinction between the two: weight per running unit will be proportionately greater than weight per square unit as the fabric width is greater than the unit. Today, most fabrics are wider than a metre or yard, while interior furnishing fabrics and those from the wool family have always been made wide. (See *Fabric Glossary,* Range of Fabric Weights.) Conversion factors between metric and English systems are as follows:

$1 \text{ g/m}^2 = 0.0295 \text{ oz./sq. yd.}$
$1 \text{ oz./sq. yd.} = 33.9 \text{ g/m}^2$

Here is a "rule of thumb" for conversion: 100 g/m² is close to 3 oz./sq. yd.

Momme is a unit of weight used for silk; it is equal to 4.33 g/m² (see discussion under *Silk Quality* in Section 2).

Carpet Pile Height and Density. Pile height is measured in millimetres. Pile density is expressed as the closeness of the tufts. In woven carpets this is *pitch:* warp yarns per 10 centimetres of width; and *wires:* tufts per 10 centimetres of length.

Thermal Insulation. Two values are used:

Tog value measures the thermal resistance of a textile, which is ten times the temperature difference between two faces of a textile, when the flow of heat is one watt per square metre.[5]

[5]C. Cooper, "Textiles as Protection against Extreme Wintry Weather, Part 1—Fabrics," *Textiles,* 8/3, 1979: 74.

Clo value measures insulating efficiency, or resistance to heat loss; this value is similar to the more familiar "R-value" used to rate housing insulation, with R-value equal to 0.88 Clo.[6] Calculations for the two values are as follows:

1 Clo = (0.18°C × m^2 × hr.) ÷ Kcal

R-value = (°F × ft.^{2} × hr.) ÷ BTU

Clo values can be related to consumer products as follows:[7]

[6]Technical data and testing report, THINSULATE™ LITE-LOFT, 3M, 1994.

[7]Work done on sleeping bags for Woods, Inc., makers of camping and survival equipment, at Ontario Research Foundation (now ORTECH), 1983, plus (4 Clo clothing value) brochure "From the Inside Out," DuPont Canada Inc., 1995.

1 Clo is the value of business clothing worn indoors (about 20°C or 68°F).

2 Clo is the value needed for skiwear for use in about –5°C (23°F).

4 Clo is the value needed in clothing for –20°C (–4°F); if the person is not moving, this should include long underwear and insulated outerwear. It is also the insulation value of a sleeping bag for ordinary camping conditions.

8–9 Clo is the value needed in a sleeping bag for Arctic survival.

Color; Dyeing, Color Matching. Wavelengths of light are expressed in nanometres, which in SI replaces the Ångström Unit.

1 nanometre (nm) = 10^{-9} m (1 Ångström unit [1 A] = 10^{-10} m)

References and Resources

References

AATCC Technical Manual (annual edition, see *Associations* for address).

Anstey, Helen, and Terry Weston. *The Anstey Weston Guide to Textile Terms* (London: Weston Publishing, 1997). Short definitions of some 1,000 terms; aimed at the fashion and retail sectors.

Anquetil, Jacques. *Silk* (Flammarion, 1996). Translated from French. History of silk in Western Europe, lavishly illustrated in color.

Ashelford, J. *Care of Clothes* (UK, National Trust, 1997). Describes historical methods for clothes care, but includes tips on looking after old and valued items today.

ASTM Standards, Section 7—Textiles (annual edition, Vol. 07.01/Textiles (I): D76–D3218, Vol. 07.02/Textiles (II) D3333–latest, see *Associations* for address).

ATI Directory (Billian Publishing Company). Lists textile firms in the U.S., Canada, and Mexico.

Barnett, Anne. *Examining Textiles Technology* (Oxford: Butterworth/Heinemann, 1997). Brand-name and market oriented but little on nonapparel textiles.

Brackenbury, T. *Knitted Clothing Technology* (Oxford: Blackwell Science, 1992). Information for those involved in knitted garment manufacture.

Braddock, Sarah E., and Marie O'Mahony. *Techno Textiles: Revolutionary Fabrics for Fashion and Design* (London: Thames & Hudson, 1998). Application of information such as is found in Hongu and Phillips *New Fibres,* but from a design viewpoint. Reference section and bibliography.

Brunnschweiler, D., and J. W. S. Hearle, editors. *Polyester: Fifty Years of Achievement: Tomorrow's Ideas and Profits* (Manchester: the Textile Institute, 1993).

Canadian Textile Manual (annual, from CTJ-Inc., see *Periodicals* for address).

Cohen, Allen C. *Beyond Basic Textiles* (New York: Fairchild Books & Visuals, 1982).

Davison's Textile Blue Book (Davison Publishing Company). Directory of firms in the U.S. connected with textile manufacturing.

Dictionary of Fiber & Textile Technology (Charlotte, NC: Hoechst Celanese, 1990). Fills a special need; quite a number of line drawings.

Dyeing Primer, reprinted from *Textile Chemist & Colorist* (Research Triangle Park, NC: AATCC, 1981).

Earnshaw, Pat. *A Dictionary of Lace* (Aylesbury, U.K.: Shire Publications Ltd., 1982).

———. *The Identification of Lace* (Aylesbury, U.K.: Shire Publications Ltd., 1984).

Elsasser, Virginia. *Textiles: Concepts and Principles* (Albany: Delmar Publishers, 1997). Sketchy, many errors, simple experiments or records offered as "laboratory assignments." Inverse relation between content and price (it is soft cover); center insert of eight color pages of fabric pieces may contribute to relatively high cost.

Encyclopedia of Textiles, American Fabrics, 3rd ed. (Englewood Cliffs, NJ: Prentice Hall, 1980).

Finch, K., and G. Putnam. *The Care and Preservation of Textiles* (London: Batsford, 1985).

Hardingham, Martin. *The Fabric Catalog* (New York: Pocket Books, 1978). Sadly, out of print; a uniquely useful fabric dictionary.

Harrison, E. P. *Scottish Estate Tweeds* (Elgin, Johnstons of Elgin, 1995). History (200 years), 185 color photos of checks by name, cashmere information—unique reference. Johnstons, Newmill, Elgin, Morayshire, Scotland 1V30 2AF; 0134-355-4040.

Hatch, Kathryn L. *Textile Science* (St. Paul, MN: West Publishing Co., 1993). An astonishingly detailed, complete (for its date), clearly written and well-illustrated reference—brava!

Hongu, Tatsuya, and Glyn O. Phillips. *New Fibres,* 7th ed. (Bradford, U.K.: Woodhead Publishing/ the Textile Institute 1997). New "superfibers" and industrial use, more *Shingosen* or new synthetic fibers, and new cellulosic MF fibers plus new frontiers.

Hudson, Peyton, B., Anne C. Clapp, and Darlene Kness. *Joseph's Introductory Textile Science,* 6th ed. (Orlando, FL: Harcourt Brace Jovanovich, 1993). Thorough, competent treatment of the field for its date.

Humphries, Mary. *Fabric Glossary,* 2nd ed. (Upper Saddle River, NJ: Prentice Hall, 1999). A fabric dictionary that may be used on its own or as a "companion" book to *Fabric Reference*—Prentice Hall markets the two books together as a "Value Package" (separate ISBN) at an attractive price advantage. On the principle that the best outcome of textiles study is a meaningful connection with specific fabrics, *Fabric Glossary* gives detailed descriptions of major "name fabrics" or categories, plus comprehensive listings of which fabrics are suitable for many end uses, in clothing as well as for interiors. 125 main *Fabric Files* define or explain, describe, and provide illustrations for some 600 fabric names and terms. The selection has been designed to touch on all aspects of textile production and behavior, so that fabrics known by name illustrate major fiber types; most kinds of yarns including novelty yarns; all categories of weaves, knits, other constructions such as tufted, twisted lace, felt, nonwoven, stitch-knit, and others, plus the "natural fabric" leather; fabrics whose character is made by finishing, including examples related to dyeing, plus printing and other applied design. However, *Fabric Glossary* can be enjoyed simply as a unique presentation of the characteristics, uses, and background (including origin of names) of materials that fascinate most people. For this Second Edition, names have been added from current fashion use. Almost all of the b/w illustrations are photos or computer scans of actual fabrics selected by the author, with many unraveled or arranged to reveal structure. But there is nothing to equal an actual swatch of fabric for "illustration"—fabric that can be examined, dissected or tested during textiles study or just for curiosity in self-learning. *Fabric Glossary* as published by Prentice Hall is printed on heavier paper, and provides templates to aid the mounting of samples for each File, and includes thorough discussion of sampling and mounting techniques. Although the individual will almost certainly mount a personal selection of fabric samples in the ample space available, there is a Swatch Set available designed to provide a valid, accurately cut and packed sample for each of 125 Files; see *Teaching Aids & Resources,* plus order information and form in back of this book or in *Fabric Glossary.*

Hunter, L. *Mohair: A Comprehensive Review* (Manchester, U.K.: the Textile Institute, 1993).

Issenman, Betty Kobayashi. *Sinews of Survival: The Living Legacy of Inuit Clothing* (Vancouver: University of British Columbia Press, 1997). Marvelously detailed examination in words, drawings, and photographs of this unique clothing of the Arctic.

Jerde, Judith. *Encyclopedia of Textiles* (New York: Facts on File, Inc.: 1992). Considerably lacking in completeness or quality of information, although the illustrations are ravishing.

Kadolph, Sara J., and Anna L. Langford. *Textiles,* 8th ed. (Upper Saddle River, NJ: Merrill/Prentice Hall, 1998). Complete, readable coverage, thoughtfully updated regarding industry needs.

Landi, Sheila. *The Textile Conservator's Manual,* 2nd ed. (Oxford: Butterworth/Heinemann, 1997).

Lebeau, Caroline. *Fabrics: The Decorative Art of Textiles* (New York: Clarkson Potter, 1994). Sumptuous book explores textiles for interior designers, with glossary of terms and source listings.

Linton, G. E. *The Modern Textile and Apparel Dictionary* (Plainfield, NJ: Textile Book Service, 1973). Quite out of date in many respects, but still encyclopedic in coverage.

Metric usage ASTM standard for the U.S., see under *SI Usage* in Section 9; see American Society for Testing and Materials under *Associations* for address.

Miles, Leslie W. C., editor. *Textile Printing,* 2nd ed. (Bradford, U.K.: Society of Dyers & Colourists, 1994). Historical overview added, processes and machines described and explained; new chapters include growing role of computers.

Miller, E. *Textiles: Properties and Behaviour in Use* (London: Batsford, 1992). General information aimed at those in clothing production.

Peigler, Dr. Richard S. "Wild Silks of the World." *American Entomologist,* 39/3, Fall 1993: 151–161. Everything you ever wanted to know about wild silks; lucid, fascinating.

Perkins, Warren S., *Textile Coloration and Finishing* (Durham, NC: Carolina Academic Press, 1996). Clear introductory text covering theory and practice.

Price, Arthur, and Allen C. Cohen. *Pizzuto's Fabric Science,* 6th ed. (New York: Fairchild Books & Visuals, 1994). Much of the most industry-oriented information, including reference directories. Looseleaf workbook format, poor index. Information recent when it was last revised is patched in, emphasis on interiors but not in depth.

Rheinberg, L. "The Romance of Silk." *Textile Progress,* Vol. 21, No. 4 (Manchester, U.K.: the Textile Institute, 1991). Misleading title for a review of developments (1991) in the silk industry worldwide. Useful glossary of silk terms but no index.

Scott, P. *The Book of Silk* (London: Thames & Hudson, 1993). History of silk worldwide.

Slater, Keith. "Chemical Testing." *Textile Progress,* Vol. 25, No. 1/2 (Manchester, U.K.: the Textile Institute, 1994). Literature review from the late 1970s to 1991.

————. "Comfort Properties of Textiles." *Textile Progress,* Vol. 9, No. 4 (Manchester, U.K.: the Textile Institute, 1977). Literature review.

————. "Textile Degradation." *Textile Progress,* Vol. 21, No. 1/2 (Manchester, U.K.: the Textile Institute, 1991). Literature review.

Spencer, D. J. *Knitting Technology,* 2nd ed. rev. (Bradford, U.K.: Woodhead Publishing/The Textile Institute, 1996). Well-illustrated handbook; covers basics and advanced applications such as CAD/CAM.

Storey, Joyce. *Manual of Textile Printing,* 2nd ed. (London: Thames & Hudson Ltd., 1992). 1974 edition updated with developments in CAD, jet printing, and laser engraving.

Textile Terms and Definitions, 10th ed. (Manchester: The Textile Institute, 1995). Standard terminology reference worldwide; includes many line drawings.

Textile test methods, see Section 8 for names.

Tortora, Phyllis G., and Billie J. Collier. *Understanding Textiles,* 5th ed. (Upper Saddle River, NJ: Merrill/Prentice Hall, 1997). Good presentation of basic coverage, well updated, includes "case studies" of specific end uses.

Tortora, Phyllis G., author, Robert S. Merkel, consultant. *Fairchild's Dictionary of Textiles,* 7th ed. (New York: Fairchild Books & Visuals, 1995). Over 14,000 entries in this updated standard.

Trotman, E. R. *Dyeing and Chemical Technology of Textile Fibres,* 6th ed. (New York: John Wiley & Sons, Ltd., 1984, reprinted Hodder & Stoughton, 1991). Solid reference that first presents fibers and their reactions, then dyes and dyeing methods, but significant developments, however, since this edition.

Ukponmwan, J. O. *The Thermal Insulation Properties of Fabrics* (Manchester, U.K.: the Textile Institute, 1993).

I found two older references useful in trying to simplify the workings of the jacquard mechanism:

Clarke, Leslie J. *The Craftsman in Textiles* (New York: Frederick A. Praeger, 1968).

Nisbet, H. *Grammar of Textile Design,* 2nd ed. (London: Scott, Greenwood & Son, 1919).

Another older book, William Watson's *Textile Design and Colour* (Burrow Green, Sevenoaks, Kent: Butterworth & Co. Publishers Ltd., 1946) is cited as reference for a diagram illustrating the principle of the jacquard mechanism that appears in the article "Jacquards for Weaving," *Textiles,* 10/1, 1981 (referred to in Footnote 5, Section 4).

Catalogs

Batsford *New Books,* periodic catalogs from a specialist in books on costume and fashion. BT Batsford, 583 Fulham Road, London SW6 5BY, U.K. Agent for some titles: Hushion House, Toronto, ON (416) 285-6100.

Fairchild Books & Visuals Catalog, exclusively publications on textiles and clothing, but does not specify date of each publication! FB&V, 7 West 34th Street, New York, NY 10001; 1-800-932-4724.

Textile Titles of the World (The Textile Institute Mail Order Book Service, annual). Titles may be ordered from the NCSU Bookstore, P.O. Box 7224, Raleigh, NC 27606-7224, Tel. 1 (919) 515-3588, as well as from the original agent, Austicks University Bookshop, 21 Blenheim Terrace, Leeds LS2 9HJ, West Yorkshire, UK; Fax +44/(0)113 243 0661. Covers clothing production and design, computers, all aspects of fiber and fabric production.

World Textile Publications Ltd. catalog showing the many specialist periodicals and directories put out by this company, with a separate folder describing their abstract database, available as CD-ROM, in print or on-line. World Textile Publications Ltd., Perkin House, 1 Longlands Street, Bradford BD1 2TP, West Yorkshire, UK.

Periodicals

American Dyestuff Reporter, SAF International, Inc., Harmon Cove Towers, Secaucus, NJ 07094.

American Sportswear & Knitting Times, National Knitwear & Sportswear Association, 386 Park Avenue South, New York, NY 10016.

America's Textiles International, Billian Publishing Inc., 2100 Powers Ferry Road, Suite 125, Atlanta, GA 30339.

Canadian Apparel Magazine, 555 Chabanel West, #801, Montreal, QC H2N 2H8.

Canadian Home Economics Journal (see CHEA under *Associations* for address).

Canadian Textile Journal, and *Canadian Textile Manual,* CTJ-Inc., 3000 Boullé, St. Hyacinthe, QC J2S 1H9.

Clothes Care Gazette, from International Fabricare Institute (see *Associations* for address). Monthly consumer information folder, authoritative regarding dry cleaning but not dependable for textiles information.

Clothing and Textiles Research Journal, from ITAA (see *Associations* for address).

Fabricare Canada, P.O. Box 968, Oakville, ON L6J 5E8.

Family and Consumer Sciences Research Journal, American Association of Family and Consumer Sciences, SAGE Publications, Inc., 2455 Teller Road, Thousand Oaks, CA 91320.

Fiber Organon (formerly *Textile Organon*), Fiber Economics Bureau, 1150 17th Street NW, Ste. 310, Washington, DC 20086.

Home Textiles Today, Cahners Business Newspapers, subscribe to Box 1424, Riverton, NJ 08077.

Journal of Interior Design, Interior Design Education Council, c/o Denise Guerin, University of Minnesota, 240 McNeal Hall, 1985 Buford Avenue, St. Paul, MN 55108.

Journal of the Textile Institute, 10 Blackfriars Street, Manchester M3 5DR, UK.

Textile Chemist and Colorist (see AATCC under *Associations* for address).

Textile Horizons (World Textile Publications Ltd., see *Catalogs* for address).

Textiles Magazine (formerly *Textiles*) (The Textile Institute, see *Journal* above).

Textile Progress (the Textile Institute, see *Journal* above).

Textile Research Journal, TRI/Princeton, P.O. Box 625, Princeton, NJ 08542.

Textile World, PRIMEDIA Intertec, 6151 Powers Ferry Road, Ste. 200, Atlanta, GA 30339-2941.

Associations

American Apparel Manufacturers Association, 2500 Wilson Blvd., Ste. 301, Arlington, VA 22201.

American Association of Family and Consumer Sciences (formerly AHEA), 1555 King Street, Alexandria, VA 22314-2738.

American Association of Textile Chemists and Colorist (AATCC), P.O. Box 12215, #1 Davis Drive, Research Triangle Park, NC 27709-2215.

American Fiber Manufacturers Association, 1150 17th Street NW, Ste. 310, Washington, DC 20036.

American Sheep Industry Association (formed from American Sheep Producers Council and the National Wool Growers Association), 6911 S. Yosemite Street, Englewood, CO 80112-1414.

American Society for Testing and Materials, 100 Barr Harbor Drive, West Conshohocken, PA 19428-2959.

American Textile Manufacturers Institute (ATMI), 1130 Connecticut Ave. NW, Ste. 1200, Washington, DC 20036.

British Textile Technology Group (BTTG), Shirley House, Wilmslow Road, Didsbury, Manchester M20 8RS, UK. Formed in 1989 by the union of the Wool Industry Research Association, formed in Leeds, and the Shirley Institute, formed in Manchester to work for cotton.

Canadian Apparel Federation, 130 Slater Street, #1050, Ottawa, ON K1P 6E2.

Canadian Fabricare Association, P.O. Box 24026, Kitchener, ON N2M 5P1.

Canadian Home Economics Association (CHEA), 901-151 Slater Street, Ottawa, ON K1P 5H3.

Canadian Textiles Institute, 66 Slater Street, Ste. 1720, Ottawa, ON K1P 6E2.

Carpet & Rug Institute, P.O. Box 2048, Dalton, GA 30722.

Cotton Incorporated, 1370 Avenue of the Americas, 34th Floor, New York, NY 10019-4641.

Industrial Fabrics Association International, 345 Cedar Street, Ste. 800, St. Paul, MN 55101-1088.

International Fabricare Institute (IFI), 12251 Tech Road, Silver Spring, MD 20904.

International Textile and Apparel Association (ITAA), P.O. Box 1360, Monument, CO 80132-1360.

International Wool Secretariat (IWS) see the Woolmark Company.

National Association of Hosiery Manufacturers, 200 North Sharon Amity Road, Charlotte, NC 28211.

National Cotton Council of America, Box 820285, Memphis, TN 38182.

National Knitwear & Sportswear Association, 386 Park Avenue South, New York, NY 10016.

Supima Association of America, 4141 East Broadway Road, Phoenix, AZ 85040.

The Woolmark Company (formerly IWS), Valley Drive, Ilkley, West Yorkshire LS29 8PB, UK.

The Woolmark Company (formerly Wool Bureau), 330 Madison Avenue, 19th Floor, New York, NY 10017-5001.

The Woolmark Company (formerly Wool Bureau of Canada Ltd.), 33 Yonge Street, Ste. 820, Toronto, ON M5E 1G4.

Teaching Aids & Resources

AATCC Quality Control Aids and Publications, send for brochure (see *Associations* for address).

A Guide to Wool, excellent booklet available to instructors and libraries on request (see the Woolmark Company under *Associations* for address).

Booklet *America's Textiles,* also *All About Textiles: A Guide to Educational Resources,* including videos and other material such as contact information, from Communications Division, American Textile Manufacturers Institute, Inc. (see *Associations* for address).

Dictionary of Textile Terms, 19th ed. (Dan River Inc., from 1325 Sixth Avenue, New York, NY 10019). 19th ed., $2.00 each; not always accurate, but a good deal of information for students for the low price.

Metric usage ASTM standard for the U.S., see Section 9; see American Society of Testing and Materials under *Associations* for address.

Multifiber cloth sources, see Section 8.

Price, Arthur, and Allen Cohen. *Textiles: From Source to Consumer,* 2nd ed. (New York: Fairchild Books & Visuals, 1993). Multimedia learning package: 180 color slides in three programs (or on one VHS video) with instructor's guide.

Qiviuq price list and sample on request from Folknits, 2151 2nd Avenue, Whitehorse, Yukon Y1A 1C6.

Textile World charts and guides (see *Periodicals* for address).

Test Kit: Absorbency and speed of drying of fabric with INTERA® compared to two other fabrics, Intera Corporation, 211 Summit Parkway, Ste. 105, Birmingham, AL 35209.

Swatch Sets:

Basic Textiles Swatch Kit, for use with Tortora and Collier, *Understanding Textiles,* 5th ed. Fabric Consultants Inc., P.O. Box 111431, Nashville, TN 37222.

Fabric Glossary Swatch Set (125), available through the author of *Fabric Glossary* and *Fabric Reference* (Prentice Hall, 1999). This swatch set has been designed to provide both name fabric samples for *Fabric Glossary* and examples of all aspects of fabric study for use with these companion books. Order information and form in back of this book.

Fabric Science Swatch Kit, 6th ed., 1994. 105 swatches, 20 mounting pages, three-ring binder. Fairchild Books & Visuals (see *Catalogs* for address).

INDEX

This Index covers both the *Fabric Reference* and its companion book *Fabric Glossary*. Page numbers in bold-face indicate pages with illustrations.

	Reference	Glossary
Intl. Standardization Organization— see ISO		
Intl. Wool Secretariat—see Woolmark Company		
interval—see progression		
Inuit clothing	**236, 237,** 238, **239**	
ion	254	
iridescence, iridescent	70, 186	**55**
Irish appliqué lace	146	
Irish tweed		249
iron (press)	28, 195, 197, 198, 200, 266	
irregular twill—see broken islands-in-a-sea; see matrix/fibril		
ISO	**222, 223,** 224	
ISOVYL	61	
IVORY SNOW	198, 205, 206	
IWS—see Woolmark Company		
jac cloth		155
jacket fabrics		9, 10
jaconet		15
jacquard knit	136, 138, **141, 142,** 186	**127**
jacquard woven	108, 122, 123—126, **129**	**21, 71, 129, 159, 237**
Java canvas, cloth		29, 81
JAVEX	206	
J-CLOTH		167
jean		73
jersey	107, 135, 136, 138, 140, 141, 170, 264	**131**
jersey "double"	138	**125**
jersey tricot	**140**	249
jet dye	187	
print	190	
jig dye	187	
Jouy—see toile de Jouy		
jute	12, 14, 19–21, 28, 29, 148, **150**	2, 3, **23**
jusi cloth	31	
KANECARON, KANEKARON	61	
kapok	12, 14, 26	
KAPTON	163	
kasha flannel		**101**
kasha satin		201
Kashmir	39	175
kasuri		179
kemp, kempy wool	32	**257**
kenaf	30, 248	

	Reference	Glossary
keratin	**32,** 47, 157	
kersey		161
KERMEL	66	
KEVLAR	**66,** 67, 75, 250	
K-KOTE	175	
knickerbocker		257, 259
knit compared to woven	**132,** 133, 201	
knit-deknit	101, **102,** 186	
knit lace	140, 141, 144	133, **139**
knits, knitting	107, **132,** 133, **134–143,** 144, 146, 153, **155,** 201, 265, 267	**85, 103, 109, 117, 125, 127, 131, 139, 185, 187, 225, 226, 227, 229, 249, 261**
knit-sew—see stitch-knit		
knop, knot yarn	103	
knots (carpet)	130, **131**	
knotted—see lace twisted		
KODEL	60	
KODOFILL, KODOSOFF	70	
KOLORBON	77	
KORATRON	178	
Kunit	153, **154, 155**	167, 225, **226**
KURALON	61, 75	
KYNOL	67	
labeling		
care	**216,** 218, **219,** 220, **221–226**	
fiber content	11, 13, 16, 37, 38	
low- or under-trademark	221	
	16, 28, 37–39, 54, 61, 62, 64, 67, 69, 71, 76, 78, 80, 143, 163, 165, 166, 175, 176, 180, 181, 221, 222, 225, 226, 233, 236, 240, 243, 245, 247, 249	
lace	144, **145–147,** 150, 193, 197, 198, 201	133, 135, 137, 139, 141
laid-in—see laying-in		
lamb's wool fabric		**103**
fiber	37	
lamé, LAMÉ	68, 104	**143**
laminated, -ing—see compound fabrics		
LAMOUS	74	
lampshade fabrics		6
Lanese	102	

	Reference	Glossary
mock leno	126, **123**	**81**
mock matelassé		**57**
modacrylic	12, 13, 15, 17–19, 61, 80, 83, 84, **88,** 89, 195	
modal—see HWM		
modifications—see under MF		
modulus	9, 53, 54, 58, 59, 62, 66	
mohair	12, 14, 38, 39, 70, 76, **87,** 91, 217	2, 3, **17**
moiré	116, 192, 201	**129, 163,** 191, 235
mold—see mildew		
moldable	19, 20, 35, 70, 159	
molecular structure	9, 22, **23, 32,** 49, **50, 51, 55–58, 61**	
moleskin	156	59, 61
molleton		161, 226
molt (caterpillar)	43, **44**	
molt (hair)	39, 40	
momie cloth, weave		66
momme, mommie	47, 267	4
Mongolian lamb look		109
monk's cloth	116	**123**
monofilament	91, 105, 131	**17**
monomer	9, 57	
Monvelle	79	
moquette	130	265
mordant	182, 217	
Morocco crepe—see marocain		
morpho structured	**70**	
mosquito netting	127	147
moss crepe		65
MOSSO	74, 153	
motes—see trash		
mother-of-pearl		55
moth balls, crystals	229	
moth larvae, -proofing	33, 169, **227,** 228, 229	
mountain sheep	**34**	
mouflon		105
mounting swatches		12,13
mousseline de laine		35
mousseline de soie	173	171
mudmee		179
muga, muggah	47, **48**	255
mulberry	**31,** 43, 45	255
mule spinning	95, 96	
mull		15
multi-component— see compound fabrics		
multifiber cloth	**82, 255**	
multifilament	43, 91, 105	

	Reference	Glossary
Multiknit	153, 154, **155,** 156	
multi-component, multi-layer, multiplex—see compound fabrics		
multi-phase loom	110, **111,** 112	
musk ox fiber	39, **41**	
muslin	114, 161, 168	147, **215,** 216, 217
MYLAR	104	
nacre velvet		267
nainsook		15
nanduti	146	
nanofiber	72, 251	
naphthol dyes	184, 216	
nap (-ped), napping	117, 170 **172,** 201, 251	**89, 99, 101, 103, 105, 155**
natté	121, **123**	**81**
NATURAL BLEND	79	
natural dyes		**245**
natural fibers	6, 11–14, 18–48	
natural polymer	12, 14, 15, 20, 48, 49	
NAUTEX	175	
neck cord	122, **124**	
neckwear fabrics	185	10
needled, needle "felt"	**153**	167
needlepoint lace	145	**133,** 141
needlepunched, needle-woven—see needled		
needles, hand knitting	265	
machine knitting	**134, 135,** 137, **138,** 139–141	
needles, sewing	133, 263, **264**	
NEOCHROME	182	
neoprene	63, **166**	
nep (yarn)	103	
net	**144,** 145, 146	133, **165**
net (nett) silk	**45**	
NEWCELL	22, 53	
New Zealand "flax" or "hemp"	12, 14, 30	
NEXTEC	176	
nightwear fabrics		7
ninon		**107,** 170
node (bast fiber)	**87**	
noil, noile, noils	47, 152	95, **223**
NOMEX	68, 131	
nonround cross section—see lobal		
nonwoven	2, **31,** 62, 78, **80, 152–155**	167
notation (yarn)	94	
Nottingham lace	145	**141**
NOVALENE	56	

Term	Reference	Glossary
permeable—see also VPMR	175, 232, 233, 240	
PERMIA	175	
perspiration	6, 17, 19, 47, 73, 77, 133, 159, **163–165,** 170, 175, 202, 228, **232, 233,** 241, 242, 255, **256**	
Persian lamb look		43
PET polyester	58	
PET-AGREE	148, 202, **225**	
petal-shaped bicomponent	**75,** 78, 154	
petrochemicals re fibers	21, 57, 235	
petroleum solvent	211, 212, **219,** 220	
pH	254	
phase change materials —see microthermal		
phosphates	204–206, 246	
PHOTOFABRIC	191	
photoluminescent	175	
pick—see weft		
pick-and-pick		41, **251**
pick counter—see thread counter		
picker lap	**95**	
picker stick	108	
picks per minute—see speed of weaving		
picot edge, picots	145, **147**	133, 135, **141**
piece dye	**187**	
pigment "dye"	184	
pigment print	185, 188, 217	
pile knit	142, **143,** 174	**109, 261**
pile stitch-knit	150, **151, 152,** 153, **154, 155**	225, **226**
pile tufted	147, **148–150**	**253**
pile woven	**128–131,** 174, 201	**43, 59, 61, 263–269**
pillar-and-inlay	**141**	**185**
pilling	6, **8,** 18, 19, 35, 58, 74, 75, **76,** 91, 96, 143, 171	
PIL-TROL	75, **76**	
pillow lace—see bobbin lace		
Pima cotton	23, 26	
pin check, pinhead		39, 41
piña	12, 14, 31	
PINSONIC	163	57
pinwale corduroy		59, **61**
piqué knit—see doubleknit		
piqué woven	**122, 123**	**77**
pirn—see bobbin		
pitch (carpet)	130, 267	
plaid, plain weave		119, **157, 179,** 240
plaid, twill weave	117, **118**	55, 240
plain stitch knit	107, **132,** 135, **136, 138,** 140, 141, 153, **155**	13, **127, 131**
plain weave	107, **109, 115–117, 126, 127, 132**	see basket, rib + *many!* more
plaited	150	133
plaiting (knit)—see plating		
plangi		177
plate (fur, leather)	157, **158,** 162	
plating (knit)	134	
pleating	**193**	
plissé	117, 192	65, **181**
plumage	14, **42,** 43, **88**	
plush knit	136, 142	261
plush stitch-knit	153, **154**	225, **227**
plush woven	130	**263**
ply (yarn)	39, 91, **92,** 97, 98	
pneumatic—see air-jet loom		
pocket cloth		75
pocket fabric	**122**	
point d'esprit	144, 192	**165**
point diagram	114, **115, 117–120, 127**	
point laces	145	**133,** 135, **137**
pointelle	**142**	
POLARGUARD HV	70, **71**	
POLARTEC	142, **143,** 154, 165, 247	
polished cotton		49
pollution (water, air)	53, 245–247	
polo cloth		89
polyacryl, polyacrylonitrile— see acrylic		
polyamide—see nylon		
polyarylate	68	
polybenzimidazole— see PBI		
polychlal	78	
polychromatic	72, 190	
polyester, general	12–19, 23, 42, **50,** 58–60, **73–76,** 79, 83, 85, **88,** 89, 102, 104, 105, 165, 171, 179, 181, 183, 187, **188,** 192, 195, 217, 218, 240	
polyetheretherketone	68	
polyethylene	12, 15, 61, 62, 75, 154, 162	
polyimide	68	

ℱABRIC 𝒢LOSSARY

𝒮WATCH 𝒮ET

SET OF 125 SWATCHES
Designed to give examples of actual fabrics for *Fabric Glossary* which also help clarify *Fabric Reference* text.

This is a Swatch Set with a difference: It provides a fabric example for each of 125 main **Fabric Files** in the *Fabric Glossary* dictionary—files that also define or explain, describe, and provide black and white illustrations* for some 600 fabric names and terms.

However, the Swatch Set has also been designed (and examples selected) to represent all the components of fabric study as followed through in most textbooks. This is particularly true for *Fabric Reference* where the appropriate *Glossary* Files are cited as an illustration of characteristics of various fibers, yarns, fabrics, and finishes, including dyeing and printing effects, when each of these is discussed.

The **Swatch Mounting Key** lists a page on which there is a template to mount each of the swatches in the set, with the name of that particular fabric if it is distinct or different from the File name. There are also notes as to identification and best mounting methods.

Application listings come next (eight pages), to indicate to the student or instructor who may be using *Fabric Glossary* independent of *Fabric Reference* which swatches provide good examples of specific fibers, distinctive yarn types, particular weaves, knit stitches, or other fabric constructions, plus results of individual finishing processes such as napping, stages and effects of dyeing, types of print, and other applied design.

*The **illustrations** are almost all either computer scans or photographs of actual fabrics, chosen by the author, many unraveled or arranged to reveal structure, such as the relative closeness of warp yarns compared to weft, or differences between fabric face and back.

Order form on back of this page.

Fabric Glossary Swatch Set

Set of 125 Swatches, selected as examples of *Fabric Glossary* name fabrics and to provide samples for textiles study in *Fabric Reference*.

U.S.A. (US$)	**Canada** (CND)	**U.K.** (£)
$20.10	$26.45	£12.40

–20% orders of 10 or more

Shipping & handling extra, min. $7.50. (£5.00).

Order from:
Mary Humphries
Tel. or Fax (416) 449-7631
49–6A The Donway West, Ste. 419, Toronto, ON Canada M3C 2E8

✂ ✂

SEND PO, CHEQUE, OR MONEY ORDER payable to Mary Humphries to:

Mary Humphries, 49–6A The Donway West, Ste. 419, Toronto, ON Canada M3C 2E8

Tel. or Fax (416) 449-7631

Send ______ Swatch Set(s)

NOTE: Instructors who have adopted *Fabric Glossary* for a course are welcome to request a complimentary copy of the Swatch Set. ______ Comp.

Name ____

Business/School Affiliation ____

Address ____

street, apt. number **city** **state/province**

____ (   ) ____________ (   ) ____________

country **zip/postal code** **telephone** **fax**